American Prisoners of War

Held in
Montreal and Quebec
during the War of 1812

Transcribed by
Eric Eugene Johnson

Society of the War of 1812
in the
State of Ohio

HERITAGE BOOKS
2015

HERITAGE BOOKS
AN IMPRINT OF HERITAGE BOOKS, INC.

Books, CDs, and more—Worldwide

For our listing of thousands of titles see our website
at
www.HeritageBooks.com

Published 2015 by
HERITAGE BOOKS, INC.
Publishing Division
5810 Ruatan Street
Berwyn Heights, Md. 20740

Heritage Books by the Society of the War of 1812 in the State of Ohio:

Translated by Harrison Scott Baker

American Prisoners of War Held at Bermuda, Cape of Good Hope and Jamaica During the War of 1812

American Prisoners of War Held at Barbados, Newfoundland and New Providence During the War of 1812

American Prisoners of War Held at Halifax, During the War of 1812, Volume I and II

Translated by Eric Eugene Johnson

American Prisoners of War Held in Montreal and Quebec during the War of 1812

American Prisoners of War Held at Quebec During the War of 1812, 8 June 1813–11 December 1814

Ohio and the War of 1812: A Collection of Lists, Musters and Essays

Ohio's Regulars in the War of 1812

International Standard Book Numbers
Paperbound: 978-0-7884-5599-5
Clothbound: 978-0-7884-6072-2

- Table of Contents -

Introduction i
The Dead vi
American sources 1
American records 3
Soldiers listed by regiments 71
British records 97

Introduction

This is a transcription of prisoner of war records of American soldiers, sailors, marines and civilians held by the British Empire at their internment facilities in either Montreal, Lower Canada or in Quebec, Lower Canada, during the War of 1812. All of these men were captured during the various land battles or naval actions on or around the Great Lakes or Lake Champlain.

The first part of this book was compiled from a copy of the *Records Relating to War of 1812 Prisoners of War* from the National Archives in Washington, DC (Microfilm Publication M2019 in Record Group 94). This file contains clothing reports, capture lists, exchange lists, parole lists, and death lists from Montreal and Quebec.

It was each nation's duty to supply new clothing to their men being held in the enemy's prison camps. A large portion of this file consists of clothing reports listing the American prisoners being held in Montreal organized by their regiments. The second group of reports are the exchange lists from Montreal and Quebec of Americans being traded for British prisoners of war who were being held in the United States. Another set of reports are for Americans who were sent back to the United States without being exchanged. These men were placed on 'parole' which meant that they could not take up arms against Great Britain until their names appeared on a prisoner exchange list.

Also included in this file are lists of men who were captured by the British at Black Rock, NY, Buffalo, NY, Prairie de Chien, IL, Fort Sullivan, ME, French Town (River Raisin), MI and Detroit, MI. Finally, there are lists of American prisoners who died in either Montreal or Quebec.

The second part of this book was compiled from a copy of the *Miscellaneous Lists and Records* of the British Admiralty made by the Public Record Office in London, Great Britain (ADM 103 / 465, part 2). Three different types of reports contain information on the American prisoners of war who were interned between 3 July 1813 and 13 March 1815 at Quebec. The first type of report is the receipt musters, listing the men being transferred from Montreal to Quebec. The second type of report is the discharge musters, listing the men who were exchanged at Quebec and being sent back to the United States, or men who were being transferred to a prison facility in either Halifax (Nova Scotia) or in England. The final reports are the listing of men who died at Quebec.

The *Records Relating to War of 1812 Prisoners of War* contains the names of 2,285 American prisoners of war while the *Miscellaneous Lists and Records* lists 1,412 Americans being held in Quebec. No attempts have been made to combine these two lists of prisoners into a single listing. Many of the names of the same men can be found in both the American and in the British records.

Likewise, most of the men in the *Miscellaneous Lists and Records* can be found in a previous volume of the prisoners of war series of books entitled *American Prisoners of War held at Quebec during the War of 1812*. This book lists the American prisoners of war listed in the *General Entry Book of American Prisoners of War* ledger at Quebec. There are men in the *Miscellaneous Lists and Records* who are not found in the *American Prisoners of War held at Quebec during the War of 1812*. Also, the *Miscellaneous Lists and Records* contains information not found in the other book. As an example: the age, birth place and cause of death of the men who died at Quebec can only be found in the *Miscellaneous Lists and Records*. The second part of this book can be regarded as a supplement to the *American Prisoners of War held at Quebec during the War of 1812*.

Seventy-one men died while interned at Quebec while another thirty-two died at Montreal based upon the reports found in these two sources. A total of thirty men volunteered to serve with the New Brunswick Fencibles rather than staying in a POW facility. The New Brunswick Fencibles was a regiment in the British Army. Ten American soldiers were classified at British subjects (deserters) and sent to England.

Death of Mrs. Joseph Bledsoe

A clothing report for the 24th Regiment of U.S. Infantry for American prisoners of war who were held in Montreal lists the death of an American woman. The report states that Mrs. Bledsoe, the wife of a private in the 24th Infantry died on 22 April 1814. Mrs. Bledsoe was probably a washerwomen in this regiment, who was captured when Fort Niagara, NY, fell to the British on 19 December 1813. The 24th Infantry was raised in Tennessee.

The identify of this woman was revealed two days later in a letter written on 24 April 1814 by Robert Gardner, the agent for the American prisoners of war in Canada, to his superior, John Mason, the Commissary General of Prisoners. Gardner states, "to the men I have paid each a small sum, $4; to one man of the 24 regiment whose wife died here two days since, $9 (Joseph Bledsoe)". Besides receiving new clothing, the American prisoners of war also received $4 each from Gardner, however, Bledsoe received an additional $5 because of the death of his wife.

Bledsoe applied for a pension after the war, which was rejected. He states in his pension papers that he was wounded during the Battle of Fort Niagara and that he was made a prisoner of war by the British. He makes no mention of his wife in his pension application, even though she had died in captivity in Montreal.

Any errors or omissions are regretted and are the fault of the transcriber.

Eric Eugene Johnson

President (2008-2011)
Society of the War of 1812 in the State of Ohio

Historian General (2011-2014)
General Society of the War of 1812

- In memory of those who did not return -

The Dead (Montreal)

Barry, Sampson	Lane, Benjamin
Beatie, William	Lark, John
Abrahams, Cyrus	Martin, Delancy
Aycaulh, James	McArthur, Alexander
Bledsoe, Mrs. Joseph	McGarley, Jesse
Couther, Jonathan	Messenger, Grove
Demolunt, Alexander	Mooney, Peter
Easter, Stephen	Mountain, Michael B.
Ferguson, William	Mullen, Enoch
Friend, John D.	Nichols, Thomas
Hargrove, John	Norton, John
Harraday, Elisha	Ogden, Thomas
Hewlett, William	Schufelt, David
Hicks, John R.	Roberts, John
Holmes, Daniel	Sanborn, Charles
Jones, Phineas	Scott, John

The Dead (Quebec)

Amling, Ezra	Foster, Hulet	Martin, Silvanus
Ayres, John	Foster, Nathaniel	McIntyre, James
Bacon, Jabbec	Goodman, Elisha	McMillan, Archibald
Bascomb, Samuel	Green, Eli	Merrill, Elijah
Bently, William	Halted, John	Mitchell, William
Bow, Stephen	Harrodon, Elisha	Moore, Joshua
Burkand, John	Hazard, Zekiel	Parker, Edward
Butler, Michael	Herrick, Eli	Paul, Simeon
Carver, William	Hooker, George	Potter, John
Churchill, Oliver	Hooker, Horace	Pratt, Nathaniel
Clark, William	Howard, Joseph	Pratt, Walter
Clement, David	Hunt, Solomon	Reed, Isaac
Cogswell, Allanson	Ingalls, Jonathan	Root, John
Coomb, Isaac	Judd, William	Rowe, Benjamin
Cotton, Seth	Kail, Horace	Sanborn, John L.
Davis, Stephen	Kimball, Benjamin	Shaver, George
Dearborne, Solomon	Knight, Andrew	Sinclair, Jacob
Dearing, John	Lackey, Amasa	Smith, John
DeFriend, John	Lamb, Joshua F.	Smith, Stephen
Dyer, Isaac	Lander, Charles	Smith, William
Eaton, William	Lane, Benjamin	Till, James
Fenning, Charles	Lawton, Perry	Wells, Caleb
Finney, Elihua	Lewis, John	Welsh, Russell
	Libby, Thomas	Young, Ephraim

- Those who die in service to the United States should not be forgotten –

American Sources

Code	Title
AS-1	Account of clothing furnished to American prisoners of war held in Canada, Robert Gardner, agent; reports by regiment with various dates
AS-2	List of American prisoners of war taken at Black Rock (New York) and Buffalo (New York) on 30th December 1814 belonging to the militia of the United States
AS-3	List of officers, non-commissioned officers, musicians and privates who surrendered to his Britannic Majesty's forces under the command of Lieutenant Colonel William McKay at Prairie de Chien (Illinois) on 20th July 1814
AS-4	List of officers, non-commissioned officers, musicians and privates who surrendered at Fort Sullivan (Maine) on 11 July 1814
AS-4a	List of non-commissioned officers and privates who escaped from Fort Sullivan (Maine) after the surrender of that post
AS-5	List of American prisoners of war on parole at Boston, 13 July 1814
AS-6	American prisoners who died at Quebec
AS-7	List of American prisoners who have died at the hospital in Montreal since November 1813
AS-8	Names, Rank, etc., of a detachment of U.S. troops paroled at Quebec on 19th November 1812. Embarked on 20th for Boston in the transport ship, Regulus
AS-9	A list of prisoners received from Quebec, 26 October 1814
AS-10	A list of prisoners received from Quebec, 29 October 1814
AS-11	A list of prisoners captured at French Town (Michigan), 22 January 1813 (Officers)
AS-12	List of American prisoners of war sent to the United States to be exchanged agreeable to cartel, Montreal, 25 April 1814
AS-13	A list of officers of the Kentucky, Ohio and Michigan militias who surrendered at Detroit under the capitulation of General Hull on 16 August 1812
AS-14	A list of officers and men's names embarked on board the Matilda transport cartel, Halifax harbor, 31 May 1814
AS-15	A list of the recruits of the 27th Regiment of Infantry who were made prisoners at the surrender of Detroit by Brigadier General Hull, 16 June 1813
AS-16	Return of United States troops who being prisoners of war to the British government and sent on parole from Quebec, have been landed on Castle Island in the harbor of Boston between the dates of November 24th and November 30th 1812
AS-17	A list of commissioned officers, non-commissioned officers, musicians and private who arrived last month in cartels from Quebec and who are now quartered at Charlestown, Massachusetts, 20 December 1812
AS-18	List of officers of militia who surrendered at Detroit under the capitulation of General Hull on the 16 August 1812

American Records

American Prisoners of War held at Montreal and Quebec during the War of 1812

Abbott, Luther - Regiment: 3rd Artillery - Source(s): AS-1.

Abrahams, Cyrus - Date of death: 13 Jan 1814 - Source(s): AS-7.

Ackley, Benjamin - Rank: Private - Source(s): AS-8.

Atchley, Joshua - Regiment: 24th Infantry - Source(s): AS-1.

Adams, John - Regiment: 4th Infantry - Rank: Private - Source(s): AS-16.

Adams, Samuel - Regiment: 2nd Light Dragoons - Rank: Private - Source(s): AS-1; AS-12.

Adams, William - Rank: Private - Source(s): AS-8.

Ager, Winthrop D. - Regiment: 4th Infantry - Rank: Second Lieutenant - Source(s): AS-11; AS-17.

Albert, Warren - Regiment: 30th Infantry - Rank: Private - Source(s): AS-12.

Alderson, Moses - Regiment: 24th Infantry - Rank: Private - Source(s): AS-1; AS-12.

Alexander, James - Rank: Private - Source(s): AS-8.

Alexander, Jonathan - Regiment: 24th Infantry - Rank: Private - Source(s): AS-1; AS-12.

Alger, John - Regiment: Militia - Rank: Private - Source(s): AS-2.

Alison, Howard - Regiment: 4th Infantry - Source(s): AS-1.

Allen, Alva - Regiment: NY Militia - Rank: Private - Source(s): AS-12.

Allen, Edward - Regiment: 4th Infantry - Rank: Corporal - Source(s): AS-17.

Allen, Ira - Rank: Citizen - Source(s): AS-10.

Allen, Isaac - Regiment: McCobb's Volunteers - Rank: Private - Source(s): AS-1; AS-14.

Allen, John - Regiment: 1st Artillery - Rank: Private - Enlistment date: 29 Mar 1810 - Enlistment period: 5 years - Name of prison ship: Lord Cathcart - Source(s): AS-1; AS-5; AS-14.

Allen, John - Regiment: 21st Infantry - Rank: Private - Enlistment date: 10 Feb 1813 - Enlistment period: 5 years - Source(s): AS-1; AS-5; AS-14.

Allen, John - Regiment: 11th Infantry - Rank: Private - Source(s): AS-10.

Allen, Joseph - Regiment: 1st Infantry - Rank: Private - Source(s): AS-16.

Allen, Philip - Regiment: 4th Infantry - Rank: Private - Source(s): AS-17.

Allen, Samuel - Regiment: 11th Infantry - Rank: Private - Source(s): AS-10.

Allen, Samuel - Rank: Private - Source(s): AS-8.

Allsworth, Philip - Regiment: 15th Infantry - Rank: Private - Source(s): AS-1; AS-12.

Alodget, Sylvester - Regiment: Militia - Rank: Private - Source(s): AS-2.

Anderson, Jeremiah - Regiment: 16th Infantry - Rank: Sergeant - Source(s): AS-1; AS-12.

Anderson, John - Regiment: 19th Infantry - Rank: Lieutenant - Source(s): AS-11 - Comments: now a Topographical Engineer.

Anderson, John - Regiment: Militia - Rank: Private - Source(s): AS-2.

Anderson, Peter - Regiment: 21st Infantry - Source(s): AS-1.

Anderson, Robert - Regiment: 1st Infantry - Rank: Private - Source(s): AS-16.

Anderson, Thomas - Regiment: 26th Infantry - Rank: Private - Source(s): AS-12.

Andrews, E. T. - Regiment: 4th Infantry - Rank: Private - Source(s): AS-17.

Andrews, Eli - Regiment: Militia - Rank: Private - Source(s): AS-3.

Andrews, Otis - Regiment: 4th Infantry - Rank: Private - Source(s): AS-17.

Andrews, Samuel - Regiment: 1st Artillery - Rank: Corporal - Source(s): AS-8; AS-12.

Andrews, William - Regiment: 4th Infantry - Rank: Private - Source(s): AS-17.

Andries, Samuel - Regiment: 1st Artillery - Source(s): AS-1.

Archer, Isaac - Regiment: 24th Infantry - Source(s): AS-1.

Archer, Robert - Regiment: 24th Infantry - Source(s): AS-1.

Armes, Thomas - Regiment: Militia - Name of prison ship: Lord Cathcart - Where taken: Black Rock, NY - Source(s): AS-1.

Armstrong, Thomas - Regiment: KY or TN Militia - Where taken: Miami Rapids, OH or River Raison, MI - Source(s): AS-1.

Arnes, Oliver - Regiment: 9th Infantry - Rank: Private - Enlistment date: 13 Feb 1813 - Enlistment period: 5 years - Source(s): AS-5, AS-14.

Arnold, James - Regiment: 24th Infantry - Source(s): AS-1.

Arrall, Richard - Regiment: 14th Infantry - Rank: First Lieutenant - Source(s): AS-14.

Ashton, John - Regiment: 4th Infantry - Rank: Private - Source(s): AS-17.

Atchison, Joseph - Regiment: 24th Infantry - Rank: Corporal - Source(s): AS-1; AS-12.

Atchley, Daniel - Regiment: 24th Infantry - Source(s): AS-1.

Atherton, William - Regiment: KY or TN Militia - Where taken: Miami Rapids, OH or River Raison, MI - Source(s): AS-1.

Ausper, John - Regiment: 9th Infantry - Rank: Private - Source(s): AS-14.

Austin, John - Regiment: 4th Infantry - Rank: Private - Source(s): AS-16.

Avery, Alexander - Regiment: 29th Infantry - Rank: Private - Source(s): AS-9.

Avery, Muttuttos - Regiment: 13th Infantry - Rank: Private - Enlistment date: 8 Feb 1813 - Enlistment period: 5 years - Source(s): AS-5.

Avery, Nicholas - Regiment: 13th Infantry - Rank: Private - Source(s): AS-14.

Avery, Richard - Regiment: 13th Infantry - Rank: Private - Enlistment date: 13 Mar 1813 - Enlistment period: 5 years - Name of prison ship: Lord Cathcart - Source(s): AS-1; AS-5.

Aycaulh, James - Date of death: 23 Feb 1814 - Source(s): AS-7.

Ayres, John - Date of death: 15 Aug 1813 - Source(s): AS-6 - Comments: Died at Quebec.

Bachelar, Aaron - Regiment: 9th Infantry - Rank: Private - Source(s): AS-14.

Bacon Jabbec - Date of death: 6 Aug 1813 - Source(s): AS-6 - Comments: Died at Quebec.

Bacon, Josiah - Regiment: 4th Infantry - Rank: Lieutenant - Source(s): AS-11.

Badgrove, John - Rank: Private - Source(s): AS-8.

Bailey, George - Regiment: 4th Infantry - Rank: Private - Source(s): AS-17.

Bailey, Levi - Regiment: 1st Infantry - Rank: Private - Source(s): AS-16.

Baines, John - Rank: Private - Source(s): AS-8.

Baish, Lewis - Regiment: 1st Infantry - Rank: Corporal - Source(s): AS-16.

Baker, Daniel - Regiment: 1st Infantry - Rank: Captain - Source(s): AS-11; AS-16.

Baker, Daniel - Regiment: 23rd Infantry - Rank: Private - Enlistment date: 23 Jun 1812 - Enlistment period: 5 years

- Name of prison ship: Lord Cathcart - Source(s): AS-1; AS-5; AS-14.

Baker, George - Regiment: 1st Artillery - Name of prison ship: Lord Cathcart - Source(s): AS-1.

Baker, Greenberry - Regiment: Militia - Rank: Private - Source(s): AS-3.

Baker, Robert - Regiment: 25th Infantry - Source(s): AS-6 - Comments: Died on prison ship.

Ball, Seth - Regiment: 15th Infantry - Source(s): AS-1.

Ballard, John - Regiment: 11th Infantry - Rank: Private - Enlistment date: 28 May 1812 - Enlistment period: 5 years - Source(s): AS-1; AS-5; AS-14.

Ballou, Darius - Regiment: 4th Infantry - Rank: Private - Source(s): AS-17.

Balts, George - Regiment: 14th Infantry - Rank: Private - Enlistment date: 7 Aug 1812 - Enlistment period: 5 years - Source(s): AS-5.

Bander, Thomas - Regiment: 15th Infantry - Rank: Private - Enlistment date: 18 May 1812 - Enlistment period: 5 years - Name of prison ship: Lord Cathcart - Source(s): AS-1; AS-5; AS-14.

Bangs, Seth - Regiment: 9th Infantry - Rank: Private - Enlistment date: 1 Jan 1813 - Enlistment period: During the war - Source(s): AS-5; AS-14.

Barb, George - Regiment: 13th Infantry - Rank: Ensign - Source(s): AS-8.

Barber, Charles - Regiment: 16th Infantry - Rank: Private - Source(s): AS-1; AS-12.

Barber, John - Regiment: 14th Infantry - Rank: Private - Enlistment date: 22 Jan 1813 - Enlistment period: 5 years - Source(s): AS-5:AS-14.

Bare, Thomas - Enlistment date: 7 Oct 1812 - Source(s): AS-5.

Barfield, Richard - Regiment: 40th Infantry - Rank: Musician - Source(s): AS-4a.

Barker, Christopher - Regiment: 1st Artillery - Source(s): AS-1.

Barker, Ephraim - Regiment: NY Militia - Rank: Private - Source(s): AS-12.

Barker, Joseph - Rank: Private - Source(s): AS-8.

Barnes, Ezra - Regiment: Militia - Rank: Private - Source(s): AS-10.

Barnes, John - Regiment: 24th Infantry - Rank: Private - Source(s): AS-1; AS-12.

Barnes, Michael - Regiment: 22nd Infantry - Rank: Private - Source(s): AS-10.

Barnes, Seth - Regiment: 15th Infantry - Rank: Sergeant - Source(s): AS-1; AS-9.

Barnet, William - Regiment: 4th Infantry - Rank: Private - Source(s): AS-17.

Barnhart, Henry - Regiment: 7th Infantry - Rank: Private - Source(s): AS-3.

Barrett, Elias - Regiment: 4th Infantry - Rank: Private - Source(s): AS-16.

Barrick, George W. - Regiment: 24th Infantry - Source(s): AS-1.

Barrier, George W. - Regiment: OH Militia - Rank: Captain - Source(s): AS-18 - Comments: McArthur's Regiment.

Barron, John - Regiment: 16th Infantry - Rank: Private - Name of prison ship: Lord Cathcart - Source(s): AS-1; AS-14.

Barrs, Henry - Name of prison ship: Lord Cathcart - Source(s): AS-1.

Barry, Sampson - Date of death: 26 Dec 1813 - Source(s): AS-7.

Barton, Caleb - Regiment: 4th Infantry - Rank: Private - Source(s): AS-17.

Bascler, George - Regiment: 24th Infantry - Rank: Private - Source(s): AS-12.

Basseu, Daniel - Regiment: 21st Infantry - Rank: Private - Source(s): AS-9.

Batchelder, Orin - Regiment: 15th Infantry - Source(s): AS-1.

Battles, Avery - Regiment: 27th Infantry - Rank: Recruit - Source(s): AS-15.

Battles, John - Regiment: Militia - Rank: Private - Source(s): AS-2.

Baxley, George - Regiment: 24th Infantry - Source(s): AS-1.

Bayley, Richard Mountjoy - Regiment: 3rd Artillery - Rank: First Lieutenant - Source(s): AS-8; AS-11 - Comments: Resigned.

Bays, Jacob - Name of prison ship: Lord Cathcart - Source(s): AS-1.

Beach, James - Source(s): AS-1.

Beaman, Peter - Regiment: 7th Infantry - Rank: Private - Source(s): AS-3.

Beard, William C. - Regiment: 1st Rifles - Rank: First Lieutenant - Source(s): AS-14.

Beasley, William - Regiment: 4th Infantry - Rank: Private - Source(s): AS-17.

Beatie, William - Date of death: 13 Aug 1813 - Source(s): AS-6 - Comments: Died at Quebec.

Beau, William K. - Regiment: 7th Infantry - Rank: Ensign - Source(s): AS-11.

Beck, Andrew - Regiment: 25th Infantry - Rank: Drummer - Source(s): AS-14.

Beckford, John - Regiment: 16th Infantry - Rank: Private - Enlistment date: 15 Oct 1812 - Source(s): AS-5; AS-14.

Beckwith, Gordon - Regiment: 4th Infantry - Rank: Private - Source(s): AS-16.

Becthold, Henry - Regiment: 12th Infantry - Name of prison ship: Lord Cathcart - Source(s): AS-1.

Beech, James - Regiment: 16th Infantry - Rank: Private - Enlistment date: 7 May 1812 - Source(s): AS-5; AS-14.

Been, John - Regiment: 7th Infantry - Rank: Private - Source(s): AS-3.

Beers, James - Regiment: 11th Infantry - Rank: Private - Source(s): AS-9.

Bell, Joshua H. - Regiment: 17th Infantry - Rank: Sergeant - Source(s): AS-9.

Bell, Thomas - Regiment: 1st Rifles - Rank: Private - Source(s): AS-1; AS-12.

Belluito, Levi - Regiment: 14th Infantry - Rank: Private - Enlistment date: 11 Apr 1812 - Enlistment period: 5 years - Source(s): AS-5; AS-14.

Bemis, Lewis - Regiment: 4th Infantry - Rank: Private - Source(s): AS-17.

Bennet, William - Regiment: 7th Infantry - Rank: Private - Source(s): AS-3.

Bennett, James W. - Regiment: 2nd Light Dragoons - Source(s): AS-1.

Bennett, John H. - Regiment: NY Militia - Rank: Private - Source(s): AS-12.

Bennett, Uriah W. - Regiment: NY Militia - Rank: Private - Source(s): AS-12.

Bennett, Waterman - Regiment: NY Militia - Rank: Private - Source(s): AS-12.

Berger, William - Rank: Corporal - Source(s): AS-8.

Berkford, John - Name of prison ship: Lord Cathcart - Source(s): AS-1.

Berry, Samuel - Regiment: 1st Infantry - Rank: Private - Source(s): AS-16.

Berry, Taylor - Regiment: KY Militia - Rank: Assistant Quartermaster General - Source(s): AS-18.

Bewell, William - Regiment: NY Militia - Rank: Private - Source(s): AS-12.

Beyarty, John - Regiment: 7th Infantry - Rank: Private - Source(s): AS-3.

Bigger, David - Regiment: 7th Infantry - Rank: Private - Source(s): AS-3.

Billey, Henry - Regiment: 1st Light Dragoons - Rank: Private - Source(s): AS-1; AS-14.

Billings, Jonathan - Regiment: 1st Artillery - Rank: Private - Source(s): AS-1; AS-12.

Billings, Noyes - Regiment: 4th Infantry - Rank: Private - Source(s): AS-17.

Bills, Chester - Rank: Private - Source(s): AS-8.

Bilty, Henry - Regiment: 1st Light Dragoons - Rank: Quartermaster Sergeant - Enlistment date: 5 Jul 1813 - Enlistment period: 5 years - Source(s): AS-5.

Bingham, Isaac - Regiment: KY or TN Militia - Where taken: Miami Rapids, OH or River Raison, MI - Source(s): AS-1.

Bird, William - Regiment: 4th Infantry - Rank: Private - Source(s): AS-17.

Bird, William - Regiment: 40th Infantry - Rank: Sergeant - Source(s): AS-4a.

Bishop, Joshua - Regiment: 33rd Infantry - Source(s): AS-1.

Bishop, William - Regiment: 12th Infantry - Rank: Private - Source(s): AS-1; AS-12.

Biyd, Samuel - Regiment: 14th Infantry - Rank: Private - Source(s): AS-14.

Blachard, B. R. - Rank: Private - Source(s): AS-8.

Blackman, Dwight - Regiment: NY Militia - Rank: Private - Source(s): AS-12.

Blake, George - Regiment: 1st Infantry - Rank: Private - Source(s): AS-16.

Blake, Henry - Regiment: 27th Infantry - Rank: Recruit - Source(s): AS-15.

Blake, Rehemiah - Regiment: 27th Infantry - Rank: Recruit - Source(s): AS-15.

Blake, Samuel - Regiment: 1st Infantry - Rank: Private - Source(s): AS-16.

Blakeley, Abel - Rank: Private - Source(s): AS-8.

Blancet, Levi - Regiment: 21st Infantry - Rank: Corporal - Enlistment date: 22 Feb 1813 - Enlistment period: 5 years - Source(s): AS-1; AS-5; AS-14.

Blanchard, Amos - Regiment: 4th Infantry - Rank: Private - Source(s): AS-17.

Blanchard, Reuben K. - Regiment: 40th Infantry - Rank: Second Lieutenant - Source(s): AS-4 - Comments: On parole at Charlestown, MA.

Blatenburger, Jacob - Enlistment date: 15 Oct 1812 - Source(s): AS-5.

Bledsoe, Joseph - Regiment: 24th Infantry - Rank: Private - Source(s): AS-1; AS-12.

Bledsoe, Mrs. Joseph - Regiment: 24th Infantry - Rank: Woman - Date of death: 22 Apr 1814 - Source(s): AS-7.

Blythe, John - Regiment: 24th Infantry - Source(s): AS-1.

Bogert, Gilbert - Regiment: 6th Infantry - Name of prison ship: Lord Cathcart - Source(s): AS-1.

Boggs, Lyman - Rank: Sergeant - Source(s): AS-9.

Bone, Young E. - Regiment: 24th Infantry - Rank: Private - Source(s): AS-1; AS-12.

Boothe, B. - Rank: Private - Source(s): AS-8.

Bosson, Thaddeus - Regiment: 21st Infantry - Rank: Private - Source(s): AS-1, AS-14.

Botchford, Buford - Regiment: Militia - Rank: Private - Source(s): AS-2.

Bouse, Samuel - Regiment: 1st Infantry - Rank: Corporal - Source(s): AS-16 - Comments: Formerly from the 19th Infantry.

Boutwell, Henry - Regiment: 11th Infantry - Rank: Corporal - Source(s): AS-9.

Boutwell, Nathaniel - Regiment: 11th Infantry - Source(s): AS-1.

Bowen, Joseph - Regiment: 1st Infantry - Source(s): AS-1.

Bowen, Thomas - Regiment: 2nd Artillery - Rank: Private - Source(s): AS-14.

Bowers, Joseph - Regiment: 3rd Artillery - Source(s): AS-1.

Bowers, Joshua - Regiment: 3rd Artillery - Rank: Private - Source(s): AS-10.

Bowles, William - Regiment: 4th Infantry - Rank: Private - Source(s): AS-17.

Bowman, Thaddeus - Regiment: Militia - Rank: Private - Source(s): AS-14.

Bowyon, George - Regiment: 16th Infantry - Rank: Private - Source(s): AS-14.

Boyce, George - Name of prison ship: Lord Cathcart - Source(s): AS-1.

Boyce, Jacob - Name of prison ship: Lord Cathcart - Source(s): AS-1.

Boyce, John - Regiment: 9th Infantry - Rank: Private - Enlistment date: 4 Mar 1813 - Enlistment period: During the war - Source(s): AS-5; AS-14.

Boyd, Dennis - Rank: Private - Source(s): AS-8.

Boyd, Thomas D. - Regiment: Militia - Rank: Private - Source(s): AS-14.

Boyd, William - Regiment: 24th Infantry - Source(s): AS-1.

Brabstone, William B. - Regiment: 24th Infantry - Rank: Private - Source(s): AS-1; AS-12.

Bradford, Augustus - Regiment: 4th Infantry - Rank: Corporal - Source(s): AS-17.

Bradford, John - Regiment: 22nd Infantry - Rank: Private - Enlistment date: 12 Feb 1813 - Enlistment period: 5 years - Source(s): AS-1; AS-5; AS-14.

Bradford, Lemuel - Regiment: 21st Infantry - Rank: Captain - Source(s): AS-14.

Bradley, Simeon - Regiment: 21st Infantry - Rank: Private - Source(s): AS-10.

Bradshaw, Edward - Regiment: 14th Infantry - Rank: Private - Enlistment date: 18 May 1812 - Enlistment period: 5 years - Source(s): AS-5; AS-14.

Brakeman, Roderick - Regiment: Militia - Rank: Private - Source(s): AS-14.

Branch, Thomas B. - Regiment: 40th Infantry - Rank: Private - Source(s): AS-4a.

Brandon, Samuel - Regiment: 24th Infantry - Source(s): AS-1.

Branton, John - Regiment: 24th Infantry - Source(s): AS-1.

Brasbridge, George - Regiment: 4th Infantry - Rank: Private - Source(s): AS-16.

Brasier, Edward - Regiment: 7th Infantry - Rank: Private - Source(s): AS-3.

Brason, David - Regiment: 7th Infantry - Rank: Private - Source(s): AS-3.

Breechman, Lemerick - Regiment: 23rd Infantry - Rank: Musician - Enlistment date: 3 May 1813 - Enlistment period: During the war - Source(s): AS-5.

Brenough, Thomas - Regiment: KY or TN Militia - Where taken: Miami Rapids, OH or River Raison, MI - Source(s): AS-1.

Brewer, John - Regiment: 4th Infantry - Rank: Private - Source(s): AS-16.

Bridge, Franklin - Regiment: McCobb's Volunteers - Rank: Sergeant - Source(s): AS-1; AS-14.

Bridgeman, William - Regiment: 21st Infantry - Rank: Private - Source(s): AS-10.

Briee, James - Regiment: 4th Infantry - Rank: Private - Source(s): AS-16.

Briggs, Samuel - Regiment: 4th Infantry - Rank: Private - Source(s): AS-17.

Briggs, William - Regiment: 11th Infantry - Source(s): AS-1.

Brink, Orson - Regiment: 11th Infantry - Source(s): AS-1.

Brink, Orson - Regiment: Volunteers - Rank: Private - Source(s): AS-14.

Bristol, Abram - Rank: Private - Source(s): AS-8.

Bristol, Anson - Regiment: Militia - Rank: Private - Source(s): AS-2.

Brocor, Stephen - Regiment: 4th Infantry - Rank: Private - Source(s): AS-17.

Broghter, Levi - Regiment: Militia - Rank: Private - Source(s): AS-2.

Bromer, Abram - Rank: Private - Source(s): AS-8.

Brooks, Roswell - Rank: Private - Source(s): AS-8.

Brothorritt, Jonathan - Regiment: 11th Infantry - Rank: Private - Enlistment date: 2 Apr 1813 - Enlistment period: 5 years - Source(s): AS-5.

Broton, Alexander - Regiment: 4th Infantry - Rank: Private - Source(s): AS-17.

Brower, James - Rank: Private - Source(s): AS-8.

Brown, Abel - Regiment: 4th Infantry - Rank: Private - Source(s): AS-17.

Brown, Daniel - Regiment: 24th Infantry - Rank: Private - Source(s): AS-1; AS-12.

Brown, Ephraim - Regiment: OH Militia - Rank: Captain - Source(s): AS-18 - Comments: Findlay's Regiment.

Brown, George - Regiment: 1st Artillery - Rank: Private - Source(s): AS-16 - Comments: Died aboard transport.

Brown, Henry - Regiment: 16th Infantry - Rank: Private - Name of prison ship: Lord Cathcart - Source(s): AS-1: AS-14.

Brown, James - Regiment: 27th Infantry - Rank: Recruit - Source(s): AS-15.

Brown, John - Rank: Private - Source(s): AS-8.

Brown, John - Regiment: Militia - Rank: Private - Source(s): AS-2 - Comments: Ohio Volunteers.

Brown, John - Source(s): AS-3 - Comments: British deserter.

Brown, John - Regiment: 3rd Artillery - Rank: Corporal - Source(s): AS-1; AS-10.

Brown, John - Regiment: 40th Infantry - Rank: Private - Source(s): AS-4 - Comments: POW at Eastport, ME.

Brown, Llewellyn - Rank: Contractor Agent - Source(s): AS-3 - Comments: Paroled.

Brown, Nathan - Regiment: 4th Infantry - Rank: Musician - Source(s): AS-16.

Brown, R. - Regiment: 17th Infantry - Rank: Private - Source(s): AS-9.

Brown, Return B. - Regiment: 4th Infantry - Rank: Captain - Source(s): AS-17.

Brown, Thomas - Regiment: 2nd Artillery - Rank: Private - Enlistment date: 18 May 1812 - Enlistment period: 5 years - Source(s): AS-5.

Brown, Thomas - Regiment: Rifles - Rank: Private - Source(s): AS-12.

Brown, Thomas - Rank: Citizen - Source(s): AS-10.

Brown, William - Name of prison ship: Lord Cathcart - Source(s): AS-1.

Brown, William - Regiment: 4th Infantry - Rank: Private - Source(s): AS-16 - Comments: Died at Fort Independence, MA.

Browne, Joseph - Regiment: 1st Rifles - Source(s): AS-1.

Browne, Thomas - Regiment: 1st Rifles - Source(s): AS-1.

Browne, William - Regiment: 1st Artillery - Source(s): AS-1.

Brownel, Wantan - Regiment: NY Militia - Rank: Private - Source(s): AS-12.

Brownwell, David - Regiment: 2nd Artillery - Rank: Private - Source(s): AS-9.

Bruce, William - Regiment: Pennsylvania Volunteers - Rank: Private - Source(s): AS-10.

Bruner, Edward - Regiment: 7th Infantry - Rank: Private - Source(s): AS-3.

Bryant, Samuel - Regiment: Militia - Rank: Private - Source(s): AS-14.

Bryant, Thomas - Regiment: 13th Infantry - Source(s): AS-1.

Bryne, Michael - Regiment: 44th Infantry - Source(s): AS-1.

Buck, Abraham - Regiment: NY Militia - Rank: Private - Source(s): AS-12.

Buck, Robert - Regiment: 12th Infantry - Rank: Private - Source(s): AS-1; AS-12.

Buckingham, Jared - Rank: Private - Source(s): AS-8.

Buckover, Peter - Regiment: 19th Infantry - Rank: Private - Source(s): AS-12.

Budewood, James - Regiment: 1st Infantry - Rank: Private - Source(s): AS-16.

Butler, William O. - Regiment: 2nd Infantry - Rank: Lieutenant - Source(s): AS-11 - Comments: now Captain, 17th Infantry.

Burers, Michael - Regiment: 4th Infantry - Rank: Private - Source(s): AS-16.

Burger, John - Regiment: 23rd Infantry - Name of prison ship: Lord Cathcart - Source(s): AS-1.

Burgh, Samuel - Regiment: Militia - Rank: Private - Source(s): AS-2.

Burke, John - Regiment: 14th Infantry - Rank: Private - Enlistment date: 8 Jan 1812 - Enlistment period: 5 years - Source(s): AS-5; AS-14.

Burnell, Nelson - Regiment: 24th Infantry - Rank: Private - Source(s): AS-1; AS-12.

Burnham, Benjamin - Regiment: 4th Infantry - Rank: Private - Source(s): AS-17.

Burns, James - Regiment: 24th Infantry - Source(s): AS-1.

Burns, John - Regiment: 4th Infantry - Rank: Private - Source(s): AS-17.

Burr, Andrew - Regiment: 1st Infantry - Rank: Sergeant - Source(s): AS-16.

Burrell, James - Rank: Private - Source(s): AS-8.

Burthole, Henry - Regiment: 12th Infantry - Rank: Private - Enlistment date: 15 Jul 1812 - Enlistment period: 5 years - Source(s): AS-5.

Burton, Oliver G. - Regiment: 4th Infantry - Rank: Captain - Source(s): AS-11; AS-17.

Bush, John - Regiment: 1st Artillery - Rank: Private - Source(s): AS-1; AS-12.

Bustrill, David - Regiment: 1st Artillery - Source(s): AS-1.

Butler, Asaph - Regiment: 27th Infantry - Rank: Recruit - Source(s): AS-15.

Butler, Michael - Date of death: 27 Jul 1813 - Source(s): AS-6 - Comments: Died at Quebec.

Butler, Samuel - Regiment: 1st Infantry - Rank: Private - Source(s): AS-16.

Buttman, David - Regiment: 21st Infantry - Rank: Private - Source(s): AS-9.

Buxton, Daniel - Regiment: NY Militia - Rank: Private - Source(s): AS-12.

Byard, Anthony W. - Regiment: 7th Infantry - Rank: Private - Source(s): AS-3.

Byler, Howard - Regiment: 16th Infantry - Rank: Private - Source(s): AS-14.

Byrne, Philip - Regiment: KY or TN Militia - Where taken: Miami Rapids, OH or River Raison, MI - Source(s):

AS-1.

Byron, John - Regiment: 27th Infantry - Rank: Recruit - Source(s): AS-15.

Cahill, Edward - Regiment: 24th Infantry - Rank: Private - Source(s): AS-1; AS-9.

Cairns, Joseph - Regiment: 27th Infantry and OH Militia - Rank: Captain - Source(s): AS-15; AS-18 - Comments: Cass' Regiment.

Cairns, Richard - Regiment: 27th Infantry - Rank: Recruit - Source(s): AS-15.

Caldwell, Isaac - Regiment: 1st Artillery - Rank: Private - Source(s): AS-1; AS-12.

Caldwell, James - Regiment: Militia Riflemen - Source(s): AS-1.

Calmes, Marquis - Regiment: NY Militia - Rank: Private - Source(s): AS-12.

Campbell, Frederick - Regiment: 16th Infantry - Rank: Private - Source(s): AS-1; AS-9.

Campbell, James - Regiment: 24th Infantry - Source(s): AS-1.

Campbell, James - Regiment: McCobb's Volunteers - Source(s): AS-1.

Campbell, James - Regiment: Volunteers - Rank: Private - Source(s): AS-14.

Campbell, James - Regiment: Civilian - Rank: Custom House Officer - Source(s): AS-12.

Campbell, James - Regiment: 16th Infantry - Rank: Private - Source(s): AS-1; AS-12.

Campbell, Joseph - Regiment: 16th Infantry - Rank: Private - Name of prison ship: Lord Cathcart - Source(s): AS-1; AS-14.

Campbell, William - Regiment: 21st Infantry - Rank: Private - Source(s): AS-14.

Campbell, William - Regiment: McCobb's Volunteers - Rank: Private - Source(s): AS-1; AS-14.

Can, Samuel - Rank: Private - Source(s): AS-8.

Canada, William - Regiment: 24th Infantry - Source(s): AS-1.

Carley, William - Regiment: 1st Artillery - Source(s): AS-1.

Carpenter, Isaac - Regiment: 40th Infantry - Rank: Ensign - Source(s): AS-4 - Comments: On parole at Weston, ME.

Carr, Daniel - Rank: Private - Source(s): AS-8.

Carr, John - Regiment: 40th Infantry - Rank: Private - Source(s): AS-4 - Comments: POW at Eastport, ME.

Carr, William D. - Regiment: 13th Infantry - Rank: Lieutenant - Source(s): AS-11.

Carrier, Kneeland - Regiment: 4th Infantry - Rank: Sergeant - Source(s): AS-17.

Carroll, Peter - Rank: Private - Source(s): AS-8.

Carroll, Timothy - Regiment: 15th Infantry - Rank: Private - Source(s): AS-9.

Carter, D. - Rank: Private - Source(s): AS-8.

Carter, Enoch - Regiment: 4th Infantry - Rank: Private - Source(s): AS-17.

Carter, J. F. - Rank: Corporal - Source(s): AS-8.

Cary, Daniel - Regiment: 11th Infantry - Rank: Private - Source(s): AS-1; AS-14.

Casey, Archibald - Regiment: 27th Infantry - Rank: Recruit - Source(s): AS-15.

Cass, Cornelius D. - Regiment: 4th Infantry - Rank: Private - Source(s): AS-17.

Cass, Ira - Regiment: 27th Infantry - Rank: Recruit - Source(s): AS-15.

Cass, Lewis - Regiment: OH Militia - Rank: Colonel - Source(s): AS-18.

Cassidy, Patrick - Regiment: 1st Infantry - Rank: Private - Source(s): AS-16.

Castler, A. - Rank: Private - Source(s): AS-8.

Castler, J. - Rank: Private - Source(s): AS-8.

Cawthorn, Eleazer - Regiment: KY or TN Militia - Where taken: Miami Rapids, OH or River Raison, MI - Source(s): AS-1.

Cease, John - Regiment: 12th Infantry - Name of prison ship: Lord Cathcart - Source(s): AS-1.

Chadwick, Thomas - Regiment: 27th Infantry - Rank: Private - Source(s): AS-1; AS-12.

Chambers, Samuel - Regiment: 16th Infantry - Rank: Private - Enlistment date: 10 Feb 1813 - Source(s): AS-1; AS-5; AS-14.

Chamberlain, Jonathan - Regiment: NY Militia - Rank: Private - Source(s): AS-12.

Chamberlain, Rufus - Rank: Private - Source(s): AS-8.

Champion, Elias - Regiment: Civilian - Rank: Private - Source(s): AS-9.

Champlain, Dodwick - Regiment: Militia - Rank: Private - Source(s): AS-2.

Chapel, Seth - Regiment: Militia - Rank: Private - Source(s): AS-2.

Chapman, James - Regiment: 40th Infantry - Rank: Private - Source(s): AS-4 - Comments: On parole at Machias, ME.

Chappel, Joseph - Rank: Private - Source(s): AS-8.

Cheek, William - Regiment: 24th Infantry - Source(s): AS-1.

Chipman, Samuel - Regiment: Militia - Rank: Private - Source(s): AS-2.

Christian, Humphrey - Regiment: 5th Infantry - Source(s): AS-1.

Christie, John M. - Regiment: 13th Infantry - Name of prison ship: Lord Cathcart - Source(s): AS-1.

Church, Logan - Regiment: Militia - Rank: Private - Source(s): AS-2.

Churchill, Ephraim - Regiment: 4th Infantry - Rank: Sergeant - Source(s): AS-16.

Churchill, Oliver - Date of death: 28 Jul 1813 - Source(s): AS-6 - Comments: Died at Quebec.

Cilley, Joseph - Regiment: OH Militia - Rank: Lieutenant, Paymaster - Source(s): AS-18 - Comments: Findlay's Regiment.

Cilly, Paul - Regiment: 1st Artillery - Rank: Private - Enlistment date: 23 Mar 1812 - Enlistment period: 5 years - Source(s): AS-5.

Clark, Almarin - Regiment: 4th Infantry - Rank: Private - Source(s): AS-17.

Clark, George - Regiment: 28th Infantry - Rank: Private - Source(s): AS-12.

Clark, J. - Rank: Private - Source(s): AS-8.

Clark, Perry - Rank: Private - Source(s): AS-8.

Clark, Samuel - Regiment: Militia - Rank: Private - Source(s): AS-2.

Clark, William - Regiment: 23rd Infantry - Rank: Lieutenant - Source(s): AS-11.

Clarke, Andrew - Regiment: 1st Artillery - Source(s): AS-1.

Clarke, Benjamin - Regiment: 21st Infantry - Source(s): AS-1.

Clarke, Charles - Regiment: 24th Infantry - Source(s): AS-1.

Clarke, Henry - Regiment: 24th Infantry - Source(s): AS-1.

Clarke, James - Regiment: 1st Artillery - Rank: Artificer - Source(s): AS-16.

Clarke, Jesse - Regiment: 4th Infantry - Rank: Private - Source(s): AS-17.

Clarke, John - Regiment: 21st Infantry - Sent to hospital - Source(s): AS-1.

Clarke, John G. - Regiment: 5th Infantry - Rank: Second Lieutenant - Source(s): AS-14.

Clay, Elijah - Regiment: 5th Infantry - Rank: Private - Enlistment date: 13 Apr 1812 - Enlistment period: 5 years - Source(s): AS-5; AS-14.

Clay, Elisha - Regiment: 5th Infantry - Name of prison ship: Lord Cathcart - Source(s): AS-1.

Clear, William - Regiment: 2nd Light Dragoons - Rank: Private - Source(s): AS-1; AS-12.

Clement, David - Rank: Sergeant - Date of death: 3 Aug 1813 - Source(s): AS-6 - Comments: Died at Quebec.

Clough, William - Regiment: 4th Infantry - Rank: Private - Source(s): AS-16.

Clyne, Isaac - Regiment: 13th Infantry - Name of prison ship: Lord Cathcart - Source(s): AS-1.

Coates, Elijah - Regiment: 24th Infantry - Source(s): AS-1.

Cobb, John - Regiment: 21st Infantry - Rank: Private - Source(s): AS-14.

Cobb, John - Regiment: McCobb's Volunteers - Rank: Private - Source(s): AS-1; AS-14.

Coe, James - Regiment: 3rd Artillery - Source(s): AS-1.

Coffin, Samuel - Regiment: 4th Infantry - Rank: Private - Source(s): AS-17.

Colbaugh, Michael - Regiment: 2nd Light Dragoons - Source(s): AS-1.

Colbern, Jacob - Regiment: 1st Artillery - Name of prison ship: Lord Cathcart - Source(s): AS-1.

Cole, Daniel S. - Regiment: Militia - Rank: Private - Source(s): AS-2.

Cole, James - Regiment: 1st Artillery - Rank: Musician - Source(s): AS-12.

Cole, Samuel - Regiment: 1st Artillery - Source(s): AS-1; AS-16.

Cole, Thomas - Regiment: 24th Infantry - Source(s): AS-1.

Coleman, Charles - Regiment: 21st Infantry - Rank: Sergeant - Source(s): AS-1.

Coleman, Charles - Rank: Corporal - Source(s): AS-9.

Coles, Robert - Regiment: 4th Infantry - Rank: Private - Source(s): AS-17.

Collins, Jacob - Regiment: 4th Infantry - Rank: Private - Source(s): AS-16.

Colver, Peter - Rank: Private - Source(s): AS-8.

Colwell, John - Regiment: 40th Infantry - Rank: Sergeant - Source(s): AS-4a.

Comfort, Richard - Regiment: 1st Volunteer Dragoons - Rank: Private - Source(s): AS-10.

Conant, John - Regiment: Militia - Rank: Private - Source(s): AS-2.

Conkley, Joshua - Regiment: NY Volunteers - Rank: Captain - Source(s): AS-14.

Connelly, Hugh M. - Regiment: 1st Infantry - Rank: Private - Source(s): AS-9.

Conner, James H. - Regiment: 24th Infantry - Rank: Private - Source(s): AS-1; AS-12.

Conner, John - Regiment: 12th Infantry - Rank: Private - Enlistment date: 11 May 1812 - Enlistment period: 5 years - Source(s): AS-5; AS-14.

Conner, John - Regiment: 12th Infantry - Name of prison ship: Lord Cathcart - Source(s): AS-1.

Conner, Michael - Regiment: 24th Infantry - Source(s): AS-1.

Conner, Thomas - Regiment: 13th Infantry - Rank: Private - Source(s): AS-5; AS-8; AS-14.

Converse, K. - Rank: Private - Source(s): AS-8.

Cook, Joel - Regiment: 4th Infantry - Rank: Captain - Source(s): AS-16.

Cook, John - Regiment: 23rd Infantry - Rank: Private - Source(s): AS-14.

Cook, Joseph - Regiment: Militia - Rank: Private - Name of prison ship: Lord Cathcart - Where taken: Sackets Harbor, NY - Source(s): AS-1; AS-14.

Cook, Robert - Regiment: 21st Infantry - Source(s): AS-1.

Cooke, Samuel - Regiment: 4th Infantry - Rank: Private - Source(s): AS-16.

Coombs, George - Regiment: 24th Infantry - Rank: Private - Source(s): AS-1; AS-12.

Coon, John - Rank: Corporal - Source(s): AS-8.

Coop, Benjamin - Regiment: 7th Infantry - Rank: Private - Source(s): AS-3.

Cooper, James - Regiment: 24th Infantry - Rank: Private - Source(s): AS-1; AS-12.

Copner, John - Regiment: Militia - Rank: Private - Source(s): AS-10.

Copps, Darius - Regiment: 40th Infantry - Rank: Ensign - Source(s): AS-4 - Comments: Discharged from the service.

Corben, Fielding - Regiment: 1st Infantry - Source(s): AS-1.

Corben, James - Regiment: 1st Infantry - Source(s): AS-1.

Corey, Amos - Regiment: 4th Infantry - Rank: Musician - Source(s): AS-17.

Corey, Philip - Regiment: NY Militia - Rank: Private - Source(s): AS-12.

Corker, Daniel - Regiment: Militia - Rank: Private - Source(s): AS-14.

Corkins, Joel - Regiment: 25th Infantry - Rank: Private - Enlistment date: 19 Mar 1813 - Enlistment period: During the war - Source(s): AS-5; AS-14.

Corley, William - Regiment: 1st Artillery - Rank: Private - Source(s): AS-12.

Corlis, Ira C. - Rank: Private - Source(s): AS-8.

Cotter, Edward - Regiment: Militia - Name of prison ship: Lord Cathcart - Where taken: Sackets Harbor, NY - Source(s): AS-1.

Countryman, Elias - Regiment: 23rd Infantry - Rank: Private - Enlistment date: 16 Sep 1813 - Enlistment period: 5 years - Source(s): AS-5; AS-14.

Courser, John - Regiment: 4th Infantry - Rank: Private - Source(s): AS-17.

Courson, Ivory - Regiment: 4th Infantry - Rank: Private - Source(s): AS-17.

Couther, Jonathan - Date of death: 16 Mar 1814 - Source(s): AS-7.

Cowder, David - Rank: Private - Source(s): AS-8.

Cox, John - Regiment: 23rd Infantry - Name of prison ship: Lord Cathcart - Source(s): AS-1.

Craft, Geoge B. - Regiment: 12th Infantry - Source(s): AS-1.

Craig, Charles - Regiment: 1st Artillery - Rank: Private - Source(s): AS-16.

Craighton, William - Regiment: 25th Infantry - Rank: Private - Source(s): AS-14.

Crail, Thomas - Regiment: 1st Infantry - Rank: Private - Source(s): AS-16.

Crandell, Joseph - Regiment: 1st Infantry - Rank: Private - Source(s): AS-16.

Cranston, John - Regiment: 13th Infantry - Name of prison ship: Lord Cathcart - Source(s): AS-1.

Crawford, Thomas - Regiment: 40th Infantry - Rank: Private - Source(s): AS-4 - Comments: POW at Eastport, ME.

Crawford, William - Regiment: 23rd Infantry - Rank: Private - Source(s): AS-10.

Crayton, William - Regiment: 25th Infantry - Rank: Private - Enlistment date: 11 May 1812 - Enlistment period: 5 years - Source(s): AS-5.

Crews, Jonathan - Regiment: Rifles - Rank: Sergeant - Source(s): AS-12.

Crise, Adam - Regiment: 1st Infantry - Rank: Private - Source(s): AS-16.

Crocker, John - Regiment: 33rd Infantry - Source(s): AS-1.

Cromer, Anthony - Rank: Private - Source(s): AS-8.

Cronigu, John - Name of prison ship: Lord Cathcart - Source(s): AS-1.

Crosby, James - Regiment: 16th Infantry - Rank: Private - Enlistment date: 2 Feb 1812 - Name of prison ship: Lord Cathcart - Source(s): AS-1; AS-5; AS-14.

Cross, Barnabas - Regiment: 1st Artillery - Source(s): AS-1.

Crow, Jonathan - Regiment: 1st Rifles - Source(s): AS-1.

Crowley, Timothy - Regiment: 1st Infantry - Rank: Private - Source(s): AS-16.

Crystic, John - Regiment: 13th Infantry - Rank: Lieutenant Colonel - Source(s): AS-8.

Cudder, Stephen - Regiment: 23rd Infantry - Rank: Private - Source(s): AS-14.

Cullum, John - Regiment: Militia - Rank: Private - Source(s): AS-14.

Cummins, Nathan - Regiment: 31st Infantry - Rank: Private - Source(s): AS-12.

Cunningham, Cornelius - Rank: Surgeon's Mate - Source(s): AS-11.

Curfrey, Daniel G. - Regiment: Militia - Name of prison ship: Hospital - Source(s): AS-1.

Curran, James - Regiment: 23rd Infantry - Rank: Private - Source(s): AS-12.

Curtis, Morgan - Regiment: 2nd Light Dragoons - Source(s): AS-1.

Cushing, William - Regiment: 23rd Infantry - Rank: Private - Source(s): AS-10.

Custis, Daniel - Rank: Private - Source(s): AS-8.

Cutebeth, Caleb - Regiment: 4th Infantry - Rank: Private - Source(s): AS-16.

Cuther, Leonard - Regiment: 3rd Militia - Rank: Private - Source(s): AS-10.

Cutler, Robert - Regiment: 4th Infantry - Rank: Private - Source(s): AS-17.

Cutter, Leonard - Regiment: 3rd Artillery - Source(s): AS-1.

Cuylu, John - Name of prison ship: Lord Cathcart - Source(s): AS-1.

Cyrtiss, Leba - Regiment: 31st Infantry - Rank: Private - Source(s): AS-9.

Daggett, Josiah - Regiment: 9th Infantry - Rank: Private - Enlistment date: 2 Feb 1813 - Enlistment period: During the war - Source(s): AS-5.

Daggett, Lewis - Regiment: 9th Infantry - Rank: Corporal - Enlistment date: 16 Mar 1813 - Enlistment period: During the war - Source(s): AS-5.

Dailey, John - Regiment: 19th Infantry - Rank: Private - Source(s): AS-12.

Dailey, John - Regiment: 40th Infantry - Rank: Private - Source(s): AS-4 - Comments: POW at Eastport, ME.

Dalaby, James - Regiment: 1st Artillery - Rank: Second Lieutenant - Source(s): AS-16.

Dallas, David - Regiment: 22nd Infantry - Rank: Private - Source(s): AS-10.

Danforth, Joseph - Regiment: 11th Infantry - Source(s): AS-1.

Darling, Thomas - Regiment: 21st Infantry - Source(s): AS-1.

Darnsforth, Joseph - Regiment: Volunteers - Rank: Private - Source(s): AS-14.

Darrah, Archibald - Regiment: 1st Artillery - Rank: Lieutenant - Source(s): AS-11.

Davaurex, James - Regiment: 7th Infantry - Rank: Private - Source(s): AS-3.

Daven, Stephen - Regiment: 24th Infantry - Rank: Private - Source(s): AS-12.

Davenport, Joseph - Regiment: 44th Infantry - Source(s): AS-1.

Davey, Herman - Regiment: 25th Infantry - Rank: Private - Source(s): AS-9.

Davidson, John - Regiment: 14th Infantry - Rank: Private - Enlistment date: 24 Jul 1812 - Enlistment period: 5 years - Source(s): AS-5; AS-14.

Davidson, John - Regiment: 6th Infantry - Rank: Private - Source(s): AS-1; AS-12.

Davis, Bookes - Regiment: 7th Infantry - Rank: Private - Source(s): AS-3.

Davis, David - Rank: Private - Source(s): AS-8.

Davis, Elnathan - Regiment: 13th Infantry - Rank: Private - Enlistment date: 29 Sep 1812 - Enlistment period: 5 years - Source(s): AS-1; AS-5; AS-14.

Davis, J. J. - Rank: Corporal - Source(s): AS-8.

Davis, John - Regiment: 4th Infantry - Rank: Private - Source(s): AS-17.

Davis, John - Enlistment date: Aug 1812 - Source(s): AS-5.

Davis, John - Regiment: 12th Infantry - Rank: Private - Source(s): AS-14.

Davis, John - Regiment: 4th Infantry - Rank: Corporal - Source(s): AS-16.

Davis, John - Name of prison ship: Lord Cathcart - Source(s): AS-1.

Davis, Samuel - Rank: Private - Source(s): AS-8.

Davis, Stephen - Date of death: 10 Aug 1813 - Source(s): AS-6 - Comments: Died at Quebec.

Davis, Thomas - Regiment: 12th Infantry - Rank: Private - Enlistment date: 7 May 1812 - Enlistment period: 5 years - Name of prison ship: Lord Cathcart - Source(s): AS-1; AS-5; AS-14.

Davis, William - Regiment: 2nd Infantry - Rank: Private - Source(s): AS-10.

Davis, William - Rank: Private - Source(s): AS-8.

Day, John - Regiment: 1st Artillery - Source(s): AS-1.

Day, Sylvester - Regiment: 4th Infantry - Rank: Surgeon's Mate - Source(s): AS-11 - Comments: now Surgeon.

De Masters, Foster - Regiment: 1st Rifles - Rank: Sergeant - Source(s): AS-10.

Dean, Randall - Rank: Private - Source(s): AS-8.

Deane, Joseph - Regiment: Militia - Rank: Private - Source(s): AS-2.

Dear, George - Regiment: 1st Infantry - Rank: Sergeant - Source(s): AS-16.

Dear, Jonathan - Regiment: 1st Artillery - Rank: Sergeant - Source(s): AS-16.

Dearborn, David - Regiment: 9th Infantry - Rank: Private - Source(s): AS-10.

Dearborn, Solomon - Rank: Sergeant - Date of death: 23 Jul 1813 - Source(s): AS-6 - Comments: Died at Quebec.

DeBogert, J. N. - Rank: Private - Source(s): AS-8 - Comments: Died on the passage.

Delaurier, John B. - Regiment: 27th Infantry - Rank: Recruit - Source(s): AS-15.

Demolunt, Alexander - Date of death: 13 Nov 1813 in Montreal - Source(s): AS-7.

Dennis, Samuel - Regiment: 27th Infantry - Rank: Recruit - Source(s): AS-15.

Dennison, Benjamin - Regiment: 15th Infantry - Rank: Private - Source(s): AS-14.

Dennison, Simon - Regiment: 1st Rifles - Rank: Private - Source(s): AS-9.

Denny, James - Regiment: OH Militia - Rank: Major - Source(s): AS-18 - Comments: McArthur's Regiment.

Dent, Abner - Regiment: OH Militia - Rank: Lieutenant, Paymaster - Source(s): AS-18 - Comments: Cass' Regiment.

Deprew, John - Rank: Corporal - Source(s): AS-8.

Derker, Celey - Name of prison ship: Lord Cathcart - Source(s): AS-1.

Derren, John - Regiment: 24th Infantry - Rank: Private - Source(s): AS-12.

Derrill, John - Regiment: 24th Infantry - Source(s): AS-1.

Devault, Isaac - Regiment: 27th Infantry - Rank: Private - Source(s): AS-12.

Devore, Enos - Regiment: 27th Infantry - Rank: Recruit - Source(s): AS-15.

Dewall, Alvin - Rank: Corporal - Source(s): AS-9.

Dibble, Nathaniel - Rank: Private - Source(s): AS-8.

Dickenson, John - Regiment: 24th Infantry - Rank: Private - Source(s): AS-9.

Dicker, Lelia - Regiment: 16th Infantry - Rank: Private - Source(s): AS-14.

Dickinson, John - Rank: Private - Source(s): AS-8.

Diesser, Thomas - Regiment: McCobb's Volunteers - Source(s): AS-1.

Diffenderfer, Frederick - Regiment: 1st Artillery - Source(s): AS-1.

Dill, Peter - Regiment: 14th Infantry - Rank: Private - Enlistment date: 31 Aug 1812 - Enlistment period: 5 years - Source(s): AS-5.

Diller, Robert - Regiment: 13th Infantry - Source(s): AS-1.

Dillon, John - Regiment: 1st Infantry - Rank: Private - Source(s): AS-16.

Diver, David - Regiment: 23rd Infantry - Name of prison ship: Lord Cathcart - Source(s): AS-1.

Divers, Stephen - Regiment: 24th Infantry - Source(s): AS-1.

Dixon, Henry C. - Regiment: 1st Artillery - Rank: Private - Source(s): AS-1; AS-12.

Dixon, James - Regiment: 14th Infantry - Rank: Private - Enlistment date: 27 Mar 1812 - Enlistment period: 5 years - Source(s): AS-5; AS-14.

Docker, Zelia - Enlistment date: 29 Oct 1812 - Source(s): AS-5.

Dockham, Ephraim D. - Regiment: 4th Infantry - Rank: Corporal - Source(s): AS-17.

Dodemead, John - Regiment: 1st Infantry - Rank: Sergeant - Source(s): AS-16 - Comments: Formerly from the 19th Infantry.

Dodge, John - Regiment: 6th Infantry - Rank: Private - Source(s): AS-9.

Doherty, James - Regiment: 7th Infantry - Rank: Private - Source(s): AS-3.

Dolf, Joshua - Regiment: 3rd Artillery - Rank: Private - Source(s): AS-10.

Dolph, Joseph - Regiment: 3rd Artillery - Source(s): AS-1.

Donaldson, Frederick - Regiment: 40th Infantry - Rank: Private - Source(s): AS-4 - Comments: On parole at Salem, MA.

Donaldson, Thomas - Regiment: 6th Infantry - Rank: Private - Enlistment date: 28 Mar 1812 - Enlistment period: 5

years - Name of prison ship: Lord Cathcart - Source(s): AS-1; AS-5; AS-14.

Donoff, David - Regiment: 11th Infantry - Source(s): AS-1.

Donohue, John - Regiment: 4th Infantry - Rank: Private - Source(s): AS-17.

Doors, F. - Rank: Private - Source(s): AS-8.

Dosery, Jonathan - Rank: Private - Source(s): AS-8.

Doty, John - Regiment: NY Militia - Rank: Private - Source(s): AS-12.

Doty, Joseph - Rank: Private - Source(s): AS-8.

Dougherty, Dennis - Regiment: 1st Artillery - Rank: Artificer - Source(s): AS-16.

Dougherty, James - Regiment: 1st Rifles - Source(s): AS-1.

Dougherty, Jared - Regiment: KY or TN Militia - Where taken: Miami Rapids, OH or River Raison, MI - Source(s): AS-1.

Dougherty, Robert - Regiment: 19th Infantry - Rank: Sergeant - Source(s): AS-17.

Dougherty, William - Regiment: 14th Infantry - Rank: Private - Enlistment date: 13 Jul 1812 - Enlistment period: 5 years - Source(s): AS-5; AS-14.

Dougherty, William - Regiment: 1st Infantry - Rank: Private - Source(s): AS-16.

Doughty, Elias - Regiment: 2nd Artillery - Rank: Private - Source(s): AS-1; AS-14.

Douglas, James - Regiment: 3rd Artillery - Source(s): AS-1.

Douglass, Caleb - Regiment: 31st Infantry - Rank: Private - Source(s): AS-9.

Douglass, Robert - Regiment: OH Militia - Rank: Lieutenant, Quartermaster - Source(s): AS-18 - Comments: McArthur's Regiment.

Dove, David - Regiment: 1st Rifles - Rank: Private - Source(s): AS-10.

Dow, Frederick - Regiment: 40th Infantry - Rank: Private - Source(s): AS-4 - Comments: POW at Eastport, ME.

Downes, John - Regiment: 19th Infantry - Rank: Private - Source(s): AS-12.

Drake, Elisha - Regiment: McCobb's Volunteers - Rank: Private - Source(s): AS-1; AS-14.

Drake, Elisha - Regiment: 21st Infantry - Rank: Private - Source(s): AS-14.

Drake, George W. - Regiment: 24th Infantry - Source(s): AS-1.

Drake, John - Regiment: NY Militia - Rank: Private - Source(s): AS-12.

Drake, William - Regiment: 2nd Infantry - Rank: Private - Source(s): AS-10.

Dressen, Thomas - Regiment: Volunteers - Rank: Private - Source(s): AS-14.

Drew, Ira - Regiment: 21st Infantry - Rank: Second Lieutenant - Source(s): AS-14.

Dudley, Ebenezer - Regiment: Militia - Rank: Private - Source(s): AS-2.

Dugan, James - Regiment: 5th Infantry - Rank: Private - Enlistment date: 27 May 1812 - Enlistment period: 5 years - Name of prison ship: Lord Cathcart - Source(s): AS-1; AS-5; AS-14.

Dugan, John - Regiment: 27th Infantry - Rank: Recruit - Source(s): AS-15.

Dugan, Thomas - Regiment: OH Militia - Rank: Lieutenant, Quartermaster - Source(s): AS-18 - Comments: Findlay's Regiment.

Dugat, A. - Rank: Private - Source(s): AS-8.

Duncan, Benjamin - Regiment: 16th Infantry - Rank: Private - Name of prison ship: Lord Cathcart - Source(s): AS- ; AS-14.

Dunham, Reuben - Regiment: NY Militia - Rank: Captain - Source(s): AS-12.

Dunkelburg, John - Regiment: 17th Infantry - Rank: Private - Source(s): AS-10.

Dunlap, James - Regiment: 19th Infantry - Rank: Private - Source(s): AS-17.

Dunning, Jesse - Regiment: 23rd Infantry - Rank: Private - Name of prison ship: Lord Cathcart - Source(s): AS-1; AS-14.

Dunton, Peleg - Regiment: 40th Infantry - Rank: Private - Source(s): AS-4 - Comments: POW at Eastport, ME.

Durant, Reuben - Regiment: 4th Infantry - Rank: Private - Source(s): AS-17.

Durrill, Joel - Regiment: 4th Infantry - Rank: Musician - Source(s): AS-17.

Dustin, Moody - Regiment: 40th Infantry - Rank: Private - Source(s): AS-4 - Comments: POW at Eastport, ME.

Dutcher, James - Rank: Private - Source(s): AS-8.

Dutrow, Jacob - Regiment: 1st Rifles - Rank: Private - Source(s): AS-1; AS-12.

Duvall, Francis - Regiment: 1st Infantry - Rank: Private - Source(s): AS-16.

Duvall, Jacob - Regiment: 22nd Infantry - Rank: Private - Source(s): AS-9.

Duvalt, Isaac - Regiment: 27th Infantry - Source(s): AS-1.

Dyer, Daniel - Regiment: McCobb's Volunteers - Source(s): AS-1.

Dyer, Daniel - Regiment: 12th Infantry - Rank: Private - Source(s): AS-14.

Dyson, Dyer - Regiment: 1st Infantry - Source(s): AS-1.

Dyson, John - Regiment: 1st Artillery - Rank: Lieutenant - Source(s): AS-11.

Eades, Thomas - Regiment: 33rd Infantry - Source(s): AS-1.

Eagan, John - Regiment: 27th Infantry - Rank: Ensign - Source(s): AS-15.

Eagan, John - Regiment: 27th Infantry - Rank: Recruit - Source(s): AS-15.

Earp, Leonard - Regiment: 4th Infantry - Rank: Private - Source(s): AS-17.

Easter, Stephen - Date of death: 28 Jun 1813 - Source(s): AS-6 - Comments: Died at Quebec.

Eastman, John A. - Regiment: 4th Infantry - Rank: Lieutenant - Source(s): AS-11.

Eastman, Jonathan - Regiment: 1st Artillery - Rank: Lieutenant - Source(s): AS-11.

Easton, George - Regiment: 23rd Infantry - Rank: Private - Source(s): AS-9.

Easton, Moses - Regiment: 4th Infantry - Source(s): AS-1.

Eastwood, Amariah - Regiment: 9th Infantry - Rank: Private - Source(s): AS-10.

Eaton, Clement - Regiment: 24th Infantry - Rank: Private - Source(s): AS-1; AS-12.

Eaton, Henry P. - Regiment: 23rd Infantry - Rank: Private - Source(s): AS-10.

Eaton, Hubbard - Regiment: 40th Infantry - Rank: Private - Source(s): AS-4 - Comments: POW at Eastport, ME.

Eaton, William - Regiment: 2nd Artillery - Source(s): AS-1.

Edging, Marting - Regiment: 17th Infantry - Rank: Private - Source(s): AS-9.

Edson, Levi - Regiment: NY Militia - Rank: Private - Source(s): AS-12.

Edson, Luther - Regiment: 27th Infantry - Rank: Recruit - Source(s): AS-15.

Edson, Nathan - Regiment: 1st Infantry - Source(s): AS-1.

Edwards, Abraham - Regiment: 19th Infantry - Rank: Captain - Source(s): AS-11.

Edwards, John - Regiment: 1st Infantry - Rank: Private - Source(s): AS-16.

Edwards, Joshua - Regiment: 1st Infantry - Rank: Private - Source(s): AS-16.

Egans, James - Regiment: 40th Infantry - Rank: Private - Source(s): AS-4 - Comments: POW at Eastport, ME.

Elass, Joseph - Regiment: 24th Infantry - Source(s): AS-1.

Elkins, Jonathan - Regiment: 4th Infantry - Rank: Private - Source(s): AS-17.

Elliot, Thomas - Regiment: 24th Infantry - Rank: Private - Source(s): AS-1; AS-12.

Elliott, John - Regiment: Militia - Rank: Private - Source(s): AS-14.

Ellis, John - Regiment: 9th Infantry - Rank: Private - Enlistment date: 5 Apr 1813 - Enlistment period: During the war - Source(s): AS-5; AS-14.

Elsworth, William - Regiment: NY Militia - Rank: Private - Source(s): AS-12.

Emerson, Jeremiah - Regiment: 4th Infantry - Rank: Private - Source(s): AS-17.

Emery, James - Regiment: McCobb's Volunteers - Source(s): AS-1.

Emery, Stephen - Regiment: 23rd Infantry - Name of prison ship: Lord Cathcart - Source(s): AS-1.

Emmit, Abraham - Regiment: 27th Infantry - Rank: Recruit - Source(s): AS-15.

Emmons, Samuel - Regiment: 1st Artillery - Rank: Musician - Source(s): AS-16.

English, John - Regiment: 21st Infantry - Name of prison ship: Hospital - Source(s): AS-1.

English, John - Regiment: 14th Infantry - Rank: Private - Source(s): AS-14.

Ennett, William - Rank: Private - Source(s): AS-8.

Ennis, James - Rank: Private - Source(s): AS-8.

Ersking, Robert - Regiment: 40th Infantry - Rank: Corporal - Source(s): AS-4a.

Erwin, John - Regiment: 1st Artillery - Rank: Private - Source(s): AS-14.

Estas, Edward - Regiment: 1st Light Dragoons - Rank: Private - Source(s): AS-14.

Estie, (-----) - Regiment: OH Militia - Rank: Surgeon - Source(s): AS-18 - Comments: McArthur's Regiment.

Evans, Thomas - Regiment: 9th Infantry - Rank: Private - Source(s): AS-14.

Evelith, Benjamin M. - Regiment: 40th Infantry - Rank: Private - Source(s): AS-4 - Comments: POW at Eastport, ME.

Evenor, Christian - Regiment: 13th Infantry - Source(s): AS-1.

Evenor, Christopher - Regiment: 13th Infantry - Rank: Private - Enlistment date: 10 Apr 1812 - Enlistment period: 5 years – Source(s): AS-5.

Everton, Benjamin - Regiment: 6th Infantry - Rank: Private - Name of prison ship: Lord Cathcart - Source(s): AS-1; AS-5; AS-14.

Ewing, James - Regiment: 24th Infantry - Source(s): AS-1.

Ewing, John - Regiment: 1st Artillery - Name of prison ship: Lord Cathcart - Source(s): AS-1.

Ewing, Patrick - Regiment: KY or TN Militia - Where taken: Miami Rapids, OH or River Raison, MI - Source(s): AS-1.

Ewings, James B. - Regiment: 2nd Artillery - Source(s): AS-1.

Fairchild, Cedric - Regiment: 2nd Light Dragoons - Rank: Private - Source(s): AS-14.

Fairchild, Cyrus B. - Regiment: 1st Light Dragoons - Rank: Quartermaster Sergeant - Enlistment date: 10 Sep 1812 - Enlistment period: 5 years - Source(s): AS-1; AS-5.

Fanning, Charles - Regiment: 1st Artillery - Source(s): AS-1.

Farien, M. - Regiment: 1st Artillery - Source(s): AS-1.

Farl, Henry - Regiment: 13th Infantry - Rank: Private - Source(s): AS-14.

Farmer, Henry - Regiment: 16th Infantry - Rank: Private - Source(s): AS-1; AS-12.

Farmham, Louis - Regiment: Militia - Rank: Private - Source(s): AS-2.

Farnham, Gaius - Regiment: 34th Infantry - Source(s): AS-1.

Farrell, John - Regiment: 1st Infantry - Rank: Private - Source(s): AS-16.

Farrell, Michael - Regiment: 14th Infantry - Rank: Private - Enlistment date: 12 May 1812 - Enlistment period: 5 years - Source(s): AS-5; AS-14.

Farrow, Joseph - Regiment: 4th Infantry - Rank: Private - Source(s): AS-16.

Favour, John - Regiment: 40th Infantry - Rank: Private - Source(s): AS-4 - Comments: On parole at Machias, ME.

Fay, Hezekiah - Regiment: Militia - Rank: Private - Source(s): AS-9.

Fellows, Philip - Regiment: NY Militia - Rank: Private - Source(s): AS-12.

Fenner, Charles - Regiment: 1st Artillery - Source(s): AS-1.

Fenton, Davidson - Regiment: 27th Infantry - Rank: Private - Source(s): AS-1; AS-12.

Ferguson, John - Regiment: 13th Infantry - Rank: Sergeant - Name of prison ship: Lord Cathcart - Source(s): AS-1.

Ferguson, John - Regiment: 13th Infantry - Rank: Corporal - Source(s): AS-9.

Ferguson, William - Date of death: 13 Apr 1814 - Source(s): AS-7.

Ferris, Barney - Regiment: 16th Infantry - Rank: Private - Enlistment date: 27 Jul 1812 - Source(s): AS-5; AS-14.

Ferris, John - Regiment: OH Militia - Rank: Captain - Source(s): AS-18 - Comments: Findlay's Regiment.

Fields, Ebenezer - Regiment: 4th Infantry - Rank: Private - Source(s): AS-17.

Fields, Elisha - Regiment: 2nd Light Dragoons - Rank: Sergeant - Enlistment date: 1813 - Enlistment period: During the war - Source(s): AS-5.

Fields, Elisha - Regiment: 2nd Light Dragoons - Rank: Private - Name of prison ship: Hospital - Source(s): AS-1; AS-14.

Figg, John - Regiment: 1st Artillery - Rank: Private - Source(s): AS-1; AS-12.

Fike, Nathan - Regiment: 24th Infantry - Source(s): AS-1.

Fillebrown, John Jr - Regiment: 40th Infantry - Rank: Captain - Source(s): AS-4 - Comments: On parole at Boston, MA.

Fillebrown, Richard - Regiment: 40th Infantry - Rank: Sergeant - Source(s): AS-4a.

Fillebrown, Richard - Regiment: 4th Infantry - Rank: Sergeant - Source(s): AS-16.

Fillebrown, Samuel S. - Regiment: 40th Infantry - Rank: Corporal - Source(s): AS-4 - Comments: POW at Eastport, ME.

Finch, Henry - Regiment: Unknown - Source(s): AS-1.

Finch, Henry - Regiment: 1st Artillery - Rank: Private - Source(s): AS-12.

Fincher, Jesse - Regiment: 13th Infantry - Source(s): AS-1.

Findlay, James - Regiment: OH Militia - Rank: Colonel - Source(s): AS-18.

Fink, Daniel - Regiment: 7th Infantry - Rank: Private - Source(s): AS-3.

Fink, John L. - Regiment: 13th Infantry - Rank: First Lieutenant - Source(s): AS-8; AS-11.

Finney, Elihua - Date of death: 26 Jul 1813 - Source(s): AS-6 - Comments: Died at Quebec.

Fisher, Anthony - Regiment: 2nd Artillery - Rank: Private - Enlistment date: 4 Aug 1812 - Enlistment period: 5 years - Source(s): AS-5; AS-14.

Fisk, John J. - Rank: Private - Source(s): AS-8.

Fisk, Thomas R. - Regiment: NY Militia - Rank: Private - Source(s): AS-12.

FitzGerald, James - Regiment: 14th Infantry - Rank: Private - Enlistment date: Jul 1812 - Enlistment period: 5 years - Source(s): AS-5.

Fitzpatrick, Edward - Regiment: 1st Artillery - Rank: Private - Source(s): AS-1; AS-12.

Flanagan, Bryan - Regiment: 4th Infantry - Rank: Private - Source(s): AS-17.

Fleming, Jacob - Rank: Private - Source(s): AS-8.

Fleming, John - Regiment: 1st Artillery - Rank: Private - Source(s): AS-1; AS-12.

Fleming, Joseph - Regiment: 16th Infantry - Rank: Private - Enlistment date: 16 Oct 1812 - Name of prison ship: Lord Cathcart - Source(s): AS-1; AS-5; AS-14.

Fleming, William - Regiment: 22nd Infantry - Source(s): AS-1.

Fleming, William - Regiment: 1st Infantry - Rank: Private - Source(s): AS-16.

Flood, Joseph - Regiment: 4th Infantry - Rank: Private - Source(s): AS-16.

Fobes, Levin - Regiment: 21st Infantry - Name of prison ship: Hospital - Source(s): AS-1.

Foens, Daniel B. - Regiment: 19th Infantry - Rank: Sergeant - Source(s): AS-12.

Folks, John - Regiment: 3rd Artillery - Rank: Private - Source(s): AS-1; AS-10.

Follett, Abel - Regiment: NY Militia - Rank: Private - Source(s): AS-12.

Foote, Henry - Regiment: 13th Infantry - Rank: Private - Enlistment date: 1 Feb 1813 - Enlistment period: During the war - Source(s): AS-1; AS-5.

For-----, Thomas - Regiment: 21st Infantry - Rank: Private - Source(s): AS-14.

Forender, John - Regiment: 4th Infantry - Rank: Private - Source(s): AS-16.

Forrest, John - Regiment: 4th Infantry - Rank: Private - Source(s): AS-17.

Forrester, Robert - Regiment: 1st Artillery - Rank: Private - Source(s): AS-16.

Forsythe, Alexander - Regiment: 1st Infantry - Rank: Sergeant - Source(s): AS-16.

Forsythe, John - Regiment: Militia - Rank: Private - Source(s): AS-2 - Comments: Ohio Volunteers.

Fort, Abram - Rank: Private - Source(s): AS-8.

Foster, Edla - Regiment: 40th Infantry - Rank: Corporal - Source(s): AS-4a.

Foster, George - Regiment: 2nd Artillery - Rank: Private - Enlistment date: 17 Jun 1812 - Enlistment period: 5 years - Source(s): AS-1; AS-5; AS-14.

Foster, Lot - Regiment: 7th Infantry - Rank: Fifer - Source(s): AS-3.

Foster, Timothy - Regiment: 4th Infantry - Rank: Private - Source(s): AS-17.

Foster, William - Regiment: 40th Infantry - Rank: Private - Source(s): AS-4 - Comments: POW at Eastport, ME.

Foster, William L. - Regiment: 4th Infantry - Rank: Private - Source(s): AS-17.

Fowler, Alfred - Regiment: NY Militia - Rank: Private - Source(s): AS-12.

Fowler, James - Regiment: 21st Infantry - Rank: Corporal - Source(s): AS-9.

Fowler, John - Regiment: 16th Infantry - Rank: Private - Source(s): AS-1; AS-12.

Fowler, Samuel - Regiment: 4th Infantry - Rank: Private - Source(s): AS-17.

Fowler, Similius - Regiment: Militia - Rank: Private - Source(s): AS-2.

Fox, Ezra - Regiment: 4th Infantry - Rank: Private - Source(s): AS-17.

Fox, John - Regiment: 21st Infantry - Source(s): AS-1.

Francis, Joseph - Regiment: 4th Infantry - Rank: Private - Source(s): AS-16.

Francis, Seth - Rank: Private - Source(s): AS-8.

Fray, Jonathan - Regiment: Volunteers - Rank: Private - Source(s): AS-14.

Frazier, Edward - Regiment: 14th Infantry - Rank: Private - Enlistment date: 28 May 1812 - Enlistment period: 5 years - Source(s): AS-5; AS-14.

Freeman, Jacob - Regiment: 2nd Artillery - Source(s): AS-1.

French, Samuel - Regiment: 4th Infantry - Rank: Private - Source(s): AS-16.

Friend, John D. - Date of death: 17 Jul 1813 - Source(s): AS-6 - Comments: Died at Quebec.

Frost, Dennis - Regiment: Militia - Rank: Private - Source(s): AS-2.

Frost, Richard - Regiment: 40th Infantry - Rank: Private - Source(s): AS-4 - Comments: POW at Eastport, ME.

Fry, Jacob - Regiment: 3rd Artillery - Rank: Sergeant - Source(s): AS-1; AS-10.

Fullard, Hiram H. - Regiment: NY Militia - Rank: Private - Source(s): AS-12.

Fuller, Charles - Regiment: 4th Infantry - Rank: Captain - Source(s): AS-11.

Fuller, Chester - Regiment: 23rd Infantry - Rank: Private - Source(s): AS-9.

Fuller, John - Rank: Private - Source(s): AS-8.

Fuller, Jonathan - Regiment: 1st Infantry - Rank: Private - Source(s): AS-16.

Furbush, Aaron W. - Regiment: 4th Infantry - Rank: Sergeant - Source(s): AS-17.

Furbush, Joshua - Regiment: 11th Infantry - Source(s): AS-1.

Furlong, William - Regiment: 21st Infantry - Rank: Private - Source(s): AS-1; AS-12.

Furman, Jeremiah - Rank: Private - Source(s): AS-8.

Furrey, Jacob - Regiment: 1st Infantry - Rank: Musician - Source(s): AS-16.

Futhey, Isaac - Regiment: 27th Infantry - Rank: Recruit - Source(s): AS-15.

Gady, Martin - Enlistment date: 14 Oct 1812 - Source(s): AS-5.

Gafford, Elijah - Regiment: 1st Artillery - Rank: Private - Source(s): AS-16.

Gahan, Jeremiah - Regiment: 40th Infantry - Rank: Private - Source(s): AS-4 - Comments: POW at Eastport, ME.

Gaiger, John N. - Regiment: 1st Artillery - Rank: Private - Source(s): AS-1; AS-12.

Gain, John - Regiment: 24th Infantry - Source(s): AS-1.

Gale, John G. - Regiment: 21st Infantry - Rank: Private - Source(s): AS-9.

Gall, Andrew - Regiment: 40th Infantry - Rank: Private - Source(s): AS-4 - Comments: POW at Eastport, ME.

Gamblin, John - Regiment: 7th Infantry - Rank: Private - Source(s): AS-3.

Garner, William - Regiment: 24th Infantry - Rank: Private - Source(s): AS-1; AS-12.

Garrett, Ashton - Regiment: 17th Infantry - Rank: Lieutenant - Source(s): AS-11.

Garrison, James - Regiment: 16th Infantry - Rank: Private - Enlistment date: 16 Jul 1812 - Source(s): AS-1; AS-5; AS-14.

Garrotson, Garrot - Regiment: 1st Infantry - Rank: Musician - Source(s): AS-16.

Gass, Charles - Regiment: 24th Infantry - Source(s): AS-1.

Gear, John - Regiment: 24th Infantry - Rank: Sergeant - Source(s): AS-1; AS-12.

Gee, George W. - Regiment: 23rd Infantry - Rank: Private - Source(s): AS-14.

Gemenvery, Roswell - Regiment: 4th Infantry - Rank: Private - Source(s): AS-17.

Gentry, John - Regiment: 24th Infantry - Source(s): AS-1.

George, John - Regiment: 12th Infantry - Source(s): AS-1.

George, Stone - Regiment: Militia - Rank: Private - Source(s): AS-2.

German, James - Regiment: 25th Infantry - Rank: Private - Source(s): AS-9.

Gibbs, Ezekiel - Regiment: Militia - Rank: Private - Source(s): AS-3.

Gibbs, Reuben - Rank: Private - Source(s): AS-8.

Gibson, Fortune - Regiment: Militia - Rank: Private - Source(s): AS-14.

Gifford, Francis - Regiment: 24th Infantry - Source(s): AS-1.

Gilchrist, James - Regiment: 22nd Infantry - Source(s): AS-1.

Giles, John - Regiment: 11th Infantry - Rank: Private - Source(s): AS-9.

Gill, William - Regiment: OH Militia & 27th Infantry - Rank: Captain - Source(s): AS-15; AS-18 - Comments: Cass' Militia Regiment.

Gillaway, H. - Rank: Private - Source(s): AS-8.

Gillerman, Gabriel - Rank: Private - Source(s): AS-8.

Gillett, Solomon - Regiment: NY Militia - Where taken: Niagara or Buffalo, NY - Source(s): AS-1; AS-12.

Gillis, Samuel - Regiment: Militia - Rank: Corporal - Source(s): AS-2.

Gillispie, William - Regiment: 16th Infantry - Rank: Private - Enlistment date: Jun 1812 - Name of prison ship: Lord Cathcart - Source(s): AS-1; AS-5; AS-14.

Gilman, Elias - Regiment: 27th Infantry - Rank: Lieutenant - Source(s): AS-15.

Glass, Joseph - Regiment: 24th Infantry - Rank: Private - Source(s): AS-12.

Gleason, Levi - Regiment: 4th Infantry - Rank: Private - Source(s): AS-16.

Glenn, James - Regiment: 24th Infantry - Source(s): AS-1.

Goddard, Lewis - Regiment: NY Volunteers - Rank: Lieutenant - Source(s): AS-14.

Godwin, Kimmel - Regiment: 14th Infantry - Rank: Second Lieutenant - Source(s): AS-14.

Golden, Benjamin - Rank: Private - Source(s): AS-8.

Goodall, Joshua - Regiment: 21st Infantry - Rank: Private - Source(s): AS-9.

Goodenow, E. - Rank: Private - Source(s): AS-8.

Goodenow, Rufus - Regiment: 4th Infantry - Rank: Private - Source(s): AS-16.

Gooding, George - Regiment: 4th Infantry - Rank: Lieutenant - Source(s): AS-11.

Goodman, John - Regiment: 24th Infantry - Rank: Private - Source(s): AS-1; AS-12.

Goodson, Archibald - Regiment: 24th Infantry - Rank: Private - Source(s): AS-1; AS-12.

Goodwin, James - Regiment: 12th Infantry - Rank: Private - Source(s): AS-14.

Goodwin, James - Regiment: 27th Infantry - Source(s): AS-1.

Goodwin, Richard - Regiment: 23rd Infantry - Rank: Private - Name of prison ship: Lord Cathcart - Source(s): AS-1; AS-14.

Goodwin, Simon - Regiment: Militia - Rank: Private - Name of prison ship: Hospital - Source(s): AS-1; AS-14.

Gordon, John - Regiment: 22nd Infantry - Rank: Private - Source(s): AS-10.

Gordon, John L. - Regiment: 27th Infantry - Rank: Recruit - Source(s): AS-15.

Gossetts, Stephen - Regiment: 2nd Artillery - Rank: Private - Enlistment date: 3 Jun 1812 - Enlistment period: 5 years - Source(s): AS-1; AS-5; AS-14.

Gould, Daniel G. - Regiment: Militia - Rank: Private - Source(s): AS-2.

Gowen, Thomas - Regiment: 24th Infantry - Rank: Private - Source(s): AS-1; AS-9.

Grady, Martin - Regiment: 16th Infantry - Rank: Private - Name of prison ship: Lord Cathcart - Source(s): AS-1; AS-14.

Graham Edward - Regiment: 4th Infantry - Source(s): AS-1.

Grant, Amasa T. - Rank: Citizen - Source(s): AS-9.

Grant, William - Regiment: 19th Infantry - Rank: Private - Source(s): AS-12.

Grave, Michael - Regiment: 2nd Artillery - Rank: Private - Source(s): AS-14.

Graves, Abraham - Regiment: NY Volunteers - Rank: Ensign - Source(s): AS-14.

Gray, Benjamin - Regiment: 3rd Artillery - Source(s): AS-1 - Comments: Enlistment date with the British.

Gray, Isaiah - Regiment: 3rd Artillery - Rank: Private - Source(s): AS-14.

Gray, Jonathan - Regiment: 21st Infantry - Rank: Private - Source(s): AS-14.

Gray, Samuel - Regiment: 7th Infantry - Rank: Private - Source(s): AS-3.

Gray, William - Regiment: 3rd Artillery - Source(s): AS-1.

Grayson, John - Regiment: 24th Infantry - Source(s): AS-1.

Green, Caleb - Rank: Private - Source(s): AS-8.

Green, Elias - Date of death: 23 Jul 1813 - Source(s): AS-6 - Comments: Died at Quebec.

Green, Elijah - Regiment: NY Militia - Rank: Private - Source(s): AS-12.

Green, Joshua - Regiment: Militia - Rank: Private - Source(s): AS-2.

Green, Thomas - Regiment: 14th Infantry - Rank: Sergeant - Enlistment date: 1 Apr 1812 - Enlistment period: 5 years - Source(s): AS-5.

Green, Thomas - Regiment: 6th Infantry - Rank: Private - Enlistment date: 1 May 1812 - Enlistment period: 5 years - Name of prison ship: Lord Cathcart - Source(s): AS-1; AS-5.

Green, William - Rank: Private - Source(s): AS-8.

Greene, Gacher - Regiment: 4th Infantry - Rank: Private - Source(s): AS-17.

Greene, John - Regiment: 4th Infantry - Rank: Private - Source(s): AS-17.

Greene, John - Regiment: 1st Artillery - Rank: Private - Name of prison ship: Lord Cathcart - Source(s): AS-1; AS-14.

Greene, Peter - Regiment: 1st Infantry - Rank: Private - Source(s): AS-16.

Greeney, Peter - Regiment: 4th Infantry - Rank: Private - Source(s): AS-17.

Greenleaf, Samuel - Rank: Private - Source(s): AS-8.

Greenley, William - Regiment: 24th Infantry - Source(s): AS-1.

Grenor, Christian - Regiment: 13th Infantry - Rank: Private - Source(s): AS-14.

Gribble, James - Regiment: 24th Infantry - Rank: Private - Source(s): AS-1; AS-12.

Griffen, Andrew - Regiment: 4th Infantry - Rank: Private - Source(s): AS-17.

Griffen, Levi - Regiment: 4th Infantry - Rank: Private - Source(s): AS-17 - Comments: Since dead.

Griffen, Peter - Regiment: 4th Infantry - Rank: Private - Source(s): AS-17.

Griffith, John - Rank: Private - Source(s): AS-8.

Griggs, William - Rank: Private - Source(s): AS-8.

Griggs, William - Regiment: 4th Infantry - Rank: Private - Source(s): AS-17.

Groves, George - Regiment: 21st Infantry - Source(s): AS-1.

Groves, Solomon - Regiment: 27th Infantry - Rank: Recruit - Source(s): AS-15.

Grummo, Paul - Regiment: 1st Infantry - Source(s): AS-1.

Guile, David - Rank: Corporal - Source(s): AS-8.

Guiles, Joseph - Regiment: 1st Infantry - Rank: Private - Source(s): AS-16.

Guinnup, John - Regiment: 13th Infantry - Name of prison ship: Lord Cathcart - Source(s): AS-1.

Gunison, Samuel - Regiment: 4th Infantry - Rank: Private - Source(s): AS-17.

Gurrill, John - Regiment: 4th Infantry - Rank: Private - Source(s): AS-17.

Guthrie, William - Regiment: OH Militia - Rank: Lieutenant - Source(s): AS-18 - Comments: Findlay's Regiment.

Guynup, John - Regiment: 13th Infantry - Rank: Private - Enlistment date: 9 May 1812 - Enlistment period: 5 years - Source(s): AS-5; AS-14.

Gwinn, Benjamin - Regiment: 1st Artillery - Source(s): AS-1.

Habbett, Lotha - Regiment: 3rd Artillery - Rank: Private - Source(s): AS-10.

Hackett, William - Rank: Private - Source(s): AS-8.

Hader, Samuel - Regiment: 4th Infantry - Rank: Private - Source(s): AS-16.

Hagar, Henry - Regiment: 2nd Light Dragoons - Rank: Private - Source(s): AS-1; AS-14.

Hagar, Jonathan - Regiment: NY Militia - Rank: Private - Source(s): AS-12.

Hagar, Perry - Regiment: 2nd Light Dragoons - Rank: Corporal - Enlistment date: 1 Apr 1812 - Enlistment period: 5 years - Source(s): AS-5.

Haines, Daniel - Rank: Private - Source(s): AS-8.

Hale, Lott - Regiment: 21st Infantry - Rank: Private - Enlistment date: 1 Feb 1813 - Enlistment period: 5 years - Source(s): AS-1; AS-5; AS-14.

Hall, Allen - Regiment: 34th Infantry - Source(s): AS-1.

Hall, Farmington - Rank: Private - Source(s): AS-8.

Hall, Henry - Regiment: 7th Infantry - Rank: Private - Source(s): AS-3.

Hall, John - Regiment: 27th Infantry - Rank: Recruit - Source(s): AS-15.

Hall, John (1) - Regiment: 7th Infantry - Rank: Private - Source(s): AS-3.

Hall, John (2) - Regiment: 7th Infantry - Rank: Private - Source(s): AS-3.

Hall, John D. - Regiment: 4th Infantry - Rank: Private - Source(s): AS-17.

Hall, Joseph - Regiment: 24th Infantry - Rank: Private - Source(s): AS-1; AS-12.

Hall, Orrin - Regiment: 13th Infantry - Name of prison ship: Lord Cathcart - Source(s): AS-1.

Hall, Samuel - Rank: Private - Source(s): AS-8.

Hall, Silas - Regiment: 40th Infantry - Rank: Private - Source(s): AS-4 - Comments: On parole at Machias, ME.

Hall, William - Regiment: 24th Infantry - Source(s): AS-1.

Halle, John - Rank: Sergeant - Date of death: 5 Jul 1813 - Source(s): AS-6 - Comments: Died at Quebec.

Halls, James - Regiment: 1st Artillery - Rank: Private - Source(s): AS-16.

Ham, Robert - Regiment: McCobb's Volunteers - Name of prison ship: Hospital - Source(s): AS-1.

Ham, Rufus - Regiment: McCobb's Volunteers - Name of prison ship: Hospital - Source(s): AS-1.

Hamblin, Ezra - Regiment: 11th Infantry - Source(s): AS-1.

Hamilton, James - Regiment: 6th Infantry - Rank: Private - Enlistment date: 2 Mar 1811 - Enlistment period: 5 years - Source(s): AS-5.

Hamilton, John - Regiment: 21st Infantry - Source(s): AS-1.

Hamilton, John - Regiment: 40th Infantry - Rank: Private - Source(s): AS-4a.

Hammatt, John - Regiment: 24th Infantry - Source(s): AS-1.

Hammond, Seneca - Regiment: 23rd Infantry - Rank: Private - Source(s): AS-10.

Hammond, Thomas - Rank: Private - Source(s): AS-8.

Hammonds, Jonathan - Regiment: 3rd Artillery - Rank: Private - Source(s): AS-1; AS-10.

Hamp, Jonathan - Regiment: 4th Infantry - Rank: Private - Source(s): AS-16.

Handy, Nathan - Rank: Private - Source(s): AS-8.

Handy, P. - Rank: Private - Source(s): AS-8.

Haney, Charles - Regiment: 3rd Artillery - Source(s): AS-1.

Hankins, Gilbert - Regiment: 2nd Light Dragoons - Source(s): AS-1.

Hann, Robert - Regiment: Volunteers - Rank: Private - Source(s): AS-14.

Hann, Rufus - Regiment: Volunteers - Rank: Private - Source(s): AS-14.

Hannion, Jacob - Regiment: 1st Artillery - Source(s): AS-1.

Hanson, Samuel - Regiment: 40th Infantry - Rank: Private - Source(s): AS-4 - Comments: POW at Eastport, ME.

Harding, Amasa - Regiment: 16th Infantry - Source(s): AS-1.

Hardy, Elisha - Regiment: 11th Infantry - Source(s): AS-1.

Hardy, Reuben - Regiment: 40th Infantry - Rank: Private - Source(s): AS-4 - Comments: On parole at Machias, ME.

Hargrove, John - Date of death: 24 Jan 1813 - Source(s): AS-7.

Harley, George - Regiment: KY or TN Militia - Where taken: Miami Rapids, OH or River Raison, MI - Source(s): AS-1.

Harmon, Ranson - Regiment: NY Militia - Rank: Captain - Source(s): AS-12.

Harraday, Elisha - Date of death: 15 Jul 1813 - Source(s): AS-6 - Comments: Died at Quebec.

Harrick, Oliver - Regiment: 12-Month Volunteers - Rank: Captain - Source(s): AS-14.

Harrington, Estes N. - Regiment: 13th Infantry - Name of prison ship: Lord Cathcart - Source(s): AS-1.

Harrington, Jason - Regiment: 40th Infantry - Rank: Private - Source(s): AS-4 - Comments: POW at Eastport, ME.

Harris, J. - Rank: Private - Source(s): AS-8.

Harris, John - Regiment: Militia - Rank: Private - Source(s): AS-2.

Harris, Joseph - Regiment: 1st Infantry - Rank: Private - Source(s): AS-16.

Harris, Stephen - Regiment: 4th Infantry - Rank: Private - Source(s): AS-17.

Harris, Thomas - Regiment: NY Militia - Rank: Private - Source(s): AS-12.

Hart, John - Regiment: 1st Artillery - Rank: Private - Source(s): AS-1; AS-9; AS-12.

Hartland, William - Rank: Private - Source(s): AS-8.

Hartley, Joseph - Regiment: 1st Rifles - Source(s): AS-1; AS-12.

Harvey, Calvin - Regiment: 9th Infantry - Rank: Private - Source(s): AS-14.

Harvey, Luther - Regiment: 9th Infantry - Rank: Musician - Enlistment date: 5 Feb 1813 - Enlistment period: 5 years - Source(s): AS-5; AS-14.

Harvey, Peter - Regiment: 4th Infantry - Rank: Private - Source(s): AS-17.

Harvey, William - Regiment: 11th Infantry - Rank: Private - Enlistment date: 15 Jul 1812 - Enlistment period: 5 years - Source(s): AS-1; AS-5.

Harvey, William - Regiment: Volunteers - Rank: Private - Source(s): AS-14.

Haskel, William - Regiment: 40th Infantry - Rank: Private - Source(s): AS-4 - Comments: On parole at Salem, MA.

Haslet, Joseph - Regiment: 1st Infantry - Rank: Private - Source(s): AS-16.

Hathaway, William G. - Regiment: Militia - Rank: Private - Source(s): AS-2.

Hawkins, Abraham - Regiment: 4th Infantry - Rank: First Lieutenant - Source(s): AS-11; AS-17.

Hawkins, John - Rank: Private - Source(s): AS-8.

Hawkins, Robert - Rank: Private - Source(s): AS-8.

Hawkins, Samuel - Regiment: 4th Infantry - Rank: Private - Source(s): AS-17.

Hawley, Luther - Regiment: Militia - Rank: Private - Source(s): AS-2.

Haynes, Carlisle - Regiment: 19th Infantry - Rank: Private - Source(s): AS-12.

Haynes, Daniel - Regiment: McCobb's Volunteers - Rank: Private - Source(s): AS-1; AS-14.

Hays, Patrick - Regiment: 1st Artillery - Rank: Private - Source(s): AS-1; AS-16.

Hazard, Ezekiel - Regiment: 1st Artillery - Name of prison ship: Lord Cathcart - Source(s): AS-1.

Hazlett, John - Rank: Private - Source(s): AS-8.

Head, William - Regiment: 1st Rifles - Source(s): AS-1.

Headley, Robert - Regiment: 1st Infantry - Rank: Private - Source(s): AS-16.

Healy, William - Regiment: 4th Infantry - Rank: Private - Source(s): AS-16.

Heath, David - Regiment: 4th Infantry - Rank: Private - Source(s): AS-17.

Heath, John - Regiment: 2nd Light Dragoons - Source(s): AS-1.

Heath, Noah - Regiment: 1st Infantry - Rank: Private - Source(s): AS-16.

Heaton, Samuel - Regiment: 1st Artillery - Rank: Artificer - Source(s): AS-16.

Hedrick, George - Regiment: 2nd Artillery - Rank: Private - Enlistment date: 13 Apr 1812 - Enlistment period: 5 years - Source(s): AS-1; AS-5; AS-14.

Heckerwelder, Thomas - Regiment: OH Militia - Rank: Ensign - Source(s): AS-18 - Comments: Cass' Regiment.

Heist, David - Rank: Private - Source(s): AS-8.

Helm, Daniel W. - Regiment: 16th Infantry - Source(s): AS-1.

Henderson, John - Regiment: 40th Infantry - Rank: Private - Source(s): AS-4 - Comments: POW at Eastport, ME.

Henderson, John - Regiment: 24th Infantry - Rank: Private - Source(s): AS-1; AS-12.

Henrick, John - Regiment: 13th Infantry - Name of prison ship: Lord Cathcart - Source(s): AS-1.

Herbaugh, John - Regiment: 24th Infantry - Rank: Private - Source(s): AS-1; AS-12.

Herrick, Eli - Rank: Corporal - Date of death: 30 Jul 1813 - Source(s): AS-6 - Comments: Died at Quebec.

Herrick, John - Regiment: 4th Infantry - Rank: Private - Source(s): AS-17.

Herring, William - Regiment: 24th Infantry - Source(s): AS-1.

Herrington, Daniel - Rank: Private - Source(s): AS-8.

Herron, James - Regiment: 14th Infantry - Rank: Private - Enlistment date: 18 Sep 1812 - Enlistment period: 5 years - Source(s): AS-5.

Herron, Luke - Regiment: 1st Artillery - Rank: Private - Source(s): AS-1; AS-12.

Herron, William - Regiment: 24th Infantry - Rank: Private - Source(s): AS-12.

Hewens, Thomas - Regiment: 33rd Infantry - Source(s): AS-1.

Hewett, Caleb - Regiment: Militia - Rank: Private - Source(s): AS-2.

Hewlett, William - Date of death: 2 Dec 1813 - Source(s): AS-7.

Hews, Elias - Rank: Private - Source(s): AS-8.

Hews, Joseph - Rank: Corporal - Source(s): AS-8.

Hibbard, J. W. - Rank: Private - Source(s): AS-8.

Hickman, Harris H. - Regiment: 19th Infantry - Rank: Captain - Source(s): AS-11.

Hicks, James - Regiment: 24th Infantry - Rank: Private - Source(s): AS-12.

Hicks, John R. - Date of death: 7 Apr 1814 - Source(s): AS-7.

Hidby, S. - Rank: Private - Source(s): AS-8.

Higgly, Eber - Rank: Private - Source(s): AS-8.

High, Joel - Rank: Sergeant - Source(s): AS-8.

Hight, Isaac - Rank: Private - Source(s): AS-8.

Hightower, Richard - Regiment: 17th Infantry - Rank: Captain - Source(s): AS-11.

Hile, Artemus - Rank: Corporal - Source(s): AS-8.

Hill, Allen - Regiment: 24th Infantry - Source(s): AS-1.

Hill, Jeremiah - Regiment: 24th Infantry - Rank: Sergeant - Source(s): AS-1; AS-12.

Hill, Jeremiah - Regiment: 40th Infantry - Rank: Private - Source(s): AS-4 - Comments: On parole at Salem, MA.

Hill, Timothy - Regiment: 4th Infantry - Rank: Private - Source(s): AS-16.

Hill, William - Regiment: 16th Infantry - Rank: Private - Enlistment date: 7 Aug 1812 - Source(s): AS=1; AS-5; AS-14.

Hillard, Samuel - Regiment: 4th Infantry - Rank: Private - Source(s): AS-17.

Hilliard, David - Rank: Sergeant - Source(s): AS-8.

Hillray, Abner - Regiment: Militia - Rank: Private - Source(s): AS-2.

Hilton, Moses - Regiment: 24th Infantry - Source(s): AS-1.

Hinds, Nathan S. - Regiment: 11th Infantry - Source(s): AS-1.

Hines, William - Regiment: 7th Infantry - Rank: Private - Source(s): AS-3.

Hisler, Mathew - Regiment: 1st Infantry - Rank: Private - Source(s): AS-16.

Hitchcock, William - Regiment: Militia - Rank: Private - Source(s): AS-2.

Hitchinson, Joseph - Regiment: 40th Infantry - Rank: Private - Source(s): AS-4 - Comments: POW at Eastport, ME.

Hitchler, John - Regiment: Militia - Rank: Private - Source(s): AS-2.

Hitt, Walter T. - Regiment: 4th Infantry - Rank: Private - Source(s): AS-17.

Hodge, Benjamin - Rank: Citizen - Source(s): AS-9.

Hogelan, William - Rank: Private - Source(s): AS-8.

Hogg, Elijah - Regiment: 40th Infantry - Rank: Private - Source(s): AS-4 - Comments: POW at Eastport, ME.

Holcomb, Leonard - Regiment: 29th Infantry - Rank: Private - Source(s): AS-9.

Holder, Caleb H. - Regiment: 17th Infantry - Rank: Lieutenant - Source(s): AS-11.

Holdersfield, James - Regiment: 26th Infantry - Rank: Private - Source(s): AS-12.

Hollaman, Edmund - Regiment: 7th Infantry - Rank: Corporal - Source(s): AS-3.

Hollender, Isaac - Regiment: NY Militia - Rank: Private - Source(s): AS-12.

Hollister, Jesse W. - Regiment: 1st Artillery - Rank: Sergeant - Source(s): AS-1; AS-12.

Holloby, John - Regiment: 24th Infantry - Source(s): AS-1.

Holloway, John - Regiment: 13th Infantry - Rank: Private - Enlistment date: 12 Apr 1812 - Enlistment period: 5 years - Name of prison ship: Lord Cathcart - Source(s): AS-1; AS-5; AS-14.

Holmes, Charles - Regiment: 1st Artillery - Source(s): AS-1.

Holmes, Daniel - Date of death: 13 Feb 1813 - Source(s): AS-7.

Holmes, Thomas - Regiment: 24th Infantry - Source(s): AS-1.

Holton, James - Rank: Private - Source(s): AS-8.

Holton, John - Regiment: 24th Infantry - Rank: Private - Source(s): AS-1; AS-12.

Holtzboun, Garret - Rank: Private - Source(s): AS-8.

Hood, Frederick - Regiment: 14th Infantry - Rank: Private - Enlistment date: 7 Sep 1812 - Enlistment period: 5 years - Source(s): AS-5.

Hooker, George - Date of death: Died - Source(s): AS-6 - Comments: Died at Quebec.

Hooper, John - Regiment: 9th Infantry - Rank: Private - Source(s): AS-14.

Hooper, Joshua - Regiment: 24th Infantry - Rank: Private - Source(s): AS-1; AS-12.

Hope, John - Regiment: 24th Infantry - Rank: Private - Source(s): AS-12.

Hopkins, Henry - Regiment: 7th Infantry - Rank: Corporal - Source(s): AS-3.

Hopkins, John - Regiment: 1st Artillery - Source(s): AS-1.

Hopkins, Samuel - Regiment: Militia - Rank: Private - Source(s): AS-14.

Hord, Daniel - Regiment: 1st Light Dragoons - Source(s): AS-1.

Hord, John - Regiment: 7th Infantry - Rank: Private - Source(s): AS-3.

Horn, Andrew - Regiment: 21st Infantry - Source(s): AS-1.

Horn, Wentworth - Regiment: 21st Infantry - Rank: Musician - Enlistment date: 25 Feb 1813 - Enlistment period: During the war - Source(s): AS-1; AS-5; AS-14.

Horney, David - Regiment: 5th Infantry - Rank: Private - Enlistment date: 6 Jan 1812 - Enlistment period: 5 years - Name of prison ship: Lord Cathcart - Source(s): AS-1; AS-5; AS-14.

Horton, Barnabas - Regiment: 9th Infantry - Rank: Private - Source(s): AS-10.

Hoss, Isaac - Regiment: 24th Infantry - Rank: Private - Source(s): AS-1; AS-12.

Hoty, Joseph D. - Regiment: Militia - Rank: Private - Source(s): AS-2.

Houck, Michael - Regiment: 4th Infantry - Rank: Private - Source(s): AS-17.

Hounshall, John - Regiment: 24th Infantry - Source(s): AS-1.

House, William - Regiment: 2nd Light Dragoons - Rank: Sergeant - Enlistment date: 15 Mar 1813 - Enlistment period: 5 years - Source(s): AS-5.

Houser, William - Regiment: 22nd Infantry - Source(s): AS-1.

Hovington, Willis - Regiment: 24th Infantry - Rank: Private - Source(s): AS-12.

Howard, Barnabas - Rank: Private - Source(s): AS-8.

Howard, Edward - Regiment: 2nd Light Dragoons - Source(s): AS-1.

Howard, Joseph - Date of death: 3 Jul 1813 - Source(s): AS-6 - Comments: Died at Quebec.

Howard, Josiah - Regiment: 9th Infantry - Rank: Private - Source(s): AS-14.

Howard, Lewis - Regiment: 21st Infantry - Source(s): AS-1.

Howard, Thomas H. - Regiment: 3rd Artillery - Source(s): AS-1.

Howard, William - Regiment: 1st Infantry - Rank: Private - Source(s): AS-16 - Comments: Formerly from the 19th Infantry.

Howe, Calvin - Regiment: 9th Infantry - Rank: Private - Source(s): AS-14.

Howe, John - Regiment: 21st Infantry - Rank: Private - Source(s): AS-1; AS-14.

Howe, William - Regiment: 2nd Light Dragoons - Rank: Private - Source(s): AS-14.

Howe, Willis - Regiment: 25th Infantry - Rank: Private - Source(s): AS-9.

Howell, John D. - Rank: Private - Source(s): AS-8.

Howell, William - Regiment: 7th Infantry - Rank: Private - Source(s): AS-3.

Hox, James - Regiment: 24th Infantry - Source(s): AS-1.

Hubbard, Thomas - Regiment: 21st Infantry - Rank: Private - Source(s): AS-1; AS-14.

Huber, Jacob - Rank: Corporal - Source(s): AS-9.

Hugeman, Daniel - Regiment: 13th Infantry - Rank: Second Lieutenant - Source(s): AS-8.

Huggins, William - Regiment: 4th Infantry - Rank: Sergeant Major - Source(s): AS-17.

Hughes, Elias - Regiment: 27th Infantry - Rank: Recruit - Source(s): AS-15.

Hughes, John - Regiment: 2nd Artillery - Rank: Private - Source(s): AS-9.

Hull, Jabez - Regiment: NY Militia - Rank: Private - Source(s): AS-12.

Hull, Warner - Rank: Private - Source(s): AS-8.

Humes, Daniel - Rank: Private - Source(s): AS-8.

Hunt, Henry - Regiment: 22nd Infantry - Rank: Private - Source(s): AS-10.

Hunt, John - Regiment: Militia - Rank: Private - Source(s): AS-14.

Hunt, John - Regiment: 11th Infantry - Source(s): AS-1.

Hunt, Solomon - Rank: Sergeant - Date of death: 11 Aug 1813 - Source(s): AS-6 - Comments: Died at Quebec.

Hunt, William - Regiment: 24th Infantry - Source(s): AS-1.

Hunter, William - Regiment: 24th Infantry - Rank: Private - Source(s): AS-12.

Hunter, William - Regiment: 4th Infantry - Rank: Corporal - Source(s): AS-17.

Hunter, William - Regiment: 1st Artillery - Rank: Private - Source(s): AS-1; AS-12.

Hutchinson, Elisha - Regiment: 14th Infantry - Rank: Private - Source(s): AS-9.

Hutchinson, Samuel - Regiment: 40th Infantry - Rank: Private - Source(s): AS-4 - Comments: On parole at Salem, MA.

Hutchinson, Seth - Regiment: 40th Infantry - Rank: Private - Source(s): AS-4 - Comments: On parole at Salem, MA.

Hutchinson, William - Regiment: Militia - Rank: Private - Source(s): AS-2.

Hyatt, Joseph - Regiment: 14th Infantry - Rank: Private - Enlistment date: Oct 1812 - Enlistment period: 5 years - Source(s): AS-5.

Hyde, Abel - Regiment: Militia - Rank: Private - Source(s): AS-2.

Hyde, Nathan - Regiment: 4th Infantry - Source(s): AS-1.

Hydendry, Henry - Regiment: 16th Infantry - Rank: Private - Name of prison ship: Lord Cathcart - Source(s): AS-1; AS-14.

Hyer, James - Regiment: 1st Infantry - Rank: Private - Source(s): AS-16.

Hymer, Jacob - Regiment: 2nd Light Dragoons - Rank: Private - Source(s): AS-1; AS-12.

Ingall, Jonathan - Date of death: 14 Aug 1813 - Source(s): AS-6 - Comments: Died at Quebec.

Ingalls, Benjamin - Regiment: 13th Infantry - Rank: Private - Source(s): AS-14.

Ingraham, Benjamin - Regiment: 13th Infantry - Rank: Private - Enlistment date: 20 Feb 1813 - Enlistment period: During the war - Name of prison ship: Lord Cathcart - Source(s): AS-1; AS-5.

Ipsam, Ebenezer - Regiment: Volunteers - Rank: Private - Source(s): AS-14.

Ireland, Jonas - Regiment: 21st Infantry - Rank: Private - Enlistment date: 12 Feb 1813 - Enlistment period: During the war - Source(s): AS-1; AS-5; AS-12.

Irvine, James B. - Regiment: 2nd Artillery - Rank: Sergeant - Enlistment date: 5 May 1812 - Enlistment period: 5 years - Source(s): AS-14; AS-5.

Irvine, John - Regiment: 5th Militia - Rank: Private - Source(s): AS-10.

Irwin, Lewis - Regiment: 16th Infantry - Rank: Private - Enlistment date: 5 Oct 1812 - Source(s): AS-5; AS-14.

Isbell, Chancey - Regiment: 1st Infantry - Rank: Musician - Source(s): AS-16.

Ives, Amos - Rank: Waggoner - Source(s): AS-10.

Jack, Henry - Regiment: KY or TN Militia - Where taken: Miami Rapids, OH or River Raison, MI - Source(s): AS-1.

Jackruder, William - Regiment: 4th Infantry - Rank: Private - Source(s): AS-16.

Jackson, Enoch - Regiment: 21st Infantry - Rank: Private - Enlistment date: 1 Apr 1813 - Enlistment period: During the war - Source(s): AS-1; AS-5.

Jackson, Enoch - Regiment: 9th Infantry - Rank: Private - Source(s): AS-14.

Jackson, Henry - Regiment: 3rd Artillery - Rank: Private - Source(s): AS-1; AS-10.

Jackson, Jacob - Regiment: NY Militia - Rank: Private - Where taken: Niagara or Buffalo, NY - Source(s): AS-1; AS-12.

Jackson, Josiah - Regiment: 1st Infantry - Rank: Private - Source(s): AS-16.

Jackson, Robert - Rank: Private - Source(s): AS-8.

James, John - Rank: Private - Source(s): AS-8.

Janehill, Zachariah - Regiment: 24th Infantry - Source(s): AS-1.

Jarnile, Samuel - Regiment: 44th Infantry - Source(s): AS-1.

Jassar, George - Rank: Sergeant - Source(s): AS-9.

Jefferies, Jonas - Regiment: 27th Infantry - Rank: Recruit - Source(s): AS-15.

Jefferson, Thomas M. - Regiment: 7th Infantry - Rank: Private - Source(s): AS-3.

Jemmison, Levi - Regiment: 4th Infantry - Rank: Sergeant - Source(s): AS-17.

Jenney, Samuel - Regiment: 21st Infantry - Source(s): AS-1.

Jennings, Edward - Regiment: 19th Infantry - Rank: Private - Source(s): AS-12.

Jepson, Ebenezer - Regiment: McCobb's Volunteers - Source(s): AS-1.

Jerris, Barney - Name of prison ship: Lord Cathcart - Source(s): AS-1.

Jesup, Thomas J. - Regiment: 7th Infantry - Rank: Lieutenant - Source(s): AS-11 - Comments: now Major, 19th Infantry.

Jinpthrum, Bernard - Regiment: 1st Infantry - Rank: Private - Source(s): AS-16.

Johnson, Abraham - Regiment: 4th Infantry - Rank: Private - Source(s): AS-16.

Johnson, Benjamin - Regiment: 1st Rifles - Rank: Private - Source(s): AS-10.

Johnson, Daniel - Rank: Private - Source(s): AS-8.

Johnson, David - Regiment: 3rd Artillery - Source(s): AS-1.

Johnson, Friend - Regiment: Militia - Rank: Corporal - Source(s): AS-2.

Johnson, Jason - Regiment: 14th Infantry - Rank: Private - Source(s): AS-14.

Johnson, Joel - Rank: Private - Source(s): AS-8.

Johnson, John - Regiment: 9th Infantry - Rank: Private - Source(s): AS-14.

Johnson, Mark - Regiment: NY Militia - Rank: Private - Source(s): AS-12.

Johnson, Solomon - Regiment: 4th Infantry - Rank: Corporal - Source(s): AS-17.

Johnson, Solomon - Regiment: 4th Infantry - Rank: Private - Source(s): AS-17.

Johnson, Thomas - Regiment: KY or TN Militia - Where taken: Miami Rapids, OH or River Raison, MI - Source(s): AS-1.

Johnson, William - Regiment: 22nd Infantry - Source(s): AS-1.

Johnson, William - Regiment: 21st Infantry - Source(s): AS-1.

Johnston, James - Regiment: 7th Infantry - Rank: Private - Source(s): AS-3.

Johnston, John - Regiment: 27th Infantry - Rank: Recruit - Source(s): AS-15.

Johnston, Noble - Regiment: 14th Infantry - Rank: Private - Enlistment date: 9 May 1812 - Enlistment period: 5

years - Source(s): AS-5; AS-14.

Johnston, Samuel - Regiment: 27th Infantry - Rank: Recruit - Source(s): AS-15.

Johnston, Truman - Regiment: 1st Artillery - Rank: Private - Enlistment date: 15 Dec 1810 - Enlistment period: 5 years - Name of prison ship: Lord Cathcart - Source(s): AS-1; AS-5; AS-14.

Jones, Enoch - Regiment: 2nd Artillery - Rank: Private - Enlistment date: 2 May 1812 - Enlistment period: 5 years - Source(s): AS-1; AS-5; AS-14.

Jones, Henry - Regiment: Militia - Rank: Private - Source(s): AS-14.

Jones, Henry - Rank: Private - Source(s): AS-8.

Jones, John - Regiment: KY or TN Militia - Where taken: Miami Rapids, OH or River Raison, MI - Source(s): AS-1.

Jones, John - Regiment: 4th Infantry - Rank: Private - Source(s): AS-17.

Jones, Nathan - Regiment: 9th Infantry - Rank: Corporal - Source(s): AS-9.

Jones, Philoster - Regiment: Militia - Rank: Private - Source(s): AS-14.

Jones, Phineas - Date of death: 10 Mar 1814 - Source(s): AS-7.

Jones, Thomas - Regiment: 25th Infantry - Rank: Private - Source(s): AS-14.

Jones, William - Regiment: 5th Infantry - Rank: Private - Enlistment date: 4 Aug 1812 - Enlistment period: 5 years - Source(s): AS-1; AS-5; AS-14.

Jones, William - Regiment: 19th Infantry - Rank: Sergeant - Source(s): AS-12.

Joseph, John - Regiment: 12th Infantry - Rank: Private - Enlistment date: 30 Jun 1812 - Enlistment period: 5 years - Name of prison ship: Lord Cathcart - Source(s): AS-1; AS-5.

Joslen, Israel - Regiment: OH Militia - Rank: Lieutenant - Source(s): AS-18 - Comments: Findlay's Regiment.

Justice, William K. - Regiment: 1st Infantry - Rank: Private - Source(s): AS-16.

Kairns, John - Regiment: 14th Infantry - Rank: Private - Source(s): AS-14.

Kane, Robert - Regiment: Militia - Rank: Private - Source(s): AS-2.

Kay, Ebenezer - Regiment: 4th Infantry - Rank: First Lieutenant - Source(s): AS-17.

Kean, (-----) - Regiment: OH Militia - Rank: Lieutenant - Source(s): AS-18 - Comments: Cass' Regiment.

Kearney, Stephen W. - Regiment: 13th Infantry - Rank: Lieutenant - Source(s): AS-11 - Comments: now Captain.

Kearns, James - Regiment: 7th Infantry - Rank: Sergeant - Source(s): AS-3.

Keith, Nehemiah - Regiment: 9th Infantry - Rank: Private - Source(s): AS-14.

Keith, Zephariah - Regiment: 9th Infantry - Rank: Private - Enlistment date: 15 Feb 1813 - Enlistment period: During the war - Source(s): AS-5.

Keller, William - Regiment: 5th Infantry - Rank: Private - Enlistment date: 15 Jan 1812 - Enlistment period: 5 years - Source(s): AS-5.

Kelley, Allson - Regiment: 24th Infantry - Source(s): AS-1.

Kellog, Daniel - Regiment: 4th Infantry - Rank: Musician - Source(s): AS-17.

Kelly, Allen - Regiment: 24th Infantry - Rank: Private - Source(s): AS-12.

Kelly, Ezra - Regiment: 27th Infantry - Rank: Recruit - Source(s): AS-15.

Kelly, James - Name of prison ship: Lord Cathcart - Source(s): AS-1.

Kelly, John - Enlistment date: 25 Jul 1812 - Source(s): AS-5.

Kelly, Paul - Regiment: 1st Artillery - Rank: Private - Source(s): AS-14.

Kelly, William - Regiment: 5th Infantry - Rank: Private - Name of prison ship: Lord Cathcart - Source(s): AS-1; AS-14.

Kelly, William - Regiment: 4th Infantry - Rank: Quartermaster Sergeant - Source(s): AS-17.

Kemble, Abel - Regiment: 2nd Light Dragoons - Source(s): AS-1.

Kemble, Hannibal - Regiment: 21st Infantry - Source(s): AS-1.

Kemper, Edward Y. - Regiment: OH Militia - Rank: Surgeon's Mate - Source(s): AS-18 - Comments: Findlay's Regiment.

Kemper, Prestley - Regiment: OH Militia - Rank: Wagon master - Source(s): AS-18.

Kendal, Reason - Regiment: KY or TN Militia - Where taken: Miami Rapids, OH or River Raison, MI - Source(s): AS-1.

Kendall, Silas - Regiment: 4th Infantry - Rank: Private - Source(s): AS-17.

Kennedy, George - Regiment: Militia - Rank: Captain - Source(s): AS-3.

Kennedy, James - Regiment: 7th Infantry - Rank: Private - Source(s): AS-3.

Kennedy, James - Regiment: Militia - Rank: Lieutenant - Source(s): AS-3.

Kenzie, John - Regiment: Militia - Source(s): AS-1.

Ketch, Klaus - Rank: Private - Source(s): AS-8.

Keys, William - Regiment: OH Militia - Rank: Captain - Source(s): AS-18 - Comments: McArthur's Regiment.

Keyser, Jacob - Regiment: 4th Infantry - Rank: Private - Source(s): AS-17.

Kicker, Isaac - Regiment: 4th Infantry - Rank: Sergeant - Source(s): AS-17.

Kihill, William - Regiment: 1st Infantry - Rank: Private - Source(s): AS-16.

Kiler, John - Enlistment date: 16 Oct 1812 - Source(s): AS-5.

Killeg, James - Regiment: 16th Infantry - Rank: Private - Source(s): AS-14.

Killen, John - Regiment: 16th Infantry - Rank: Private - Source(s): AS-14.

Kimbal, Moses - Rank: Sergeant - Source(s): AS-8.

Kimball, Benjamin - Date of death: 6 Aug 1813 - Source(s): AS-6 - Comments: Died at Quebec.

Kimball, Bradbury - Regiment: 40th Infantry - Rank: Private - Source(s): AS-4 - Comments: POW at Eastport, ME.

Kimball, Nathaniel - Regiment: 21st Infantry - Rank: Private - Source(s): AS-1; AS-14.

King, Willis - Regiment: 24th Infantry - Rank: Corporal - Source(s): AS-1; AS-12.

Kingman, Ebenezer - Regiment: 21st Infantry - Rank: Private - Enlistment date: 9 Mar 1813 - Enlistment period: During the war - Name of prison ship: Lord Cathcart - Source(s): AS-1; AS-5; AS-14.

Kingsland, Joseph - Regiment: 6th Infantry - Rank: Private - Enlistment date: 27 Arp 1812 - Enlistment period: 5 years - Name of prison ship: Lord Cathcart - Source(s): AS-1; AS-5; As-14.

Kinter, Solomon - Rank: Private - Source(s): AS-8.

Kirk, John - Regiment: 22nd Infantry - Rank: Corporal - Source(s): AS-10.

Knapp, Abraham - Regiment: 1st Artillery - Rank: Corporal - Source(s): AS-17 - Comments: Since dead.

Knapp, John - Rank: Private - Source(s): AS-8.

Knapp, Silas - Regiment: NY Militia - Rank: Private - Source(s): AS-12.

Knapp, Titus - Regiment: 4th Infantry - Rank: Private - Source(s): AS-17 - Comments: Since dead.

Knapp, William - Regiment: 4th Infantry - Rank: Private - Source(s): AS-17.

Knight, Asa - Regiment: 4th Infantry - Rank: Private - Source(s): AS-17.

Knight, Hudson - Regiment: 21st Infantry - Rank: Musician - Enlistment date: 16 Mar 1813 - Enlistment period: During the war - Source(s): AS-1; AS-5; AS-14.

Knight, William - Regiment: 5th Infantry - Rank: Musician - Enlistment date: May 1812 - Enlistment period: 5 years - Name of prison ship: Lord Cathcart - Source(s): AS-1; AS-5.

Knoningen, John - Regiment: 16th Infantry - Rank: Private - Source(s): AS-14.

Knowles, John - Regiment: 1st Infantry - Source(s): AS-1.

Knowles, Seth - Regiment: 3rd Artillery - Rank: Private - Enlistment date: 3 Jun 1812 - Enlistment period: 5 years - Source(s): AS-5.

Knowly, Joseph - Regiment: 3rd Artillery - Source(s): AS-1.

Kothrock, Isaac - Regiment: 1st Infantry - Rank: Private - Source(s): AS-16.

Kowington, Willis - Regiment: 24th Infantry - Source(s): AS-1.

Kyle, Samuel B. - Regiment: OH Militia - Rank: Captain - Source(s): AS-18 - Comments: Findlay's Regiment.

Lacey, Fielding - Regiment: 26th Infantry - Rank: Private - Source(s): AS-12.

Lackey, Andrew - Regiment: 27th Infantry - Rank: Recruit - Source(s): AS-15.

Lackey, Hugh - Regiment: 27th Infantry - Rank: Recruit - Source(s): AS-15.

Ladd, Aaron - Regiment: 4th Infantry - Rank: Private - Source(s): AS-17.

Ladd, Peter - Regiment: 4th Infantry - Rank: Private - Source(s): AS-17 - Comments: Died aboard transport.

Ladd, Samuel - Regiment: 4th Infantry - Rank: Private - Source(s): AS-17.

Lafferty, Archibald - Regiment: 27th Infantry - Rank: Recruit - Source(s): AS-15.

Laforge, Charles - Regiment: 12th Infantry - Rank: Private - Source(s): AS-14.

Laforge, Stephen - Rank: Private - Source(s): AS-8.

Lambe, Oliver - Regiment: 40th Infantry - Rank: Private - Source(s): AS-4 - Comments: POW at Eastport, ME.

Lamont, John - Regiment: NY Militia - Rank: Private - Source(s): AS-12.

Lamson, John - Rank: Corporal - Source(s): AS-9.

Lanabee, Asa - Regiment: 4th Infantry - Rank: Private - Source(s): AS-16.

Lancaster, William - Regiment: 21st Infantry - Rank: Private - Source(s): AS-9.

Land, Joshua - Regiment: 1st Rifles - Rank: Private - Source(s): AS-10.

Lander, Charles - Date of death: 22 Jul 1813 - Source(s): AS-6 - Comments: Died at Quebec.

Landon, D. - Rank: Private - Source(s): AS-8.

Landrum, Younger - Regiment: 2nd Light Dragoons - Source(s): AS-1.

Lane, Benjamin - Date of death: 23 Jul 1813 - Source(s): AS-6 - Comments: Died at Quebec.

Lane, Isaac - Regiment: 24th Infantry - Source(s): AS-1.

Lark, John - Date of death: 12 Feb 1814 - Source(s): AS-7.

Larney, Joseph - Regiment: 5th Infantry - Rank: Private - Source(s): AS-14.

Larrabee, Abraham - Regiment: 4th Infantry - Rank: Private - Source(s): AS-16.

Larsons, Samuel - Regiment: 5th Infantry - Rank: Private - Source(s): AS-14.

Latham John - Regiment: 3rd Militia - Rank: Private - Source(s): AS-10.

Latham, John - Regiment: 3rd Artillery - Source(s): AS-1.

Laughlin, John - Regiment: 2nd Artillery - Rank: Private - Source(s): As-1; AS-12.

Lawrence, Abel - Rank: Sergeant - Source(s): AS-9.

Lawton, Perry - Date of death: 21 Jul 1813 - Source(s): AS-6 - Comments: Died at Quebec.

Lay, John - Regiment: Militia - Rank: Private - Source(s): AS-2.

Layman, Joseph - Regiment: 4th Infantry - Rank: Private - Source(s): AS-16.

Layman, William - Regiment: 4th Infantry - Rank: Private - Source(s): AS-16.

Le Duck, Peter - Regiment: 17th Infantry - Rank: Private - Source(s): AS-9.

Le Forge, Charles - Regiment: 12th Infantry - Name of prison ship: Lord Cathcart - Source(s): AS-1.

Leatt, Abraham - Regiment: 23rd Infantry - Rank: Private - Source(s): AS-14.

Leders, Jacob - Regiment: 3rd Artillery - Rank: Private - Source(s): AS-1; AS-10.

Lee, Abram - Rank: Private - Source(s): AS-8.

Lee, Daniel - Regiment: 13th Infantry - Rank: Private - Source(s): AS-1; AS-14.

Lee, George - Regiment: 40th Infantry - Rank: Private - Source(s): AS-4 - Comments: On parole at Salem, MA.

Lee, Isaac - Rank: Corporal - Source(s): AS-8.

Lee, William R. - Regiment: Militia - Rank: Private - Source(s): AS-14.

Leggs, David - Regiment: 1st Rifles - Rank: Private - Enlistment date: 9 Dec 1812 - Enlistment period: 5 years - Name of prison ship: Lord Cathcart - Source(s): AS-1; AS-5.

Leisse, John - Regiment: 12th Infantry - Rank: Private - Source(s): AS-14.

Leister, Jonathan - Regiment: 19th Infantry - Rank: Private - Source(s): AS-12.

Leonard, Isaac - Regiment: 22nd Infantry - Source(s): AS-1.

Leonard, Jacob - Regiment: 40th Infantry - Rank: Private - Source(s): AS-4 - Comments: On parole at Salem, MA.

Leonard, Martin - Regiment: 1st Artillery - Rank: Sergeant - Source(s): AS-16.

Leonard, Samuel - Regiment: 40th Infantry - Rank: Private - Source(s): AS-4 - Comments: On parole at Salem, MA.

Lerney, Joseph K. - Regiment: 15th Infantry - Name of prison ship: Lord Cathcart - Source(s): AS-1.

Leroy, Charles - Regiment: 13th Infantry - Rank: Private - Source(s): AS-14.

Leroy, Charles M. - Rank: Private - Source(s): AS-8 - Comments: Deserted at Cape Breton, Nova Scotia.

Leti, Puff - Regiment: 24th Infantry - Source(s): AS-1.

Lewis, Levi - Regiment: 1st Artillery - Source(s): AS-1; AS-12.

Lewis, Ria - Rank: Private - Source(s): AS-8.

Lewis, William - Regiment: NY Militia - Rank: Private - Source(s): AS-12.

Leyss, David - Regiment: 5th Infantry - Rank: Private - Source(s): AS-14.

Licker, Francis - Source(s): AS-3 - Comments: British subject.

Lighter, Jacob - Regiment: 14th Infantry - Rank: Sergeant - Enlistment date: 11 May 1812 - Enlistment period: 5 years - Source(s): AS-5; AS-14.

Likens, Thomas - Regiment: 1st Artillery - Source(s): AS-1.

Lincoln, Gideon - Regiment: 4th Infantry - Rank: Private - Source(s): AS-16.

Lincoln, William - Rank: Private - Source(s): AS-8.

Lindsay, David - Regiment: 40th Infantry - Rank: Sergeant - Source(s): AS-4 - Comments: POW at Eastport, ME.

Lindsay, William - Regiment: 2nd Artillery - Rank: Private - Enlistment date: 1 Jan 1813 - Enlistment period: 5 years - Source(s): AS-5; AS-14.

Linet, Samuel - Regiment: Militia - Name of prison ship: Lord Cathcart - Where taken: Sackets Harbor, NY - Source(s): AS-1.

Linnell, Samuel - Regiment: Militia - Rank: Private - Source(s): AS-14.

Little, Solomon - Regiment: 23rd Infantry - Rank: Sergeant - Enlistment date: 12 May 1813 - Enlistment period: During the war - Source(s): AS-5; AS-14.

Lloyd, Thompson C. - Regiment: 1st Rifles - Source(s): AS-1.

Lloyd, William - Regiment: 13th Infantry - Rank: Private - Enlistment date: 22 Apr 1812 - Enlistment period: 5 years - Name of prison ship: Lord Cathcart - Source(s): AS-1; AS-5.

Lockard, Thomas - Regiment: 1st Artillery - Source(s): AS-1.

Lockhard, Josiah - Regiment: OH Militia - Rank: Captain - Source(s): AS-18 - Comments: McArthur's Regiment.

Lockyear, Benjamin - Rank: Private - Source(s): AS-8.

Londred, Lewis - Regiment: 1st Infantry - Rank: Private - Source(s): AS-16.

Loomis, Daniel - Regiment: 25th Infantry - Rank: Corporal - Enlistment date: 23 Jul 1812 - Enlistment period: 5 years - Source(s): AS-5; AS-14.

Loomis, Jacob - Regiment: Militia - Rank: Private - Source(s): AS-2.

Lord, Horatio - Regiment: 11th Infantry - Source(s): AS-1.

Lord, Joseph - Rank: Private - Source(s): AS-8.

Lounsbury, Samuel - Regiment: 2nd Light Dragoons - Name of prison ship: Lord Cathcart - Source(s): AS-1.

Louran, Thomas - Regiment: 14th Infantry - Rank: Private - Enlistment date: 25 Jan 1813 - Enlistment period: 5 years - Source(s): AS-5; AS-14.

Loury, James - Regiment: 1st Infantry - Rank: Private - Source(s): AS-16.

Lovejoy, Jacob - Regiment: McCobb's Volunteers - Rank: Private - Source(s): AS-1; AS-14.

Loveland, Anson - Regiment: 1st Artillery - Rank: Corporal - Source(s): AS-16.

Loveland, Asa - Regiment: Civilian - Rank: Custom House Officer - Source(s): AS-12.

Lovell, Sylvanus - Regiment: 11th Infantry - Rank: Private - Source(s): AS-10.

Lovering, Joshua - Regiment: 4th Infantry - Rank: Private - Source(s): AS-17.

Lowe, Samuel - Regiment: 14th Infantry - Rank: Private - Source(s): AS-14.

Lozier, Abraham - Regiment: 2nd Artillery - Rank: Private - Enlistment date: 31 Jan 1813 - Enlistment period: 5 years - Source(s): AS-5; AS-14.

Lucas, Ephraim - Regiment: 21st Infantry - Rank: Private - Source(s): AS-1; AS-14.

Lucas, Robert - Regiment: OH Militia - Rank: Captain - Source(s): AS-18 - Comments: McArthur's Regiment.

Luckitt, Alexander - Regiment: 1st Infantry - Rank: Private - Source(s): AS-16.

Ludden, Eley - Regiment: NY Militia - Rank: Private - Source(s): AS-12.

Lusk, John - Regiment: NY Militia - Rank: Lieutenant - Source(s): AS-12.

Lyles, William - Regiment: 12th Infantry - Name of prison ship: Lord Cathcart - Source(s): AS-1.

Lyles, William - Regiment: Marine Corps - Rank: Sergeant - Source(s): AS-9.

Lynn, James - Regiment: Militia - Rank: Private - Source(s): AS-2.

Lynn, Joshua - Regiment: 21st Infantry - Rank: Private - Source(s): AS-9.

Lyon, William - Regiment: Militia - Rank: Private - Source(s): AS-2.

Lythe, Daniel - Regiment: Volunteers - Rank: Private - Source(s): AS-14.

Lyttle, Daniel - Regiment: 1st Rifles - Rank: Private - Enlistment date: 31 Aug 1812 - Enlistment period: 5 years - Name of prison ship: Lord Cathcart - Source(s): AS-1; AS-5.

Mack, Abner - Regiment: Militia - Rank: Private - Source(s): AS-14.

Madden, Thomas - Regiment: Volunteers - Rank: Private - Source(s): AS-14.

Magary, Edward - Regiment: 4th Infantry - Rank: Private - Source(s): AS-16.

Magee, George - Regiment: 23rd Infantry - Name of prison ship: Lord Cathcart - Source(s): AS-1.

Magee, William - Name of prison ship: Lord Cathcart - Source(s): AS-1.

Magerman, J. N. - Rank: Private - Source(s): AS-8.

Mahan, Francis - Regiment: KY or TN Militia - Where taken: Miami Rapids, OH or River Raison, MI - Source(s): AS-1.

Mahoney, Thomas - Regiment: 1st Artillery - Rank: Artificer - Source(s): AS-16.

Maloney, John - Regiment: 24th Infantry - Source(s): AS-1.

Manchester, Noah - Regiment: 1st Rifles - Source(s): AS-1.

Mandeville, Peter - Regiment: 6th Infantry - Rank: Private - Enlistment date: Jan 1810 - Enlistment period: 5 years - Name of prison ship: Lord Cathcart - Source(s): AS-1; AS-5; AS-14.

Mann, Neely - Regiment: 1st Artillery - Rank: Private - Source(s): AS-16.

Manrow, John - Regiment: 2nd Light Dragoons - Rank: Corporal - Enlistment date: 11 Apr 1812 - Enlistment period: During the war - Source(s): AS-5.

Maramond, Chester - Regiment: Militia - Rank: Private - Source(s): AS-2.

Marks, Abraham - Regiment: 1st US Volunteers - Source(s): AS-1.

Marks, Henry - Regiment: 13th Infantry - Source(s): AS-1.

Marks, Ira - Regiment: 21st Infantry - Rank: Sergeant - Source(s): AS-1; AS-9.

Marsh, Ormond - Regiment: 1st Infantry - Rank: Ensign - Source(s): AS-11 - Comments: now Lieutenant.

Marsh, William - Regiment: 7th Infantry - Rank: Private - Source(s): AS-3.

Marshall, Joseph - Regiment: 14th Infantry - Rank: First Lieutenant - Source(s): AS-14.

Marshall, Thomas - Regiment: 7th Infantry - Rank: Private - Source(s): AS-3.

Martin, Asahel - Regiment: Militia - Rank: Private - Source(s): AS-2.

Martin, John - Regiment: 7th Infantry - Rank: Private - Source(s): AS-3.

Martin, Delancy - Date of death: 3 Aug 1813 - Source(s): AS-6 - Comments: Died at Quebec.

Martin, Robert - Regiment: 19th Infantry - Rank: Private - Source(s): AS-12.

Martin, William - Regiment: NY Militia - Rank: Ensign - Source(s): AS-12.

Martin, William - Regiment: Militia - Rank: Private - Source(s): AS-2.

Mason, John - Rank: Private - Source(s): AS-8.

Mason, Moses - Regiment: 4th Infantry - Rank: Private - Source(s): AS-17.

Mason, Richard - Source(s): AS-3 - Comments: British deserter.

Masters, John - Regiment: KY or TN Militia - Where taken: Miami Rapids, OH or River Raison, MI - Source(s): AS-1.

Masters, William - Rank: Private - Source(s): AS-8.

Mathews, William - Regiment: 4th Infantry - Source(s): AS-1.

Matson, Thomas F. - Regiment: 1st Infantry - Rank: Private - Source(s): AS-16.

McArthur, Alexander - Date of death: 28 Dec 1813 - Source(s): AS-7.

McArthur, Duncan - Regiment: OH Militia - Rank: Colonel - Source(s): AS-18.

McArthur, John - Regiment: 4th Infantry - Rank: Private - Source(s): AS-17.

McBride, Alexander - Regiment: NY Militia - Rank: Private - Source(s): AS-12.

McBride, James - Rank: Private - Source(s): AS-8.

McBride, James - Regiment: 7th Infantry - Rank: Private - Source(s): AS-3.

McBride, John - Regiment: NY Militia - Rank: Lieutenant - Source(s): AS-12.

McBride, Samuel - Regiment: 7th Infantry - Rank: Private - Source(s): AS-3.

McCabe, Robert - Regiment: 1st Infantry - Rank: Ensign - Source(s): AS-11; AS-16 - Comments: now Lieutenant.

McCall, Preserved - Regiment: NY Militia - Rank: Private - Source(s): AS-12.

McCammon, Robert - Regiment: 24th Infantry - Rank: Private - Source(s): AS-1; AS-12.

McCann, Edward - Regiment: 6th Infantry - Rank: Private - Enlistment date: Jul 1812 - Enlistment period: 5 years - Name of prison ship: Lord Cathcart - Source(s): AS-1; AS-5; AS-14.

McCann, Robert - Regiment: 22nd Infantry - Rank: Private - Enlistment date: 15 Jun 1812 - Enlistment period: 5 years - Source(s): AS-5; AS-14.

McCarey, Lewis - Regiment: 7th Infantry - Rank: Private - Source(s): AS-3.

McCarl, Isaac - Regiment: 24th Infantry - Source(s): AS-1.

McCarty, John - Regiment: 23rd Infantry - Rank: First Lieutenant - Source(s): AS-8; AS-11.

McChristie, Jesse - Regiment: 1st Artillery - Rank: Private - Source(s): AS-1; AS-9; AS-12.

McClaine, Thomas - Regiment: 7th Infantry - Rank: Private - Source(s): AS-3.

McCoomb, George - Regiment: NY Militia - Rank: Private - Source(s): AS-12.

McCord, Bernard - Regiment: 1st Infantry - Rank: Private - Source(s): AS-16.

McCormick, James - Rank: Private - Source(s): AS-8.

McCormick, Samuel - Regiment: OH Militia - Rank: Lieutenant, Adjutant - Source(s): AS-18 - Comments: Findlay's Regiment.

McCoy, Jacob - Regiment: 24th Infantry - Source(s): AS-1; AS-12.

McCraig, Thomas - Regiment: 24th Infantry - Source(s): AS-1.

McCulloch, Samuel - Regiment: 22nd Infantry - Rank: Private - Source(s): AS-10.

McCune, William - Regiment: 12th Infantry - Rank: Corporal - Source(s): AS-9.

McCurdy, Robert - Regiment: 22nd Infantry - Source(s): AS-1.

McDoad, James - Regiment: 22nd Infantry - Rank: Private - Source(s): AS-10.

McDonald, Francis - Regiment: 15th Infantry - Rank: Private - Enlistment date: 7 Jun 1812 - Enlistment period: 5 years - Name of prison ship: Lord Cathcart - Source(s): AS-1; AS-5; AS-14.

McDonald, James - Regiment: 4th Infantry - Rank: Private - Source(s): AS-16.

McDonald, John - Regiment: NY Militia - Rank: Private - Source(s): AS-12.

McDonald, John - Regiment: OH Militia - Rank: Lieutenant, Paymaster - Source(s): AS-18 - Comments: McArthur's Regiment.

McDonald, Peter - Regiment: 14th Infantry - Rank: Private - Source(s): AS-14.

McDonald, Stephen - Regiment: 27th Infantry - Rank: Recruit - Source(s): AS-15.

McElhaney, William - Regiment: 1st Infantry - Rank: Private - Source(s): AS-16.

McElroy, Charles - Regiment: 13th Infantry - Rank: Private - Enlistment date: 9 May 1812 - Enlistment period: 5 years - Source(s): AS-5.

McEwen, William - Regiment: 1st Rifles - Name of prison ship: Lord Cathcart - Source(s): AS-1.

McFadden, Neal - Regiment: 27th Infantry - Rank: Recruit - Source(s): AS-15.

McFarland, Stephen - Regiment: OH Militia - Rank: Lieutenant - Source(s): AS-18 - Comments: Cass' Regiment.

McGarley, Jesse - Date of death: 8 Apr 1814 - Source(s): AS-7.

McGee, P. - Rank: Private - Source(s): AS-8.

McGee, Truman - Regiment: 11th Infantry - Source(s): AS-1.

McGee, William - Enlistment date: Oct 1812 - Source(s): AS-5.

McGill, Hiram - Regiment: 24th Infantry - Rank: Private - Source(s): AS-1; AS-12.

McGill, Patrick - Regiment: 24th Infantry - Source(s): AS-1 - Comments: Since dead.

McGlaughlin, Mark - Regiment: 22nd Infantry - Source(s): AS-1.

McGonnegal, Michael - Regiment: 16th Infantry - Source(s): AS-1.

McGriffen, John - Regiment: 2nd Artillery - Rank: Private - Source(s): AS-1; AS-12.

McIlroy, James - Regiment: KY or TN Militia - Where taken: Miami Rapids, OH or River Raison, MI - Source(s): AS-1.

McInelly, John - Regiment: 11th Infantry - Source(s): AS-1.

McIntire, Ledich - Regiment: 22nd Infantry - Rank: Private - Source(s): AS-14.

McIntire, Zadock - Regiment: 22nd Infantry - Rank: Private - Enlistment date: 19 May 1812 - Enlistment period: 5 years - Source(s): AS-1; AS-5.

McIntosh, Robert - Regiment: 4th Infantry - Rank: Private - Source(s): AS-16.

McInturff, William - Regiment: 24th Infantry - Source(s): AS-1.

McKay, Robert - Regiment: NY Militia - Rank: Captain - Source(s): AS-12.

McKay, William - Rank: Private - Source(s): AS-8.

McKenize, John - Regiment: 7th Infantry - Rank: Sergeant - Source(s): AS-3.

McKenzy, Thomas - Regiment: 13th Infantry - Rank: Private - Enlistment date: 15 Jun 1813 - Enlistment period: 5 years - Name of prison ship: Lord Cathcart - Source(s): AS-1; AS-5; AS-14.

McKinley, William - Regiment: 4th Infantry - Source(s): AS-1.

McLean, Richard - Regiment: 1st Artillery - Rank: Private - Source(s): AS-1; AS-12.

McManey, John - Regiment: 1st Artillery - Source(s): AS-1.

McMellon, William - Regiment: KY or TN Militia - Where taken: Miami Rapids, OH or River Raison, MI - Source(s): AS-1.

McMullen, Archibald - Date of death: 18 Aug 1813 - Source(s): AS-6 - Comments: Died at Quebec.

McNutt, James - Regiment: 22nd Infantry - Rank: Volunteer - Source(s): AS-10.

McQuay, Daniel - Regiment: 24th Infantry - Rank: Private - Source(s): AS-1; AS-12.

McQuegtion, Hugh - Regiment: 9th Infantry - Rank: Private - Source(s): AS-10.

McWade, Edward - Regiment: 1st Artillery - Source(s): AS-1.

McWilliams, William - Regiment: 1st Artillery - Source(s): AS-1.

McWithy, John - Regiment: 4th Infantry - Rank: Corporal - Source(s): AS-17.

Meacham, Jesse - Regiment: Militia - Name of prison ship: Lord Cathcart - Where taken: Black Rock, NY - Source(s): AS-1.

Medae, Thomas - Regiment: McCobb's Volunteers - Source(s): AS-1.

Medell, Alden - Regiment: 9th Infantry - Rank: Private - Source(s): AS-10.

Mellen, Aaron - Regiment: 4th Infantry - Rank: Corporal - Source(s): AS-17.

Mellens, Daniel D. - Regiment: 40th Infantry - Rank: Private - Source(s): AS-4 - Comments: On parole at Salem, MA.

Melvine, Thomas - Regiment: 24th Infantry - Rank: Private - Source(s): AS-1; AS-12.

Menill, Abraham - Regiment: 33rd Infantry - Source(s): AS-1.

Mercer, James - Regiment: 24th Infantry - Rank: Private - Source(s): AS-1; AS-12.

Meriar, James F. - Regiment: 40th Infantry - Rank: Private - Source(s): AS-4 - Comments: POW at Eastport, ME.

Meriar, Samuel - Regiment: 40th Infantry - Rank: Private - Source(s): AS-4 - Comments: POW at Eastport, ME.

Merrier, Jacob - Regiment: 24th Infantry - Rank: Private - Source(s): AS-1; AS-12.

Merrill, Jacob - Regiment: McCobb's Volunteers - Rank: Private - Source(s): AS-1; AS-14.

Merrill, Jacob - Regiment: 21st Infantry - Rank: Private - Enlistment date: 26 Jan 1813 - Enlistment period: 5 years - Source(s): AS-1; AS-5; AS-14.

Merrill, James - Regiment: 4th Infantry - Rank: Private - Source(s): AS-16.

Merrill, Mathias - Rank: Private - Source(s): AS-8.

Merrill, Theodosius - Regiment: McCobb's Volunteers – Sent to hospital - Source(s): AS-1.

Merritt, Jonathan - Regiment: Volunteers - Rank: Private - Source(s): AS-14.

Merritt, Jonathan B. - Regiment: 11th Infantry - Source(s): AS-1.

Merry, Anson, - Regiment: Militia - Rank: Private - Source(s): AS-2.

Messenger, Grove - Date of death: 29 Jan 1814 - Source(s): AS-7.

Messenger, W. S. - Regiment: 11th Infantry - Rank: Private - Source(s): AS-10.

Metadow, Samuel - Regiment: OH Militia - Rank: Surgeon - Source(s): AS-18 - Comments: McArthur's Regiment.

Millard, Almon H. - Regiment: NY Militia - Rank: Major - Source(s): AS-12.

Miller, (-----) - Regiment: OH Militia - Rank: Lieutenant - Source(s): AS-18 - Comments: Findlay's Regiment.

Miller, Alexander - Regiment: NY Militia - Rank: Private - Source(s): AS-12.

Miller, Benjamin - Regiment: 27th Infantry - Rank: Private - Source(s): AS-1; AS-12.

Miller, Gordon - Rank: Private - Source(s): AS-8.

Miller, Jacob - Regiment: 19th Infantry - Rank: Private - Source(s): AS-12.

Miller, James - Rank: Private - Source(s): AS-8.

Miller, John - Regiment: 1st Infantry - Rank: Corporal - Source(s): AS-16.

Miller, Reuben - Regiment: 24th Infantry - Source(s): AS-1.

Miller, William - Regiment: Militia - Rank: Private - Source(s): AS-2.

Miller, William - Regiment: 1st Infantry - Rank: Private - Source(s): AS-16.

Millineuse, Thomas - Regiment: 6th Infantry - Rank: Private - Enlistment date: 18 Jun 1812 - Enlistment period: 5 years - Name of prison ship: Lord Cathcart - Source(s): AS-1; AS-5; AS-14.

Million, Rodney - Regiment: KY or TN Militia - Where taken: Miami Rapids, OH or River Raison, MI - Source(s): AS-1.

Mills, Elias - Regiment: 1st Infantry - Source(s): AS-1.

Mills, Henry - Regiment: NY Militia - Rank: Private - Source(s): AS-12.

Mills, John - Regiment: 4th Infantry - Rank: Musician - Source(s): AS-16.

Mills, Joseph - Rank: Private - Source(s): AS-8.

Mineher, William - Regiment: 40th Infantry - Rank: Private - Source(s): AS-4 - Comments: POW at Eastport, ME.

Minor, Harris - Regiment: 11th Infantry - Rank: Private - Source(s): AS-9.

Minor, Lewis - Regiment: Militia - Rank: Private - Source(s): AS-14.

Minor, Lewis - Regiment: 15th Infantry - Source(s): AS-1.

Mirak, J. - Rank: Private - Source(s): AS-8.

Misner, Oscar - Rank: Private - Source(s): AS-8.

Mitchell, Hugh - Regiment: 22nd Infantry - Rank: Private - Source(s): AS-10.

Mitchell, Nathan - Regiment: 4th Infantry - Rank: Private - Source(s): AS-17.

Mitchell, William - Date of death: 4 Aug 1813 - Source(s): AS-6 - Comments: Died at Quebec.

Moire, Thomas - Regiment: NY Militia - Rank: Private - Source(s): AS-12.

Moire, William - Regiment: 24th Infantry - Rank: Private - Source(s): AS-12.

Monroe, John - Regiment: 2nd Light Dragoons - Rank: Private - Name of prison ship: Hospital - Source(s): AS-1; AS-14.

Moody, John - Regiment: McCobb's Volunteers - Source(s): AS-1.

Moody, John - Regiment: 1st Artillery - Rank: Private - Source(s): AS-16.

Moody, John - Rank: Corporal - Source(s): AS-9.

Moody, John - Rank: Private - Source(s): AS-8.

Mooney, Peter - Date of death: 13 Jan 1814 - Source(s): AS-7.

Moor, Obadiah - Regiment: 40th Infantry - Rank: Private - Source(s): AS-4 - Comments: POW at Eastport, ME.

Moore, Abel - Regiment: 21st Infantry - Source(s): AS-1.

Moore, Abraham - Regiment: 26th Infantry - Rank: Private - Source(s): AS-12.

Moore, Joshua - Regiment: 21st Infantry - Rank: Private - Source(s): AS-10; AS-14.

Moore, Larrond - Regiment: 14th Infantry - Rank: Corporal - Enlistment date: 12 May 1812 - Enlistment period: 5 years - Source(s): AS-5; AS-14.

Moore, Thomas - Regiment: 24th Infantry - Source(s): AS-1.

Moore, Thomas - Regiment: OH Militia - Rank: Major - Source(s): AS-18 - Comments: Findlay's Regiment.

Moore, Thomas - Regiment: 7th Infantry - Rank: Private - Source(s): AS-3.

Moran, William - Regiment: 1st Rifles - Source(s): AS-1.

Moray, Pliny - Regiment: 1st Artillery - Rank: Private - Source(s): AS-14.

Moren, John - Regiment: Militia - Rank: Private - Source(s): AS-9.

Morgan, John - Regiment: 4th Infantry - Rank: Private - Source(s): AS-16.

Morriett, Joseph - Regiment: 24th Infantry - Source(s): AS-1.

Morris, Jacob - Rank: Private - Source(s): AS-8.

Morris, James - Regiment: 24th Infantry - Source(s): AS-1.

Morris, Maurice - Regiment: 14th Infantry - Rank: Private - Enlistment date: 26 Nov 1812 - Enlistment period: 5 years - Source(s): AS-5; AS-14.

Morrisett, Joshua - Regiment: 24th Infantry - Rank: Private - Source(s): AS-9.

Morrison, Robert - Rank: Private - Source(s): AS-8.

Morrison, Robert - Regiment: OH Militia & 27th Infantry - Rank: Major - Source(s): AS-15; AS-18 - Comments: Cass' Militia Regiment.

Morrison, Robert - Regiment: 24th Infantry - Rank: Sergeant - Source(s): AS-3.

Morrison, William - Regiment: 1st Artillery - Source(s): AS-1.

Morrow, Edward - Regiment: 5th Infantry - Rank: Private - Source(s): AS-10.

Morrow, Joseph - Regiment: 18th Infantry - Rank: Private - Source(s): AS-10.

Morse, Jesse - Regiment: McCobb's Volunteers - Source(s): AS-1.

Morse, Joshua - Regiment: Volunteers - Rank: Private - Source(s): AS-14.

Morss, William - Regiment: 24th Infantry - Source(s): AS-1.

Moses, John - Regiment: 11th Infantry - Rank: Private - Source(s): AS-10.

Moulthrop, Jerry - Regiment: 4th Infantry - Rank: Private - Source(s): AS-17.

Mountain, Michael B. - Regiment: 2nd Artillery - Date of death: 22 Apr 1814 - Source(s): AS-1; AS-7.

Moutton, Elisha - Rank: Private - Source(s): AS-8.

Mower, Ebenezer - Regiment: 4th Infantry - Rank: Sergeant - Source(s): AS-16.

Mudge, Ebenezer - Regiment: 11th Infantry - Name of prison ship: Hospital - Source(s): AS-1.

Mullarey, James R. - Regiment: 23rd Infantry - Rank: Major - Source(s): AS-11 - Comments: now Lieutenant Colonel.

Mullen, Charles - Regiment: 19th Infantry - Rank: Private - Source(s): AS-12.

Mullen, Enoch - Date of death: 22 Apr 1814 - Source(s): AS-7.

Mullett, Isaac - Regiment: 40th Infantry - Rank: Private - Source(s): AS-4 - Comments: On parole at Salem, MA.

Mum, Joel - Regiment: Militia - Rank: Private - Source(s): AS-2.

Munday, James - Regiment: 17th Infantry - Rank: Ensign - Source(s): AS-11.

Munger, Horace - Regiment: 13th Infantry - Rank: Private - Enlistment date: 2 Feb 1813 - Enlistment period: 5 years - Name of prison ship: Lord Cathcart - Source(s): AS-1; AS-5.

Munn, Harvey - Regiment: 4th Infantry - Rank: Sergeant - Source(s): AS-16.

Munroe, Ephraim - Regiment: 13th Infantry - Rank: Private - Source(s): AS-9.

Munroe, William - Regiment: Militia - Name of prison ship: Lord Cathcart - Where taken: Oswego, NY - Source(s): AS-1.

Munson, Jeremiah R. - Regiment: OH Militia & 27th Infantry - Rank: Major - Source(s): AS-15; AS-18 - Comments: Cass' Militia Regiment.

Murphy, James - Regiment: 7th Infantry - Rank: Private - Source(s): AS-3.

Murray, James - Regiment: Volunteers - Rank: Private - Source(s): AS-14.

Murray, James - Regiment: 21st Infantry - Rank: Private - Source(s): AS-14.

Mutair, Lewis - Regiment: 24th Infantry - Source(s): AS-1.

Nance, Eaton - Regiment: 7th Infantry - Rank: Corporal - Source(s): AS-3.

Nash, Bartlett - Regiment: 2nd Light Dragoons - Rank: Private - Source(s): AS-1; AS-12.

Nate, Daniel - Regiment: Militia - Rank: Private - Source(s): AS-2.

Nate, Jonathan - Regiment: 21st Infantry - Source(s): AS-1.

Nearing, Lyman W. - Regiment: 23rd Infantry - Name of prison ship: Lord Cathcart - Source(s): AS-1.

Neighbors, John - Regiment: 24th Infantry - Source(s): AS-1.

Neilson, Jon - Regiment: 24th Infantry - Source(s): AS-1.

Neiodle, Alpheus - Rank: Private - Source(s): AS-8.

Nelson, James - Regiment: 1st Light Dragoons - Rank: Quartermaster Sergeant - Enlistment date: 28 Jul 1812 - Enlistment period: 5 years - Source(s): AS-1; AS-5; AS-14.

Nelson, John - Regiment: OH Militia - Rank: Lieutenant - Source(s): AS-18 - Comments: Findlay's Regiment.

Nesbett, James - Regiment: NY Militia - Rank: Private - Source(s): AS-12.

Neuman, Stokely - Regiment: 14th Infantry - Rank: Private - Enlistment date: 12 Aug 1812 - Enlistment period: 5 years - Source(s): AS-5; AS-14.

Nevill, William - Regiment: 4th Infantry - Rank: Private - Source(s): AS-17.

Newman, Henry - Regiment: 23rd Infantry - Source(s): AS-1.

Newton, Asa - Rank: Private - Source(s): AS-8.

Newton, Reuben - Regiment: 4th Infantry - Rank: Sergeant - Source(s): AS-17.

Nicholas, Jacob - Regiment: 40th Infantry - Rank: Private - Source(s): AS-4a.

Nichols, Elijah - Rank: Private - Source(s): AS-8.

Nichols, John - Regiment: 24th Infantry - Rank: Private - Source(s): AS-1; AS-12.

Nichols, Thomas - Date of death: 11 Mar 1814 - Source(s): AS-7.

Nicholson, Solomon - Regiment: 21st Infantry - Rank: Private - Enlistment date: 7 Mar 1813 - Enlistment period: During the war - Source(s): AS-1; AS-5; AS-14.

Nicloge, Paschal - Rank: Citizen - Source(s): AS-9.

Nicnard, Peter - Rank: Private - Source(s): AS-9.

Nisbett, Shedrick - Regiment: 14th Infantry - Rank: Corporal - Enlistment date: 19 May 1812 - Enlistment period: 5 years - Source(s): AS-5; AS-14.

Nixon, James - Regiment: 27th Infantry - Rank: Recruit - Source(s): AS-15.

Nobel, Horace - Regiment: 4th Infantry - Rank: Private - Source(s): AS-17.

Noble, Isaac - Regiment: 4th Infantry - Rank: Private - Source(s): AS-17.

Nobles, Stephen - Regiment: 23rd Infantry - Rank: Private - Source(s): AS-10.

Nope, John - Regiment: 24th Infantry - Source(s): AS-1.

Norris, James - Rank: Private - Source(s): AS-8.

Northup, Henry - Regiment: OH Militia - Rank: Lieutenant, Adjutant - Source(s): AS-18 - Comments: Cass' Regiment.

Northup, Henry - Regiment: 27th Infantry - Rank: Captain - Source(s): AS-15.

Norton, Daniel B. - Regiment: Porter's Volunteers - Rank: Private - Source(s): AS-10.

Norton, John - Date of death: 15 Dec 1813 - Source(s): AS-7.

Norton, Patrick - Regiment: 4th Infantry - Rank: Private - Source(s): AS-17.

Nourse, Benjamin - Regiment: 29th Infantry - Rank: Private - Source(s): AS-10.

Nourse, Thomas W. - Regiment: 4th Infantry - Source(s): AS-1.

Numm. Richard - Regiment: 1st Artillery - Source(s): AS-1.

Nutter, Henry - Regiment: 4th Infantry - Rank: Private - Source(s): AS-17.

Nutting, Simni - Regiment: 40th Infantry - Rank: Private - Source(s): AS-4 - Comments: POW at Eastport, ME.

Nutting, Cyrus - Regiment: 40th Infantry - Rank: Private - Source(s): AS-4 - Comments: POW at Eastport, ME.

Nye, George - Regiment: 3rd Artillery - Rank: Private - Source(s): AS-1; AS-10.

Oakley, Jonathan - Rank: Private - Source(s): AS-8.

Octettree, Thomas - Regiment: 1st Rifles - Rank: Private - Source(s): AS-1, AS-12.

Ogden, Thomas - Date of death: 7 Mar 1814 - Source(s): AS-7.

Ogle, Howard - Enlistment date: 1 Sep 1812 - Source(s): AS-1; AS-5.

O'Hara, John - Regiment: 1st Infantry - Rank: Private - Source(s): AS-16.

Oliver, Henry - Regiment: 24th Infantry - Rank: Private - Source(s): AS-1; AS-12.

Olley, Nathaniel - Regiment: Militia - Rank: Private - Source(s): AS-14.

Ongy, Peter - Rank: Indian Interpreter - Source(s): AS-3 - Comments: Paroled.

Orkins, James - Regiment: 40th Infantry - Rank: Private - Source(s): AS-4 - Comments: POW at Eastport, ME.

Orne, Ebenezer - Regiment: 11th Infantry - Source(s): AS-1.

Orne, Joseph - Regiment: 11th Infantry - Source(s): AS-1.

Orr, Montgomery - Regiment: 4th Infantry - Rank: Sergeant - Source(s): AS-16 - Comments: Died at Fort Independence, MA.

Osgood, Richard - Regiment: 2nd Light Dragoons - Rank: Corporal - Enlistment date: 20 Feb 1813 - Enlistment period: During the war - Name of prison ship: Hospital - Source(s): AS-1; AS-5.

Ostender, Jones - Regiment: 5th Infantry - Rank: Private - Source(s): AS-14.

Ostender, Justus - Regiment: 5th Infantry - Name of prison ship: Lord Cathcart - Source(s): AS-1.

Ostenger, Robert - Regiment: 21st Infantry - Rank: Private - Source(s): AS-9.

Owen, Amasa - Regiment: 11th Infantry - Source(s): AS-1.

Owens, Jeremiah - Regiment: 24th Infantry - Source(s): AS-1.

Pace, William - Regiment: 24th Infantry - Source(s): AS-1 - Comments: A boy.

Page, Achilles - Regiment: 1st Infantry - Rank: Private - Source(s): AS-16.

Page, David - Regiment: 24th Infantry - Rank: Private - Source(s): AS-1; AS-12.

Page, David - Regiment: 40th Infantry - Rank: Private - Source(s): AS-4 - Comments: On parole at Machias, ME.

Page, John - Regiment: 7th Infantry - Rank: Private - Source(s): AS-3.

Page, John - Regiment: 29th Infantry - Rank: Private - Source(s): AS-9.

Paine, Reuben - Regiment: 11th Infantry - Rank: Private - Enlistment date: 18 May 1812 - Enlistment period: 5 years - Source(s): AS-5.

Paleifer, Joseph - Regiment: 40th Infantry - Rank: Private - Source(s): AS-4 - Comments: On parole at Salem, MA.

Palmer, Nicholas - Regiment: 23rd Infantry - Source(s): AS-1.

Park, Luther - Regiment: 11th Infantry - Source(s): AS-1.

Park, Luther - Regiment: Volunteers - Rank: Private - Source(s): AS-14.

Parker, Abel - Regiment: 1st Artillery - Rank: Private - Source(s): AS-16.

Parker, Cornelius - Regiment: 16th Infantry - Source(s): AS-1.

Parker, James - Regiment: 4th Infantry - Rank: Private - Source(s): AS-16.

Parker, John - Regiment: 40th Infantry - Rank: Private - Source(s): AS-4a.

Parker, William - Rank: Corporal - Source(s): AS-8.

Parkins, Samuel R. - Regiment: Militia - Rank: Private - Source(s): AS-2.

Parks, John - Regiment: 22nd Infantry - Rank: Private - Source(s): AS-9.

Parks, Roger - Regiment: 12th Infantry - Name of prison ship: Lord Cathcart - Source(s): AS-1.

Parmlee, Ezekiel - Regiment: Militia - Rank: Private - Source(s): AS-2.

Parrish, Peter - Source(s): AS-3 - Comments: British subject.

Parsons, Elisha - Regiment: 4th Infantry - Rank: Private - Source(s): AS-17.

Parsons, Paul - Rank: Private - Source(s): AS-8.

Partridge, ---- - Rank: Private - Source(s): AS-8.

Paskiel, Ezekiel D. - Regiment: 40th Infantry - Rank: Private - Source(s): AS-4 - Comments: On parole at Salem, MA.

Paste, William - Regiment: 24th Infantry - Rank: Private - Source(s): AS-12.

Pastor, Christian - Regiment: 27th Infantry - Rank: Recruit - Source(s): AS-15.

Patch, David - Regiment: 11th Infantry - Rank: Corporal - Source(s): AS-10.

Patterson, H. - Rank: Private - Source(s): AS-8.

Patterson, J. - Rank: Private - Source(s): AS-8.

Patterson, John - Regiment: 24th Infantry - Source(s): AS-1.

Patterson, Tillender - Regiment: 1st Artillery - Rank: Private - Source(s): AS-16.

Paul, David - Regiment: 40th Infantry - Rank: Private - Source(s): AS-4 - Comments: On parole at Salem, MA.

Pausey, Morgan - Regiment: 24th Infantry - Rank: Private - Source(s): AS-12.

Pawley, Francis - Rank: Sergeant - Source(s): AS-8.

Payne, Reuben - Regiment: 11th Infantry - Source(s): AS-1.

Payne, Reuben - Regiment: Volunteers - Rank: Private - Source(s): AS-14.

Payons, Samuel - Regiment: 5th Infantry - Name of prison ship: Lord Cathcart - Source(s): AS-1.

Pays, Jacob - Regiment: 16th Infantry - Rank: Private - Source(s): AS-14.

Peabody, Stephen P. - Regiment: NY Militia - Rank: Private - Where taken: Niagara or Buffalo, NY - Source(s): AS-1; AS-12.

Peake, John - Regiment: 2nd Light Dragoons - Rank: Private - Source(s): AS-1; AS-9.

Pearl, John - Regiment: 11th Infantry - Rank: Private - Source(s): AS-9.

Pearl, John - Regiment: 9th Infantry - Rank: Private - Enlistment date: 3 Oct 1812 - Enlistment period: 5 years - Source(s): AS-5; AS-14.

Pearson, William - Rank: Sergeant - Source(s): AS-8.

Peck, Andrew - Regiment: 25th Infantry - Rank: Musician - Enlistment date: 20 Jan 1813 - Enlistment period: 5 years - Source(s): AS-5.

Peck, Mathias - Regiment: Militia - Rank: Private - Source(s): AS-2.

Peckham, John - Regiment: McCobb's Volunteers - Source(s): AS-1.

Peckham, Lewis - Regiment: 4th Infantry - Rank: First Lieutenant - Source(s): AS-16.

Pelton, Benjamin F. - Regiment: NY Militia - Rank: Private - Source(s): AS-12.

Penley, Joseph - Regiment: Militia - Rank: Private - Source(s): AS-14.

Pennington, Levi - Regiment: 22nd Infantry - Rank: Private - Source(s): AS-9.

Penny, Samuel - Regiment: 21st Infantry - Rank: Private - Source(s): AS-14.

Pentz, Henry - Regiment: OH Militia - Rank: Lieutenant - Source(s): AS-18 - Comments: Findlay's Regiment.

Perkins, John - Regiment: KY or TN Militia - Where taken: Miami Rapids, OH or River Raison, MI - Source(s): AS-1.

Perkins, Joseph - Regiment: 24th Infantry - Rank: Lieutenant - Source(s): AS-3.

Perkins, Thomas - Regiment: 3rd Artillery - Rank: Private - Source(s): AS-1; AS-10.

Perkins, William - Regiment: 4th Infantry - Rank: Private - Source(s): AS-17.

Perley, Joseph - Regiment: McCobb's Volunteers - Source(s): AS-1.

Perry, Calvin - Regiment: 1st Infantry - Rank: Corporal - Source(s): AS-16.

Perry, Daniel - Regiment: Militia - Rank: Private - Source(s): AS-2.

Perry, David - Regiment: 1st Infantry - Rank: Private - Source(s): AS-16.

Perry, Richard - Regiment: 4th Infantry - Rank: Private - Source(s): AS-17.

Peters, George P. - Regiment: 4th Infantry - Rank: First Lieutenant - Source(s): AS-11; AS-16.

Peterson, Peter - Regiment: 9th Infantry - Rank: Private - Source(s): AS-14.

Pettingall, Joseph - Regiment: 4th Infantry - Rank: Private - Source(s): AS-16.

Pettis, Samuel - Regiment: 4th Infantry - Rank: Private - Source(s): AS-17.

Pettit, Joseph - Regiment: 27th Infantry - Rank: Recruit - Source(s): AS-15.

Phelps, Henry - Regiment: 25th Infantry - Rank: Private - Source(s): AS-10.

Phelps, John - Regiment: McCobb's Volunteers - Source(s): AS-1.

Phelps, John - Regiment: 24th Infantry - Rank: Private - Source(s): AS-1; AS-12.

Pheuhugan, Thomas - Regiment: 2nd Artillery - Rank: Private - Source(s): AS-14.

Philips, Alford - Regiment: 13th Infantry - Rank: Lieutenant - Source(s): AS-11.

Philips, Asher - Regiment: 19th Infantry - Rank: Ensign - Source(s): AS-16.

Philips, Isaac - Regiment: 1st Infantry - Rank: Corporal - Source(s): AS-16.

Philips, Pleasant - Regiment: 7th Infantry - Rank: Private - Source(s): AS-3.

Phillips, John C. - Regiment: Volunteers - Rank: Private - Source(s): AS-14.

Phillips, John Capin - Regiment: 2nd Light Dragoons - Rank: Corporal - Enlistment date: 16 Feb 1813 - Enlistment period: 5 years - Name of prison ship: Hospital - Source(s): AS-1; AS-5; AS-14.

Phillips, Joseph - Rank: Private - Source(s): AS-8.

Phills, Curtis - Regiment: 4th Infantry - Rank: Private - Source(s): AS-17.

Pichicen, Anthony - Regiment: 3rd Artillery - Source(s): AS-1; AS-10.

Pickett, Lester - Regiment: 30th Infantry - Rank: Private - Source(s): AS-9.

Pickham, Lewis - Regiment: 4th Infantry - Rank: Lieutenant - Source(s): AS-11.

Pierce, Elias - Rank: Sergeant - Source(s): AS-9.

Pierce, John - Regiment: 3rd Artillery - Source(s): AS-1.

Pierce, Moses - Regiment: 4th Infantry - Rank: Private - Source(s): AS-17.

Pierce, William - Regiment: 21st Infantry - Rank: Sergeant - Source(s): AS-1.

Pigman, John G. - Regiment: 27th Infantry - Rank: Recruit - Source(s): AS-15.

Pinkley, John - Regiment: 4th Infantry - Rank: Private - Source(s): AS-17.

Plants, Edward - Regiment: 2nd Artillery - Rank: Private - Enlistment date: 6 Mar 1813 - Enlistment period: 5 years - Source(s): AS-1; AS-5; AS-14.

Platenburgh, Jacob - Regiment: 16th Infantry - Rank: Private - Name of prison ship: Lord Cathcart - Source(s): AS-1; AS-14.

Plotts, John - Regiment: 12th Infantry - Rank: Corporal - Enlistment date: 25 Nov 1812 - Enlistment period: 5 years - Name of prison ship: Lord Cathcart - Source(s): AS-1; AS-5; AS-5.

Plummer, Isaac - Regiment: McCobb's Volunteers - Rank: Private - Name of prison ship: Hospital - Source(s): AS-1; AS-14.

Pomers, John - Rank: Private - Source(s): AS-8.

Pomroy, Richard C. - Regiment: NY Militia - Rank: Private - Source(s): AS-12.

Pomroy, William - Regiment: 4th Infantry - Rank: Private - Source(s): AS-17.

Pooler, Orange - Regiment: 4th Infantry - Rank: Sergeant - Source(s): AS-17.

Pope, Mathew - Regiment: 24th Infantry - Rank: Private - Source(s): AS-1; AS-12.

Porter, Lincoln - Regiment: 1st Infantry - Rank: Private - Source(s): AS-16.

Porter, Nathan - Regiment: 40th Infantry - Rank: Private - Source(s): AS-4 - Comments: POW at Eastport, ME.

Porter, Samuel - Regiment: 4th Infantry - Rank: Private - Source(s): AS-16.

Posey, Harrison - Regiment: 24th Infantry - Rank: Private - Source(s): AS-1; AS-12.

Posey, Morgan - Regiment: 24th Infantry - Source(s): AS-1.

Post, Cornelius - Regiment: 27th Infantry - Rank: Recruit - Source(s): AS-15.

Pratt, Charles - Regiment: McCobb's Volunteers - Rank: Private - Name of prison ship: Hospital - Source(s): AS-1; AS-14.

Pratt, Charles - Regiment: 21st Infantry - Rank: Private - Source(s): AS-14.

Pratt, Jeremiah - Regiment: 24th Infantry - Source(s): AS-1.

Pratt, Nathaniel - Date of death: 23 Jul 1813 - Source(s): AS-6 - Comments: Died at Quebec.

Prentice, James - Regiment: 21st Infantry - Source(s): AS-1.

Prentiss, Ella - Regiment: 4th Infantry - Rank: Musician - Source(s): AS-17.

Prestman, Daniel - Regiment: 16th Infantry - Source(s): AS-1.

Preston, David - Rank: Private - Source(s): AS-8.

Price, Hurd - Regiment: 24th Infantry - Rank: Private - Source(s): AS-1; AS-12.

Price, Johnson - Regiment: 14th Infantry - Rank: Private - Source(s): AS-12.

Price, Obadiah - Rank: Private - Source(s): AS-8.

Price, Robert - Regiment: 23rd Infantry - Rank: Private - Name of prison ship: Lord Cathcart - Source(s): AS-1; AS-14.

Price, Rulon - Regiment: Militia - Rank: Private - Source(s): AS-2.

Prouty, Jacob - Regiment: 4th Infantry - Rank: Corporal - Source(s): AS-17.

Pruitt, Gabriel - Regiment: 24th Infantry - Source(s): AS-1.

Pruitt, Jesse - Regiment: 24th Infantry - Source(s): AS-1; As-12.

Purdy, Henry - Regiment: Militia - Rank: Private - Source(s): AS-2.

Purge, John - Regiment: 3rd Artillery - Rank: Private - Source(s): AS-10.

Purnell, Samuel - Regiment: 21st Infantry - Rank: Corporal - Enlistment date: 29 Jan 1813 - Enlistment period: During the war - Source(s): AS-1; AS-5; AS-14.

Puthuff, William H. - Regiment: OH Militia - Rank: Lieutenant, Adjutant - Source(s): AS-18 - Comments: McArthur's Regiment.

Putnam, Benjamin - Regiment: 11th Infantry - Source(s): AS-1.

Putnam, John - Regiment: Militia - Rank: Private - Source(s): AS-2.

Putnam, Perley - Regiment: 40th Infantry - Rank: Major - Source(s): AS-4 - Comments: On parole at Salem, MA.

Pyke, Nathan - Regiment: 24th Infantry - Rank: Private - Source(s): AS-12.

Quire, Raymond - Regiment: 2nd Light Dragoons - Rank: Private - Source(s): AS-1; AS-12.

Race, Jonathan - Regiment: 23rd Infantry - Rank: Private - Enlistment date: 14 Feb 1813 - Enlistment period: During the war - Name of prison ship: Lord Cathcart - Source(s): AS-1 ; AS-5.

Rambo, Peter - Regiment: 24th Infantry - Source(s): AS-1.

Ramsdale, Anthony - Regiment: 40th Infantry - Rank: Private - Source(s): AS-4 - Comments: POW at Eastport, ME.

Ramsdale, Samuel - Regiment: 9th Infantry - Rank: Private - Source(s): AS-14.

Rand, Daniel - Regiment: 9th Infantry - Rank: Private - Source(s): AS-10.

Rand, Jacob D. - Regiment: 4th Infantry - Rank: Sergeant - Source(s): AS-16.

Randall, Isaiah - Regiment: 3rd Artillery - Source(s): AS-1.

Randall, Joshua - Regiment: 3rd Militia - Rank: Private - Source(s): AS-10.

Ranney, William - Rank: Private - Source(s): AS-8.

Rannselaer, John - Regiment: 11th Infantry - Rank: Private - Enlistment date: 5 Mar 1813 - Enlistment period: 5 years - Source(s): AS-5; AS-14.

Ranson, Rothbane - Regiment: NY Militia - Rank: Private - Source(s): AS-12.

Ranyard, Francis - Regiment: KY or TN Militia - Where taken: Miami Rapids, OH or River Raison, MI - Source(s): AS-1.

Rasdon, Timothy - Regiment: Militia - Rank: Private - Source(s): AS-10.

Rath, Anthony - Regiment: 1st Infantry - Rank: Private - Source(s): AS-16.

Rathbone, Jeremiah - Regiment: 23rd Infantry - Rank: Private - Enlistment date: 11 Jul 1812 - Enlistment period: 5 years - Name of prison ship: Lord Cathcart - Source(s): AS-1; AS-5; AS-14.

Rawl, William - Regiment: 27th Infantry - Rank: Recruit - Source(s): AS-15.

Ray, John - Regiment: 23rd Infantry - Source(s): AS-1.

Ray, John - Regiment: NY Militia - Rank: Private - Source(s): AS-12.

Ray, Jonathan - Regiment: McCobb's Volunteers - Source(s): AS-1.

Ray, Robert - Regiment: 3rd Artillery - Rank: Private - Source(s): AS-1; AS-10.

Reab, George - Regiment: 13th Infantry - Rank: Ensign - Source(s): AS-11.

Read, James - Regiment: 22nd Infantry - Source(s): AS-1.

Read, John P. - Regiment: McCobb's Volunteers - Rank: Sergeant - Source(s): AS-1.

Read, John T. - Rank: Sergeant - Source(s): AS-9.

Reader, Thomas - Regiment: 1st Artillery - Rank: Private - Source(s): AS-1; AS-12.

Reall, Abner - Rank: Private - Source(s): AS-8.

Ream, Jacob - Regiment: 1st Infantry - Rank: Private - Source(s): AS-16.

Rear, John - Regiment: 16th Infantry - Source(s): AS-1.

Redfield, A. C. - Regiment: 11th Infantry - Source(s): AS-1.

Redman, Alonzo - Regiment: 40th Infantry - Rank: Corporal - Source(s): AS-4a.

Reece, Henry - Regiment: 2nd Artillery - Source(s): AS-6 - Comments: Died on prison ship.

Reed, Charles W. - Regiment: 23rd Infantry - Rank: Sergeant Major - Source(s): AS-10.

Reed, Daniel - Regiment: 4th Infantry - Rank: Sergeant - Source(s): AS-17.

Reed, Isaac - Date of death: 4 Aug 1813 - Source(s): AS-6 - Comments: Died at Quebec.

Reed, James - Regiment: 11th Infantry - Rank: Private - Source(s): AS-10.

Reed, Samuel R. - Regiment: McCobb's Volunteers - Rank: Corporal - Source(s): AS-1; AS-14.

Reed, William - Regiment: 4th Infantry - Rank: Private - Source(s): AS-17.

Reese, Henry - Regiment: 7th Infantry - Rank: Private - Source(s): AS-3.

Remmington, Ira - Regiment: 21st Infantry - Rank: Private - Source(s): AS-10.

Reynolds, George - Regiment: 24th Infantry - Source(s): AS-1.

Reynolds, Gilbert - Regiment: 5th Infantry - Rank: Musician - Enlistment date: 13 Jan 1812 - Enlistment period: 5

years - Name of prison ship: Lord Cathcart - Source(s): AS-1; AS-5; AS-14.

Reynolds, James - Rank: Private - Source(s): AS-8.

Reynolds, John - Regiment: NY Militia - Rank: Private - Source(s): AS-12.

Reynolds, William - Regiment: 24th Infantry - Source(s): AS-1.

Reynolds, William - Rank: Private - Source(s): AS-8.

Rice, Charles - Regiment: 1st Infantry - Rank: Private - Source(s): AS-16.

Rice, John P. - Regiment: 1st Infantry - Rank: Private - Source(s): AS-16 - Comments: Formerly from the 19th Infantry.

Rice, Nathaniel - Regiment: 11th Infantry - Source(s): AS-1.

Rice, Robert - Regiment: 23rd Infantry - Rank: Private - Enlistment date: 11 Sep 1812 - Enlistment period: 5 years - Source(s): AS-5.

Rice, Samuel - Regiment: Volunteers - Rank: Private - Source(s): AS-14.

Rice, Samuel - Regiment: 11th Infantry - Rank: Private - Enlistment date: 14 Mar 1812 - Enlistment period: 5 years - Source(s): AS-1; AS-5.

Rice, William - Rank: Private - Source(s): AS-8.

Richards, Francis - Regiment: 23rd Infantry - Rank: Private - Source(s): AS-10.

Richards, Stephen - Regiment: Volunteers - Rank: Private - Source(s): AS-14.

Richards, Stephen - Regiment: Militia - Source(s): AS-1.

Richardson, Ephraim - Regiment: 7th Infantry - Rank: Private - Source(s): AS-3.

Richardson, John - Enlistment date: Aug 1812 - Source(s): AS-5.

Richardson, John - Regiment: 16th Infantry - Rank: Private - Name of prison ship: Lord Cathcart - Source(s): AS-1; AS-14.

Richardson, Jonathan - Regiment: Militia - Rank: Private - Source(s): AS-2.

Richardson, Moses - Regiment: 40th Infantry - Rank: Private - Source(s): AS-4 - Comments: POW at Eastport, ME.

Richardson, Simeon - Regiment: McCobb's Volunteers - Source(s): AS-1.

Richardson, William - Regiment: KY or TN Militia - Where taken: Miami Rapids, OH or River Raison, MI - Source(s): AS-1.

Riddle, Elihu - Regiment: 11th Infantry - Rank: Private - Source(s): AS-10.

Ridenour, Conrad - Regiment: 14th Infantry - Rank: Private - Source(s): AS-14.

Ridge, William - Regiment: 24th Infantry - Source(s): AS-1.

Ridgley, William - Rank: Sergeant - Source(s): AS-8.

Riggs, Cyrus - Regiment: 24th Infantry - Rank: Private - Source(s): AS-1; AS-12.

Riley, Charles - Regiment: 3rd Artillery - Source(s): AS-1.

Riley, James - Regiment: Militia - Source(s): AS-1.

Riley, William - Regiment: 4th Infantry - Source(s): AS-1.

Roach, James - Rank: Private - Source(s): AS-8.

Roach, William - Rank: Private - Source(s): AS-8.

Robb, Samuel - Regiment: 22nd Infantry - Rank: Private - Enlistment date: 21 Aug 1812 - Enlistment period: 5

years - Name of prison ship: Hospital - Source(s): AS-1; AS-5; AS-14.

Robbins, Conrad - Rank: Private - Source(s): AS-8.

Roberts, John - Date of death: 26 Mar 1814 - Source(s): AS-7.

Roberts, Jorum - Regiment: 23rd Infantry - Name of prison ship: Lord Carthart - Source(s): AS-1.

Robertson, Henry - Regiment: Militia - Rank: Private - Source(s): AS-14.

Robertson, James - Regiment: 7th Infantry - Rank: Private - Source(s): AS-3.

Robins, Jordan - Regiment: 23rd Infantry - Rank: Private - Source(s): AS-14.

Robinson, David - Regiment: 4th Infantry - Rank: Sergeant - Source(s): AS-17.

Robinson, James - Regiment: 21st Infantry - Source(s): AS-1.

Robinson, John - Regiment: OH Militia - Rank: Captain - Source(s): AS-18 - Comments: Findlay's Regiment.

Rockway, John - Regiment: 3rd Artillery - Rank: Private - Source(s): AS-1; AS-10.

Roe, Michael - Regiment: 2nd Artillery - Rank: Private - Enlistment date: 18 May 1812 - Enlistment period: 5 years - Source(s): AS-5.

Rogers, Daniel - Regiment: 4th Infantry - Rank: Private - Source(s): AS-17.

Rogers, Elenus - Regiment: 40th Infantry - Rank: Sergeant - Source(s): AS-4a.

Rogers, Robert - Regiment: 1st Artillery - Source(s): AS-1.

Roiva, Jonathan - Regiment: 9th Infantry - Rank: Private - Source(s): AS-14.

Roland, Alexander - Regiment: 2nd Light Dragoons - Rank: Private - Source(s): AS-14.

Roles, Rezin - Regiment: 14th Infantry - Rank: Private - Source(s): AS-14.

Rollapaugh, Cornelius - Regiment: 2nd Artillery - Source(s): AS-1.

Rollings, Mayhew - Regiment: 4th Infantry - Rank: Private - Source(s): AS-16.

Rollins, John M. - Regiment: 4th Infantry - Rank: Private - Source(s): AS-17.

Rollins, Thomas - Regiment: 1st Artillery - Source(s): AS-1.

Romaine, Job - Regiment: 1st Rifles - Source(s): AS-1; AS-12.

Rome, Asa R. - Rank: Private - Source(s): AS-8.

Roney, Matthias - Regiment: 3rd Militia - Rank: Private - Source(s): AS-10.

Rood, Amos - Rank: Private - Source(s): AS-8.

Rooney, John - Regiment: NY Militia - Rank: Private - Source(s): AS-12.

Rooney, Mathias - Regiment: 3rd Artillery - Source(s): AS-1.

Rose, John - Regiment: 14th Infantry - Rank: Private - Source(s): AS-14.

Rose, Levi - Regiment: OH Militia - Rank: Captain - Source(s): AS-18 - Comments: Cass' Regiment.

Roseman, Edward - Regiment: 23rd Infantry - Rank: Private - Source(s): AS-10.

Rowe, Benjamin - Regiment: 21st Infantry - Date of death: 14 Aug 1813 - Source(s): AS-1; AS-6 - Comments: Died at Quebec.

Rowe, Jonathan - Regiment: 9th Infantry - Rank: Private - Source(s): AS-14.

Rowe, Michael - Regiment: 2nd Artillery - Source(s): AS-1.

Rowells, John - Regiment: 4th Infantry - Rank: Private - Source(s): AS-16.

Rowley, Ira - Regiment: NY Militia - Rank: Captain - Source(s): AS-12.

Rucark, Thomas - Regiment: 2nd Artillery - Rank: Private - Enlistment date: 10 Aug 1812 - Enlistment period: 5 years - Source(s): AS-1; AS-5.

Rudd, Levi - Regiment: 30th Infantry - Rank: Private - Source(s): AS-9.

Rudderkesk, K. - Rank: Private - Source(s): AS-8.

Rumrell, A. B. - Rank: Private - Source(s): AS-8.

Rumsey, Nathaniel - Rank: Citizen - Source(s): AS-9.

Rumsey, Peter - Rank: Private - Source(s): AS-8.

Runnion, Thomas - Regiment: 24th Infantry - Source(s): AS-1.

Runnolds, John - Regiment: 7th Infantry - Rank: Private - Source(s): AS-3.

Rupe, David - Regiment: OH Militia - Rank: Captain - Source(s): AS-18 - Comments: McArthur's Regiment.

Rusk, Richard H. - Regiment: 2nd Light Dragoons - Source(s): AS-1.

Russell, Thaddeus B. - Regiment: 4th Infantry - Rank: Private - Source(s): AS-17.

Rust, William - Regiment: 22nd Infantry - Rank: Private - Source(s): AS-10.

Ruthner, John - Regiment: 22nd Infantry - Rank: Private - Source(s): AS-10.

Ryan, James - Regiment: 1st Artillery - Rank: Private - Source(s): AS-16.

Rye, Thomas - Regiment: 24th Infantry - Rank: Private - Source(s): AS-12.

Sabin, Daniel - Regiment: NY Militia - Where taken: Niagara or Buffalo, NY - Source(s): AS-1.

Sabin, Oliver - Rank: Private - Source(s): AS-8.

Sabine, Daniel - Regiment: NY Militia - Rank: Private - Source(s): AS-12.

Sabrey, Ephraim - Regiment: 9th Infantry - Rank: Private - Source(s): AS-14.

Sallis, Lucius - Regiment: 4th Infantry - Rank: Corporal - Source(s): AS-17.

Sammons, Jacob - Regiment: 13th Infantry - Rank: Second Lieutenant - Source(s): AS-8; AS-11.

Samson, John - Regiment: 21st Infantry - Rank: Corporal - Source(s): AS-1.

Sanborn, Charles - Rank: Sergeant - Date of death: 23 Jul 1813 - Source(s): AS-6 - Comments: Died at Quebec.

Sanborn, John - Regiment: 4th Infantry - Rank: Corporal - Source(s): AS-16.

Sanders, William G. - Regiment: 14th Infantry - Rank: Second Lieutenant - Source(s): AS-14.

Sanders, Zebulon - Regiment: 4th Infantry - Rank: Musician - Source(s): AS-17.

Sanderson, George - Regiment: OH Militia - Rank: Captain - Source(s): AS-18 - Comments: Cass' Regiment.

Sanford, L. - Rank: Private - Source(s): AS-8.

Saunderson, John - Regiment: 1st Artillery - Rank: Private - Name of prison ship: Lord Cathcart - Source(s): AS-1; AS-14.

Savory, Solomon - Rank: Private - Source(s): AS-8.

Sawyer, Charles W. - Regiment: 2nd Light Dragoons - Rank: Corporal - Enlistment date: 13 Oct 1812 - Enlistment period: 5 years - Name of prison ship: Lord Cathcart - Source(s): AS-1; AS-5; AS-13.

Sawyer, William - Regiment: OH Militia - Rank: Lieutenant - Source(s): AS-18 - Comments: Cass' Regiment.

Schenck, Peter L. - Regiment: OH Militia - Rank: Lieutenant, Clerk - Source(s): AS-18 - Comments: Findlay's Regiment.

Schenk, Henry - Rank: Sergeant - Source(s): AS-8.

Schivers, Luther - Regiment: 24th Infantry - Source(s): AS-1.

Schooley, William - Name of prison ship: Lord Cathcart - Source(s): AS-1.

Schufelt, David - Date of death: 30 Nov 1813 - Source(s): AS-6 - Comments: Died at Montreal.

Sciecr, John - Regiment: 12th Infantry - Rank: Private - Enlistment date: 19 May 1812 - Enlistment period: 5 years - Source(s): AS-5.

Scirven, Joel - Regiment: KY or TN Militia - Where taken: Miami Rapids, OH or River Raison, MI - Source(s): AS-1.

Scott, Abraham - Regiment: 23rd Infantry - Rank: Corporal - Enlistment date: 27 Jan 1813 - Enlistment period: During the war - Name of prison ship: Lord Cathcart - Source(s): AS-1; AS-5.

Scott, Charles - Regiment: 24th Infantry - Rank: Private - Source(s): AS-1; AS-12.

Scott, John - Date of death: 12 Apr 1814 - Source(s): AS-7.

Scott, John - Regiment: 1st Infantry - Rank: Private - Source(s): AS-16.

Scott, Solomon - Regiment: 5th Infantry - Source(s): AS-1.

Scott, W. - Regiment: 2nd Artillery - Rank: Lieutenant Colonel - Source(s): AS-8.

Scott, William - Rank: Private - Source(s): AS-8.

Scudder, Stephen - Regiment: 23rd Infantry - Name of prison ship: Lord Cathcart - Source(s): AS-1.

Seales, William - Regiment: 9th Infantry - Rank: Private - Source(s): AS-10.

Seaman, Chauncey - Rank: Private - Source(s): AS-8.

Sedman, Francis - Regiment: 1st Rifles - Name of prison ship: Lord Cathcart - Source(s): AS-1.

See, Daniel - Regiment: 13th Infantry - Rank: Private - Enlistment date: 19 Jun 1812 - Enlistment period: 5 years - Source(s): AS-5.

Seeney, King - Regiment: 1st Artillery - Rank: Private - Source(s): AS-16.

Seers, Harrison - Regiment: 7th Infantry - Rank: Private - Source(s): AS-3.

Seldon, Temri - Regiment: 31st Infantry - Source(s): AS-1.

Self, Charles - Regiment: 19th Infantry - Rank: Private - Source(s): AS-12.

Selman, David - Regiment: 24th Infantry - Source(s): AS-1.

Seward, (-----) - Regiment: OH Militia - Rank: Ensign - Source(s): AS-18 - Comments: Findlay's Regiment.

Seycant, Seth - Regiment: 4th Infantry - Rank: Private - Source(s): AS-16.

Shadley, Henry - Regiment: 27th Infantry - Rank: Recruit - Source(s): AS-15.

Shadock, John - Regiment: 21st Infantry - Rank: Private - Source(s): AS-14.

Shall, Henry - Regiment: 6th Infantry - Rank: First Lieutenant - Source(s): AS-14.

Shannon, Archibald - Regiment: 24th Infantry - Rank: Private - Source(s): AS-1; AS-12.

Sharp, John - Regiment: OH Militia - Rank: Captain - Source(s): AS-18 - Comments: Cass' Regiment.

Sharp, Solomon - Regiment: 11th Infantry - Source(s): AS-1.

Shator, Anthony - Regiment: 2nd Light Dragoons - Name of prison ship: Lord Cathcart - Source(s): AS-1.

Shattock, Eli - Regiment: Militia - Rank: Private - Source(s): AS-2.

Shattuck, John - Regiment: 21st Infantry - Source(s): AS-1.

Shaver, George - Date of death: 26 Jul 1813 - Source(s): AS-6 - Comments: Died at Quebec.

Shead, Isaac - Regiment: 2nd Light Dragoons - Rank: Corporal - Enlistment date: 23 Mar 1813 - Enlistment period: During the war - Name of prison ship: Hospital - Source(s): AS-1; AS-5; AS-14.

Sheets, Ishmael - Regiment: 14th Infantry - Rank: Private - Enlistment date: 18 May 1812 - Enlistment period: 5 years - Source(s): AS-5; AS-14.

Sheets, John - Regiment: OH Militia - Rank: Captain - Source(s): AS-18 - Comments: Findlay's Regiment.

Sheffield, Joseph - Regiment: Unknown - Source(s): AS-1.

Sheffield, Joseph - Regiment: 1st Artillery - Rank: Private - Source(s): AS-12.

Sheldon, James - Regiment: 4th Infantry - Rank: Private - Source(s): AS-16.

Sheldon, William - Regiment: NY Militia - Rank: Captain - Source(s): AS-12.

Sheller, Samuel - Regiment: 2nd Artillery - Rank: Private - Source(s): AS-1; AS-12.

Shendohl, Daniel - Regiment: 1st Infantry - Rank: Private - Source(s): AS-16.

Shepherd, David - Regiment: 22nd Infantry - Rank: Private - Source(s): AS-14.

Shepherd, Samuel - Regiment: Militia Riflemen - Source(s): AS-1.

Sheppard, Elias - Regiment: 1st Artillery - Rank: Musician - Source(s): AS-1; AS-12.

Sherman, Joel - Regiment: 19th Infantry - Rank: Corporal - Source(s): AS-12.

Sherry, Jacob - Regiment: 11th Infantry - Name of prison ship: Hospital - Source(s): AS-1.

Sheyres, David - Regiment: 22nd Infantry - Source(s): AS-1.

Shields, Barnel - Regiment: 4th Infantry - Rank: Private - Source(s): AS-17.

Shivers, Luke - Regiment: 24th Infantry - Rank: Private - Source(s): AS-12.

Shoemaker, Henry - Regiment: Militia - Name of prison ship: Lord Cathcart - Where taken: Oswego, NY - Source(s): AS-1.

Shoops, David - Regiment: 22nd Infantry - Rank: Private - Enlistment date: 28 Jun 1812 - Enlistment period: 5 years - Source(s): AS-5.

Short, Henry - Regiment: 24th Infantry - Source(s): AS-1.

Sickle, George M. - Regiment: 27th Infantry - Rank: Recruit - Source(s): AS-15.

Sighendall, Peter - Regiment: 1st Infantry - Rank: Private - Source(s): AS-16.

Sigs, Nathaniel - Regiment: 11th Infantry - Source(s): AS-1.

Silver, Obed. - Regiment: 4th Infantry - Rank: Corporal - Source(s): AS-16.

Simmons, Levi - Regiment: 29th Infantry - Rank: Private - Source(s): AS-9.

Simonds, Josiah - Regiment: 40th Infantry - Rank: Private - Source(s): AS-4 - Comments: On parole at Salem, MA.

Simpson, Francis - Regiment: 40th Infantry - Rank: Private - Source(s): AS-4 - Comments: POW at Eastport, ME.

Simpson, John - Rank: Corporal - Source(s): AS-8.

Simpson, Nathaniel - Regiment: 4th Infantry - Rank: Private - Source(s): AS-17.

Simpson, Robert - Regiment: 24th Infantry - Rank: Private - Source(s): AS-1; AS-12.

Skeels, Henry - Regiment: 27th Infantry - Rank: Recruit - Source(s): AS-15.

Skinner, Benjamin - Regiment: 23rd Infantry - Rank: Private - Source(s): AS-10.

Slater, Anthony - Regiment: 2nd Light Dragoons - Rank: Sergeant - Enlistment date: 24 Jun 1812 - Enlistment period: 5 years - Source(s): AS-5.

Slaughter, John - Regiment: 2nd Artillery - Source(s): AS-1.

Slaughter, Jonathan - Regiment: 2nd Artillery - Rank: Private - Source(s): AS-12.

Sliter, J. - Rank: Sergeant - Source(s): AS-8.

Sloan, James W. - Regiment: OH Militia - Rank: Captain - Source(s): AS-18 - Comments: Light Dragoons.

Sloan, Reuben - Rank: Private - Source(s): AS-8.

Sloan, Silvester - Rank: Private - Source(s): AS-8.

Small, Henry - Regiment: 1st Infantry - Rank: Private - Source(s): AS-16.

Smilley, Thomas - Regiment: 6th Infantry - Rank: Private - Source(s): AS-14.

Smith, Abraham - Regiment: 40th Infantry - Rank: Private - Source(s): AS-4 - Comments: On parole at Machias, ME.

Smith, Alexander - Rank: Private - Source(s): AS-8.

Smith, Benjamin - Rank: Private - Source(s): AS-8.

Smith, Benjamin - Regiment: 1st Artillery - Rank: Private - Source(s): AS-14.

Smith, Benjamin - Regiment: 1st Rifles - Rank: Private - Enlistment date: 4 Oct 1812 - Enlistment period: 5 years - Name of prison ship: Lord Cathcart - Source(s): AS-1; AS-5.

Smith, Caleb - Regiment: 1st Artillery - Rank: Private - Source(s): AS-16.

Smith, Charles - Regiment: 27th Infantry - Rank: Private - Source(s): AS-1; AS-12.

Smith, Cornelius - Regiment: 23rd Infantry - Rank: Private - Enlistment date: 7 Apr 1813 - Enlistment period: 5 years - Name of prison ship: Lord Cathcart - Source(s): AS-1; AS-5; AS-14.

Smith, Daniel - Regiment: McCobb's Volunteers - Rank: Private - Source(s): AS-1; AS-14.

Smith, David - Regiment: NY Militia - Rank: Private - Source(s): AS-12.

Smith, Elijah - Regiment: 13th Infantry - Rank: Private - Enlistment date: 23 Feb 1813 - Enlistment period: During the war - Source(s): AS-1; AS-5.

Smith, Frederick - Regiment: 6th Infantry - Rank: Private - Enlistment date: 4 Sep 1812 - Name of prison ship: Lord Cathcart - Source(s): AS-1; AS-5; AS-14.

Smith, Gustavo's - Regiment: 7th Infantry - Rank: Private - Source(s): AS-3.

Smith, Ira - Regiment: Militia - Rank: Sergeant - Source(s): AS-2.

Smith, James - Regiment: 1st Artillery - Rank: Artificer - Source(s): AS-16.

Smith, John - Regiment: 1st Artillery - Source(s): AS-1.

Smith, John - Regiment: 4th Infantry - Rank: First Lieutenant - Source(s): AS-11; AS-16.

Smith, Jonathan - Regiment: 34th Infantry - Source(s): AS-1.

Smith, Joseph - Regiment: 9th Infantry - Rank: Private - Enlistment date: 25 May 1812 - Enlistment period: 5 years - Source(s): AS-5; AS-14.

Smith, Joseph - Regiment: 15th Infantry - Source(s): AS-1.

Smith, Justus - Rank: Private - Source(s): AS-8.

Smith, Nathan - Rank: Private - Source(s): AS-8.

Smith, Noah - Regiment: 11th Infantry - Rank: Private - Source(s): AS-10.

Smith, Richard - Regiment: 21st Infantry - Rank: Private - Source(s): AS-1; AS-14.

Smith, Samuel - Regiment: 4th Infantry - Rank: Private - Source(s): AS-16.

Smith, William - Date of death: 16 Jul 1813 - Source(s): AS-6 - Comments: Died at Quebec.

Smith, William - Regiment: 29th Infantry - Rank: Private - Source(s): AS-9.

Smith, William H. - Regiment: 21st Infantry - Source(s): AS-1.

Snow, Daniel G. - Rank: Private - Source(s): AS-8.

Snyder, George - Enlistment date: 6 Feb 1812 - Source(s): AS-5.

Sonellie, Thomas - Regiment: 6th Infantry - Name of prison ship: Lord Cathcart - Source(s): AS-1.

Southack, William - Regiment: 1st Artillery - Source(s): AS-1.

Southerick, Joshua - Regiment: 31st Infantry - Rank: Private - Source(s): AS-9.

Southerland, Sylvester - Rank: Private - Source(s): AS-8.

Sparhawk, Rowland - Regiment: 4th Infantry - Rank: Private - Source(s): AS-17.

Spark, Joseph - Rank: Private - Source(s): AS-8.

Speey, Jacob - Regiment: Volunteers - Rank: Private - Source(s): AS-14.

Spencer, Andrew - Regiment: 21st Infantry - Name of prison ship: Hospital - Source(s): AS-1.

Spencer, Daniel - Regiment: 4th Infantry - Rank: Private - Source(s): AS-17.

Spencer, John - Regiment: 28th Infantry - Rank: Sergeant - Source(s): AS-12.

Spencer, John - Regiment: OH Militia and 27th Infantry - Rank: Captain - Source(s): AS-15; AS-18 - Comments: Cass' Regiment.

Spencer, Nathan - Regiment: 25th Infantry - Rank: Musician - Enlistment date: 9 Mar 1813 - Enlistment period: During the war - Source(s): AS-5.

Spencer, Samuel - Regiment: 25th Infantry - Rank: Private - Source(s): AS-14.

Sperry, Jacob - Regiment: 11th Infantry - Rank: Private - Enlistment date: 12 Jun 1812 - Enlistment period: 5 years - Source(s): AS-5.

Spink, Anthony - Regiment: 25th Infantry - Rank: Private - Enlistment date: 15 Jun 1812 - Enlistment period: 5 years - Source(s): AS-5; AS-14.

Sprague, John - Regiment: 4th Infantry - Rank: Private - Source(s): AS-17.

Spriggs, Leven - Regiment: 1st Artillery - Rank: Sergeant - Source(s): AS-12.

Spriggs, Nelson - Regiment: 1st Artillery - Source(s): AS-1.

Sproat, Peter W. - Regiment: Militia - Rank: Private - Source(s): AS-2.

Sprouts, James - Regiment: 2nd Light Dragoons - Rank: Private - Source(s): AS-1; AS-12.

Stadler, Joseph - Regiment: 27th Infantry - Rank: Recruit - Source(s): AS-15.

Stanhope, Curtis L. - Regiment: 1st Artillery - Name of prison ship: Lord Cathcart - Source(s): AS-1.

Stanley, Lorner - Regiment: 1st Rifles - Rank: Private - Source(s): AS-10.

Stansbury, Dixon - Regiment: 1st Infantry - Rank: Second Lieutenant - Source(s): AS-16; AS-16.

Stansbury, Samuel - Regiment: 2nd Artillery - Rank: Private - Enlistment date: 15 Apr 1812 - Enlistment period: 5 years - Name of prison ship: Hospital - Source(s): AS-1; AS-5; AS-14.

Stearns, Nathan - Regiment: 11th Infantry - Source(s): AS-1.

Steele, George G. - Regiment: 16th Infantry - Rank: Captain - Source(s): AS-14.

Steele, Joshua D. - Regiment: Civilian - Rank: Private - Source(s): AS-9.

Steer, John - Regiment: 24th Infantry - Rank: Private - Source(s): AS-1; AS-12.

Stephens, T. - Rank: Private - Source(s): AS-8.

Stephens, William - Regiment: 21st Infantry - Rank: Sergeant - Enlistment date: 25 jan 1813 - Enlistment period: During the war - Source(s): AS-5; AS-14.

Stephenson, Robert - Regiment: 1st Infantry - Rank: Private - Source(s): AS-16.

Stephenson, William - Regiment: 4th Infantry - Rank: Private - Source(s): AS-17.

Sternberg, Christian - Regiment: 13th Infantry - Source(s): AS-1.

Stetson, Oliver - Regiment: Militia - Rank: Private - Source(s): AS-2.

Stevens, Benjamin W. - Regiment: 2nd Light Dragoons - Name of prison ship: Hospital - Source(s): AS-1.

Stevens, Benjamin W. - Rank: Sergeant - Source(s): AS-9.

Stevens, J. - Regiment: 24th Infantry - Source(s): AS-1.

Stevens, Joshua - Regiment: 13th Infantry - Source(s): AS-1.

Stevens, Roswell - Rank: Private - Source(s): AS-8.

Stevens, William - Regiment: 21st Infantry - Source(s): AS-1.

Stewart, John - Regiment: 22nd Infantry - Rank: Private - Source(s): AS-10.

Stewart, Samuel - Regiment: OH Militia - Rank: Captain - Source(s): AS-18 - Comments: Findlay's Regiment.

Stewart, William M. - Rank: Private - Source(s): AS-8.

Stickney, Abijah - Regiment: 1st Artillery - Source(s): AS-1.

Stiles, William - Regiment: 2nd Artillery - Rank: Private - Enlistment date: 15 Aug 1812 - Enlistment period: 5 years - Source(s): AS-5; AS-14.

Stocker, Jesse L. - Rank: Sergeant - Source(s): AS-9.

Stockwell, Luther - Regiment: 11th Infantry - Rank: Private - Source(s): AS-9.

Stokes, Berimon - Regiment: 24th Infantry - Source(s): AS-1.

Stokes, Damon - Regiment: 24th Infantry - Rank: Private - Source(s): AS-12.

Stone, Henry - Regiment: 13th Infantry - Source(s): AS-1.

Stone, John F. - Regiment: Unknown - Source(s): AS-1.

Stone, John F. W. - Regiment: 1st Artillery - Rank: Private - Source(s): AS-12.

Stone, Westerly - Rank: Private - Source(s): AS-8.

Stoors, Stephen - Regiment: 13th Infantry - Source(s): AS-1.

Storier, John - Regiment: 1st Infantry - Rank: Sergeant - Source(s): AS-16.

Story, Pliney - Regiment: 1st Rifles - Name of prison ship: Lord Cathcart - Source(s): AS-1.

Strain, Thomas - Regiment: 1st Infantry - Rank: Private - Source(s): AS-16.

Stratton, Anthony - Regiment: 2nd Light Dragoons - Rank: Private - Source(s): AS-14.

Stratton, Gardner - Rank: Private - Source(s): AS-8.

Stratton, Thomas - Regiment: 2nd Artillery - Rank: Private - Source(s): AS-1; AS-12.

Stribbs, Henry - Regiment: 5th Infantry - Rank: Private - Source(s): AS-10.

Strickland, Richard - Regiment: Militia - Name of prison ship: Lord Cathcart - Where taken: Black Rock, NY - Source(s): AS-1.

Strong, Cyrus - Regiment: 1st Infantry - Rank: Musician - Source(s): AS-16.

Strong, Timothy - Regiment: Militia - Rank: Private - Source(s): AS-2.

Stubes, Timothy S. - Regiment: 40th Infantry - Rank: Corporal - Source(s): AS-4 - Comments: POW at Eastport, ME.

Sturgess, Zed. - Regiment: NY Militia - Rank: Private - Source(s): AS-12.

Sullivan, Daniel - Regiment: 24th Infantry - Rank: Private - Source(s): AS-1; AS-12.

Summers, William - Regiment: 1st Artillery - Source(s): AS-1.

Summit, Dennis - Rank: Private - Source(s): AS-8.

Swain, John - Regiment: NY Militia - Rank: Private - Source(s): AS-12.

Swartout, Perry - Rank: Private - Source(s): AS-8.

Swift, Socrates - Regiment: NY Militia - Rank: Private - Source(s): AS-12.

Swill, William - Rank: Private - Source(s): AS-8.

Talbot, David - Rank: Private - Source(s): AS-8.

Talley, Thomas - Regiment: 1st Light Dragoons - Source(s): AS-1.

Tanner, Asa - Regiment: 1st Rifles - Rank: Private - Source(s): AS-10.

Tanner, Eli - Regiment: 1st Rifles - Rank: Private - Source(s): AS-1; AS-12.

Taylor, Isaac - Regiment: KY or TN Militia - Where taken: Miami Rapids, OH or River Raison, MI - Source(s): AS-1.

Taylor, James - Regiment: KY Militia - Rank: Quartermaster General - Source(s): AS-18.

Taylor, John - Regiment: 3rd Artillery - Rank: Private - Source(s): AS-1; AS-10.

Taylor, Reuben - Regiment: 1st Artillery - Rank: Private - Source(s): AS-16.

Taylor, Richard - Rank: Corporal - Source(s): AS-9.

Taylor, Thomas - Regiment: McCobb's Volunteers - Rank: Private - Source(s): AS-1; AS-14.

Taylor, William - Regiment: 16th Infantry - Rank: Private - Enlistment date: Oct 1812 - Source(s): AS-5; AS-14.

Taylor, William - Name of prison ship: Lord Cathcart - Source(s): AS-1.

Temple, Dixon - Regiment: 1st Rifles - Source(s): AS-1.

Temple, Lorain - Regiment: Volunteers - Rank: Private - Source(s): AS-14.

Temple, Loren - Regiment: 11th Infantry - Source(s): AS-1.

Temple, William - Regiment: 1st Light Dragoons - Source(s): AS-1.

Templin, John D. - Regiment: 1st Light Dragoons - Rank: Quartermaster Sergeant - Enlistment date: 21 Aug 1812 - Enlistment period: 5 years - Source(s): AS-1; AS-5; AS-14.

Terrick, Benjamin - Regiment: 15th Infantry - Name of prison ship: Lord Cathcart - Source(s): AS-1.

Thayer, Abraham - Regiment: 11th Infantry - Rank: Private - Source(s): AS-10.

Thayer, Martin - Regiment: 4th Infantry - Rank: Private - Source(s): AS-17.

Thejon, Joshua - Regiment: 23rd Infantry - Rank: Corporal - Source(s): AS-9.

Thing, Samuel - Regiment: 4th Infantry - Rank: Private - Source(s): AS-17.

Thomas, Allen - Regiment: Unknown - Source(s): AS-1.

Thomas, Bennett - Rank: Private - Source(s): AS-8.

Thomas, James - Rank: Corporal - Source(s): AS-8.

Thomberg, Thomas - Regiment: 19th Infantry - Rank: Private - Source(s): AS-9.

Thompson, Amos - Regiment: Militia - Rank: Private - Source(s): AS-2.

Thompson, Curtis - Regiment: 21st Infantry - Rank: Private - Source(s): AS-1; AS-12.

Thompson, David - Regiment: 27th Infantry - Rank: Recruit - Source(s): AS-15.

Thompson, James - Regiment: 17th Infantry - Rank: Sergeant - Source(s): AS-10.

Thompson, John - Regiment: 2nd Light Dragoons - Rank: Corporal - Enlistment date: 28 Dec 1812 - Enlistment period: 5 years - Name of prison ship: Lord Cathcart - Source(s): AS-1; AS-5; AS-14.

Thompson, Jonathan J. - Regiment: 22nd Infantry - Source(s): AS-1.

Thompson, Robert - Regiment: 4th Infantry - Rank: Private - Source(s): AS-16.

Thompson, Robert - Rank: Private - Source(s): AS-8.

Thornburg, John - Regiment: 24th Infantry - Source(s): AS-1.

Thornton, Reuben - Rank: Private - Source(s): AS-8.

Thurber, D. - Regiment: 2nd Light Dragoons - Source(s): AS-1.

Thurston, George Washington - Rank: Private - Source(s): AS-8.

Thurston, Nathaniel - Regiment: 4th Infantry - Rank: Musician - Source(s): AS-16.

Tignar, Jason - Regiment: Militia - Rank: Private - Source(s): AS-2.

Tillaban, William - Rank: Private - Source(s): AS-8.

Tilton, Israel - Regiment: 4th Infantry - Rank: Private - Source(s): AS-17.

Tinner, Peter - Regiment: 14th Infantry - Rank: Corporal - Enlistment date: 4 Aug 1812 - Enlistment period: 5 years - Source(s): AS-5; AS-14.

Tinney, Samuel - Regiment: 21st Infantry - Rank: Private - Enlistment date: 20 Mar 1813 - Enlistment period: During the war - Source(s): AS-5.

Tinnord, Jon - Regiment: 1st Infantry - Rank: Private - Source(s): AS-16.

Tompkins, James - Regiment: 24th Infantry - Rank: Private - Source(s): AS-1; AS-12.

Tone, Christopher - Regiment: 11th Infantry - Source(s): AS-1.

Toney, Joseph - Regiment: 12th Infantry - Name of prison ship: Lord Cathcart - Source(s): AS-1.

Tormell, William - Regiment: 2nd Light Dragoons - Name of prison ship: Hospital - Source(s): AS-1.

Torry, Abner - Rank: Private - Source(s): AS-8.

Tortham, Apollo - Regiment: Militia - Rank: Private - Source(s): AS-2.

Towiner, Samuel - Regiment: 23rd Infantry - Rank: Corporal - Source(s): AS-10.

Town, George C. - Regiment: 23rd Infantry - Rank: Sergeant - Source(s): AS-10.

Tox, Ambrose P. - Regiment: NY Militia - Rank: Private - Source(s): AS-12.

Tracksell, Jacob - Regiment: 2nd Light Dragoons - Rank: Corporal - Enlistment date: 4 May 1813 - Enlistment period: 5 years - Name of prison ship: Lord Cathcart - Source(s): AS-1; AS-5; As-14.

Tracy, James - Regiment: 4th Infantry - Rank: Sergeant - Source(s): AS-17.

Trader, Elisha - Regiment: 7th Infantry - Rank: Private - Source(s): AS-3.

Trainer, James - Regiment: 2nd Artillery - Source(s): AS-1.

Trames, Hugh - Regiment: 7th Infantry - Rank: Private - Source(s): AS-3.

Trark, Howard - Regiment: McCobb's Volunteers - Source(s): AS-1.

Trasher, John - Regiment: 4th Infantry - Rank: Private - Source(s): AS-16.

Trasher, Philip - Regiment: 4th Infantry - Rank: Private - Source(s): AS-16.

Traux, J. B. - Rank: Sergeant - Source(s): AS-8.

Trayman, James - Regiment: 2nd Artillery - Rank: Private - Enlistment date: 12 Apr 1812 - Enlistment period: 5 years - Source(s): AS-5; AS-14.

Tree, Almond - Regiment: 13th Infantry - Rank: Private - Name of prison ship: Lord Cathcart - Source(s): AS-1; AS-14.

Trimble, William - Regiment: OH Militia - Rank: Major - Source(s): AS-18 - Comments: McArthur's Regiment.

Tromell, William - Rank: Sergeant - Source(s): AS-9.

Troop, Alexander - Regiment: 24th Infantry - Rank: Private - Source(s): AS-1; AS-12.

Truelove, Barney - Rank: Private - Source(s): AS-8.

Truman, Gaius - Regiment: 1st Artillery - Rank: Private - Source(s): AS-16.

Tucker, Aaron - Regiment: 4th Infantry - Rank: Sergeant - Source(s): AS-17.

Tucker, Frederick - Regiment: 27th Infantry - Rank: Recruit - Source(s): AS-15.

Tucker, Henry - Regiment: 4th Infantry - Rank: Corporal - Source(s): AS-17.

Tuffs, William - Regiment: 13th Infantry - Rank: Private - Source(s): AS-1; AS-14.

Tull, Elijah - Regiment: 7th Infantry - Rank: Private - Source(s): AS-3.

Tundy, Jacob - Rank: Private - Source(s): AS-8.

Turkee, Marshall S. - Regiment: 4th Infantry - Rank: Sergeant - Source(s): AS-17.

Turnald, John - Rank: Private - Source(s): AS-8.

Turner, Abner - Rank: Private - Source(s): AS-8.

Turner, Cornelius - Rank: Surgeon's Mate - Source(s): AS-11.

Turner, Horace - Regiment: Militia - Rank: Corporal - Source(s): AS-2.

Turner, Isaac - Regiment: 1st Artillery - Source(s): AS-1.

Turner, Israel - Regiment: 13th Infantry - Rank: First Lieutenant - Source(s): AS-8; As-11.

Turner, John - Rank: Private - Source(s): AS-8.

Turner, John - Regiment: KY or TN Militia - Where taken: Miami Rapids, OH or River Raison, MI - Source(s): AS-1.

Turner, Nathan - Rank: Private - Source(s): AS-8.

Turner, William - Regiment: OH Militia - Rank: Surgeon - Source(s): AS-18 - Comments: Findlay's Regiment.

Twitchell, Anson - Regiment: 4th Infantry - Rank: Corporal - Source(s): AS-16.

Tyler, John - Regiment: Militia - Rank: Private - Source(s): AS-2.

Updegraff, John - Regiment: 1st Infantry - Rank: Private - Source(s): AS-16.

Valentine, Elijah - Regiment: 1st Artillery - Source(s): AS-1.

Valentine, John - Regiment: 13th Infantry - Source(s): AS-1; AS-12.

Valley, Nathan - Regiment: 1st US Volunteers - Source(s): AS-1.

Valurence, Joseph - Regiment: 16th Infantry - Source(s): AS-1.

Van Curen, Edward - Rank: Citizen - Source(s): AS-10.

Van Horne, Thomas B. - Regiment: OH Militia - Rank: Major - Source(s): AS-18 - Comments: Findlay's Regiment.

Van Meter, John - Regiment: 27th Infantry - Rank: Recruit - Source(s): AS-15.

Van Naleknburgh, J. - Rank: Private - Source(s): AS-8.

Van Severance, Joseph - Regiment: 16th Infantry - Rank: Private - Source(s): AS-12.

Van Swearingen, Henry - Regiment: 1st Rifles - Rank: First Lieutenant - Source(s): AS-14.

Van Tile, John - Rank: Private - Source(s): AS-8.

Van Winkle, James - Regiment: 27th Infantry - Rank: Recruit - Source(s): AS-15.

Vanderford, Benjamin - Regiment: 4th Infantry - Rank: Private - Source(s): AS-17.

Vandermark, Charles - Rank: Private - Source(s): AS-8.

VanGuilder, Abram - Rank: Private - Source(s): AS-8.

Vanhorn James - Regiment: 1st Infantry - Source(s): AS-1.

Vanslyck, Nicholas - Rank: Private - Source(s): AS-8.

Varley, Joseph - Source(s): AS-1.

Varnum, Jacob B. - Regiment: 40th Infantry - Rank: Captain - Source(s): AS-4 - Comments: On parole at Boston, MA.

Varnum, Samuel M. - Regiment: 40th Infantry - Rank: Private - Source(s): AS-4 - Comments: On parole at Machias, ME.

Vasure, Jove - Regiment: 3rd Artillery - Rank: Private - Source(s): AS-10.

Vaughn, Samuel - Regiment: 1st Artillery - Rank: Private - Enlistment date: 31 Dec 1811 - Enlistment period: 5 years - Name of prison ship: Lord Cathcart - Source(s): AS-1; AS-5; As-14.

Vaughn, Thursten - Regiment: 7th Infantry - Rank: Private - Source(s): AS-3.

Vazier, Joseph - Regiment: 3rd Artillery - Source(s): AS-1.

Venderheaon, Garham - Regiment: NY Militia - Rank: Private - Source(s): AS-12.

Venice, Philip - Rank: Private - Source(s): AS-8.

Verssin, Charles - Regiment: 21st Infantry - Source(s): AS-1.

Vicar, William - Regiment: 1st Infantry - Rank: Private - Source(s): AS-16.

Vicker, Philip - Regiment: NY Militia - Rank: Private - Source(s): AS-12.

Vickery, John - Regiment: 4th Infantry - Rank: Private - Source(s): AS-17.

Victory, Thomas - Regiment: NY Militia - Rank: Private - Source(s): AS-12.

Vinton, Ezekiel - Regiment: 13th Infantry - Rank: Private - Enlistment date: 15 Mar 1813 - Enlistment period: During the war - Name of prison ship: Lord Cathcart - Source(s): AS-1; AS-5.

Vinton, John - Regiment: 22nd Infantry - Source(s): AS-1.

Virgin, John - Regiment: 4th Infantry - Rank: Private - Source(s): AS-17.

Virgin, Levi - Regiment: 21st Infantry - Rank: Private - Enlistment date: 3 Mar 1813 - Enlistment period: During the war - Source(s): AS-5; AS-14.

Virgin, Levit C. - Regiment: 21st Infantry - Source(s): AS-1.

Voight, Thomas - Regiment: 21st Infantry - Source(s): AS-1.

Voucher, Samuel - Regiment: 1st Artillery - Name of prison ship: Lord Cathcart - Source(s): AS-1.

Waddle, George - Regiment: 24th Infantry - Rank: Private - Source(s): AS-1; AS-12.

Waddle, John - Regiment: 24th Infantry - Rank: Private - Source(s): AS-1; AS-12.

Wade, Hamilton - Regiment: 1st Artillery - Rank: Private - Source(s): AS-16.

Wade, Melvin - Regiment: 9th Infantry - Rank: Private - Enlistment date: 12 Mar 1813 - Enlistment period: 5 years - Source(s): AS-5; AS-14.

Wadleigh, Thomas - Regiment: 40th Infantry - Rank: Sergeant - Source(s): AS-4 - Comments: POW at Eastport, ME.

Waggoner, Anthony L. - Regiment: 1st Artillery - Rank: Private - Source(s): AS-16.

Wagstaff, Reuben - Regiment: 1st Infantry - Rank: Private - Source(s): AS-9.

Waire, Robert - Regiment: Rifles - Rank: Sergeant - Source(s): AS-12.

Walker, (-----) - Regiment: OH Militia - Rank: Lieutenant - Source(s): AS-18 - Comments: Light Dragoons.

Walker, Adam - Regiment: 4th Infantry - Rank: Musician - Source(s): AS-17.

Walker, Benjamin - Regiment: 1st Artillery - Source(s): AS-1.

Walker, Colman - Regiment: KY or TN Militia - Where taken: Miami Rapids, OH or River Raison, MI - Source(s): AS-1.

Walker, David - Rank: Private - Source(s): AS-8.

Walker, J. - Rank: Private - Source(s): AS-8.

Walker, John - Regiment: 24th Infantry - Rank: Private - Source(s): AS-12.

Walker, John N. - Regiment: 24th Infantry - Source(s): AS-1.

Walker, Seth - Regiment: 40th Infantry - Rank: Private - Source(s): AS-4 - Comments: On parole at Salem, MA.

Walker, Solomon S. - Regiment: 1st Artillery - Rank: Private - Source(s): AS-16.

Walker, William - Regiment: 12th Infantry - Source(s): AS-1.

Walker, William - Regiment: 2nd Light Dragoons - Rank: Sergeant - Source(s): AS-5.

Walker, William Jr. - Regiment: 2nd Light Dragoons - Name of prison ship: Hospital - Source(s): AS-1; AS-14.

Wall, Thomas - Rank: Private - Source(s): AS-8.

Wallace, Robert - Regiment: OH Militia - Rank: Aide de Camp - Source(s): AS-18.

Wallis, Samuel - Regiment: 24th Infantry - Source(s): AS-1.

Walsh, William - Regiment: 1st Infantry - Rank: Private - Source(s): AS-16.

Walter, Samuel - Regiment: 6th Infantry - Rank: Private - Enlistment date: 20 Apr 1812 - Enlistment period: 5 years - Source(s): AS-5; AS-14.

Walton, Edward - Regiment: 14th Infantry - Rank: Private - Source(s): AS-14.

Walton, George S. - Regiment: NY Militia - Rank: Private - Source(s): AS-12.

Ward, John - Regiment: KY or TN Militia - Where taken: Miami Rapids, OH or River Raison, MI - Source(s): AS-1.

Ward, Lewis - Regiment: 11th Infantry - Rank: Private - Source(s): AS-10.

Warham James - Regiment: NY Militia - Rank: Private - Source(s): AS-12.

Waring, (-----) - Regiment: OH Militia - Rank: Cornet - Source(s): AS-18 - Comments: Light Dragoons.

Waring, Jonathan - Regiment: 13th Infantry - Rank: Private - Enlistment date: 20 May 1813 - Enlistment period: During the war - Source(s): AS-1; AS-5; AS-14.

Warley, Joseph - Regiment: 16th Infantry - Rank: Private - Source(s): AS-14.

Warner, Elisha - Rank: Private - Source(s): AS-8.

Warner, Martin - Regiment: 1st Artillery - Rank: Private - Source(s): AS-10.

Warner, Wynkoop - Regiment: OH Militia and 27th Infantry - Rank: Lieutenant - Source(s): AS-15; AS-18 - Comments: Cass' Regiment.

Warner, Z. - Rank: Private - Source(s): AS-8.

Warren, Elisha - Regiment: 25th Infantry - Rank: Sergeant Major - Source(s): AS-9.

Warren, Thomas - Regiment: NY Militia - Rank: Private - Source(s): AS-12.

Washington, James - Regiment: 44th Infantry - Source(s): AS-1.

Waterman, Elisha - Regiment: 1st Artillery - Source(s): AS-1.

Wather, John - Regiment: 6th Infantry - Source(s): AS-6 - Comments: Died on prison ship.

Watson, John J. - Regiment: 4th Infantry - Rank: Private - Source(s): AS-17.

Watter, Samuel - Regiment: 6th Infantry - Name of prison ship: Lord Cathcart - Source(s): AS-1.

Way, Ebenezer - Regiment: 4th Infantry - Rank: Lieutenant - Source(s): AS-11 - Comments: now Captain.

Weadon, Luther - Regiment: 23rd Infantry - Rank: Private - Source(s): AS-10.

Wear, Robert - Regiment: 1st Rifles - Source(s): AS-1.

Webb, Andrew - Regiment: 24th Infantry - Source(s): AS-1.

Webb, John P. - Regiment: 4th Infantry - Rank: Private - Source(s): AS-16.

Webb, Joseph - Rank: Private - Source(s): AS-8.

Webb, Joseph - Regiment: 26th Infantry - Rank: Private - Source(s): AS-12.

Webb, Samuel - Rank: Private - Source(s): AS-8.

Weeks, J. - Rank: Private - Source(s): AS-8.

Weeman, Edward - Regiment: 33rd Infantry - Source(s): AS-1.

Weems, Daniel - Regiment: 14th Infantry - Rank: Private - Enlistment date: 12 Dec 1812 - Enlistment period: 5 years - Source(s): AS-5.Weiden, Joseph - Rank: Corporal - Source(s): AS-8.

Weldon, Jacob - Regiment: 24th Infantry - Rank: Sergeant - Source(s): AS-1; AS-12.

Welky, Max - Regiment: 24th Infantry - Source(s): AS-1.

Wells, Caleb - Date of death: 29 Jul 1813 - Source(s): AS-6 - Comments: Died at Quebec.

Wells, Charles C. - Regiment: Militia - Rank: Private - Source(s): AS-2.

Wells, David - Regiment: 4th Infantry - Rank: Private - Source(s): AS-16.

Wells, John - Regiment: 27th Infantry - Rank: Recruit - Source(s): AS-15.

Wells, Jonathan - Regiment: 9th Infantry - Rank: Private - Source(s): AS-12.

Wells, Silas - Regiment: 4th Infantry - Rank: Private - Source(s): AS-17.

Welsh, Andrew - Regiment: 24th Infantry - Rank: Private - Source(s): AS-12.

Wentey, Benjamin L. - Rank: Private - Source(s): AS-8.

Wentworth, Icabod - Regiment: 4th Infantry - Rank: Private - Source(s): AS-17.

Wentworth, Jediah - Regiment: 4th Infantry - Rank: Corporal - Source(s): AS-17.

West, Charles - Regiment: 14th Infantry - Rank: Sergeant - Source(s): AS-9.

West, Hugh G. - Regiment: 2nd Artillery - Rank: Private - Enlistment date: 20 May 1812 - Enlistment period: 5 years - Source(s): AS-1; AS-5.

Westbrook, Abraham - Regiment: 16th Infantry - Rank: Private - Source(s): AS-1; AS-14.

Westland, DeWitt - Rank: Private - Source(s): AS-8.

Westman, Ephraim - Regiment: Militia - Rank: Private - Source(s): AS-2.

Westwok, Abraham - Name of prison ship: Lord Cathcart - Source(s): AS-1.

Weydell, John - Regiment: 1st Artillery - Rank: Corporal - Source(s): AS-16.

Wheaton, Jared - Regiment: Militia - Rank: Private - Source(s): AS-2.

Wheeler, Stephen - Regiment: 9th Infantry - Rank: Sergeant - Source(s): AS-14.

Wheeler, Uriah - Rank: Private - Source(s): AS-8.

Wheeler, Whiteston - Regiment: 2nd Artillery - Source(s): AS-1.

Wheeler, Wilson - Regiment: 2nd Artillery - Rank: Private - Enlistment date: 18 Jun 1812 - Enlistment period: 5 years - Source(s): AS-5; AS-14.

Wheelock, Ezra - Regiment: 4th Infantry - Rank: Private - Source(s): AS-17.

Wheelock, James - Regiment: 14th Infantry - Rank: Private - Enlistment date: 23 Sep 1812 - Enlistment period: 5 years - Source(s): AS-5; AS-14.

Whelan, Mark - Regiment: 4th Infantry - Rank: Private - Source(s): AS-16.

Whistler, John - Regiment: 19th Infantry - Rank: Ensign - Source(s): AS-11; AS-16.

Whistler, William - Regiment: 1st Infantry - Rank: Lieutenant - Source(s): AS-11 - Comments: now Captain.

White, Cornelius - Regiment: 11th Infantry - Rank: Private - Source(s): AS-10.

White, Isaac - Regiment: 1st Artillery - Source(s): AS-1.

White, Jesse - Regiment: McCobb's Volunteers - Source(s): AS-1.

White, Joshua - Regiment: 21st Infantry - Rank: Private - Source(s): AS-14.

White, Joshua - Regiment: Volunteers - Rank: Private - Source(s): AS-14.

White, Richard - Rank: Citizen - Source(s): AS-10.

White, William - Regiment: 16th Infantry - Source(s): AS-1.

White, William - Name of prison ship: Lord Cathcart - Source(s): AS-1.

Whitelock, John - Regiment: 1st Infantry - Rank: Sergeant - Source(s): AS-16.

Whitely, John - Regiment: 4th Infantry - Rank: Private - Source(s): AS-16.

Whitety, Davie R. - Regiment: 2nd Artillery - Source(s): AS-1.

Whitmore, Stephen - Rank: Private - Source(s): AS-8.

Whitney, David - Regiment: 2nd Artillery - Rank: Private - Enlistment date: 11 Apr 1812 - Enlistment period: 5 years - Source(s): AS-5; AS-14.

Whitney, Isaac - Regiment: 34th Infantry - Source(s): AS-1.

Whitney, Jeremiah - Regiment: 21st Infantry - Source(s): AS-1.

Whitney, Joseph - Regiment: 21st Infantry - Rank: Sergeant - Source(s): AS-1.

Whitney, Solomon B. - Regiment: 1st Artillery - Rank: Sergeant - Source(s): AS-16.

Whitney, William - Regiment: 21st Infantry - Source(s): AS-1.

Whitten, Charles - Regiment: 21st Infantry - Source(s): AS-1.

Whitten, George - Regiment: 21st Infantry - Rank: Private - Source(s): AS-9.

Whitten, William - Regiment: 21st Infantry - Source(s): AS-1.

Whittey, G. D. - Regiment: 44th Infantry - Source(s): AS-1.

Whitton, Charles - Regiment: 21st Infantry - Rank: Private - Source(s): AS-14.

Whitton, George - Regiment: McCobb's Volunteers - Rank: Private - Source(s): AS-1, AS-14.

Wicklow, William - Rank: Private - Source(s): AS-8.

Wilber, John - Regiment: NY Militia - Where taken: Niagara or Buffalo, NY - Source(s): AS-1.

Wilcox, David - Regiment: 22nd Infantry - Source(s): AS-1.

Wilcox, Hiram - Regiment: Militia - Rank: Private - Source(s): AS-2.

Wilcox, John - Regiment: 13th Infantry - Rank: Private - Name of prison ship: Lord Cathcart - Source(s): AS-1; AS-14.

Wilder, Nathaniel - Regiment: NY Militia - Rank: Private - Source(s): AS-12.

Wilkie, Maxfield - Regiment: 24th Infantry - Rank: Private - Source(s): AS-12.

Wilkington, Robert - Regiment: McCobb's Volunteers - Source(s): AS-1.

Wilkins, Aaron - Regiment: 9th Infantry - Rank: Private - Source(s): AS-14.

Wilkins, Edward - Regiment: 34th Infantry - Source(s): AS-1.

Wilkins, William - Regiment: 14th Infantry - Rank: Private - Enlistment date: 15 Aug 1812 - Enlistment period: 5 years - Source(s): AS-5.

Wilkinson, Allison - Regiment: 13th Infantry - Rank: Private - Enlistment date: 22 Feb 1813 - Enlistment period: During the war - Source(s): AS-5.

Wilkinson, Alvin - Regiment: 13th Infantry - Source(s): AS-1.

Wilkinson, Andrew - Regiment: 21st Infantry - Source(s): AS-1.

Wilkinson, Oliver - Regiment: 13th Infantry - Rank: Private - Source(s): AS-14.

Willen, Jonathan - Regiment: 4th Infantry - Rank: Private - Source(s): AS-16.

Willett, Joseph - Regiment: 6th Infantry - Rank: Private - Enlistment date: 24 Jul 1812 - Enlistment period: 5 years - Name of prison ship: Lord Cathcart - Source(s): AS-1; AS-5; AS-14.

Willett, Phineas - Regiment: 16th Infantry - Rank: Private - Enlistment date: 1 Nov 1812 - Name of prison ship: Lord Cathcart - Source(s): AS-1; AS-5; AS-14.

William, Austin - Regiment: 11th Infantry - Rank: Private - Source(s): AS-9.

William, William H. - Regiment: 31st Infantry - Rank: Private - Source(s): AS-9.

Williams, John - Regiment: 4th Infantry - Rank: Private - Source(s): AS-17.

Williams, John - Regiment: Unknown - Source(s): AS-1.

Williams, John - Regiment: 1st Artillery - Rank: Private - Source(s): AS-12.

Williams, Robert - Regiment: 23rd Infantry - Rank: Private - Source(s): AS-10.

Williams, Samuel - Regiment: 21st Infantry - Rank: Private - Enlistment date: 10 Feb 1813 - Enlistment period: During the war - Source(s): AS-1; AS-5; AS-14.

Williams, Zadock - Regiment: 4th Infantry - Rank: Private - Source(s): AS-17.

Williamson, Robert - Regiment: 1st Infantry - Rank: Private - Source(s): AS-16.

Williamson, Thomas - Regiment: 1st Infantry - Rank: Private - Source(s): AS-16.

Williber, John - Regiment: 24th Infantry - Rank: Private - Source(s): AS-9.

Willist, William - Regiment: Militia - Rank: Private - Source(s): AS-2.

Willoughby, George - Regiment: 5th Infantry - Rank: Corporal - Enlistment date: 17 Jul 1811 - Enlistment period: 5 years - Name of prison ship: Lord Cathcart - Source(s): AS-1; AS-5; AS-14.

Wilson, Andrew - Regiment: 1st Infantry - Rank: Private - Source(s): AS-16.

Wilson, Benjamin - Rank: Private - Source(s): AS-8.

Wilson, Ephraim - Regiment: 40th Infantry - Rank: Private - Source(s): AS-4 - Comments: POW at Eastport, ME.

Wilson, George - Regiment: 4th Infantry - Rank: Private - Source(s): AS-17.

Wilson, Jonathan - Regiment: 24th Infantry - Rank: Private - Source(s): AS-1; AS-12.

Wilson, Levi - Regiment: 40th Infantry - Rank: Private - Source(s): AS-4 - Comments: On parole at Machias, ME.

Wilson, Samuel - Rank: Sergeant - Source(s): AS-8.

Wilson, William - Regiment: KY or TN Militia - Where taken: Miami Rapids, OH or River Raison, MI - Source(s): AS-1.

Wilson, William - Rank: Private - Source(s): AS-8.

Winner, John - Regiment: 27th Infantry - Rank: Recruit - Source(s): AS-15.

Winnet, George - Regiment: Indian - Source(s): AS-10.

Winter, Christopher - Regiment: 24th Infantry - Source(s): AS-1.

Winters, John - Regiment: 1st Rifles - Rank: Private - Source(s): AS-9.

Winters, Stephen - Regiment: 23rd Infantry - Rank: Corporal - Source(s): AS-10.

Winton, John - Regiment: 22nd Infantry - Rank: Private - Source(s): AS-14.

Withington, Robert - Regiment: Volunteers - Rank: Private - Source(s): AS-14.

Withington, Thomas - Regiment: KY or TN Militia - Where taken: Miami Rapids, OH or River Raison, MI - Source(s): AS-1.

Withrell, David - Regiment: 15th Infantry - Source(s): AS-1.

Witt, Ira - Rank: Private - Source(s): AS-8.

W------ngford, Jonathan - Regiment: 4th Infantry - Rank: Private - Source(s): AS-17 - Comments: Since dead.

Wood, Amory - Regiment: Militia - Name of prison ship: Lord Cathcart - Where taken: Black Rock, NY - Source(s): AS-1.

Wood, David - Regiment: Rifles - Rank: Private - Source(s): AS-12.

Wood, Eli - Regiment: NY Militia - Rank: Private - Source(s): AS-12.

Wood, Israel - Regiment: 21st Infantry - Rank: Private - Source(s): AS-1; AS-14.

Wood, James M. - Regiment: 27th Infantry - Rank: Recruit - Source(s): AS-15.

Wood, Joel - Regiment: 24th Infantry - Source(s): AS-1.

Wood, Joel - Regiment: 1st Rifles - Rank: Private - Source(s): AS-12.

Wood, Lewis - Regiment: 11th Infantry - Rank: Private - Source(s): AS-10.

Wood, Michael - Regiment: 19th Infantry - Rank: Private - Source(s): AS-17 - Comments: Since dead.

Wood, Michael - Regiment: 1st Infantry - Rank: Private - Source(s): AS-16 - Comments: Died in Charlestown, Boston harbor, on 7 Dec 1812.

Wood, Silas - Regiment: 4th Infantry - Rank: Private - Source(s): AS-17.

Wood, Thomas B. - Rank: Private - Source(s): AS-8.

Woodbridge, Asa - Regiment: Militia - Rank: Private - Source(s): AS-2.

Woodbury, Daniel - Regiment: 11th Infantry - Source(s): AS-1.

Woodcock, Charles - Regiment: 29th Infantry - Rank: Private - Source(s): AS-9.

Woodland, Labediah - Regiment: 14th Infantry - Rank: Private - Source(s): AS-14.

Woodman, Benjamin - Regiment: McCobb's Volunteers - Source(s): AS-1.

Woods, David - Regiment: 1st Rifles - Source(s): AS-1.

Woods, George W. - Regiment: 24th Infantry - Source(s): AS-1.

Woolworth, Elijah - Regiment: 13th Infantry - Source(s): AS-1.

Woolworth, Elijah - Regiment: 18th Infantry - Rank: Private - Source(s): AS-9.

Wooster, William D. - Rank: Sergeant - Source(s): AS-8.

Worther, Enoch - Regiment: 4th Infantry - Rank: Private - Source(s): AS-16.

Wright, Jabez - Regiment: 3rd Artillery - Rank: Private - Source(s): AS-1: AS-10.

Wright, Jacob - Regiment: NY Militia - Rank: Private - Source(s): AS-12.

Wright, Micajah - Regiment: 24th Infantry - Rank: Private - Source(s): AS-1; AS-12.

Wright, Oliver - Regiment: 11th Infantry - Rank: Private - Enlistment date: 1 Apr 1813 - Enlistment period: During the war - Source(s): AS-1; AS-5.

Wright, Philemon - Regiment: 4th Infantry - Rank: Sergeant - Source(s): AS-17.

Wright, Samuel - Regiment: Militia - Rank: Private - Source(s): AS-2.

Wright, Samuel - Rank: Private - Source(s): AS-8.

Wright, William - Regiment: 24th Infantry - Source(s): AS-1.

Wry, Thomas - Regiment: 24th Infantry - Source(s): AS-1.

Wyman, Amos N. - Regiment: 40th Infantry - Rank: Musician - Source(s): AS-4 - Comments: POW at Eastport, ME.

Wymess, Daniel - Regiment: 14th Infantry - Rank: Private - Source(s): AS-14.

Wyn, Abram - Rank: Sergeant - Source(s): AS-8.

Wyncy, David - Rank: Private - Source(s): AS-8.

Yager, Christian - Regiment: 1st Infantry - Rank: Private - Source(s): AS-16.

Yanger, Philip - Rank: Private - Source(s): AS-8.

Yarwood, James - Regiment: NY Militia - Rank: Private - Source(s): AS-12.

Yates, Francis - Regiment: 1st Rifles - Rank: Private - Source(s): AS-1; AS-9.

Yates, Henry D. - Rank: Sergeant - Source(s): AS-9.

Young, Ephraim - Date of death: 10 Aug 1813 - Source(s): AS-6 - Comments: Died at Quebec.

Young, Thomas - Rank: Corporal - Source(s): AS-8.

Young, Thomas - Regiment: 3rd Artillery - Rank: Private - Source(s): AS-1; AS-10.

Soldiers listed by regiments

1st U.S. Infantry

Allen, Joseph
Anderson, Robert
Bailey, Levi
Baish, Lewis
Baker, Daniel
Berry, Samuel
Blake, George
Blake, Samuel
Bouse, Samuel
Bowen, Joseph
Budewood, James
Burr, Andrew
Butler, Samuel
Cassidy, Patrick
Connelly, Hugh M.
Corben, Fielding
Corben, James
Crail, Thomas
Crandell, Joseph
Crise, Adam
Crowley, Timothy
Dear, George
Dillon, John
Dodemaid, John
Dougherty, William
Duvall, Francis
Dyson, Dyer
Edson, Nathan
Edwards, John
Edwards, Joshua
Farrell, John
Fleming, William
Forsyth, Alexander
Fuller, Jonathan
Furrey, Jacob
Garrotson, Garrot
Greene, Peter
Grummo, Paul
Guiles, Joseph
Harris, Joseph
Haslet, Joseph
Headley, Robert
Heath, Noah
Hisler, Mathew
Howard, William
Hyer, James
Isbell, Chancey

1st U.S. Infantry

Jackson, Josiah
Jinpthrum, Bernard
Justice, William K.
Kihill, William
Knowles, John
Kothrock, Isaac
Londred, Lewis
Loury, James
Luckitt, Alexander
Marsh, Ormond
Matson, Thomas F.
McCabe, Robert
McCord, Bernard
McElhaney, William
Miller, John
Miller, William
Mills, Elias
O'Hara, John
Page, Achilles
Perry, Calvin
Perry, David
Philips, Isaac
Porter, Lincoln
Rath, Anthony
Ream, Jacob
Rice, Charles
Rice, John P.
Scott, John
Shendohl, Daniel
Sighendall, Peter
Small, Henry
Stansbury, Dixon
Stephenson, Robert
Storier, John
Strain, Thomas
Strong, Cyrus
Tinnord, Jon
Updegraff, John
Vanhorn James
Vicar, William
Wagstaff, Reuben
Walsh, William
Whistler, William
Whitelock, John
Williamson, Robert
Williamson, Thomas
Wilson, Andrew

Soldiers listed by regiments

1st U.S. Infantry	Wood, Michael	4th U.S. Infantry	Coffin, Samuel
	Yager, Christian		Coles, Robert
4th U.S. Infantry	Adams, John		Collins, Jacob
	Ager, Winthrop D.		Cook, Joel
	Alison, Howard		Cooke, Samuel
	Allen, Edward		Corey, Amos
	Allen, Philip		Courser, John
	Andrews, E. T.		Courson, Ivory
	Andrews, Otis		Cutebeth, Caleb
	Andrews, William		Cutler, Robert
	Ashton, John		Davis, John
	Austin, John		Day, Sylvester
	Bacon, Josiah		Dockham, Ephraim D.
	Bailey, George		Donohue, John
	Ballou, Darius		Durant, Reuben
	Barrett, Elia		Durrill, Joel
	Barnet, William		Earp, Leonard
	Barton, Caleb		Eastman, John A.
	Beasley, William		Easton, Moses
	Beckwith, Gordon		Elkins, Jonathan
	Bemis, Lewis		Emerson, Jeremiah
	Billings, Noyes		Farrow, Joseph
	Bird, William		Fields, Ebenezer
	Blanchard, Amos		Fillebrown, Richard
	Bowles, William		Flanagan, Bryan
	Bradford, Augustus		Flood, Joseph
	Brasbridge, George		Forender, John
	Brewer, John		Forrest, John
	Briee, James		Foster, Timothy
	Briggs, Samuel		Foster, William L.
	Brocor, Stephen		Fowler, Samuel
	Broton, Alexander		Fox, Ezra
	Brown, Abel		Francis, Joseph
	Brown, Nathan		French, Samuel
	Brown, Return B.		Fuller, Charles
	Brown, William		Furbush, Aaron W.
	Burers, Michael		Gemenvery, Roswell
	Burnham, Benjamin		Gleason, Levi
	Burns, John		Goodenow, Rufus
	Burton, Oliver G.		Gooding, George
	Carrier, Kneiland		Graham Edward
	Carter, Enoch		Greene, Gpacher
	Cass, Cornelius D.		Greene, John
	Churchill, Ephraim		Greeney, Peter
	Clark, Almarin		Griffen, Andrew
	Clarke, Jesse		Griffen, Levi
	Clough, William		Griffen, Peter

Soldiers listed by regiments

4th U.S. Infantry

Griggs, William
Gunison, Samuel
Gurrill, John
Hader, Samuel
Hall, John D.
Hamp, Jonathan
Harris, Stephen
Harvey, Peter
Hawkins, Abraham
Hawkins, Samuel
Healy, William
Heath, David
Herrick, John
Hill, Timothy
Hilliard, Samuel
Hith, Waller T.
Houck, Michael
Huggins, William
Hunter, William
Hyde, Nathan
Jackruder, William
Jemmison, Levi
Johnson, Abraham
Johnson, Solomon
Jones, John
Kay, Ebenezer
Kellogg, Daniel
Kelly, William
Kendall, Silas
Keyser, Jacob
Kicker, Isaac
Knapp, Titus
Knapp, William
Knight, Asa
Ladd, Aaron
Ladd, Peter
Ladd, Samuel
Lanabee, Asa
Larrabee, Abraham
Layman, Joseph
Layman, William
Lincoln, Gideon
Lovering, Joshua
Magary, Edward
Mason, Moses
Mathews, William
McArthur, John

4th U.S. Infantry

McDonald, James
McIntosh, Robert
McKinley, William
McWithy, John
Mellen, Aaron
Merrill, James
Mills, John
Mitchell, Nathan
Morgan, John
Moulthrop, Jerry
Mower, Ebenezer
Munn, Harvey
Nevill, William
Newton, Reuben
Nobel, Horace
Noble, Isaac
Norton, Patrick
Nourse, Thomas W.
Nutter, Henry
Orr, Montgomery
Parker, James
Parsons, Elisha
Peckham, Lewis
Perkins, William
Perry, Richard
Peters, George P.
Pettingall, Joseph
Pettis, Samuel
Phills, Curtis
Pickham, Lewis
Pierce, Moses
Pinkley, John
Pomeroy, William
Pooler, Orange
Porter, Samuel
Prentiss, Ella
Prouty, Jacob
Rand, Jacob D.
Reed, Daniel
Reed, William
Riley, William
Robinson, David
Rogers, Daniel
Rollings, Mayhew
Rollins, John M.
Rowells, John
Russell, Thaddeus B.

Soldiers listed by regiments

4th U.S. Infantry		4th U.S. Infantry	Wright, Philemon
	Sallis, Lucius	5th U.S. Infantry	Christian, Humphrey
	Sanborn, John		Clarke, John G.
	Sanders, Zebulon		Clay, Elijah
	Seycant, Seth		Clay, Elisha
	Sheldon, James		Dugan, James
	Shields, Barnel		Horney, David
	Silver, Obed.		Jones, William
	Simpson, Nathaniel		Keller, William
	Smith, John		Kelly, William
	Smith, Samuel		Knight, William
	Sparhawk, Rowland		Larney, Joseph
	Spencer, Daniel		Larsons, Samuel
	Sprague, John		Leyss, David
	Stephenson, William		Morrow, Edward
	Thayer, Martin		Ostender, Jones
	Thing, Samuel		Ostender, Justus
	Thompson, Robert		Payons, Samuel
	Thurston, Nathaniel		Reynolds, Gilbert
	Tilton, Israel		Scott, Solomon
	Tracy, James		Stribbs, Henry
	Trasher, John		Willoughby, George
	Trasher, Philip	6th U.S. Infantry	Bogert, Gilbert
	Tucker, Aaron		Davidson, John
	Tucker, Henry		Dodge, John
	Turkee, Marshall S.		Donaldson, Thomas
	Twitchell, Insorp		Everton, Benjamin
	Vanderford, Benjamin		Green, Thomas
	Vickery, John		Hamilton, James
	Virgin, John		Kingsland, Joseph
	Walker, Adam		Mandeville, Peter
	Watson, John J.		McCann, Edward
	Way, Ebenezer		Millineuse, Thomas
	Webb, John P.		Shall, Henry
	Wells, David		Smiley, Thomas
	Wells, Silas		Smith, Frederick
	Wentworth, Icabod		Sonellie, Thomas
	Wentworth, Jedediah		Walter, Samuel
	Wheelock, Ezra		Wather, John
	Whelan, Mark		Watter, Samuel
	Whitely, John		Willett, Joseph
	Whood, Silas	7th U.S. Infantry	Barnhart, Henry
	Willen, Jonathan		Beaman, Peter
	Williams John		Beau, William K.
	Williams, Zadock		Been, John
	Wilson, George		Bennet, William
	W------ngford, Jonathan		Beyarty, John
	Worther, Enoch		

Soldiers listed by regiments

7th U.S. Infantry	Bigger, David	7th U.S. Infantry	Tull, Elijah
	Brasier, Edward		Vaughn, Thursten
	Brason, David	9th U.S. Infantry	Arnes, Oliver
	Bruner, Edward		Ausper, John
	Byard, Anthony W.		Bachelor, Aaron
	Coop, Benjamin		Bangs, Seth
	Davarex, James		Boyce, John
	Davis, Brookes		Daggett, Josiah
	Doherty, James		Daggett, Lewis
	Fink, Daniel		Dearborn, David
	Foster, Lot		Eastwood, Amariah
	Gamblin, John		Ellis, John
	Gray, Samuel		Evans, Thomas
	Hall, Henry		Harvey, Calvin
	Hall, John (1)		Harvey, Luther
	Hall, John (2)		Hooper, John
	Hines, William		Horton, Barnabas
	Hollaman, Edmund		Howard, Josiah
	Hopkins, Henry		Howe, Calvin
	Hord, John		Jackson, Enoch
	Howel, William		Johnson, John
	Jefferson, Thomas M.		Jones, Nathan
	Jesup, Thomas J.		Keith, Nehemiah
	Johnston, James		Keith, Zephariah
	Kearns, James		McQuegtion, Hugh
	Kennedy, James		Medell, Alden
	Marsh, William		Pearl, John
	Marshall, Thomas		Peterson, Peter
	Martin, John		Ramsdale, Samuel
	McBride, James		Rand, Daniel
	McBride, Samuel		Roiva, Jonathan
	McCarey, Lewis		Rowe, Jonathan
	McClaine, Thomas		Sabrey, Ephraim
	McKenize, John		Seales, William
	Moore, Thomas		Smith, Joseph
	Murphy, James		Wade, Melvin
	Nance, Eaton		Wells, Jonathan
	Page, John		Wheeler, Stephen
	Philips, Pleasant		Wilkins, Aaron
	Reese, Henry	11th U.S. Infantry	Allen, John
	Richardson, Ephraim		Allen, Samuel
	Robertson, James		Ballard, John
	Runnolds, John		Beers, James
	Seers, Harrison		Boutell, Nathaniel
	Smith, Gustavas		Bowtell, Henry
	Trader, Elisha		Briggs, William
	Trames, Hugh		Brink, Orson

Soldiers listed by regiments

11th U.S. Infantry		11th U.S. Infantry	
	Brothorritt, Jonathan		William Austin
	Cary, Daniel		Wood, Lewis
	Danforth, Joseph		Woodbury, Daniel
	Donoff, David		Wright, Oliver
	Furbush, Joshua	12th U.S. Infantry	Becthold, Henry
	Giles, John		Bishop, William
	Hamblin, Ezra		Buck, Robert
	Hardy, Elisha		Burthole, Henry
	Harvey, William		Cease, John
	Hinds, Nathan S.		Conner, John
	Hunt, John		Conner, John
	Lord, Horatio		Craft, George B.
	Lovell, Sylvanus		Davis, John
	McGee, Truman		Davis, Thomas
	McInelly, John		Dyer, Daniel
	Merritt, Jonathan B.		George, John
	Messenger, W. S.		Goodwin, James
	Minor, Harris		Joseph, John
	Moses, John		Laforge, Charles
	Mudge, Ebenezer		Le Forge, Charles
	Orne, Ebenezer		Leisse, John
	Orne, Joseph		Lyles, William
	Owen, Amasa		McCune, William
	Paine, Reuben		Parks, Roger
	Park, Luther		Plotts, John
	Patch, David		Sciecr, John
	Payne, Reuben		Toney, Joseph
	Pearl, John		Walker, William
	Putnam, Benjamin	13th U.S. Infantry	Avery, Muttuttos
	Rennselaer, John		Avery, Nicholas
	Redfield, A. C.		Avery, Richard
	Reed, James		Barb, George
	Rice, Nathaniel		Bryant, Thomas
	Rice, Samuel		Carr, William D.
	Riddle, Elihu		Christie, John M.
	Sharp, Solomon		Clyne, Isaac
	Sherry, Jacob		Conner, Thomas
	Sigs, Nathaniel		Cranston, John
	Smith, Noah		Crystic, John
	Sperry, Jacob		Davis, Elnathan
	Stearns, Nathan		Diller, Robert
	Stockwell, Luther		Evenor, Christian
	Temple, Loren		Evenor, Christopher
	Thayer, Abraham		Farl, Henry
	Tone, Christopher		Ferguson, John
	Ward, Lewis		Fincher, Jesse
	White, Cornelius		Fink, John L.

Soldiers listed by regiments

13th U.S. Infantry	14th U.S. Infantry
Foote, Henry	Burke, John
Grenor, Christian	Davidson, John
Guinnup, John	Dill, Peter
Guynup, John	Dixon, James
Hall, Orrin	Dougherty, William
Halloway, John	English, John
Harrington, Estes N.	Farrell, Michael
Henrick, John	FitzGerald, James
Holloway, John	Frazier, Edward
Hugenian, Daniel	Godwin, Kimmel
Ingalls, Benjamin	Green, Thomas
Ingraham, Benjamin	Herron, James
Kearney, Stephen W.	Hood, Frederick
Lee, Daniel	Hutchinson, Elisha
Leroy, Charles	Hyatt, Joseph
Lloyd, William	Johnson, Jason
Marks, Henry	Johnston, Noble
McElroy, Charles	Kairns, John
McKenzy, Thomas	Lighter, Jacob
Munger, Horace	Louran, Thomas
Munroe, Ephraim	Lowe, Samuel
Philips, Alford	Marshall, Joseph
Reab, George	McDonald, Peter
Sammons, Jacob	Moore, Larrond
See, Daniel	Morris, Maurice
Smith, Elijah	Neuman, Stokely
Sternberg, Christian	Nisbett, Shedrick
Stevens, Joshua	Price, Johnson
Stone, Henry	Ridenour, Conrad
Stoors, Stephen	Roles, Rezin
Tree, Almond	Rose, John
Tuffs, William	Sanders, William G.
Turner, Israel	Sheets, Ishmael
Valentine, John	Tinner, Peter
Vinton, Ezekiel	Walton, Edward
Waring, Jonathan	Weems, Daniel
Wilcox, John	West, Charles
Wilkinson, Allison	Wheelock, James
Wilkinson, Alvin	Wilkins, William
Wilkinson, Oliver	Woodland, Labediah
Woolworth, Elijah	Wymess, Daniel

14th U.S. Infantry	15th U.S. Infantry
Arrall, Richard	----, Harry
Balts, George	---, Philaitus
Barber, John	Allsworth, Philip
Belluito, Levi	Ball, Seth
Biyd, Samuel	Bander, Thomas
Bradshaw, Edward	Barnes, Seth

Soldiers listed by regiments

15th U.S. Infantry	Batchelder, Orin	16th U.S. Infantry	Taylor, William
	Carroll, Timothy		Valurence, Joseph
	Dennison, Benjamin		Van Severance, Joseph
	Lerney, Joseph K.		Warley, Joseph
	McDonald, Francis		Westbrook, Abraham
	Minor, Lewis		White, William
	Smith, Joseph		Willett, Phineas
	Terrick, Benjamin	17th U.S. Infantry	Bell, Joshua H.
	Withrell, David		Brown, R.
16th U.S. Infantry	Anderson, Jeremiah		Dunkelburg, John
	Barber, Charles		Edging, Marting
	Barron, John		Garrett, Ashton
	Beckford, John		Hightower, Richard
	Beech, James		Holder, Caleb H.
	Bowyon, George		Le Duck, Peter
	Brown, Henry		Munday, James
	Byler, Howard		Thompson, James
	Campbell, Frederick	18th U.S. Infantry	Morrow, Joseph
	Campbell, James		Woolworth, Elijah
	Campbell, Joseph	19th U.S. Infantry	Anderson, John
	Chambers, Samuel		Buckover, Peter
	Crosby, James		Dailey, John
	Dicker, Lelia		Dougherty, Robert
	Duncan, Benjamin		Downes, John
	Farmer, Henry		Dunlap, James
	Ferris, Barney		Edwards, Abraham
	Fleming, Joseph		Foens, Daniel B.
	Fowler, John		Grant, William
	Garrison, James		Haynes, Carlisle
	Gillispie, William		Hickman, Harris H.
	Gradey, Martin		Jennings, Edward
	Harding, Amasa		Jones, William
	Helm, Daniel W.		Leister, Jonathan
	Hill, William		Martin, Robert
	Hydendry, Henry		Miller, Jacob
	Irwin, Lewis		Mullen, Charles
	Killeg, James		Philips, Asher
	Killen, John		Self, Charles
	Kroningen, John		Sherman, Joel
	McGonnegal, Michael		Thomberg, Thomas
	Parker, Cornelius		Whistler, John
	Pays, Jacob		Wood, Michael
	Platenburgh, Jacob	21st U.S. Infantry	Allen, John
	Prestman, Daniel		Anderson, Peter
	Rear, John		Basseu, Daniel
	Richardson, John		Blancet, Levi
	Steele, George G.		Bosson, Thaddeus

American Prisoners of War held at Montreal and Quebec during the War of 1812

Soldiers listed by regiments

21st U.S. Infantry		21st U.S. Infantry	
	Bradford, Lemuel		Nicholson, Solomon
	Bradley, Simeon		Ostenger, Robert
	Bridgeman, William		Penny, Samuel
	Butman, David		Pierce, William
	Campbell, William		Pratt, Charles
	Clarke, Benjamin		Prentice, James
	Clarke, John		Purnell, Samuel
	Cobb, John		Remmington, Ira
	Coleman, Charles		Robinson, James
	Cook, Robert		Rowe, Benjamin
	Darling, Thomas		Samson, John
	Drake, Elisha		Shadock, John
	Drew, Ira		Shattuck, John
	English, John		Smith, Richard
	Fobes, Lewis		Smith, William H.
	For-----, Thomas		Spencer, Andrew
	Fowler, James		Stephens, William
	Fox, John		Stevens, William
	Furlong, William		Thompson, Curtis
	Gale, John G.		Tinney, Samuel
	Goodall, Joshua		Verssin, Charles
	Gray, Jonathan		Virgin, Levi
	Groves, George		Virgin, Levit C.
	Hale, Lott		Voight, Thomas
	Hamilton, John		White, Joshua
	Horn, Andrew		Whitney, Jeremiah
	Horn, Wentworth		Whitney, Joseph
	Howard, Lewis		Whitney, William
	Howe, John		Whitten, Charles
	Hubbard, Thomas		Whitten, George
	Ireland, Jonas		Whitten, William
	Jackson, Enoch		Whitton, Charles
	Jenney, Samuel		Wilkinson, Andrew
	Johnson, William		Williams, Samuel
	Kemble, Hannibal		Wood, Israel
	Kimball, Nathaniel	22nd U.S. Infantry	Barnes, Michael
	Kingman, Ebenezer		Bradford, John
	Knight, Hudson		Dallas, David
	Lancaster, William		Duvall, Jacob
	Lucas, Ephraim		Fleming, William
	Lynn, Joshua		Gilchrist, James
	Marks, Ira		Gordon, John
	Merrill, Jacob		Houser, William
	Moore, Abel		Hunt, Henry
	Moore, Joshua		Johnson, William
	Murray, James		Kirk, John
	Nate, Jonathan		Leonard, Isaac

Soldiers listed by regiments

22nd U.S. Infantry	McCann, Robert	23rd U.S. Infantry	Mullarey, James R.
	McCulloch, Samuel		Nearing, Lyman W.
	McCurdy, Robert		Newman, Henry
	McDoad, James		Nobles, Stephen
	McGlaughlin, Mark		Palmer, Nicholas
	McIntire, Ledich		Price, Robert
	McIntire, Zadock		Race, Jonathan
	McNutt, James		Rathbone, Jeremiah
	Mitchell, Hugh		Ray, John
	Parks, John		Reed, Charles W.
	Pennington, Levi		Rice, Robert
	Read, James		Richards, Francis
	Robb, Samuel		Roberts, Jorum
	Rust, William		Robins, Jordan
	Ruthner, John		Roseman, Edward
	Shepherd, David		Scott, Abraham
	Sheyres, David		Scudder, Stephen
	Shoops, David		Skinner, Benjamin
	Stewart, John		Smith, Cornelius
	Thompson, Jonathan J.		Thejon, Joshua
	Vinton, John		Towiner, Samuel
	Wilcox, David		Town, George C.
	Winton, John		Weadon, Luther
23rd U.S. Infantry	Baker, Daniel		Williams, Robert
	Breechman, Lemerick		Winters, Stephen
	Burger, John	24th U.S. Infantry	Atchley, Joshua
	Clark, William		Alderson, Moses
	Cook, John		Alexander, Jonathan
	Countryman, Elias		Archer, Isaac
	Cox, John		Archer, Robert
	Crawford, William		Arnold, James
	Cudder, Stephen		Atcheson, Joseph
	Curran, James		Atchley, Daniel
	Cushing, William		Barnes, John
	Diver, David		Barrick, George W.
	Dunning, Jesse		Bascler, George
	Easton, George		Baxley, George
	Eaton, Henry P.		Bledsoe, Joseph
	Emery, Stephen		Bledsoe, Mrs. (female)
	Fuller, Chester		Blythe, John
	Gee, George W.		Bone, Young E.
	Goodwin, Richard		Boyd, William
	Hammond, Seneca		Brabstone, William B.
	Leatt, Abraham		Brandon, Samuel
	Little, Solomon		Branton, John
	Magee, George		Brown, Daniel
	McCarty, John		Burnell, Nelson

Soldiers listed by regiments

24th U.S. Infantry		24th U.S. Infantry	
	Burns, James		Hill, Jeremiah
	Cahill, Edward		Hilton, Moses
	Campbell, James		Holloby, John
	Canada, William		Holmes, Thomas
	Cheek, William		Holton, John
	Clarke, Charles		Hooper, Joshua
	Clarke, Henry		Hope, John
	Coates, Elijah		Hoss, Isaac
	Cole, Thomas		Hounshall, John
	Conner, James H.		Hovington, Willis
	Conner, Michael		Hox, James
	Coombs, George		Hunt, William
	Cooper, James		Hunter, William
	Daven, Stephen		Janehill, Zachariah
	Derren, John		Kelley, Allison
	Derrill, John		Kelly, Allen
	Dickenson, John		King, Willis
	Divers, Stephens		Kowington, Willis
	Drake, George W.		Lane, Isaac
	Eaton, Clement		Leti, Puff
	Elass, Joseph		Maloney, John
	Elliot, Thomas		McCammon, Robert
	Ewing, James		McCarl, Isaac
	Fike, Nathan		McCoy, Jacob
	Gain, John		McCraig, Thomas
	Garner, William		McGill, Hiram
	Gass, Charles		McGill, Patrick
	Gear, John		McInturff, William
	Gentry, John		McQuay, Daniel
	Gifford, Francis		Melvine, Thomas
	Glass, Joseph		Mercer, James
	Glenn, James		Merrier, Jacob
	Goodman, John		Miller, Reuben
	Goodson, Archibald		Moire, William
	Gowen, Thomas		Moore, Thomas
	Grayson, John		Morriett, Joseph
	Greenley, William		Morris, James
	Gribble, James		Morrisett, Joshua
	Hall, Joseph		Morrison, Robert
	Hall, William		Morss, William
	Hammatt, John		Mutair, Lewis
	Henderson, John		Neighbors, John
	Herbaugh, John		Neilson, Jon
	Herring, William		Nichols, John
	Herron, William		Nope, John
	Hicks, James		Oliver, Henry
	Hill, Allen		Owens, Jeremiah

Soldiers listed by regiments

24th U.S. Infantry	Pace, William	24th U.S. Infantry	Wilber, John
	Page, David		Wilson, Jonathan
	Paste, William		Winter, Christopher
	Patterson, John		Wood, Joel
	Pausey, Morgan		Woods, George W.
	Perkins, Joseph		Wright, Micajah
	Phelps, John		Wright, William
	Pope, Mathew		Wry, Thomas
	Posey, Harrison	25th U.S. Infantry	Baker, Robert
	Posey, Morgan		Beck, Andrew`
	Pratt, Jeremiah		Corkins, Joel
	Price, Hurd		Craighton, William
	Pruitt, Gabriel		Crayton, William
	Pruitt, Jesse		Davey, Herman
	Pyke, Nathan		German, James
	Rambo, Peter		Howe, Willis
	Reynolds, George		Jones, Thomas
	Reynolds, William		Loomis, Daniel
	Ridge, William		Peck, Andrew
	Riggs, Cyrus		Phelps, Henry
	Runnion, Thomas		Spencer, Nathan
	Rye, Thomas		Spencer, Samuel
	Schivers, Luther		Spink, Anthony
	Scott, Charles		Warren, Elisha
	Selman, David	26th U.S. Infantry	Anderson, Thomas
	Shannon, Archibald		Holdersfield, James
	Shivers, Luke		Lacey, Fielding
	Short, Henry		Moore, Abraham
	Simpson, Robert		Webb, Joseph
	Steer, John	27th U.S. Infantry	Munson, Jeremiah R.
	Stevens, J.		Battles, Avery
	Stokes, Berimon		Blake, Henry
	Stokes, Damon		Blake, Rehemiah
	Sullivan, Daniel		Brown, James
	Thornburg, John		Butler, Asaph
	Tompkins, James		Byron, John
	Troop, Alexander		Cairns, Joseph
	Waddle, George		Cairns, Richard
	Waddle, John		Casey, Archibald
	Walker, John		Cass, Ira
	Walker, John N.		Chadwick, Thomas
	Wallis, Samuel		Delaurier, John B.
	Webb, Andrew		Dennis, Samuel
	Weldon, Jacob		Devault, Isaac
	Welky, Max		Devore, Enos
	Welsh, Andrew		Dugan, John
	Wilkie, Maxfield		Duvalt, Isaac

American Prisoners of War held at Montreal and Quebec during the War of 1812

Soldiers listed by regiments

Eagan, John
Edson, Luther
Emmit, Abraham
Fenton, Davidson
Futhey, Isaac
Gill, William
Gilman, Elias
Goodwin, James
Gordon, John L.
Groves, Solomon
Hall, John
Hughes, Elias
Jefferies, Jonas
Johnston, John
Johnston, Samuel
Kelly, Eua
Lackey, Andrew
Lackey, Hugh
Lafferty, Archibald
McDonald, Stephen
McFadden, Neal
Miller, Benjamin
Morrison, Robert
Nixon, James
Northup, Henry
Pastor, Christian
Pettit, Joseph
Pigman, John G.
Post, Cornelius
Rawl, William
Shadley, Henry
Sickle, George M.
Skeels, Henry
Smith, Charles
Spencer, John
Stadler, Joseph
Thompson, David
Tucker, Frederick
Van Meter, John
Van Winkle, James
Warner, Winthrop
Wells, John
Winner, John
Wood, James M.

28th U.S. Infantry
Clark, George
Spencer, John

29th U.S. Infantry
Avery, Alexander

29th U.S. Infantry
Holcomb, Leonard
Nourse, Benjamin
Page, John
Simmons, Levi
Smith, William
Woodcock, Charles

30th U.S. Infantry
Albert, Warren
Pickett, Lester
Rudd, Levi

31st U.S. Infantry
Cummins, Nathan
Curtiss, Leba
Douglass, Caleb
Seldon, Temri
Southerick, Joshua
William, William H.

33rd U.S. Infantry
Bishop, Joshua
Crocker, John
Eades, Thomas
Hewens, Thomas
Menill, Abraham
Weeman, Edward

34th U.S. Infantry
Farnham, Gaius
Hall, Allen
Smith, Jonathan
Whitney, Isaac
Wilkins, Edward

40th U.S. Infantry
Barfield, Richard
Bird, William
Blanchard, Reuben K.
Branch, Thomas B.
Brown, John
Carpenter, Isaac
Carr, John
Chapman, James
Colwell, John
Copps, Darius
Crawford, Thomas
Dailey, John
Donaldson, Frederick
Dow, Frederick
Dunter, Peleg
Dustin, Moody
Eaton, Hubbard
Egans, James
Ersking, Robert
Evelith, Benjamin M.
Fillebrown, John Jr

Soldiers listed by regiments

40th U.S. Infantry		40th U.S. Infantry	
	Fillebrown, Richard		Simonds, Josiah
	Fillebrown, Samuel S.		Simpson, Francis
	Foster, Edla		Smith, Abraham
	Foster, William		Stubes, Timothy S.
	Fravoar, John		Varnum, Jacob B.
	Frost, Richard		Varnum, Samuel M.
	Gahan, Jeremiah		Wadleigh, Thomas
	Gall, Andrew		Walker, Seth
	Hall, Silas		Wilson, Ephraim
	Hamilton, John		Wilson, Levi
	Hanson, Samuel		Wyman, Amos N.
	Hardy, Reuben	44th U.S. Infantry	Bryne, Michael
	Harrington, Jason		Davenport, Joseph
	Haskel, William		Jarnile, Samuel
	Henderson, John		Washington, James
	Hill, Jeremiah		Whittey, G D
	Hitchinson, Joseph	1st U.S. Light Dragoons	Billey, Henry
	Hogg, Elijah		Bilty, Henry
	Hutchenson, Samuel		Estas, Edward
	Hutchenson, Seth		Fairchild, Cyrus B.
	Kimball, Bradbury		Hord, Daniel
	Lambe, Olive		Nelson, James
	Lee, George		Talley, Thomas
	Leonard, Jacob		Temple, William
	Leonard, Samuel		Templin, John D.
	Lindsay, David	2nd U.S. Light Dragoons	Adams, Samuel
	Mellens, Daniel D.		Bennett, James W.
	Merian, James F.		Clear, William
	Meriar, Samuel		Colbaugh, Michael
	Mineher, William		Curtis, Morgan
	Moor, Obadiah		Fairchild, Cedric
	Mullett, Isaac		Fields, Elisha
	Nicholas, Jacob		Hagar, Henry
	Nutting Simni		Hagar, Perry
	Nutting, Cyrus		Hankins, Gilbert
	Orkins, James		Heath, John
	Page, David		House, William
	Paleifer, Joseph		Howard, Edward
	Parker, John		Howe, William
	Paskiel, Ezekiel D.		Hymer, Jacob
	Paul, David		Kemble, Abel
	Porter, Nathan		Landrum, Younger
	Putnam, Perley		Lounsbury, Samuel
	Ramsdale, Anthony		Manrow, John
	Redman, Alonzo		Monroe, John
	Richarson, Moses		Nash, Bartlett
	Rogers, Elenus		Osgood, Richard

Soldiers listed by regiments

1st U.S. Artillery

Peake, John	Eastman, Jonathan
Phillips, John Capin	Emmons, Samuel
Quire, Raymond	Erwin, John
Roland, Alexander	Ewing, John
Rusk, Richard H.	Fanning, Charles
Sawyer, Charles W.	Farien, M.
Shator, Anthony	Fenner, Charles
Shead, Isaac	Figg, John
Slater, Anthony	Finch, Henry
Sprouts, James	Fitzpatick, Edward
Stevens, Benjamin W.	Fleming, John
Stratton, Anthony	Forrester, Robert
Thompson, John	Gafford, Elijah
Thurber, D.	Gaiger, John N.
Tormell, William	Greene, John
Tracksell, Jacob	Gwinn, Benjamin
Walker, William	Halls, James
Walker, William Jr.	Hannion, Jacob
Allen, John	Harard, Ezekiel
Andrews, Samuel	Hart, John
Andries, Samuel	Hays, Patrick
Baker, George	Heaton, Samuel
Barker, Christopher	Herron, Luke
Billings, Jonathan	Hollister, Jesse W.
Brown, George	Holmes, Charles
Browne, William	Hopkins, John
Bush, John	Hunter, William
Bustrill, David	Johnston, Truman
Caldwell, Isaac	Kelly, Paul
Carley, William	Knapp, Abraham
Cilly, Paul	Leonard, Martin
Clarke, Andrew	Lewis, Levi
Clarke, James	Likens, Thomas
Colbern, Jacob	Lockard, Thomas
Cole, James	Loveland, Anson
Cole, Samuel	Mahoney, Thomas
Corley, William	Mann, Neely
Craig, Charles	McChristie, Jesse
Cross, Barnabas	McLean, Richard
Dalaby, James	McManey, John
Darrah, Archibald	McWade, Edward
Day, John	McWilliams, William
Dear, Jonathan	Moody, John
Diffenderfer, Frederick	Moray, Pliny
Dixon, Henry C.	Morrison, William
Dougherty, Dennis	Numm, Richard
Dyson, John	Parker, Abel

1st U.S. Artillery

American Prisoners of War held at Montreal and Quebec during the War of 1812

Soldiers listed by regiments

1st U.S. Artillery	Patterson, Tillender	1st U.S. Rifles	Dutrow, Jacob
	Reader, Thomas		Hartley, Joseph
	Rogers, Robert		Head, William
	Rollins, Thomas		Johnson, Benjamin
	Ryan, James		Land, Joshua
	Saunderson, John		Leggs, David
	Seeney, King		Lloyd, Thompson C.
	Sheffield, Joseph		Lyttle, Daniel
	Sheppard, Elias		Manchester, Noah
	Smith, Benjamin		McEwen, William
	Smith, Caleb		Moran, William
	Smith, James		Octettree, Thomas
	Smith, John		Romaine, Job
	Southack, William		Sedman, Francis
	Spriggs, Leven		Smith, Benjamin
	Spriggs, Nelson		Stanley, Lorner
	Stanhope, Curtis L.		Story, Pliney
	Stickney, Abijah		Tanner, Asa
	Stone, John F. W.		Tanner, Eli
	Summers, William		Temple, Dixon
	Taylor, Reuben		Van Swearingen, Henry
	Truman, Gaius		Waire, Robert
	Turner, Isaac		Wear, Robert
	Valentine, Elijah		Winters, John
	Vaughn, Samuel		Wood, David
	Voucher, Samuel		Wood, Joel
	Wade, Hamilton		Woods, David
	Waggoner, Anthony L.		Yates, Francis
	Walker, Benjamin	1st U.S. Volunteers	Marks, Abraham
	Walker, Solomon S.		Valley, Nathan
	Warner, Martin	1st Volunteer Dragoons	Comfort, Richard
	Waterman, Elisha	2nd U.S. Artillery	Bowen, Thomas
	Weydell, John		Brown, Thomas
	White, Isaac		Brownwell, David
	Whitney, Solomon B.		Doughty, Elias
	Williams, John		Eaton, William
1st U.S. Rifles	Beard, William C.		Ewings, James B.
	Bell, Thomas		Fisher, Anthony
	Brown, Thomas		Foster, George
	Browne, Joseph		Freeman, Jacob
	Browne, Thomas		Gossetts, Stephen
	Crews, Jonathan		Grave, Michael
	Crow, Jonathan		Hedrick, George
	De Masters, Foster		Hughes, John
	Dennison, Simon		Irvine, James B.
	Dougherty, James		Jones, Enoch
	Dove, David		Laughlin, John

Soldiers listed by regiments

2nd U.S. Artillery		3rd U.S. Artillery	
	Lindsay, William		Jackson, Henry
	Lozier, Abraham		Johnson, David
	McGriffen, John		Knowles, Seth
	Mountain, Michael B.		Knowly, Joseph
	Pheuhugan, Thomas		Latham, John
	Plants, Edward		Leders, Jacob
	Reece, Henry		Nye, George
	Roe, Michael		Perkins, Thomas
	Rollapaugh, Cornelius		Pichicen, Anthony
	Rowe, Michael		Pierce, John
	Rucark, Thomas		Purge, John
	Scott, W.		Randall, Isaiah
	Sheller, Samuel		Ray, Robert
	Slaughter, Jonathan		Riley, Charles
	Slaughter, John		Rockway, John
	Stansbury, Samuel		Rooney, Mathias
	Stiles, William		Taylor, John
	Stratton, Thomas		Vasure, Jove
	Trainer, James		Vazier, Joseph
	Trayman, James		Wright, Jabez
	West, Hugh G.		Young, Thomas
	Wheeler, Whiteston	Civilian	Campbell, James
	Wheeler, Wilson		Champion, Elias
	Whitety, Davie R.		Loveland, Asa
	Whitney, David		Steele, Joshua D.
	Bulter, William O.	Indian	Winnet, George
	Davis, William	Kentucky Militia	Berry, Taylor
	Drake, William		Taylor, James
3rd U.S. Artillery	Abbott, Luther	Kentucky or Tennessee	Armstrong, Thomas
	Bayley, Richard Mountjoy	Militia	Atherton, William
	Bowers, Joseph		Bingham, Isaac
	Bowers, Joshua		Brenough, Thomas
	Brown, John		Byrne, Philip
	Coe, James		Cawthorn, Eleazer
	Cutter, Leonard		Dougherty, Jared
	Dolf, Joshua		Ewing, Patrick
	Dolph, Joseph		Harley, George
	Douglas, James		Jack, Henry
	Folks, John		Johnson, Thomas
	Fry, Jacob		Jones, John
	Gray, Benjamin		Kendal, Reason
	Gray, Isaiah		Mahan, Francis
	Gray, William		Masters, John
	Habbett, Lotha		McIlroy, James
	Hammonds, Jonathan		McMellon, William
	Haney, Charles		Million, Rodney
	Howard, Thomas H.		Perkins, John

American Prisoners of War held at Montreal and Quebec during the War of 1812

Soldiers listed by regiments

Kentucky or Tennessee Militia

Ranyard, Francis
Richardson, William
Scirven, Joel
Taylor, Isaac
Turner, John
Walker, Colman
Ward, John
Wilson, William
Withington, Thomas

Militia

Alger, John
Alodget, Sylvester
Anderson, John
Andrews, Eli
Armes, Thomas
Baker, Greenberry
Barnes, Ezra
Battles, John
Botchford, Buford
Bowman, Thaddeus
Boyd, Thomas D.
Brakeman, Roderick
Bristol, Anson
Broghter, Levi
Brown, John
Bryant, Samuel
Burgh, Samuel
Champlain, Dodwick
Chapel, Seth
Chipman, Samuel
Church, Logan
Clark, Samuel
Cole, Daniel S.
Conant, John
Cook, Joseph
Copner, John
Corker, Daniel
Cotter, Edward
Cullum, John
Curfrey, Daniel G.
Cuther, Leonard
Deane, Joseph
Dudley, Ebenezer
Elliott, John
Farmham, Louis
Fay, Hezekiah
Forythe, John
Fowler, Similius

Militia

Frost, Dennis
George, Stone
Gibbs, Ezekiel
Gibson, Fortune
Gillis, Samuel
Goodwin, Simon
Gould, Daniel G.
Green, Joshua
Harris, John
Hathway, William G.
Hawly, Luther
Hewett, Caleb
Hillray, Abner
Hitchcock, William
Hitchler, John
Hopkins, Samuel
Hoty, Joseph D.
Hunt, John
Hutchinson, William
Hyde, Abel
Irvine, John
Johnson, Frunel
Jones, Henry
Jones, Philoster
Kane, Robert
Kennedy, George
Kennedy, James
Kenzie, John
Latham John
Lay, John
Lee, William R.
Linet, Samuel
Linnell, Samuel
Loomis, Jacob
Lynn, James
Lyon, William
Mack, Abner
Maramond, Chester
Martin, Asahel
Martin, William
Meacham, Jesse
Merry, Anson,
Miller, William
Minor, Lewis
Moren, John
Mum, Joel
Munroe, William

Soldiers listed by regiments

Militia	Nate, Daniel	McCobb's Volunteers	Dyer, Daniel
	Olley, Nathaniel		Emery, James
	Parkins, Samuel R.		Ham, Robert
	Parmlee, Ezekiel		Ham, Rufus
	Peck, Mathias		Haynes, Daniel
	Penley, Joseph		Jepson, Ebenezer
	Perry, Daniel		Lovejoy, Jacob
	Price, Rulon		Medae, Thomas
	Purdy, Henry		Merrill, Jacob
	Putnam, John		Merrill, Theodosius
	Randall, Joshua		Moody, John
	Rasdon, Timothy		Morse, Jesse
	Richards, Stephen		Peckam, John
	Richardson, Jonathan		Perley, Joseph
	Riley, James		Phelps, John
	Roberton, Henry		Plummer, Isaac
	Roney, Matthias		Pratt, Charles
	Shattock, Eli		Ray, Jonathan
	Shoemaker, Henry		Read, John P.
	Smith, Ira		Reed, Samuel R.
	Sproat, Peter W.		Richardson, Simeon
	Stetson, Oliver		Smith, Daniel
	Strickland, Richard		Taylor, Thomas
	Strong, Timothy		Trask, Howard
	Thompson, Amos		White, Jesse
	Tignar, Jason		Whitton, George
	Tortham, Apollo		Wilkington, Robert
	Turner, Horace		Woodman, Benjamin
	Tyler, John	New York Militia	Allen, Alva
	Wells, Charles C.		Barker, Ephraim
	Westman, Ephraim		Bennett, John H.
	Wheaton, Jared		Bennett, Uriah W.
	Wilcox, Hiram		Bennett, Waterman
	Willtist, William		Bewell, William
	Wood, Amory		Blackman, Dwight
	Woodbridge, Asa		Brownell, Wontan
	Wright, Samuel		Buck, Abraham
Marine Corps	Lyles, William		Buxton, Daniel
Militia Riflemen	Caldwell, James		Calmes, Marquis
	Shepherd, Samuel		Chamblerlain, Jonathan
			Corey, Philip
McCobb's Volunteers	Allen, Isaac		Doty, John
	Bridge, Franklin		Drake, John
	Campbell, James		Dunham, Reubel
	Campbell, William		Edson, Levi
	Cobb, John		Elsworth, William
	Diesser, Thomas		Fellows, Philip
	Drake, Elisha		

Soldiers listed by regiments

New York Militia

Fisk, Thomas R.
Follett, Abel
Fowler, Alfred
Fullard, Hiram H.
Gillett, Solomon
Green, Elijah
Hagar, Jonathan
Harmon, Ranson
Harris, Thomas
Hollender, Isaac
Hull, Jabez
Jackson, Jacob
Johnson, Mark
Knapp, Silas
Lamont, John
Lewis, William
Ludden, Eley
Lusk, John
Martin, William
McBride, Alexander
McBride, John
McCall, Preserved
McCoomb, George
McDonald, John
McKay, Robert
Millard, Almon H.
Miller, Alexander
Mills, Henry
Moire, Thomas
Nesbett, James
Peabody, Stephen P.
Pelton, Benjamin F.
Pomroy, Richard C.
Ranson, Rothbane
Ray, John
Reynolds, John
Rooney, John
Rowley, Ira
Sabine, Daniel
Sheldon, William
Smith, David
Sturgess, Zed.
Swain, John
Swift, Socrates
Tox, Ambrose P.
Venderheaon, Garham

New York Militia

New York Volunteers

Ohio Militia

Vicker, Philip
Victory, Thomas
Walton, George S.
Warham James
Warren, Thomas
Wilber, John
Wilder, Nathaniel
Wood, Eli
Wright, Jacob
Yarwood, James
Conkley, Joshua
Goddard, Lewis
Graves, Abraham
Barrier, George W.
Brown, Ephraim
Carins, Joseph
Cass, Lewis
Cilley, Joseph
Denny, James
Dent, Abner
Douglass, Robert
Dugan, Thomas
Estie, Charles
Ferris, John
Findlay, James
Guthrie, William
Heckerwelder, Thomas
Joslen, Israel
Kean, (-----)
Kemper, Edward Y.
Kemper, Prestley
Keys, William
Kyle, Samuel B.
Lockhard, Josiah
Lucas, Robert
McArthur, Duncan
McCormick, Samuel
McDonald, John
McFarland, Stephen
Metadow, Samuel
Miller, (-----)
Moore, Thomas
Nelson, John
Northup, Henry
Pentz, Henry
Puthuff, William H.
Robinson, John

Soldiers listed by regiments

Ohio Militia	Rose, Levi	Unknown	Adams, William
	Rupe, David		Alexander, James
	Sanderson, George		Allen, Ira
	Sawyer, William		Allen, Samuel
	Schenck, Peter L.		Aycaulh, James
	Seward, (-----)		Ayres, John
	Sharp, John		Bacon, Jabbec
	Sheets, John		Badgrove, John
	Sloan, James W.		Baines, John
	Spencer, John		Bare, Thomas
	Stewart, Samuel		Barker, Joseph
	Trimble, William		Barrs, Henry
	Turner, William		Barry, Sampson
	Van Horne, Thomas B.		Bays, Jacob
	Walker, (-----)		Beach, James
	Wallace, Robert		Beatie, William
	Waring, (-----)		Berger, William
	Warner, Wynkoop		Berkford, John
Pennsylvania Volunteers	Bruce, William		Bills, Chester
Porter's Volunteers	Norton, Daniel B.		Blachard, B. R.
Volunteers	Brink, Orson		Blakeley, Abel
	Campbell, James		Blatenburger, Jacob
	Darnsforth, Joseph		Boggs, Lyman
	Dressen, Thomas		Boothe, B.
	Fray, Jonathan		Boyce, George
	Hann, Robert		Boyce, Jacob
	Hann, Rufus		Boyd, Dennis
	Harrick, Oliver		Bristol, Abram
	Harvey, William		Bromer, Abram
	Isham, Ebenezer		Brooks, Roswell
	Lythe, Daniel		Brower, James
	Madden, Thomas		Brown, John
	Merritt, Jonathan		Brown, Llewellyn
	Morse, Joshua		Brown, Thomas
	Murray, James		Brown, William
	Park, Luther		Buckingham, Jared
	Payne, Reuben		Burrell, James
	Phillips, John C.		Butter, Michael
	Rice, Samuel		Can, Samuel
	Richards, Stephen		Carr, Daniel
	Speey, Jacob		Carroll, Peter
	Temple, Lorain		Carter, D.
	White, Joshua		Carter, J. F.
	Whitton, George		Castler, A.
	Withingston, Robert		Castler, J.
Unknown	Abrahams, Cyrus		Champberlain, Rufus
	Ackley, Benjamin		Chappel, Joseph

Soldiers listed by regiments

Unknown

Churchill, Oliver
Clark, J.
Clark, Perry
Clement, David
Coleman, Charles
Colver, Peter
Converse, K.
Coon, John
Corlis, Ira C.
Couther, Jonathan
Cowder, David
Cromer, Anthony
Cronigu, John
Cunningham, Cornelius
Custis, Daniel
Cuylu, John
Davis, David
Davis, J. J.
Davis, John
Davis, Samuel
Davis, Stephen
Davis, William
Dean, Randall
Dearborne, Solomon
DeBogert, J. N.
Demolunt, Alexander
Deprew, John
Derker, Celey
Dewall, Alvin
Dibble, Nathaniel
Dickinson, John
Docker, Zelia
Doors, F.
Dosery, Jonathan
Doty, Joseph
Dugat, A.
Dutcher, James
Easter, Stephen
Ennett, William
Ennis, James
Ferguson, William
Finch, Henry
Finney, Elihu
Fisk, John J.
Fleming, Jacob
Fort, Abram
Francis, Seth

Unknown

Friend, John D.
Fuller, John
Furman, Jeremiah
Gady, Martin
Gibbs, Reuben
Gillispie, William
Gillaway, H.
Gillerman, Gabriel
Golden, Benjamin
Goodenow, E.
Grady, Martin
Grant, Amasa T.
Green, Caleb
Green, Elias
Green, William
Greenleaf, Samuel
Griggs, William
Griffith, John
Guile, David
Hackett, William
Haines, Daniel
Hall, Farmington
Hall, Samuel
Halle, John
Hammond, Thomas
Handy, Nathan
Handy, P.
Hargrove, John
Harraday, Elisha
Harris, J.
Hartland, William
Hawkins, John
Hawkins, Robert
Hazlett, John
Herrick, Eli
Herrington, Daniel
Hewlett, William
Hews, Elias
Hews, Joseph
Hibbard, J. W.
Hicks, John R.
Hidby, S.
Hiest, David
Higgly, Eber
High, Joel
Hight, Isaac
Hile, Artimus

Soldiers listed by regiments

Unknown		Unknown	
	Hilliard, David		Lord, Joseph
	Hodge, Benjamin		Magee, William
	Hogelan, William		Magerman, J. N.
	Holmes, Daniel		Martin, Leluancy
	Holton, James		Mason, John
	Holtzboun, Garret		Mason, Richard
	Hooker, George		Masters, William
	Howard, Barnabas		McArthur, Alexander
	Howard, Joseph		McBride, James
	Howell, John D.		McCormick, James
	Huber, Jacob		McGarley, Jesse
	Hull, Warner		McGee, P.
	Humes, Daniel		McGee, William
	Hunt, Solomon		McKay, William
	Ingall, Jonathan		McMullin, Archibald
	Ives, Amos		Merrill, Mathias
	Jackson, Robert		Messenger, Grove
	James, John		Miller, Gordon
	Jassar, George		Miller, James
	Jerris, Barney		Mills, Joseph
	Johnson, Daniel		Mirak, J.
	Johnson, Joel		Misner, Oscar
	Jones, Henry		Mitchell, William
	Jones, Phinehal		Moody, John
	Kelly, James		Mooney, Peter
	Kelly, John		Morris, Jacob
	Ketch, Klaus		Morrison, Robert
	Kiler, John		Moutton, Elisha
	Kimbal, Moses		Mullen, Enoch
	Kimball, Benjamin		Neiodle, Alpheus
	Kinter, Solomon		Newton, Asa
	Knapp, John		Nichols, Elijah
	Laforge, Stephen		Nichols, Thomas
	Lamson, John		Nicloge, Parshal
	Lander, Charles		Nicnard, Peter
	Landon, D.		Norris, James
	Lane, Benjamin		Norton, John
	Lark, John		Oakley, Jonathan
	Lawrence, Abel		Ogden, Thomas
	Lawton, Terry		Ogle, Howard
	Lee, Abram		Ongy, Peter
	Lee, Isaac		Parker, William
	Leroy, Charles M.		Parrish, Peter
	Lewis, Ria		Parsons, Paul
	Licker, Francis		Partridge, (-----)
	Lincoln, William		Patterson, H.
	Lockyear, Benjamin		Patterson, J.

Soldiers listed by regiments

Unknown

Pawley, Francis
Pearson, William
Phillips, Joseph
Pierce, Elias
Pomers, John
Pratt, Nathaniel
Preston, David
Price, Obadiah
Ranney, William
Read, John T.
Reall, Abner
Reed, Isaac
Reynolds, James
Reynolds, William
Rice, William
Richardson, John
Ridgley, William
Roach, James
Roach, William
Robbins, Conrad
Roberts, John
Rome, Asa R.
Rood, Amos
Rudderkesk, K.
Rumrell, A. B.
Rumsey, Nathaniel
Rumsey, Peter
Sabin, Oliver
Sanborn, Charles
Sanford, L.
Savory, Solomon
Schenk, Henry
Schooley, William
Schufelt, David
Scott, John
Scott, William
Seaman, Chauncey
Shaver, George
Sheffield, Joseph
Simpson, John
Sliter, J.
Sloan, Reuben
Sloan, Silvester
Smith, Alexander
Smith, Benjamin
Smith, Justus
Smith, Nathan

Unknown

Smith, William
Snow, Daniel G.
Snyder, George
Southerland, Sylvester
Spark, Joseph
Stephens, T.
Stevens, Benjamin W.
Stevens, Roswell
Stewart, William M.
Stocker, Jesse L.
Stone, John F.
Stone, Westerly
Stratton, Gardner
Summit, Dennis
Swartout, Perry
Swill, William
Talbot, David
Taylor, Richard
Taylor, William
Thomas, Allen
Thomas, Bennett
Thomas, James
Thompson, Robert
Thornton, Reuben
Thurston,
    George Washington
Tillaban, William
Torry, Abner
Traux, J. B.
Tromell, William
Trulove, Barney
Tundy, Jacob
Turnald, John
Turner, Abner
Turner, Cornelius
Turner, John
Turner, Nathan
Van Curen, Edward
Van Naleknburgh, J.
Van Tile, John
Vandermark, Charles
VanGuilder, Abram
Vanslyck, Nicholas
Varley, Joseph
Venice, Philip
Walker, David
Walker, J.

Soldiers listed by regiments

Unknown

Wall, Thomas
Warner, Elisha
Warner, Z.
Webb, Joseph
Webb, Samuel
Weeks, J.
Weiden, Joseph
Wells, Caleb
Wentey, Benjamin L.
Westland, DeWitt
Westtwok, Abraham
Wheeler, Uriah
White, Richard
White, William
Whitmore, Stephen
Wicklow, William
Williams, John
Wilson, Benjamin
Wilson, Samuel
Wilson, William
Witt, Ira
Wood, Thomas B.
Wooster, William D.
Wright, Samuel
Wynn, Abram
Wyncy, David
Yanges, Philip
Yates, Henry D.
Young, Ephraim
Young, Thomas

Soldiers listed by regiments

British Records

Abbey, Horace B. Prisoner: 1895 - Rank: Corporal - Name of Prize: Land forces - By what ship or how taken: Taken on shore - Discharged: 8 Nov 1814 - By what order: George No. 515 by Sir George Prevost - Source: List of American Prisoners of War discharged at Quebec - Name of prize ship: Land forces.

Abbott, John Prisoner: 1832 - Rank: Private - Name of Prize: Land forces - By what ship or how taken: Taken on shore - Discharged: 8 Nov 1814 - By what order: George No. 515 by Sir George Prevost - Source: List of American Prisoners of War discharged at Quebec - Name of prize ship: Land forces.

Ackley, William Prisoner: 450 - Rank: Private - Name of Prize: Land forces - By what ship or how taken: Taken on shore - Discharged: 10 Aug 1813 - By what order: HMS Regales by order of his Excellency Sir George Prevost - Source: List of American Prisoners of War discharged at Quebec - Name of prize ship: Land forces.

Adney, William D. Prisoner: 1764 - Rank: Sergeant - Name of Prize: Land forces - By what ship or how taken: Taken on shore - Discharged: 8 Nov 1814 - By what order: George No. 515 by Sir George Prevost - Source: List of American Prisoners of War discharged at Quebec - Name of prize ship: Land forces.

Allen, Isaac Prisoner: 213 - Rank: Private - Name of Prize: Eagle - By what ship or how taken: Man of war - Discharged: 31 Oct 1813 - By what order: HMS Malabar Transport by order of his Excellency Sir George Prevost - Source: List of American Prisoners of War discharged at Quebec - Name of prize ship: Eagle.

Allen, John (1) Prisoner: 108 - Rank: Private - Name of Prize: Land forces - By what ship or how taken: Taken on shore - Discharged: 31 Oct 1813 - By what order: HMS Malabar Transport by order of his Excellency Sir George Prevost - Source: List of American Prisoners of War discharged at Quebec - Name of prize ship: Land forces.

Allen, John (2) Prisoner: 280 - Rank: Private - Name of Prize: Land forces - By what ship or how taken: Taken on shore - Discharged: 31 Oct 1813 - By what order: HMS Malabar Transport by order of his Excellency Sir George Prevost - Source: List of American Prisoners of War discharged at Quebec - Name of prize ship: Land forces.

Allen, Thomas Prisoner: 157 - Rank: Seaman - Name of Prize: Growler - By what ship or how taken: Man of war - Discharged: 31 Oct 1813 - By what order: HMS Malabar Transport by order of his Excellency Sir George Prevost - Source: List of American Prisoners of War discharged at Quebec - Name of prize ship: Growler.

Ames, Thomas Prisoner: 978 - Rank: Private - Name of Prize: Land forces - By what ship or how taken: Taken on shore - Discharged: 31 Oct 1813 - By what order: HMS Malabar Transport by order of his Excellency Sir George Prevost - Source: List of American Prisoners of War discharged at Quebec - Name of prize ship: Land forces.

Amling, Ezra Prisoner: 1315 - Rank: Private - Source: Account of American prisoners of war who died at Quebec between 14 February 1814 and 23 December 1814 - Ship or Corps: Land forces - Vessel: Taken on shore - Place born: Vermont - Age: 23 - Where taken: Fort Niagara - Date of death: 3 Jun 1814 - Disorder or casualty: Anasarca.

Amyet, John Prisoner: 1348 – Rank: Private - By what ship or how taken: Troops - Time when: 19 Dec 1813 - Place where: Fort Niagara - Whether man of war, privateer, or merchant vessel: Taken on shore - When received: 29 Jan 1814 - From what ship or whence received: Montreal by land carriages. - Prisoner: 1348 - Rank: Private - Name of Prize: Land forces - By what ship or how taken: Taken on shore - Discharged: 4 May 1814 - By what order: Returned to the United States - Source: List of American Prisoners of War discharged at Quebec - Name of prize ship: Land forces.

Anderson, Peter Prisoner: 1278 - Rank: Private - By what ship or how taken: Troops - Time when: 19 Dec 1813 - Place where: Fort Niagara - Whether man of war, privateer, or merchant vessel: Taken on shore - When received: 29 Jan 1814 - From what ship or whence received: Montreal by land carriages. - Prisoner: 1278 - Rank: Private - Name of Prize: Land forces - By what ship or how taken: Taken on shore - Discharged: 4 May 1814 - By what order: Returned to the United States - Source: List of American Prisoners of War discharged at Quebec - Name of prize ship: Land forces.

Andrews, David (1) Prisoner: 470 - Rank: Private - Name of Prize: Land forces - By what ship or how taken: Taken on shore - Discharged: 10 Aug 1813 - By what order: HMS Regulus by order of his Excellency Sir George Prevost - Source: List of American Prisoners of War discharged at Quebec - Name of prize ship: Land forces.

Andrews, David (2) Prisoner: 456 - Rank: Private - Name of Prize: Land forces - By what ship or how taken: Taken on shore - Discharged: 10 Aug 1813 - By what order: HMS Regulus by order of his Excellency Sir George Prevost - Source: List of American Prisoners of War discharged at Quebec - Name of prize ship: Land forces.

Andrews, Edward Prisoner: 725 - Rank: Private - Name of Prize: Land forces - By what ship or how taken: Taken on shore - Discharged: 10 Aug 1813 - By what order: HMS Regulus by order of his Excellency Sir George

Prevost - Source: List of American Prisoners of War discharged at Quebec - Name of prize ship: Land forces.

Andrews, Stephen   Prisoner: 645 - Rank: Private - Name of Prize: Land forces - By what ship or how taken: Taken on shore - Discharged: 10 Aug 1813 - By what order: HMS Regulus by order of his Excellency Sir George Prevost - Source: List of American Prisoners of War discharged at Quebec - Name of prize ship: Land forces.

Archer, Isaac   Prisoner: 1395 - Rank: Corporal - By what ship or how taken: Troops - Time when: 19 Dec 1813 - Place where: Fort Niagara - Whether man of war, privateer, or merchant vessel: Taken on shore - When received: 29 Jan 1814 - From what ship or whence received: Montreal by land carriages.
Prisoner: 1395 - Rank: Corporal - Name of Prize: Land forces - By what ship or how taken: Taken on shore - Discharged: 4 May 1814 - By what order: Returned to the United States - Source: List of American Prisoners of War discharged at Quebec - Name of prize ship: Land forces.

Archer, Robert   Prisoner: 1396 - Rank: Private - By what ship or how taken: Troops - Time when: 19 Dec 1813 - Place where: Fort Niagara - Whether man of war, privateer, or merchant vessel: Taken on shore - When received: 29 Jan 1814 - From what ship or whence received: Montreal by land carriages. - Prisoner: 1396 - Rank: Private - Name of Prize: Land forces - By what ship or how taken: Taken on shore - Discharged: 4 May 1814 - By what order: Returned to the United States - Source: List of American Prisoners of War discharged at Quebec - Name of prize ship: Land forces.

Armour, Robert   Prisoner: 1322 - Rank: Private - By what ship or how taken: Troops - Time when: 19 Dec 1813 - Place where: Fort Niagara - Whether man of war, privateer, or merchant vessel: Taken on shore - When received: 29 Jan 1814 - From what ship or whence received: Montreal by land carriages. - Prisoner: 1322 - Rank: Private - Name of Prize: Land forces - By what ship or how taken: Taken on shore - Discharged: 4 May 1814 - By what order: Returned to the United States - Source: List of American Prisoners of War discharged at Quebec - Name of prize ship: Land forces.

Armstrong, Earl   Prisoner: 1703 - Rank: Private - Name of Prize: Land forces - By what ship or how taken: Taken on shore - Discharged: 8 Nov 1814 - By what order: George No. 515 by Sir George Prevost - Source: List of American Prisoners of War discharged at Quebec - Name of prize ship: Land forces.

Armstrong, George   Prisoner: 1917 - Rank: Private - Name of Prize: Land forces - By what ship or how taken: Taken on shore - Discharged: 8 Nov 1814 - By what order: George No. 515 by Sir George Prevost - Source: List of American Prisoners of War discharged at Quebec - Name of prize ship: Land forces.

Armstrong, Isaac   Prisoner: 1915 - Rank: Private - Name of Prize: Land forces - By what ship or how taken: Taken on shore - Discharged: 8 Nov 1814 - By what order: George No. 515 by Sir George Prevost - Source: List of American Prisoners of War discharged at Quebec - Name of prize ship: Land forces.

Armstrong, Thomas   Prisoner: 1140 - Rank: Private - By what ship or how taken: Troops - Time when: 22 Jan 1813 - Place where: Rapids, River Raisin - Whether man of war, privateer, or merchant vessel: Taken on shore - When received: 25 Nov 1813 - From what ship or whence received: Town goal. - Prisoner: 1140 - Rank: Private - Name of Prize: Land forces - By what ship or how taken: Taken on shore - Discharged: 3 Apr 1814 - By what order: Returned to the United States - Source: List of American Prisoners of War discharged at Quebec - Name of prize ship: Land forces.

Armstrong, William   Prisoner: 464 - Rank: Private - Name of Prize: Land forces - By what ship or how taken: Taken on shore - Discharged: 10 Aug 1813 - By what order: HMS Regulus by order of his Excellency Sir George Prevost - Source: List of American Prisoners of War discharged at Quebec - Name of prize ship: Land forces.

Arnold, James   Prisoner: 1356 - Rank: Private - By what ship or how taken: Troops - Time when: 19 Dec 1813 - Place where: Fort Niagara - Whether man of war, privateer, or merchant vessel: Taken on shore - When received: 29 Jan 1814 - From what ship or whence received: Montreal by land carriages. - Prisoner: 1356 - Rank: Private - Name of Prize: Land forces - By what ship or how taken: Taken on shore - Discharged: 4 May 1814 - By what order: Returned to the United States - Source: List of American Prisoners of War discharged at Quebec - Name of prize ship: Land forces.

Artemus, George   Prisoner: 1955 - Rank: Musician - Name of Prize: Land forces - By what ship or how taken: Taken on shore - Discharged: 13 Mar 1815 - By what order: Returned to the United States - Source: List of American Prisoners of War discharged at Quebec - Name of prize ship: Land forces.

Arthurs, James   Prisoner: 582 - Rank: Private - Name of Prize: Land forces - By what ship or how taken: Taken on shore - Discharged: 10 Aug 1813 - By what order: HMS Regulus by order of his Excellency Sir George Prevost - Source: List of American Prisoners of War discharged at Quebec - Name of prize ship: Land forces.

Artis, John   Prisoner: 489 - Rank: Private - Name of Prize: Land forces - By what ship or how taken: Taken on shore - Discharged: 10 Aug 1813 - By what order: HMS Regulus by order of his Excellency Sir George Prevost - Source: List of American Prisoners of War discharged at Quebec - Name of prize ship: Land forces.

Ashley, Jonas   Prisoner: 1899 - Rank: Private - Name of Prize: Land forces - By what ship or how taken: Taken on shore - Discharged: 8 Nov 1814 - By what order: George No. 515 by Sir George Prevost - Source: List of American Prisoners of War discharged at Quebec - Name of prize ship: Land forces.

Atchley, Daniel   Prisoner: 1406 - Rank: Private - By what ship or how taken: Troops - Time when: 19 Dec 1813 - Place where: Fort Niagara - Whether man of war, privateer, or merchant vessel: Taken on shore - When received: 29 Jan 1814 - From what ship or whence received: Montreal by land carriages. - Prisoner: 1406 - Rank: Private - Name of Prize: Land forces - By what ship or how taken: Taken on shore - Discharged: 4 May 1814 - By what order: Returned to the United States - Source: List of American Prisoners of War discharged at Quebec - Name of prize ship: Land forces.

Atchley, Joseph   Prisoner: 1350 - Rank: Private - By what ship or how taken: Troops - Time when: 19 Dec 1813 - Place where: Fort Niagara - Whether man of war, privateer, or merchant vessel: Taken on shore - When received: 29 Jan 1814 - From what ship or whence received: Montreal by land carriages.

Atchley, Joseph   Prisoner: 1350 - Rank: Private - Name of Prize: Land forces - By what ship or how taken: Taken on shore - Discharged: 4 May 1814 - By what order: Returned to the United States - Source: List of American Prisoners of War discharged at Quebec - Name of prize ship: Land forces.

Atherton, William   Prisoner: 1157 - Rank: Private - By what ship or how taken: Troops - Time when: 5 May 1813 - Place where: Rapids, River Raisin - Whether man of war, privateer, or merchant vessel: Taken on shore - When received: 25 Nov 1813 - From what ship or whence received: Town goal. - Prisoner: 1157 - Rank: Private - Name of Prize: Land forces - By what ship or how taken: Taken on shore - Discharged: 4 May 1814 - By what order: Returned to the United States - Source: List of American Prisoners of War discharged at Quebec - Name of prize ship: Land forces.

Atkins, Henry   Prisoner: 1670 - Rank: Seaman - Name of Prize: Taken in a gig (a ship's long boat) - By what ship or how taken: Man of war - Discharged: 7 Nov 1813 - By what order: HMS Freedom No. 582 by order of his Excellency Sir George Prevost - Source: List of American Prisoners of War discharged at Quebec - Name of prize ship: Taken in a gig (a ship's long boat).

Austin, William   Prisoner: 1782 - Rank: Private - Name of Prize: Land forces - By what ship or how taken: Taken on shore - Discharged: 8 Nov 1814 - By what order: George No. 515 by Sir George Prevost - Source: List of American Prisoners of War discharged at Quebec - Name of prize ship: Land forces.

Avery, Matualas   Prisoner: 964 - Rank: Private - Name of Prize: Land forces - By what ship or how taken: Taken on shore - Discharged: 2 Nov 1813 - Source: List of Prisoners received on board the Malabar, discharged from hospital - Name of prize ship: Land forces.

Avery, Richard   Prisoner: 963 - Rank: Private - Name of Prize: Land forces - By what ship or how taken: Taken on shore - Discharged: 31 Oct 1813 - By what order: HMS Malabar Transport by order of his Excellency Sir George Prevost - Source: List of American Prisoners of War discharged at Quebec - Name of prize ship: Land forces.

Ayres, John   Prisoner: 138 - Rank: Private - Source: Account of American prisoners of war who died at Quebec in the Months of July, August & September 1813 - Ship or Corps: Land forces - Vessel: Taken on shore - Place born: New Bedford - Age: 40 - Where taken: Stoney Point - Date of death: 15 Aug 1813.

Ayres, Samuel   Prisoner: 1907 - Rank: Corporal - Name of Prize: Land forces - By what ship or how taken: Taken on shore - Discharged: 8 Nov 1814 - By what order: George No. 515 by Sir George Prevost - Source: List of American Prisoners of War discharged at Quebec - Name of prize ship: Land forces.

Bacon, Jabez   Prisoner: 40 - Rank: Private - Source: Account of American prisoners of war who died at Quebec in the Months of July, August & September 1813 - Ship or Corps: Land forces - Vessel: Taken on shore - Place born: Neddick, MA - Age: 38 - Where taken: Stoney Point - Date of death: 6 Aug 1813.

Bacon, Moses   Prisoner: 1831 - Rank: Private - Name of Prize: Land forces - By what ship or how taken: Taken on shore - Discharged: 8 Nov 1814 - By what order: George No. 515 by Sir George Prevost - Source: List of American Prisoners of War discharged at Quebec - Name of prize ship: Land forces.

Bacon, Nathan   Prisoner: 630 - Rank: Private - Name of Prize: Land forces - By what ship or how taken: Taken on shore - Discharged: 10 Aug 1813 - By what order: HMS Regulus by order of his Excellency Sir George Prevost - Source: List of American Prisoners of War discharged at Quebec - Name of prize ship: Land forces.

Baker, Daniel B.   Prisoner: 332 - Rank: Private - Name of Prize: Land forces - By what ship or how taken: Taken on shore - Discharged: 31 Oct 1813 - By what order: HMS Malabar Transport by order of his Excellency Sir George Prevost - Source: List of American Prisoners of War discharged at Quebec - Name of prize ship: Land forces.

Baker, George   Prisoner: 952 - Rank: Private - Name of Prize: Land forces - By what ship or how taken: Taken on shore - Discharged: 31 Oct 1813 - By what order: HMS Malabar Transport by order of his Excellency Sir

George Prevost - Source: List of American Prisoners of War discharged at Quebec - Name of prize ship: Land forces.

Baker, John   Prisoner: 676 - Rank: Private - Name of Prize: Land forces - By what ship or how taken: Taken on shore - Discharged: 10 Aug 1813 - By what order: HMS Regulus by order of his Excellency Sir George Prevost - Source: List of American Prisoners of War discharged at Quebec - Name of prize ship: Land forces.

Baker, Lloyd   Prisoner: 1791 - Rank: Private - Name of Prize: Land forces - By what ship or how taken: Taken on shore - Discharged: 8 Nov 1814 - By what order: George No. 515 by Sir George Prevost - Source: List of American Prisoners of War discharged at Quebec - Name of prize ship: Land forces.

Baker, Samuel (1)   Prisoner: 1030 - Rank: Seaman - Name of Prize: Growler - By what ship or how taken: Man of war - Discharged: 31 Oct 1813 - By what order: HMS Malabar Transport by order of his Excellency Sir George Prevost - Source: List of American Prisoners of War discharged at Quebec - Name of prize ship: Growler.

Baker, Samuel (2)   Prisoner: 1778 - Rank: Corporal - Name of Prize: Land forces - By what ship or how taken: Taken on shore - Discharged: 8 Nov 1814 - By what order: George No. 515 by Sir George Prevost - Source: List of American Prisoners of War discharged at Quebec - Name of prize ship: Land forces.

Baldwyn, John   Prisoner: 1752 - Rank: Private - Name of Prize: Tigress - By what ship or how taken: Man of war - Discharged: 8 Nov 1814 - By what order: George No. 515 by Sir George Prevost - Source: List of American Prisoners of War discharged at Quebec - Name of prize ship: Tigress.

Ballard, James H.   Prisoner: 1667 - Rank: Lieutenant - Name of Prize: Land forces - By what ship or how taken: Taken on shore - Discharged: 10 Nov 1814 - By what order: Stately No. 400 to Halifax by order of Sir George Prevost - Source: List of American Prisoners of War discharged at Quebec - Name of prize ship: Land forces.

Ballard, John   Prisoner: 188 - Rank: Private - Name of Prize: Growler - By what ship or how taken: Man of war - Discharged: 31 Oct 1813 - By what order: HMS Malabar Transport by order of his Excellency Sir George Prevost - Source: List of American Prisoners of War discharged at Quebec - Name of prize ship: Growler.

Banger, Thomas   Prisoner: 1093 - Rank: Private - Name of Prize: Land forces - By what ship or how taken: Taken on shore - Discharged: 31 Oct 1813 - By what order: HMS Malabar Transport by order of his Excellency Sir George Prevost - Source: List of American Prisoners of War discharged at Quebec - Name of prize ship: Land forces.

Bangs, Seth   Prisoner: 41 - Rank: Private - Name of Prize: Land forces - By what ship or how taken: Taken on shore - Discharged: 31 Oct 1813 - By what order: HMS Malabar Transport by order of his Excellency Sir George Prevost - Source: List of American Prisoners of War discharged at Quebec - Name of prize ship: Land forces.

Banker, Christopher   Prisoner: 1236 - Rank: Sergeant - By what ship or how taken: Troops - Time when: 19 Dec 1813 - Place where: Fort Niagara - Whether man of war, privateer, or merchant vessel: Taken on shore - When received: 29 Jan 1814 - From what ship or whence received: Montreal by land carriages. - Prisoner: 1236 - Rank: Sergeant - Name of Prize: Land forces - By what ship or how taken: Taken on shore - Discharged: 4 May 1814 - By what order: Returned to the United States - Source: List of American Prisoners of War discharged at Quebec - Name of prize ship: Land forces.

Baptiste, John   Prisoner: 1786 - Rank: Private - Name of Prize: Land forces - By what ship or how taken: Taken on shore - Discharged: 8 Nov 1814 - By what order: George No. 515 by Sir George Prevost - Source: List of American Prisoners of War discharged at Quebec - Name of prize ship: Land forces.

Barber, John   Prisoner: 840 - Rank: Private - Name of Prize: Land forces - By what ship or how taken: Taken on shore - Discharged: 31 Oct 1813 - By what order: HMS Malabar Transport by order of his Excellency Sir George Prevost - Source: List of American Prisoners of War discharged at Quebec - Name of prize ship: Land forces.

Barnes, Jacob   Prisoner: 1361 - Rank: Private - By what ship or how taken: Troops - Time when: 19 Dec 1813 - Place where: Fort Niagara - Whether man of war, privateer, or merchant vessel: Taken on shore - When received: 29 Jan 1814 - From what ship or whence received: Montreal by land carriages. - Prisoner: 1361 - Rank: Private - Name of Prize: Land forces - By what ship or how taken: Taken on shore - Discharged: 4 May 1814 - By what order: Returned to the United States - Source: List of American Prisoners of War discharged at Quebec - Name of prize ship: Land forces.

Barnes, Thomas   Prisoner: 732 - Rank: Private - Name of Prize: Land forces - By what ship or how taken: Taken on shore - Discharged: 10 Aug 1813 - By what order: HMS Regulus by order of his Excellency Sir George Prevost - Source: List of American Prisoners of War discharged at Quebec - Name of prize ship: Land forces.

Barrell, Dyer   Prisoner: 1792 - Rank: Sergeant - Name of Prize: Land forces - By what ship or how taken: Taken on shore - Discharged: 8 Nov 1814 - By what order: George No. 515 by Sir George Prevost - Source: List of American Prisoners of War discharged at Quebec - Name of prize ship: Land forces.

Barron, John   Prisoner: 364 - Rank: Private - Name of Prize: Land forces - By what ship or how taken: Taken on shore - Discharged: 31 Oct 1813 - By what order: HMS Malabar Transport by order of his Excellency Sir George Prevost - Source: List of American Prisoners of War discharged at Quebec - Name of prize ship: Land forces.

Bascomb, Samuel   Prisoner: 1222 - Rank: Private - Source: Account of American prisoners of war who died at Quebec between 14 February 1814 and 23 December 1814 - Ship or Corps: Land forces - Vessel: Taken on shore - Place born: Massachusetts - Age: 19 - Where taken: Fort Niagara - Date of death: 21 Apr 1814 - Disorder or casualty: Gun shot wound.

Bassell, John   Prisoner: 1276 - Rank: Corporal - By what ship or how taken: Troops - Time when: 19 Dec 1813 - Place where: Fort Niagara - Whether man of war, privateer, or merchant vessel: Taken on shore - When received: 29 Jan 1814 - From what ship or whence received: Montreal by land carriages. - Prisoner: 1276 - Rank: Corporal - Name of Prize: Land forces - By what ship or how taken: Taken on shore - Discharged: 24 Feb 1814 - By what order: Volunteered for the New Brunswick Fencibles - Source: List of American Prisoners of War discharged at Quebec - Name of prize ship: Land forces.

Batch, George   Prisoner: 462 - Rank: Private - Name of Prize: Land forces - By what ship or how taken: Taken on shore - Discharged: 31 Oct 1813 - By what order: HMS Malabar Transport by order of his Excellency Sir George Prevost - Source: List of American Prisoners of War discharged at Quebec - Name of prize ship: Land forces.

Batchelor, Orson   Prisoner: 50 - Rank: Private - Name of Prize: Land forces - By what ship or how taken: Taken on shore - Discharged: 31 Oct 1813 - By what order: HMS Malabar Transport by order of his Excellency Sir George Prevost - Source: List of American Prisoners of War discharged at Quebec - Name of prize ship: Land forces.

Batty, Joseph   Prisoner: 153 - Rank: Seaman - Name of Prize: Growler - By what ship or how taken: Man of war - Discharged: 31 Oct 1813 - By what order: HMS Malabar Transport by order of his Excellency Sir George Prevost - Source: List of American Prisoners of War discharged at Quebec - Name of prize ship: Growler.

Bayley, Moses   Prisoner: 1733 - Rank: Seaman - Name of Prize: Scorpion - By what ship or how taken: Man of war - Discharged: 7 Nov 1813 - By what order: HMS Freedom No. 582 by order of his Excellency Sir George Prevost - Source: List of American Prisoners of War discharged at Quebec - Name of prize ship: Scorpion.

Bays, Jacob   Prisoner: 288 - Rank: Private - Name of Prize: Land forces - By what ship or how taken: Taken on shore - Discharged: 31 Oct 1813 - By what order: HMS Malabar Transport by order of his Excellency Sir George Prevost - Source: List of American Prisoners of War discharged at Quebec - Name of prize ship: Land forces.

Beall, John   Prisoner: 469 - Rank: Private - Name of Prize: Land forces - By what ship or how taken: Taken on shore - Discharged: 10 Aug 1813 - By what order: HMS Regulus by order of his Excellency Sir George Prevost - Source: List of American Prisoners of War discharged at Quebec - Name of prize ship: Land forces.

Beals, William   Prisoner: 1192 - By what ship or how taken: Citizen - When received: 12 Dec 1813 - From what ship or whence received: Town goal. - Prisoner: 1192 - Rank: Private - Name of Prize: Land forces - By what ship or how taken: Taken on shore - Discharged: 4 May 1814 - By what order: Returned to the United States - Source: List of American Prisoners of War discharged at Quebec - Name of prize ship: Land forces.

Bear, Henry   Prisoner: 291 - Rank: Private - Name of Prize: Land forces - By what ship or how taken: Taken on shore - Discharged: 31 Oct 1813 - By what order: HMS Malabar Transport by order of his Excellency Sir George Prevost - Source: List of American Prisoners of War discharged at Quebec - Name of prize ship: Land forces.

Beard, John   Prisoner: 509 - Rank: Private - Name of Prize: Land forces - By what ship or how taken: Taken on shore - Discharged: 10 Aug 1813 - By what order: HMS Regulus by order of his Excellency Sir George Prevost - Source: List of American Prisoners of War discharged at Quebec - Name of prize ship: Land forces.

Beard, Richard   Prisoner: 434 - Rank: Private - Name of Prize: Land forces - By what ship or how taken: Taken on shore - Discharged: 10 Aug 1813 - By what order: HMS Regulus by order of his Excellency Sir George Prevost - Source: List of American Prisoners of War discharged at Quebec - Name of prize ship: Land forces.

Beck, Andrew   Prisoner: 276 - Rank: Musician - Name of Prize: Land forces - By what ship or how taken: Taken on shore - Discharged: 31 Oct 1813 - By what order: HMS Malabar Transport by order of his Excellency Sir George Prevost - Source: List of American Prisoners of War discharged at Quebec - Name of prize ship: Land forces.

Beckford, John   Prisoner: 1080 - Rank: Private - Name of Prize: Land forces - By what ship or how taken: Taken on shore - Discharged: 31 Oct 1813 - By what order: HMS Malabar Transport by order of his Excellency Sir George Prevost - Source: List of American Prisoners of War discharged at Quebec - Name of prize ship: Land forces.

Beech, James   Prisoner: 1116 - Rank: Private - Name of Prize: Land forces - By what ship or how taken: Taken on shore - Discharged: 31 Oct 1813 - By what order: HMS Malabar Transport by order of his Excellency Sir George Prevost - Source: List of American Prisoners of War discharged at Quebec - Name of prize ship: Land forces.

Bell, Orling   Prisoner: 1906 - Rank: Private - Name of Prize: Land forces - By what ship or how taken: Taken on shore - Discharged: 8 Nov 1814 - By what order: George No. 515 by Sir George Prevost - Source: List of American Prisoners of War discharged at Quebec - Name of prize ship: Land forces.

Bellville, Levi   Prisoner: 815 - Rank: Private - Name of Prize: Land forces - By what ship or how taken: Taken on shore - Discharged: 31 Oct 1813 - By what order: HMS Malabar Transport by order of his Excellency Sir George Prevost - Source: List of American Prisoners of War discharged at Quebec - Name of prize ship: Land forces.

Bench, Levi   Prisoner: 1967 - Rank: Private - Name of Prize: Land forces - By what ship or how taken: Taken on shore - Discharged: 13 Mar 1815 - By what order: Returned to the United States - Source: List of American Prisoners of War discharged at Quebec - Name of prize ship: Land forces.

Benedict, Henry   Prisoner: 1797 - Rank: Corporal - Name of Prize: Land forces - By what ship or how taken: Taken on shore - Discharged: 8 Nov 1814 - By what order: George No. 515 by Sir George Prevost - Source: List of American Prisoners of War discharged at Quebec - Name of prize ship: Land forces.

Bennett, James W.   Prisoner: 1235 - Rank: Private - By what ship or how taken: Troops - Time when: 19 Dec 1813 - Place where: Fort Niagara - Whether man of war, privateer, or merchant vessel: Taken on shore - When received: 29 Jan 1814 - From what ship or whence received: Montreal by land carriages. - Prisoner: 1235 - Rank: Private - Name of Prize: Land forces - By what ship or how taken: Taken on shore - Discharged: 28 Feb 1814 - By what order: Transferred to John Thomas No. 23 Transport - Source: List of American Prisoners of War discharged at Quebec - Name of prize ship: Land forces.

Bennett, John   Prisoner: 1971 - Rank: Citizen - Discharged: 13 Mar 1815 - By what order: Returned to the United States - Source: List of American Prisoners of War discharged at Quebec.

Bent, John   Prisoner: 940 - Rank: Private - Name of Prize: Land forces - By what ship or how taken: Taken on shore - Discharged: 4 May 1814 - By what order: Returned to the United States - Source: List of American Prisoners of War discharged at Quebec - Name of prize ship: Land forces.

Bentley, William   Prisoner: 361 - Rank: Private - Source: Account of American prisoners of war who died at Quebec in the Months of July, August & September 1813 - Ship or Corps: Land forces - Vessel: Taken on shore - Place born: Chester, PA - Age: 48 - Where taken: Stoney Point - Date of death: 13 Aug 1813.

Benton, John   Prisoner: 1838 - Rank: Private - Name of Prize: Land forces - By what ship or how taken: Taken on shore - Discharged: 8 Nov 1814 - By what order: George No. 515 by Sir George Prevost - Source: List of American Prisoners of War discharged at Quebec - Name of prize ship: Land forces.

Bertel, George   Prisoner: 967 - Rank: Private - Name of Prize: Land forces - By what ship or how taken: Taken on shore - Discharged: 31 Oct 1813 - By what order: HMS Malabar Transport by order of his Excellency Sir George Prevost - Source: List of American Prisoners of War discharged at Quebec - Name of prize ship: Land forces.

Berwick, George W.   Prisoner: 1355 - Rank: Private - By what ship or how taken: Troops - Time when: 19 Dec 1813 - Place where: Fort Niagara - Whether man of war, privateer, or merchant vessel: Taken on shore - When received: 29 Jan 1814 - From what ship or whence received: Montreal by land carriages. - Prisoner: 1355 - Rank: Private - Name of Prize: Land forces - By what ship or how taken: Taken on shore - Discharged: 4 May 1814 - By what order: Returned to the United States - Source: List of American Prisoners of War discharged at Quebec - Name of prize ship: Land forces.

Bevins, John H.   Prisoner: 1822 - Rank: Private - Name of Prize: Land forces - By what ship or how taken: Taken on shore - Discharged: 8 Nov 1814 - By what order: George No. 515 by Sir George Prevost - Source: List of American Prisoners of War discharged at Quebec - Name of prize ship: Land forces.

Bilby, Henry   Prisoner: 1107 - Rank: Private - Name of Prize: Land forces - By what ship or how taken: Taken on shore - Discharged: 31 Oct 1813 - By what order: HMS Malabar Transport by order of his Excellency Sir George Prevost - Source: List of American Prisoners of War discharged at Quebec - Name of prize ship: Land forces.

Bingham, Isaac   Prisoner: 1126 - Rank: Private - By what ship or how taken: Troops - Time when: 5 May 1813 -

Place where: Rapids, River Raisin - Whether man of war, privateer, or merchant vessel: Taken on shore - When received: 25 Nov 1813 - From what ship or whence received: Town goal. - Prisoner: 1126 - Rank: Private - Name of Prize: Land forces - By what ship or how taken: Taken on shore - Discharged: 4 May 1814 - By what order: Returned to the United States - Source: List of American Prisoners of War discharged at Quebec - Name of prize ship: Land forces.

Bird, John D. Prisoner: 1570 - Rank: Midshipman - Name of Prize: Somers - By what ship or how taken: Man of war - Discharged: 10 Nov 1814 - By what order: Lord Cathcart No. 161 for Halifax by order of Sir George Prevost - Source: List of American Prisoners of War discharged at Quebec - Name of prize ship: Somers.

Birk, John Prisoner: 539 - Rank: Private - Name of Prize: Land forces - By what ship or how taken: Taken on shore - Discharged: 31 Oct 1813 - By what order: HMS Malabar Transport by order of his Excellency Sir George Prevost - Source: List of American Prisoners of War discharged at Quebec - Name of prize ship: Land forces.

Bishop, James Prisoner: 1296 - Rank: Private - By what ship or how taken: Troops - Time when: 19 Dec 1813 - Place where: Fort Niagara - Whether man of war, privateer, or merchant vessel: Taken on shore - When received: 29 Jan 1814 - From what ship or whence received: Montreal by land carriages. - Prisoner: 1296 - Rank: Private - Name of Prize: Land forces - By what ship or how taken: Taken on shore - Discharged: 27 Feb 1814 - By what order: Volunteered for the New Brunswick Fencibles - Source: List of American Prisoners of War discharged at Quebec - Name of prize ship: Land forces.

Bishop, Jesse Prisoner: 608 - Rank: Private - Name of Prize: Land forces - By what ship or how taken: Taken on shore - Discharged: 10 Aug 1813 - By what order: HMS Regulus by order of his Excellency Sir George Prevost - Source: List of American Prisoners of War discharged at Quebec - Name of prize ship: Land forces.

Bishop, Job Prisoner: 1771 - Rank: Corporal - Name of Prize: Land forces - By what ship or how taken: Taken on shore - Discharged: 8 Nov 1814 - By what order: George No. 515 by Sir George Prevost - Source: List of American Prisoners of War discharged at Quebec - Name of prize ship: Land forces.

Bishop, Josiah Prisoner: 1327 - Rank: Sergeant - By what ship or how taken: Troops - Time when: 19 Dec 1813 - Place where: Fort Niagara - Whether man of war, privateer, or merchant vessel: Taken on shore - When received: 29 Jan 1814 - From what ship or whence received: Montreal by land carriages. - Prisoner: 1327 - Rank: Sergeant - Name of Prize: Land forces - By what ship or how taken: Taken on shore - Discharged: 4 May 1814 - By what order: Returned to the United States - Source: List of American Prisoners of War discharged at Quebec - Name of prize ship: Land forces.

Black, John Prisoner: 506 - Rank: Private - Name of Prize: Land forces - By what ship or how taken: Taken on shore - Discharged: 10 Aug 1813 - By what order: HMS Regulus by order of his Excellency Sir George Prevost - Source: List of American Prisoners of War discharged at Quebec - Name of prize ship: Land forces.

Blake, William Prisoner: 1954 - Rank: Private - Name of Prize: Land forces - By what ship or how taken: Taken on shore - Discharged: 13 Mar 1815 - By what order: Returned to the United States - Source: List of American Prisoners of War discharged at Quebec - Name of prize ship: Land forces.

Blancet, Levi (1) Prisoner: 111 - Rank: Corporal - Name of Prize: Land forces - By what ship or how taken: Taken on shore - Discharged: 31 Oct 1813 - By what order: HMS Malabar Transport by order of his Excellency Sir George Prevost - Source: List of American Prisoners of War discharged at Quebec - Name of prize ship: Land forces.

Blancet, Levi (2) Prisoner: 1768 - Rank: Corporal - Name of Prize: Land forces - By what ship or how taken: Taken on shore - Discharged: 8 Nov 1814 - By what order: George No. 515 by Sir George Prevost - Source: List of American Prisoners of War discharged at Quebec - Name of prize ship: Land forces.

Blanch, James Prisoner: 542 - Rank: Sergeant - Name of Prize: Land forces - By what ship or how taken: Taken on shore - Discharged: 4 May 1814 - By what order: Returned to the United States - Source: List of American Prisoners of War discharged at Quebec - Name of prize ship: Land forces.

Blank, Samuel Prisoner: 999 - Rank: Seaman - Name of Prize: Juliet - By what ship or how taken: Man of war - Discharged: 31 Oct 1813 - By what order: HMS Malabar Transport by order of his Excellency Sir George Prevost - Source: List of American Prisoners of War discharged at Quebec - Name of prize ship: Juliet.

Blogs, Murdock Prisoner: 485 - Rank: Private - Name of Prize: Land forces - By what ship or how taken: Taken on shore - Discharged: 10 Aug 1813 - By what order: HMS Regulus by order of his Excellency Sir George Prevost - Source: List of American Prisoners of War discharged at Quebec - Name of prize ship: Land forces.

Blyth, John Prisoner: 1411 - Rank: Private - By what ship or how taken: Troops - Time when: 19 Dec 1813 - Place where: Fort Niagara - Whether man of war, privateer, or merchant vessel: Taken on shore - When received: 29 Jan 1814 - From what ship or whence received: Montreal by land carriages. - Prisoner: 1411 - Rank: Private - Name of Prize: Land forces - By what ship or how taken: Taken on shore - Discharged: 4 May 1814

- By what order: Returned to the United States - Source: List of American Prisoners of War discharged at Quebec - Name of prize ship: Land forces.

Boehm, Joseph   Prisoner: 476 - Rank: Private - Name of Prize: Land forces - By what ship or how taken: Taken on shore - Discharged: 10 Aug 1813 - By what order: HMS Regulus by order of his Excellency Sir George Prevost - Source: List of American Prisoners of War discharged at Quebec - Name of prize ship: Land forces.

Boerstler, Charles G.   Prisoner: 927 - Rank: Lieutenant Colonel - Name of Prize: Land forces - By what ship or how taken: Taken on shore - Discharged: 16 Nov 1813 - By what order: Returned to the United States - Source: List of American Prisoners of War discharged at Quebec - Name of prize ship: Land forces.

Boget, Gilbert   Prisoner: 1072 - Rank: Private - Name of Prize: Land forces - By what ship or how taken: Taken on shore - Discharged: 4 May 1814 - By what order: Returned to the United States - Source: List of American Prisoners of War discharged at Quebec - Name of prize ship: Land forces.

Bonney, William   Prisoner: 39 - Rank: Private - Name of Prize: Land forces - By what ship or how taken: Taken on shore - Discharged: 31 Oct 1813 - By what order: HMS Malabar Transport by order of his Excellency Sir George Prevost - Source: List of American Prisoners of War discharged at Quebec - Name of prize ship: Land forces.

Booth, George   Prisoner: 494 - Rank: Private - Name of Prize: Land forces - By what ship or how taken: Taken on shore - Discharged: 10 Aug 1813 - By what order: HMS Regulus by order of his Excellency Sir George Prevost - Source: List of American Prisoners of War discharged at Quebec - Name of prize ship: Land forces.

Booth, Richard   Prisoner: 44 - Rank: Private - Name of Prize: Land forces - By what ship or how taken: Taken on shore - Discharged: 4 May 1814 - By what order: Returned to the United States - Source: List of American Prisoners of War discharged at Quebec - Name of prize ship: Land forces.

Bosson, Thaddeus   Prisoner: 116 - Rank: Private - Name of Prize: Land forces - By what ship or how taken: Taken on shore - Discharged: 31 Oct 1813 - By what order: HMS Malabar Transport by order of his Excellency Sir George Prevost - Source: List of American Prisoners of War discharged at Quebec - Name of prize ship: Land forces.

Botts, James   Prisoner: 685 - Rank: Private - Name of Prize: Land forces - By what ship or how taken: Taken on shore - Discharged: 10 Aug 1813 - By what order: HMS Regulus by order of his Excellency Sir George Prevost - Source: List of American Prisoners of War discharged at Quebec - Name of prize ship: Land forces.

Bourdineou, Elijah   Prisoner: 1731 - Rank: Seaman - Name of Prize: Scorpion - By what ship or how taken: Man of war - Discharged: 7 Nov 1813 - By what order: HMS Freedom No. 582 by order of his Excellency Sir George Prevost - Source: List of American Prisoners of War discharged at Quebec - Name of prize ship: Scorpion.

Bow, Stephen   Prisoner: 228 - Rank: Private - Source: Account of American prisoners of war who died at Quebec in the Months of July, August & September 1813 - Ship or Corps: Eagle - Vessel: Man of war - Place born: Marblehead, MA - Age: 25 - Where taken: Lake Champlain - Date of death: 27 Aug 1813 - Disorder or casualty: Typhus fever.

Bowen, Joseph   Prisoner: 1155 - Rank: Corporal - By what ship or how taken: Troops - Time when: 5 May 1813 - Place where: Rapids, River Raisin - Whether man of war, privateer, or merchant vessel: Taken on shore - When received: 25 Nov 1813 - From what ship or whence received: Town goal. - Prisoner: 1155 - Rank: Corporal - Name of Prize: Land forces - By what ship or how taken: Taken on shore - Discharged: 4 May 1814 - By what order: Returned to the United States - Source: List of American Prisoners of War discharged at Quebec - Name of prize ship: Land forces.

Bowen, Pearce   Prisoner: 1790 - Rank: Corporal - Name of Prize: Land forces - By what ship or how taken: Taken on shore - Discharged: 8 Nov 1814 - By what order: George No. 515 by Sir George Prevost - Source: List of American Prisoners of War discharged at Quebec - Name of prize ship: Land forces.

Bowes, George   Prisoner: 1634 - Rank: Private - Name of Prize: Land forces - By what ship or how taken: Taken on shore - Discharged: 8 Nov 1814 - By what order: George No. 515 by Sir George Prevost - Source: List of American Prisoners of War discharged at Quebec - Name of prize ship: Land forces.

Bowlett, Nathaniel   Prisoner: 1238 - Rank: Private - By what ship or how taken: Troops - Time when: 19 Dec 1813 - Place where: Fort Niagara - Whether man of war, privateer, or merchant vessel: Taken on shore - When received: 29 Jan 1814 - From what ship or whence received: Montreal by land carriages. - Prisoner: 1238 - Rank: Private - Name of Prize: Land forces - By what ship or how taken: Taken on shore - Discharged: 4 May 1814 - By what order: Returned to the United States - Source: List of American Prisoners of War discharged at Quebec - Name of prize ship: Land forces.

Bowyer, George   Prisoner: 302 - Rank: Private - Name of Prize: Land forces - By what ship or how taken: Taken on shore - Discharged: 31 Oct 1813 - By what order: HMS Malabar Transport by order of his Excellency Sir

George Prevost - Source: List of American Prisoners of War discharged at Quebec - Name of prize ship: Land forces.

Boyce, John   Prisoner: 22 - Rank: Private - Name of Prize: Land forces - By what ship or how taken: Taken on shore - Discharged: 31 Oct 1813 - By what order: HMS Malabar Transport by order of his Excellency Sir George Prevost - Source: List of American Prisoners of War discharged at Quebec - Name of prize ship: Land forces.

Boyce, Nelson   Prisoner: 583 - Rank: Private - Name of Prize: Land forces - By what ship or how taken: Taken on shore - Discharged: 10 Aug 1813 - By what order: HMS Regulus by order of his Excellency Sir George Prevost - Source: List of American Prisoners of War discharged at Quebec - Name of prize ship: Land forces.

Boyd, Samuel   Prisoner: 383 - Rank: Private - Name of Prize: Land forces - By what ship or how taken: Taken on shore - Discharged: 31 Oct 1813 - By what order: HMS Malabar Transport by order of his Excellency Sir George Prevost - Source: List of American Prisoners of War discharged at Quebec - Name of prize ship: Land forces.

Boyd, William   Prisoner: 1346 - Rank: Private - By what ship or how taken: Troops - Time when: 19 Dec 1813 - Place where: Fort Niagara - Whether man of war, privateer, or merchant vessel: Taken on shore - When received: 29 Jan 1814 - From what ship or whence received: Montreal by land carriages. - Prisoner: 1346 - Rank: Private - Name of Prize: Land forces - By what ship or how taken: Taken on shore - Discharged: 4 May 1814 - By what order: Returned to the United States - Source: List of American Prisoners of War discharged at Quebec - Name of prize ship: Land forces.

Brace, Stephen   Prisoner: 1152 - Rank: Private - By what ship or how taken: Troops - Time when: 5 May 1813 - Place where: Rapids, River Raisin - Whether man of war, privateer, or merchant vessel: Taken on shore - When received: 25 Nov 1813 - From what ship or whence received: Town goal. - Prisoner: 1152 - Rank: Private - Name of Prize: Land forces - By what ship or how taken: Taken on shore - Discharged: 4 May 1814 - By what order: Returned to the United States - Source: List of American Prisoners of War discharged at Quebec - Name of prize ship: Land forces.

Bradford, John   Prisoner: 360 - Rank: Private - Name of Prize: Land forces - By what ship or how taken: Taken on shore - Discharged: 31 Oct 1813 - By what order: HMS Malabar Transport by order of his Excellency Sir George Prevost - Source: List of American Prisoners of War discharged at Quebec - Name of prize ship: Land forces.

Bradshaw, Edward   Prisoner: 424 - Rank: Private - Name of Prize: Land forces - By what ship or how taken: Taken on shore - Discharged: 31 Oct 1813 - By what order: HMS Malabar Transport by order of his Excellency Sir George Prevost - Source: List of American Prisoners of War discharged at Quebec - Name of prize ship: Land forces.

Brandon, Samuel   Prisoner: 1250 - Rank: Sergeant - By what ship or how taken: Troops - Time when: 19 Dec 1813 - Place where: Fort Niagara - Whether man of war, privateer, or merchant vessel: Taken on shore - When received: 29 Jan 1814 - From what ship or whence received: Montreal by land carriages. - Prisoner: 1250 - Rank: Sergeant - Name of Prize: Land forces - By what ship or how taken: Taken on shore - Discharged: 4 May 1814 - By what order: Returned to the United States - Source: List of American Prisoners of War discharged at Quebec - Name of prize ship: Land forces. - Prisoner: 1250 - Rank: Sergeant - By what ship or how taken: Troops - Time when: 19 Dec 1813 - Place where: Fort Niagara - Whether man of war, privateer, or merchant vessel: Taken on shore - When received: 29 Jan 1814 - From what ship or whence received: Montreal by land carriages.

Brenhard, Arnold   Prisoner: 1819 - Rank: Private - Name of Prize: Land forces - By what ship or how taken: Taken on shore - Discharged: 8 Nov 1814 - By what order: George No. 515 by Sir George Prevost - Source: List of American Prisoners of War discharged at Quebec - Name of prize ship: Land forces.

Brett, Francis   Prisoner: 1430 - Rank: Passenger - Time when: Jul 1813 - Place where: St. Johns - Whether man of war, privateer, or merchant vessel: Merchant ship - When received: 24 May 1814 - From what ship or whence received: Mary Transport No. 368.

Bridge, Franklin   Prisoner: 199 - Rank: Sergeant - Name of Prize: Eagle - By what ship or how taken: Man of war - Discharged: 31 Oct 1813 - By what order: HMS Malabar Transport by order of his Excellency Sir George Prevost - Source: List of American Prisoners of War discharged at Quebec - Name of prize ship: Eagle.

Briggs, William   Prisoner: 1232 - Rank: Private - By what ship or how taken: Troops - Time when: 19 Dec 1813 - Place where: Fort Niagara - Whether man of war, privateer, or merchant vessel: Taken on shore - When received: 29 Jan 1814 - From what ship or whence received: Montreal by land carriages. - Prisoner: 1232 - Rank: Private - Name of Prize: Land forces - By what ship or how taken: Taken on shore - Discharged: 4 May 1814 - By what order: Returned to the United States - Source: List of American Prisoners of War

discharged at Quebec - Name of prize ship: Land forces.

Brill, William   Prisoner: 644 - Rank: Private - Name of Prize: Land forces - By what ship or how taken: Taken on shore - Discharged: 10 Aug 1813 - By what order: HMS Regulus by order of his Excellency Sir George Prevost - Source: List of American Prisoners of War discharged at Quebec - Name of prize ship: Land forces.

Brine, Thomas   Prisoner: 981 - Rank: Private - Name of Prize: Land forces - By what ship or how taken: Taken on shore - Discharged: 4 May 1814 - By what order: Returned to the United States - Source: List of American Prisoners of War discharged at Quebec - Name of prize ship: Land forces.

Brink, Orson   Prisoner: 180 - Rank: Private - Name of Prize: Growler - By what ship or how taken: Man of war - Discharged: 31 Oct 1813 - By what order: HMS Malabar Transport by order of his Excellency Sir George Prevost - Source: List of American Prisoners of War discharged at Quebec - Name of prize ship: Growler.

Brison, Paul   Prisoner: 433 - Rank: Private - Name of Prize: Land forces - By what ship or how taken: Taken on shore - Discharged: 10 Aug 1813 - By what order: HMS Regulus by order of his Excellency Sir George Prevost - Source: List of American Prisoners of War discharged at Quebec - Name of prize ship: Land forces.

Britt, Francis   Prisoner: 355 - Rank: Passenger - Name of Prize: Pashero - By what ship or how taken: Merchant ship - Discharged: 24 May 1813 - By what order: Mulgrave Transport No. 311 - Source: List of American Prisoners of War discharged at Quebec - Name of prize ship: Pashero.

Broadest, Moses   Prisoner: 442 - Rank: Private - Name of Prize: Land forces - By what ship or how taken: Taken on shore - Discharged: 10 Aug 1813 - By what order: HMS Regulus by order of his Excellency Sir George Prevost - Source: List of American Prisoners of War discharged at Quebec - Name of prize ship: Land forces.

Bromley, Salmon   Prisoner: 1302 - Rank: Private - By what ship or how taken: Troops - Time when: 19 Dec 1813 - Place where: Fort Niagara - Whether man of war, privateer, or merchant vessel: Taken on shore - When received: 29 Jan 1814 - From what ship or whence received: Montreal by land carriages. - Prisoner: 1302 - Rank: Private - Name of Prize: Land forces - By what ship or how taken: Taken on shore - Discharged: 27 Feb 1814 - By what order: Volunteered for the New Brunswick Fencibles - Source: List of American Prisoners of War discharged at Quebec - Name of prize ship: Land forces.

Bronaugh, Thomas   Prisoner: 1133 - Rank: Private - By what ship or how taken: Troops - Time when: 5 May 1813 - Place where: Rapids, River Raisin - Whether man of war, privateer, or merchant vessel: Taken on shore - When received: 25 Nov 1813 - From what ship or whence received: Town goal. - Prisoner: 1133 - Rank: Private - Name of Prize: Land forces - By what ship or how taken: Taken on shore - Discharged: 4 May 1814 - By what order: Returned to the United States - Source: List of American Prisoners of War discharged at Quebec - Name of prize ship: Land forces.

Brookes, Joseph   Prisoner: 1914 - Rank: Private - Name of Prize: Land forces - By what ship or how taken: Taken on shore - Discharged: 8 Nov 1814 - By what order: George No. 515 by Sir George Prevost - Source: List of American Prisoners of War discharged at Quebec - Name of prize ship: Land forces.

Brown, Henry (1)   Prisoner: 1071 - Rank: Corporal - Name of Prize: Land forces - By what ship or how taken: Taken on shore - Discharged: 31 Oct 1813 - By what order: HMS Malabar Transport by order of his Excellency Sir George Prevost - Source: List of American Prisoners of War discharged at Quebec - Name of prize ship: Land forces.

Brown, Henry (2)   Prisoner: 1735 - Rank: Seaman - Name of Prize: Scorpion - By what ship or how taken: Man of war - Discharged: 7 Nov 1813 - By what order: HMS Freedom No. 582 by order of his Excellency Sir George Prevost - Source: List of American Prisoners of War discharged at Quebec - Name of prize ship: Scorpion.

Brown, James   Prisoner: 348 - Rank: Private - Name of Prize: Land forces - By what ship or how taken: Taken on shore - Discharged: 4 May 1814 - By what order: Returned to the United States - Source: List of American Prisoners of War discharged at Quebec - Name of prize ship: Land forces.

Brown, John   Prisoner: 1704 - Rank: Private - Name of Prize: Land forces - By what ship or how taken: Taken on shore - Discharged: 8 Nov 1814 - By what order: George No. 515 by Sir George Prevost - Source: List of American Prisoners of War discharged at Quebec - Name of prize ship: Land forces.

Brown, Joseph   Prisoner: 1347 - Rank: Private - By what ship or how taken: Troops - Time when: 19 Dec 1813 - Place where: Fort Niagara - Whether man of war, privateer, or merchant vessel: Taken on shore - When received: 29 Jan 1814 - From what ship or whence received: Montreal by land carriages.

Brown, Joshua   Prisoner: 1347 - Rank: Private - Name of Prize: Land forces - By what ship or how taken: Taken on shore - Discharged: 4 May 1814 - By what order: Returned to the United States - Source: List of American Prisoners of War discharged at Quebec - Name of prize ship: Land forces.

Brown, Rufus   Prisoner: 1811 - Rank: Private - Name of Prize: Land forces - By what ship or how taken: Taken on shore - Discharged: 8 Nov 1814 - By what order: George No. 515 by Sir George Prevost - Source: List of

American Prisoners of War discharged at Quebec - Name of prize ship: Land forces.

Brown, Thomas   Prisoner: 1028 - Rank: Seaman - Name of Prize: Growler - By what ship or how taken: Man of war - Discharged: 1 Nov 1813 - By what order: HMS Hero by order of his Excellency Sir George Prevost - Source: List of American prisoners sent to England on the HMS Hero - Name of prize ship: Growler. - Prisoner: 1028 - Rank: Able Seaman - Name of Prize: Growler - By what ship or how taken: Man of war - Discharged: 4 May 1814 - By what order: Returned to the United States - Source: List of American Prisoners of War discharged at Quebec - Name of prize ship: Growler.

Brown, William (1)   Prisoner: 430 - Rank: Private - Name of Prize: Land forces - By what ship or how taken: Taken on shore - Discharged: 10 Aug 1813 - By what order: HMS Regulus by order of his Excellency Sir George Prevost - Source: List of American Prisoners of War discharged at Quebec - Name of prize ship: Land forces.

Brown, William (2)   Prisoner: 1253 - Rank: Private - By what ship or how taken: Troops - Time when: 19 Dec 1813 - Place where: Fort Niagara - Whether man of war, privateer, or merchant vessel: Taken on shore - When received: 29 Jan 1814 - From what ship or whence received: Montreal by land carriages. - Prisoner: 1253 - Rank: Private - Name of Prize: Land forces - By what ship or how taken: Taken on shore - Discharged: 4 May 1814 - By what order: Returned to the United States - Source: List of American Prisoners of War discharged at Quebec - Name of prize ship: Land forces.

Brown, William (3)   Prisoner: 1692 - Rank: Musician - Name of Prize: Land forces - By what ship or how taken: Taken on shore - Discharged: 8 Nov 1814 - By what order: George No. 515 by Sir George Prevost - Source: List of American Prisoners of War discharged at Quebec - Name of prize ship: Land forces.

Bruntsman, Daniel   Prisoner: 1256 - Rank: Private - By what ship or how taken: Troops - Time when: 19 Dec 1813 - Place where: Fort Niagara - Whether man of war, privateer, or merchant vessel: Taken on shore - When received: 29 Jan 1814 - From what ship or whence received: Montreal by land carriages. - Prisoner: 1256 - Rank: Private - Name of Prize: Land forces - By what ship or how taken: Taken on shore - Discharged: 4 May 1814 - By what order: Returned to the United States - Source: List of American Prisoners of War discharged at Quebec - Name of prize ship: Land forces.

Bryan, Philip   Prisoner: 1129 - Rank: Sergeant - By what ship or how taken: Troops - Time when: 5 May 1813 - Place where: Rapids, River Raisin - Whether man of war, privateer, or merchant vessel: Taken on shore - When received: 25 Nov 1813 - From what ship or whence received: Town goal. - Prisoner: 1129 - Rank: Sergeant - Name of Prize: Land forces - By what ship or how taken: Taken on shore - Discharged: 4 May 1814 - By what order: Returned to the United States - Source: List of American Prisoners of War discharged at Quebec - Name of prize ship: Land forces.

Bryant, Lemuel   Prisoner: 994 - Rank: Seaman - Name of Prize: Juliet - By what ship or how taken: Man of war - Discharged: 31 Oct 1813 - By what order: HMS Malabar Transport by order of his Excellency Sir George Prevost - Source: List of American Prisoners of War discharged at Quebec - Name of prize ship: Juliet.

Bryce, James   Prisoner: 657 - Rank: Private - Name of Prize: Land forces - By what ship or how taken: Taken on shore - Discharged: 10 Aug 1813 - By what order: HMS Regulus by order of his Excellency Sir George Prevost - Source: List of American Prisoners of War discharged at Quebec - Name of prize ship: Land forces.

Buchanan, John   Prisoner: 1380 - Rank: Private - By what ship or how taken: Troops - Time when: 19 Dec 1813 - Place where: Fort Niagara - Whether man of war, privateer, or merchant vessel: Taken on shore - When received: 29 Jan 1814 - From what ship or whence received: Montreal by land carriages. - Prisoner: 1380 - Rank: Private - Name of Prize: Land forces - By what ship or how taken: Taken on shore - Discharged: 4 May 1814 - By what order: Returned to the United States - Source: List of American Prisoners of War discharged at Quebec - Name of prize ship: Land forces.

Buckley, Elias   Prisoner: 1883 - Rank: Private - Name of Prize: Land forces - By what ship or how taken: Taken on shore - Discharged: 8 Nov 1814 - By what order: George No. 515 by Sir George Prevost - Source: List of American Prisoners of War discharged at Quebec - Name of prize ship: Land forces.

Buel, Jeremiah   Prisoner: 987 - Rank: Purser Steward - Name of Prize: Growler - By what ship or how taken: Man of war - Discharged: 31 Oct 1813 - By what order: HMS Malabar Transport by order of his Excellency Sir George Prevost - Source: List of American Prisoners of War discharged at Quebec - Name of prize ship: Growler.

Bunnell, David C.   Prisoner: 1723 - Rank: Purser Steward - Name of Prize: Scorpion - By what ship or how taken: Man of war - Discharged: 7 Nov 1813 - By what order: HMS Freedom No. 582 by order of his Excellency Sir George Prevost - Source: List of American Prisoners of War discharged at Quebec - Name of prize ship: Scorpion.

Burees, Viris   Prisoner: 1226 - Rank: Private - By what ship or how taken: Troops - Time when: 19 Dec 1813 -

Place where: Fort Niagara - Whether man of war, privateer, or merchant vessel: Taken on shore - When received: 29 Jan 1814 - From what ship or whence received: Montreal by land carriages. - Prisoner: 1226 - Rank: Private - Name of Prize: Land forces - By what ship or how taken: Taken on shore - Discharged: 4 May 1814 - By what order: Returned to the United States - Source: List of American Prisoners of War discharged at Quebec - Name of prize ship: Land forces.

Burger, John   Prisoner: 319 - Rank: Private - Name of Prize: Land forces - By what ship or how taken: Taken on shore - Discharged: 31 Oct 1813 - By what order: HMS Malabar Transport by order of his Excellency Sir George Prevost - Source: List of American Prisoners of War discharged at Quebec - Name of prize ship: Land forces.

Burk, Edward   Prisoner: 1913 - Rank: Private - Name of Prize: Land forces - By what ship or how taken: Taken on shore - Discharged: 8 Nov 1814 - By what order: George No. 515 by Sir George Prevost - Source: List of American Prisoners of War discharged at Quebec - Name of prize ship: Land forces.

Burkand, John   Prisoner: 1285 - Rank: Private - Source: Account of American prisoners of war who died at Quebec between 14 February 1814 and 23 December 1814 - Ship or Corps: Land forces - Vessel: Taken on shore - Place born: Vermont - Age: 34 - Where taken: Fort Niagara - Date of death: 20 Apr 1814 - Disorder or casualty: Pneumonia.

Burke, Dorris   Prisoner: 1720 - Rank: Private - Name of Prize: Land forces - By what ship or how taken: Taken on shore - Discharged: 10 Nov 1814 - By what order: Stately No. 400 to Halifax by order of Sir George Prevost - Source: List of American Prisoners of War discharged at Quebec - Name of prize ship: Land forces.

Burnell, John   Prisoner: 452 - Rank: Private - Name of Prize: Land forces - By what ship or how taken: Taken on shore - Discharged: 10 Aug 1813 - By what order: HMS Regulus by order of his Excellency Sir George Prevost - Source: List of American Prisoners of War discharged at Quebec - Name of prize ship: Land forces.

Burns, Andrew   Prisoner: 631 - Rank: Private - Name of Prize: Land forces - By what ship or how taken: Taken on shore - Discharged: 10 Aug 1813 - By what order: HMS Regulus by order of his Excellency Sir George Prevost - Source: List of American Prisoners of War discharged at Quebec - Name of prize ship: Land forces.

Burns, John E.   Prisoner: 1835 - Rank: Private - Name of Prize: Land forces - By what ship or how taken: Taken on shore - Discharged: 8 Nov 1814 - By what order: George No. 515 by Sir George Prevost - Source: List of American Prisoners of War discharged at Quebec - Name of prize ship: Land forces.

Burtsell, David   Prisoner: 1318 - Rank: Private - By what ship or how taken: Troops - Time when: 19 Dec 1813 - Place where: Fort Niagara - Whether man of war, privateer, or merchant vessel: Taken on shore - When received: 29 Jan 1814 - From what ship or whence received: Montreal by land carriages. - Prisoner: 1318 - Rank: Private - Name of Prize: Land forces - By what ship or how taken: Taken on shore - Discharged: 27 Feb 1814 - By what order: Volunteered for the New Brunswick Fencibles - Source: List of American Prisoners of War discharged at Quebec - Name of prize ship: Land forces.

Bush, Hollower   Prisoner: 1438 - Rank: Private - Name of Prize: Land forces - By what ship or how taken: Taken on shore - Discharged: 8 Nov 1814 - By what order: George No. 515 by Sir George Prevost - Source: List of American Prisoners of War discharged at Quebec - Name of prize ship: Land forces.

Buskirk, Garrett   Prisoner: 1400 - Rank: Private - By what ship or how taken: Troops - Time when: 19 Dec 1813 - Place where: Fort Niagara - Whether man of war, privateer, or merchant vessel: Taken on shore - When received: 29 Jan 1814 - From what ship or whence received: Montreal by land carriages. - Prisoner: 1400 - Rank: Private - Name of Prize: Land forces - By what ship or how taken: Taken on shore - Discharged: 4 May 1814 - By what order: Returned to the United States - Source: List of American Prisoners of War discharged at Quebec - Name of prize ship: Land forces.

Butler, Michael   Prisoner: 110 - Rank: Private - Source: Account of American prisoners of war who died at Quebec in the Months of July, August & September 1813 - Ship or Corps: Land forces - Vessel: Taken on shore - Place born: New York - Age: 18 - Where taken: Beaver Dams - Date of death: 27 Jul 1813.

Butterfield, Abraham   Prisoner: 1818 - Rank: Private - Name of Prize: Land forces - By what ship or how taken: Taken on shore - Discharged: 8 Nov 1814 - By what order: George No. 515 by Sir George Prevost - Source: List of American Prisoners of War discharged at Quebec - Name of prize ship: Land forces.

Cady, Daniel G.   Prisoner: 977 - Rank: Private - Name of Prize: Land forces - By what ship or how taken: Taken on shore - Discharged: 31 Oct 1813 - By what order: HMS Malabar Transport by order of his Excellency Sir George Prevost - Source: List of American Prisoners of War discharged at Quebec - Name of prize ship: Land forces.

Caldwell, Nathaniel   Prisoner: 1823 - Rank: Private - Name of Prize: Land forces - By what ship or how taken: Taken on shore - Discharged: 8 Nov 1814 - By what order: George No. 515 by Sir George Prevost - Source: List of American Prisoners of War discharged at Quebec - Name of prize ship: Land forces.

Callahan, Francis Prisoner: 1211 - Rank: Boy - By what ship or how taken: Troops - Time when: 19 Dec 1813 - Place where: Fort Niagara - Whether man of war, privateer, or merchant vessel: Taken on shore - When received: 18 Jan 1814 - From what ship or whence received: Montreal by land carriages. - Prisoner: 1211 - Rank: Boy - Name of Prize: Land forces - By what ship or how taken: Taken on shore - Discharged: 4 May 1814 - By what order: Returned to the United States - Source: List of American Prisoners of War discharged at Quebec - Name of prize ship: Land forces.

Campbell, James Prisoner: 198 - Rank: Private - Name of Prize: Growler - By what ship or how taken: Man of war - Discharged: 31 Oct 1813 - By what order: HMS Malabar Transport by order of his Excellency Sir George Prevost - Source: List of American Prisoners of War discharged at Quebec - Name of prize ship: Growler.

Campbell, Jesse Prisoner: 1464 - Rank: Private - Name of Prize: Land forces - By what ship or how taken: Taken on shore - Discharged: 10 Nov 1814 - By what order: Sovereign No. 628 to Halifax by order of Sir George Prevost - Source: List of American Prisoners of War discharged at Quebec - Name of prize ship: Land forces.

Campbell, Joseph Prisoner: 1081 - Rank: Private - Name of Prize: Land forces - By what ship or how taken: Taken on shore - Discharged: 31 Oct 1813 - By what order: HMS Malabar Transport by order of his Excellency Sir George Prevost - Source: List of American Prisoners of War discharged at Quebec - Name of prize ship: Land forces.

Campbell, Oliver Prisoner: 1821 - Rank: Private - Name of Prize: Land forces - By what ship or how taken: Taken on shore - Discharged: 8 Nov 1814 - By what order: George No. 515 by Sir George Prevost - Source: List of American Prisoners of War discharged at Quebec - Name of prize ship: Land forces.

Campbell, William Prisoner: 217 - Rank: Private - Name of Prize: Growler - By what ship or how taken: Man of war - Discharged: 31 Oct 1813 - By what order: HMS Malabar Transport by order of his Excellency Sir George Prevost - Source: List of American Prisoners of War discharged at Quebec - Name of prize ship: Growler.

Cane, Thomas Prisoner: 501 - Rank: Private - Name of Prize: Land forces - By what ship or how taken: Taken on shore - Discharged: 10 Aug 1813 - By what order: HMS Regulus by order of his Excellency Sir George Prevost - Source: List of American Prisoners of War discharged at Quebec - Name of prize ship: Land forces.

Capatity, William Prisoner: 517 - Rank: Private - Name of Prize: Land forces - By what ship or how taken: Taken on shore - Discharged: 10 Aug 1813 - By what order: HMS Regulus by order of his Excellency Sir George Prevost - Source: List of American Prisoners of War discharged at Quebec - Name of prize ship: Land forces.

Carpenter, John Prisoner: 448 - Rank: Private - Name of Prize: Land forces - By what ship or how taken: Taken on shore - Discharged: 10 Aug 1813 - By what order: HMS Regulus by order of his Excellency Sir George Prevost - Source: List of American Prisoners of War discharged at Quebec - Name of prize ship: Land forces.

Carr, John (1) Prisoner: 704 - Rank: Private - Name of Prize: Land forces - By what ship or how taken: Taken on shore - Discharged: 10 Aug 1813 - By what order: HMS Regulus by order of his Excellency Sir George Prevost - Source: List of American Prisoners of War discharged at Quebec - Name of prize ship: Land forces.

Carr, John (2) Prisoner: 1751 - Rank: Private - Name of Prize: Scorpion - By what ship or how taken: Man of war - Discharged: 8 Nov 1814 - By what order: George No. 515 by Sir George Prevost - Source: List of American Prisoners of War discharged at Quebec - Name of prize ship: Scorpion.

Carr, William Prisoner: 619 - Rank: Private - Name of Prize: Land forces - By what ship or how taken: Taken on shore - Discharged: 10 Aug 1813 - By what order: HMS Regulus by order of his Excellency Sir George Prevost - Source: List of American Prisoners of War discharged at Quebec - Name of prize ship: Land forces.

Carroll, Isaac Prisoner: 681 - Rank: Private - Name of Prize: Land forces - By what ship or how taken: Taken on shore - Discharged: 10 Aug 1813 - By what order: HMS Regulus by order of his Excellency Sir George Prevost - Source: List of American Prisoners of War discharged at Quebec - Name of prize ship: Land forces.

Carroll, Martin Prisoner: 1840 - Rank: Private - Name of Prize: Land forces - By what ship or how taken: Taken on shore - Discharged: 8 Nov 1814 - By what order: George No. 515 by Sir George Prevost - Source: List of American Prisoners of War discharged at Quebec - Name of prize ship: Land forces.

Carry, Daniel Prisoner: 347 - Rank: Private - Name of Prize: Land forces - By what ship or how taken: Taken on shore - Discharged: 31 Oct 1813 - By what order: HMS Malabar Transport by order of his Excellency Sir George Prevost - Source: List of American Prisoners of War discharged at Quebec - Name of prize ship: Land forces.

Carter, Nathaniel Prisoner: 568 - Rank: Private - Name of Prize: Land forces - By what ship or how taken: Taken on shore - Discharged: 10 Aug 1813 - By what order: HMS Regulus by order of his Excellency Sir George Prevost - Source: List of American Prisoners of War discharged at Quebec - Name of prize ship: Land forces.

Cartwright, George Prisoner: 1760 - Rank: Private - Name of Prize: Tigress - By what ship or how taken: Man of war - Discharged: 8 Nov 1814 - By what order: George No. 515 by Sir George Prevost - Source: List of American Prisoners of War discharged at Quebec - Name of prize ship: Tigress.

Carver, William   Prisoner: 32 - Rank: Private - Source: Account of American prisoners of war who died at Quebec in the Months of July, August & September 1813 - Ship or Corps: Land forces - Vessel: Taken on shore - Place born: Providence, RI - Age: 28 - Where taken: Stoney Point - Date of death: 12 Sep 1813 - Disorder or casualty: Dysentery.

Case, John   Prisoner: 1714 - Rank: Lieutenant - Name of Prize: Land forces - By what ship or how taken: Taken on shore - Discharged: 10 Nov 1814 - By what order: Stately No. 400 to Halifax by order of Sir George Prevost - Source: List of American Prisoners of War discharged at Quebec - Name of prize ship: Land forces.

Catnary, James   Prisoner: 569 - Rank: Private - Name of Prize: Land forces - By what ship or how taken: Taken on shore - Discharged: 10 Aug 1813 - By what order: HMS Regulus by order of his Excellency Sir George Prevost - Source: List of American Prisoners of War discharged at Quebec - Name of prize ship: Land forces.

Catter, Edward   Prisoner: 134 - Rank: Private - Name of Prize: Land forces - By what ship or how taken: Taken on shore - Discharged: 31 Oct 1813 - By what order: HMS Malabar Transport by order of his Excellency Sir George Prevost - Source: List of American Prisoners of War discharged at Quebec - Name of prize ship: Land forces.

Cawthorn, Eleazer   Prisoner: 1134 - Rank: Private - By what ship or how taken: Troops - Time when: 5 May 1813 - Place where: Rapids, River Raisin - Whether man of war, privateer, or merchant vessel: Taken on shore - When received: 25 Nov 1813 - From what ship or whence received: Town goal. - Prisoner: 1134 - Rank: Private - Name of Prize: Land forces - By what ship or how taken: Taken on shore - Discharged: 4 May 1814 - By what order: Returned to the United States - Source: List of American Prisoners of War discharged at Quebec - Name of prize ship: Land forces.

Cedus, Francis   Prisoner: 1746 - Rank: Seaman - Name of Prize: Tigress - By what ship or how taken: Man of war - Discharged: 7 Nov 1813 - By what order: HMS Freedom No. 582 by order of his Excellency Sir George Prevost - Source: List of American Prisoners of War discharged at Quebec - Name of prize ship: Tigress.

Chambers, James   Prisoner: 1717 - Rank: Ensign - Name of Prize: Land forces - By what ship or how taken: Taken on shore - Discharged: 10 Nov 1814 - By what order: Stately No. 400 to Halifax by order of Sir George Prevost - Source: List of American Prisoners of War discharged at Quebec - Name of prize ship: Land forces.

Chambers, Samuel   Prisoner: 1051 - Rank: Private - Name of Prize: Growler - By what ship or how taken: Man of war - Discharged: 31 Oct 1813 - By what order: HMS Malabar Transport by order of his Excellency Sir George Prevost - Source: List of American Prisoners of War discharged at Quebec - Name of prize ship: Growler.

Chandler, John   Prisoner: 254 - Rank: Brigadier General - Name of Prize: Land forces - By what ship or how taken: Taken on shore - Discharged: 3 Apr 1814 - By what order: Returned to the United States - Source: List of American Prisoners of War discharged at Quebec - Name of prize ship: Land forces.

Chapin, Cyrenius   Prisoner: 1213 - Rank: Lieutenant Colonel - By what ship or how taken: Troops - Time when: 19 Dec 1813 - Place where: Fort Niagara - Whether man of war, privateer, or merchant vessel: Taken on shore - When received: 28 Jan 1814 - From what ship or whence received: Montreal by land carriages. - Prisoner: 1213 - Rank: Lieutenant Colonel - Name of Prize: Land forces - By what ship or how taken: Taken on shore - Discharged: 6 May 1814 - By what order: Returned to the United States - Source: List of American Prisoners of War discharged at Quebec - Name of prize ship: Land forces.

Chapman, Elisha   Prisoner: 584 - Rank: Private - Name of Prize: Land forces - By what ship or how taken: Taken on shore - Discharged: 10 Aug 1813 - By what order: HMS Regulus by order of his Excellency Sir George Prevost - Source: List of American Prisoners of War discharged at Quebec - Name of prize ship: Land forces.

Chase, John   Prisoner: 1221 - Rank: Private - By what ship or how taken: Troops - Time when: 19 Dec 1813 - Place where: Fort Niagara - Whether man of war, privateer, or merchant vessel: Taken on shore - When received: 29 Jan 1814 - From what ship or whence received: Montreal by land carriages. - Prisoner: 1221 - Rank: Private - Name of Prize: Land forces - By what ship or how taken: Taken on shore - Discharged: 4 May 1814 - By what order: Returned to the United States - Source: List of American Prisoners of War discharged at Quebec - Name of prize ship: Land forces.

Cheek, William   Prisoner: 1401 - Rank: Corporal - By what ship or how taken: Troops - Time when: 19 Dec 1813 - Place where: Fort Niagara - Whether man of war, privateer, or merchant vessel: Taken on shore - When received: 29 Jan 1814 - From what ship or whence received: Montreal by land carriages. - Prisoner: 1401 - Rank: Corporal - Name of Prize: Land forces - By what ship or how taken: Taken on shore - Discharged: 4 May 1814 - By what order: Returned to the United States - Source: List of American Prisoners of War

discharged at Quebec - Name of prize ship: Land forces.

Cheney, Elisha Prisoner: 1802 - Rank: Private - Name of Prize: Land forces - By what ship or how taken: Taken on shore - Discharged: 8 Nov 1814 - By what order: George No. 515 by Sir George Prevost - Source: List of American Prisoners of War discharged at Quebec - Name of prize ship: Land forces.

Chick, Nathaniel Prisoner: 1393 - Rank: Wheelwright - By what ship or how taken: Troops - Time when: 19 Dec 1813 - Place where: Fort Niagara - Whether man of war, privateer, or merchant vessel: Taken on shore - When received: 29 Jan 1814 - From what ship or whence received: Montreal by land carriages. - Prisoner: 1393 - Rank: Wheelwright - Name of Prize: Land forces - By what ship or how taken: Taken on shore - Discharged: 4 May 1814 - By what order: Returned to the United States - Source: List of American Prisoners of War discharged at Quebec - Name of prize ship: Land forces.

Christian, Charles P. Prisoner: 1680 - Rank: Sergeant - Name of Prize: Land forces - By what ship or how taken: Taken on shore - Discharged: 8 Nov 1814 - By what order: George No. 515 by Sir George Prevost - Source: List of American Prisoners of War discharged at Quebec - Name of prize ship: Land forces.

Christian, H. Prisoner: 916 - Rank: Private - Name of Prize: Land forces - By what ship or how taken: Taken on shore - Discharged: 4 May 1814 - By what order: Returned to the United States - Source: List of American Prisoners of War discharged at Quebec - Name of prize ship: Land forces.

Christopher, Samuel Prisoner: 438 - Rank: Private - Name of Prize: Land forces - By what ship or how taken: Taken on shore - Discharged: 10 Aug 1813 - By what order: HMS Regulus by order of his Excellency Sir George Prevost - Source: List of American Prisoners of War discharged at Quebec - Name of prize ship: Land forces.

Church, Jesse Prisoner: 1713 - Rank: Lieutenant - Name of Prize: Land forces - By what ship or how taken: Taken on shore - Discharged: 10 Nov 1814 - By what order: Stately No. 400 to Halifax by order of Sir George Prevost - Source: List of American Prisoners of War discharged at Quebec - Name of prize ship: Land forces.

Church, Worthy L. Prisoner: 1705 - Rank: Lieutenant Colonel - Name of Prize: Land forces - By what ship or how taken: Taken on shore - Discharged: 10 Nov 1814 - By what order: Stately No. 400 to Halifax by order of Sir George Prevost - Source: List of American Prisoners of War discharged at Quebec - Name of prize ship: Land forces.

Churchill, Oliver Prisoner: 203 - Rank: Private - Source: Account of American prisoners of war who died at Quebec in the Months of July, August & September 1813 - Ship or Corps: Land forces - Vessel: Taken on shore - Place born: Middleborough - Age: 21 - Where taken: Stoney Point - Date of death: 29 Jul 1813.

Clafflin, George Prisoner: 1794 - Rank: Corporal - Name of Prize: Land forces - By what ship or how taken: Taken on shore - Discharged: 8 Nov 1814 - By what order: George No. 515 by Sir George Prevost - Source: List of American Prisoners of War discharged at Quebec - Name of prize ship: Land forces.

Clap, Martin Prisoner: 130 - Rank: Private - Name of Prize: Land forces - By what ship or how taken: Taken on shore - Discharged: 31 Oct 1813 - By what order: HMS Malabar Transport by order of his Excellency Sir George Prevost - Source: List of American Prisoners of War discharged at Quebec - Name of prize ship: Land forces.

Clarey, Timothy Prisoner: 1969 - Rank: Corporal - Name of Prize: Land forces - By what ship or how taken: Taken on shore - Discharged: 13 Mar 1815 - By what order: Returned to the United States - Source: List of American Prisoners of War discharged at Quebec - Name of prize ship: Land forces.

Clark, Benjamin Prisoner: 76 - Rank: Private - Name of Prize: Land forces - By what ship or how taken: Taken on shore - Discharged: 31 Oct 1813 - By what order: HMS Malabar Transport by order of his Excellency Sir George Prevost - Source: List of American Prisoners of War discharged at Quebec - Name of prize ship: Land forces.

Clark, Charles Prisoner: 1413 - Rank: Drummer - By what ship or how taken: Troops - Time when: 19 Dec 1813 - Place where: Fort Niagara - Whether man of war, privateer, or merchant vessel: Taken on shore - When received: 29 Jan 1814 - From what ship or whence received: Montreal by land carriages. - Prisoner: 1413 - Rank: Drummer - Name of Prize: Land forces - By what ship or how taken: Taken on shore - Discharged: 4 May 1814 - By what order: Returned to the United States - Source: List of American Prisoners of War discharged at Quebec - Name of prize ship: Land forces.

Clark, Henry Prisoner: 1372 - Rank: Private - By what ship or how taken: Troops - Time when: 19 Dec 1813 - Place where: Fort Niagara - Whether man of war, privateer, or merchant vessel: Taken on shore - When received: 29 Jan 1814 - From what ship or whence received: Montreal by land carriages. - Prisoner: 1372 - Rank: Private - Name of Prize: Land forces - By what ship or how taken: Taken on shore - Discharged: 4 May 1814 - By what order: Returned to the United States - Source: List of American Prisoners of War discharged at Quebec - Name of prize ship: Land forces.

Clark, James   Prisoner: 460 - Rank: Private - Name of Prize: Land forces - By what ship or how taken: Taken on shore - Discharged: 10 Aug 1813 - By what order: HMS Regulus by order of his Excellency Sir George Prevost - Source: List of American Prisoners of War discharged at Quebec - Name of prize ship: Land forces.

Clark, John   Prisoner: 77 - Rank: Private - Name of Prize: Land forces - By what ship or how taken: Taken on shore - Discharged: 31 Oct 1813 - By what order: HMS Malabar Transport by order of his Excellency Sir George Prevost - Source: List of American Prisoners of War discharged at Quebec - Name of prize ship: Land forces.

Clark, Joseph   Prisoner: 1715 - Rank: Ensign - Name of Prize: Land forces - By what ship or how taken: Taken on shore - Discharged: 10 Nov 1814 - By what order: Stately No. 400 to Halifax by order of Sir George Prevost - Source: List of American Prisoners of War discharged at Quebec - Name of prize ship: Land forces.

Clark, Stephen   Prisoner: 459 - Rank: Private - Name of Prize: Land forces - By what ship or how taken: Taken on shore - Discharged: 10 Aug 1813 - By what order: HMS Regulus by order of his Excellency Sir George Prevost - Source: List of American Prisoners of War discharged at Quebec - Name of prize ship: Land forces.

Clark, William   Prisoner: 78 - Rank: Private - Source: Account of American prisoners of war who died at Quebec in the Months of July, August & September 1813 - Ship or Corps: Land forces - Vessel: Taken on shore - Place born: Berwick - Age: 18 - Where taken: Stoney Point - Date of death: 5 Sep 1813 - Disorder or casualty: Diarrhea.

Clarke, Norman   Prisoner: 1262 - Rank: Private - By what ship or how taken: Troops - Time when: 19 Dec 1813 - Place where: Fort Niagara - Whether man of war, privateer, or merchant vessel: Taken on shore - When received: 29 Jan 1814 - From what ship or whence received: Montreal by land carriages. - Prisoner: 1262 - Rank: Private - Name of Prize: Land forces - By what ship or how taken: Taken on shore - Discharged: 4 May 1814 - By what order: Returned to the United States - Source: List of American Prisoners of War discharged at Quebec - Name of prize ship: Land forces.

Clay, Elijah   Prisoner: 305 - Rank: Private - Name of Prize: Land forces - By what ship or how taken: Taken on shore - Discharged: 31 Oct 1813 - By what order: HMS Malabar Transport by order of his Excellency Sir George Prevost - Source: List of American Prisoners of War discharged at Quebec - Name of prize ship: Land forces.

Clay, Walter   Prisoner: 567 - Rank: Private - Name of Prize: Land forces - By what ship or how taken: Taken on shore - Discharged: 10 Aug 1813 - By what order: HMS Regulus by order of his Excellency Sir George Prevost - Source: List of American Prisoners of War discharged at Quebec - Name of prize ship: Land forces.

Clayton, Farmer   Prisoner: 1816 - Rank: Private - Name of Prize: Land forces - By what ship or how taken: Taken on shore - Discharged: 8 Nov 1814 - By what order: George No. 515 by Sir George Prevost - Source: List of American Prisoners of War discharged at Quebec - Name of prize ship: Land forces.

Cleaver, Seth   Prisoner: 544 - Rank: Corporal - Name of Prize: Land forces - By what ship or how taken: Taken on shore - Discharged: 10 Aug 1813 - By what order: HMS Regulus by order of his Excellency Sir George Prevost - Source: List of American Prisoners of War discharged at Quebec - Name of prize ship: Land forces.

Clement, David   Prisoner: 691 - Rank: Sergeant - Source: Account of American prisoners of war who died at Quebec in the Months of July, August & September 1813 - Ship or Corps: Land forces - Vessel: Taken on shore - Place born: Maryland - Age: 44 - Where taken: Beaver Dams - Date of death: 3 Aug 1813.

Clews, Thomas   Prisoner: 1676 - Rank: Seaman - Name of Prize: Forsyth - By what ship or how taken: Merchant Vessel - Discharged: 7 Nov 1813 - By what order: HMS Freedom No. 582 by order of his Excellency Sir George Prevost - Source: List of American Prisoners of War discharged at Quebec - Name of prize ship: Forsyth.

Clyne, Isaac   Prisoner: 960 - Rank: Private - Name of Prize: Land forces - By what ship or how taken: Taken on shore - Discharged: 31 Oct 1813 - By what order: HMS Malabar Transport by order of his Excellency Sir George Prevost - Source: List of American Prisoners of War discharged at Quebec - Name of prize ship: Land forces.

Coalbath, John L.   Prisoner: 1770 - Rank: Sergeant - Name of Prize: Land forces - By what ship or how taken: Taken on shore - Discharged: 8 Nov 1814 - By what order: George No. 515 by Sir George Prevost - Source: List of American Prisoners of War discharged at Quebec - Name of prize ship: Land forces.

Coalbough, Michael   Prisoner: 1263 - Rank: Private - By what ship or how taken: Troops - Time when: 19 Dec 1813 - Place where: Fort Niagara - Whether man of war, privateer, or merchant vessel: Taken on shore - When received: 29 Jan 1814 - From what ship or whence received: Montreal by land carriages. - Prisoner: 1263 - Rank: Private - Name of Prize: Land forces - By what ship or how taken: Taken on shore - Discharged: 4 May 1814 - By what order: Returned to the United States - Source: List of American Prisoners of War discharged at Quebec - Name of prize ship: Land forces.

Coates, Elisha   Prisoner: 1261 - Rank: Private - By what ship or how taken: Troops - Time when: 19 Dec 1813 - Place where: Fort Niagara - Whether man of war, privateer, or merchant vessel: Taken on shore - When received: 29 Jan 1814 - From what ship or whence received: Montreal by land carriages. - Prisoner: 1261 - Rank: Private - Name of Prize: Land forces - By what ship or how taken: Taken on shore - Discharged: 4 May 1814 - By what order: Returned to the United States - Source: List of American Prisoners of War discharged at Quebec - Name of prize ship: Land forces.

Cobb, John   Prisoner: 235 - Rank: Private - Name of Prize: Growler - By what ship or how taken: Man of war - Discharged: 31 Oct 1813 - By what order: HMS Malabar Transport by order of his Excellency Sir George Prevost - Source: List of American Prisoners of War discharged at Quebec - Name of prize ship: Growler.

Cogswell, Alanson   Prisoner: 1229 - Rank: Private - Source: Account of American prisoners of war who died at Quebec between 14 February 1814 and 23 December 1814 - Ship or Corps: Land forces - Vessel: Taken on shore - Place born: Vermont - Age: 21 - Where taken: Fort Niagara - Date of death: 5 Mar 1814 - Disorder or casualty: Phthisis.

Colbun, James   Prisoner: 273 - Rank: Private - Name of Prize: Land forces - By what ship or how taken: Taken on shore - Discharged: 31 Oct 1813 - By what order: HMS Malabar Transport by order of his Excellency Sir George Prevost - Source: List of American Prisoners of War discharged at Quebec - Name of prize ship: Land forces.

Colby, Jacob   Prisoner: 52 - Rank: Private - Name of Prize: Land forces - By what ship or how taken: Taken on shore - Discharged: 31 Oct 1813 - By what order: HMS Malabar Transport by order of his Excellency Sir George Prevost - Source: List of American Prisoners of War discharged at Quebec - Name of prize ship: Land forces. - Prisoner: 52 - Rank: Private - Name of Prize: Land forces - By what ship or how taken: Taken on shore - Discharged: 4 May 1814 - By what order: Returned to the United States - Source: List of American Prisoners of War discharged at Quebec - Name of prize ship: Land forces.

Cole, Benjamin   Prisoner: 1972 - Rank: Citizen - Discharged: 13 Mar 1815 - By what order: Returned to the United States - Source: List of American Prisoners of War discharged at Quebec.

Cole, Ely   Prisoner: 1827 - Rank: Private - Name of Prize: Land forces - By what ship or how taken: Taken on shore - Discharged: 8 Nov 1814 - By what order: George No. 515 by Sir George Prevost - Source: List of American Prisoners of War discharged at Quebec - Name of prize ship: Land forces.

Cole, Thomas   Prisoner: 1420 - Rank: Private - By what ship or how taken: Troops - Time when: 19 Dec 1813 - Place where: Fort Niagara - Whether man of war, privateer, or merchant vessel: Taken on shore - When received: 29 Jan 1814 - From what ship or whence received: Montreal by land carriages. - Prisoner: 1420 - Rank: Private - Name of Prize: Land forces - By what ship or how taken: Taken on shore - Discharged: 4 May 1814 - By what order: Returned to the United States - Source: List of American Prisoners of War discharged at Quebec - Name of prize ship: Land forces.

Collins, Robert   Prisoner: 708 - Rank: Private - Name of Prize: Land forces - By what ship or how taken: Taken on shore - Discharged: 10 Aug 1813 - By what order: HMS Regulus by order of his Excellency Sir George Prevost - Source: List of American Prisoners of War discharged at Quebec - Name of prize ship: Land forces.

Colville, Robert   Prisoner: 1428 - Rank: Private - By what ship or how taken: Troops - Time when: 19 Dec 1813 - Place where: Fort Niagara - Whether man of war, privateer, or merchant vessel: Taken on shore - When received: 29 Jan 1814 - From what ship or whence received: Montreal by land carriages. - Prisoner: 1428 - Rank: Private - Name of Prize: Land forces - By what ship or how taken: Taken on shore - Discharged: 6 May 1814 - By what order: Returned to the United States - Source: List of American Prisoners of War discharged at Quebec - Name of prize ship: Land forces.

Conklin, John J.   Prisoner: 1919 - Rank: Corporal - Name of Prize: Land forces - By what ship or how taken: Taken on shore - Discharged: 8 Nov 1814 - By what order: George No. 515 by Sir George Prevost - Source: List of American Prisoners of War discharged at Quebec - Name of prize ship: Land forces.

Conkling, Abraham   Prisoner: 1565 - Rank: Lieutenant - Name of Prize: Ohio - By what ship or how taken: Man of war - Discharged: 10 Nov 1814 - By what order: Lord Cathcart No. 161 for Halifax by order of Sir George Prevost - Source: List of American Prisoners of War discharged at Quebec - Name of prize ship: Ohio.

Conner, John   Prisoner: 1049 - Rank: Private - Name of Prize: Growler - By what ship or how taken: Man of war - Discharged: 31 Oct 1813 - By what order: HMS Malabar Transport by order of his Excellency Sir George Prevost - Source: List of American Prisoners of War discharged at Quebec - Name of prize ship: Growler.

Conner, William   Prisoner: 1888 - Rank: Private - Name of Prize: Land forces - By what ship or how taken: Taken on shore - Discharged: 8 Nov 1814 - By what order: George No. 515 by Sir George Prevost - Source: List of American Prisoners of War discharged at Quebec - Name of prize ship: Land forces.

Conway, Michael   Prisoner: 406 - Rank: Private - Name of Prize: Land forces - By what ship or how taken: Taken on shore - Discharged: 31 Oct 1813 - By what order: HMS Malabar Transport by order of his Excellency Sir George Prevost - Source: List of American Prisoners of War discharged at Quebec - Name of prize ship: Land forces.

Conwell, John   Prisoner: 601 - Rank: Private - Name of Prize: Land forces - By what ship or how taken: Taken on shore - Discharged: 10 Aug 1813 - By what order: HMS Regulus by order of his Excellency Sir George Prevost - Source: List of American Prisoners of War discharged at Quebec - Name of prize ship: Land forces.

Cook, Hezekiah   Prisoner: 627 - Rank: Private - Name of Prize: Land forces - By what ship or how taken: Taken on shore - Discharged: 10 Aug 1813 - By what order: HMS Regulus by order of his Excellency Sir George Prevost - Source: List of American Prisoners of War discharged at Quebec - Name of prize ship: Land forces.

Cook, Joseph   Prisoner: 135 - Rank: Private - Name of Prize: Land forces - By what ship or how taken: Taken on shore - Discharged: 31 Oct 1813 - By what order: HMS Malabar Transport by order of his Excellency Sir George Prevost - Source: List of American Prisoners of War discharged at Quebec - Name of prize ship: Land forces.

Cook, Robert   Prisoner: 72 - Rank: Private - Name of Prize: Land forces - By what ship or how taken: Taken on shore - Discharged: 31 Oct 1813 - By what order: HMS Malabar Transport by order of his Excellency Sir George Prevost - Source: List of American Prisoners of War discharged at Quebec - Name of prize ship: Land forces.

Coomb, Isaac   Prisoner: 1974 - Rank: Private - Source: Account of American prisoners of war who died at Quebec between 14 February 1814 and 23 December 1814 - Ship or Corps: Land forces - Vessel: Taken on shore - Place born: New Hampshire - Age: 20 - Where taken: Fort Erie - Date of death: 22 Dec 1814 - Disorder or casualty: Typhus fever.

Corbin, Fielding   Prisoner: 1177 - Rank: Private - By what ship or how taken: Troops - Time when: 5 May 1813 - Place where: Rapids - Whether man of war, privateer, or merchant vessel: Taken on shore - When received: 25 Nov 1813 - From what ship or whence received: Town goal. - Prisoner: 1177 - Rank: Private - Name of Prize: Land forces - By what ship or how taken: Taken on shore - Discharged: 4 May 1814 - By what order: Returned to the United States - Source: List of American Prisoners of War discharged at Quebec - Name of prize ship: Land forces.

Corbin, James   Prisoner: 1164 - Rank: Corporal - By what ship or how taken: Troops - Time when: 5 May 1813 - Place where: Fort Dearborn - Whether man of war, privateer, or merchant vessel: Taken on shore - When received: 25 Nov 1813 - From what ship or whence received: Town goal. - Prisoner: 1164 - Rank: Private - Name of Prize: Land forces - By what ship or how taken: Taken on shore - Discharged: 4 May 1814 - By what order: Returned to the United States - Source: List of American Prisoners of War discharged at Quebec - Name of prize ship: Land forces.

Cord, Jacob   Prisoner: 688 - Rank: Private - Name of Prize: Land forces - By what ship or how taken: Taken on shore - Discharged: 10 Aug 1813 - By what order: HMS Regulus by order of his Excellency Sir George Prevost - Source: List of American Prisoners of War discharged at Quebec - Name of prize ship: Land forces.

Corkins, Joel   Prisoner: 390 - Rank: Private - Name of Prize: Land forces - By what ship or how taken: Taken on shore - Discharged: 31 Oct 1813 - By what order: HMS Malabar Transport by order of his Excellency Sir George Prevost - Source: List of American Prisoners of War discharged at Quebec - Name of prize ship: Land forces.

Corsey, John   Prisoner: 991 - Rank: Seaman - Name of Prize: Juliet - By what ship or how taken: Man of war - Discharged: 31 Oct 1813 - By what order: HMS Malabar Transport by order of his Excellency Sir George Prevost - Source: List of American Prisoners of War discharged at Quebec - Name of prize ship: Juliet.

Cotton, Seth   Prisoner: 1481 - Rank: Private - Source: Account of American prisoners of war who died at Quebec between 14 February 1814 and 23 December 1814 - Ship or Corps: Land forces - Vessel: Taken on shore - Place born: Massachusetts - Age: 20 - Where taken: St. David - Date of death: 2 Sep 1814 - Disorder or casualty: Dysentery.

Count, Levin   Prisoner: 441 - Rank: Private - Name of Prize: Land forces - By what ship or how taken: Taken on shore - Discharged: 10 Aug 1813 - By what order: HMS Regulus by order of his Excellency Sir George Prevost - Source: List of American Prisoners of War discharged at Quebec - Name of prize ship: Land forces.

Cox, John   Prisoner: 335 - Rank: Private - Name of Prize: Land forces - By what ship or how taken: Taken on shore - Discharged: 31 Oct 1813 - By what order: HMS Malabar Transport by order of his Excellency Sir George Prevost - Source: List of American Prisoners of War discharged at Quebec - Name of prize ship: Land forces.

Craft, George B.   Prisoner: 1324 - Rank: Private - By what ship or how taken: Troops - Time when: 19 Dec 1813 - Place where: Fort Niagara - Whether man of war, privateer, or merchant vessel: Taken on shore - When

received: 29 Jan 1814 - From what ship or whence received: Montreal by land carriages. - Prisoner: 1324 - Rank: Private - Name of Prize: Land forces - By what ship or how taken: Taken on shore - Discharged: 4 May 1814 - By what order: Returned to the United States - Source: List of American Prisoners of War discharged at Quebec - Name of prize ship: Land forces.

Crandle, Joshua   Prisoner: 1684 - Rank: Sergeant Major - Name of Prize: Land forces - By what ship or how taken: Taken on shore - Discharged: 8 Nov 1814 - By what order: George No. 515 by Sir George Prevost - Source: List of American Prisoners of War discharged at Quebec - Name of prize ship: Land forces.

Cranston, John   Prisoner: 961 - Rank: Private - Name of Prize: Land forces - By what ship or how taken: Taken on shore - Discharged: 31 Oct 1813 - By what order: HMS Malabar Transport by order of his Excellency Sir George Prevost - Source: List of American Prisoners of War discharged at Quebec - Name of prize ship: Land forces.

Crayton, William   Prisoner: 380 - Rank: Private - Name of Prize: Land forces - By what ship or how taken: Taken on shore - Discharged: 31 Oct 1813 - By what order: HMS Malabar Transport by order of his Excellency Sir George Prevost - Source: List of American Prisoners of War discharged at Quebec - Name of prize ship: Land forces.

Creighton, Hugh   Prisoner: 1427 - Rank: Private - By what ship or how taken: Troops - Time when: 19 Dec 1813 - Place where: Fort Niagara - Whether man of war, privateer, or merchant vessel: Taken on shore - When received: 29 Jan 1814 - From what ship or whence received: Montreal by land carriages. - Prisoner: 1427 - Rank: Private - Name of Prize: Land forces - By what ship or how taken: Taken on shore - Discharged: 4 May 1814 - By what order: Returned to the United States - Source: List of American Prisoners of War discharged at Quebec - Name of prize ship: Land forces.

Crocker, Benjamin   Prisoner: 660 - Rank: Private - Name of Prize: Land forces - By what ship or how taken: Taken on shore - Discharged: 10 Aug 1813 - By what order: HMS Regulus by order of his Excellency Sir George Prevost - Source: List of American Prisoners of War discharged at Quebec - Name of prize ship: Land forces.

Crocker, John   Prisoner: 1167 - Rank: Private - By what ship or how taken: Troops - Time when: 5 May 1813 - Place where: Rapids - Whether man of war, privateer, or merchant vessel: Taken on shore - When received: 25 Nov 1813 - From what ship or whence received: Town goal. - Prisoner: 1167 - Rank: Private - Name of Prize: Land forces - By what ship or how taken: Taken on shore - Discharged: 4 May 1814 - By what order: Returned to the United States - Source: List of American Prisoners of War discharged at Quebec - Name of prize ship: Land forces.

Crosby, James   Prisoner: 1079 - Rank: Private - Name of Prize: Land forces - By what ship or how taken: Taken on shore - Discharged: 31 Oct 1813 - By what order: HMS Malabar Transport by order of his Excellency Sir George Prevost - Source: List of American Prisoners of War discharged at Quebec - Name of prize ship: Land forces.

Cross, Barnabus   Prisoner: 1378 - Rank: Private - By what ship or how taken: Troops - Time when: 19 Dec 1813 - Place where: Fort Niagara - Whether man of war, privateer, or merchant vessel: Taken on shore - When received: 29 Jan 1814 - From what ship or whence received: Montreal by land carriages. - Prisoner: 1378 - Rank: Private - Name of Prize: Land forces - By what ship or how taken: Taken on shore - Discharged: 22 Feb 1814 - By what order: Volunteered for the New Brunswick Fencibles - Source: List of American Prisoners of War discharged at Quebec - Name of prize ship: Land forces.

Crosby, William   Prisoner: 1898 - Rank: Sergeant - Name of Prize: Land forces - By what ship or how taken: Taken on shore - Discharged: 8 Nov 1814 - By what order: George No. 515 by Sir George Prevost - Source: List of American Prisoners of War discharged at Quebec - Name of prize ship: Land forces.

Crouch, Henry   Prisoner: 1712 - Rank: Captain - Name of Prize: Land forces - By what ship or how taken: Taken on shore - Discharged: 10 Nov 1814 - By what order: Stately No. 400 to Halifax by order of Sir George Prevost - Source: List of American Prisoners of War discharged at Quebec - Name of prize ship: Land forces.

Cummings, David   Prisoner: 928 - Rank: Captain - Name of Prize: Land forces - By what ship or how taken: Taken on shore - Discharged: 10 Aug 1813 - By what order: HMS Regulus by order of his Excellency Sir George Prevost - Source: List of American Prisoners of War discharged at Quebec - Name of prize ship: Land forces.

Cummings, John L.   Prisoner: 1566 - Rank: Midshipman - Name of Prize: Ohio - By what ship or how taken: Man of war - Discharged: 10 Nov 1814 - By what order: Lord Cathcart No. 161 for Halifax by order of Sir George Prevost - Source: List of American Prisoners of War discharged at Quebec - Name of prize ship: Ohio.

Cunningham, Kelley   Prisoner: 602 - Rank: Private - Name of Prize: Land forces - By what ship or how taken: Taken on shore - Discharged: 10 Aug 1813 - By what order: HMS Regulus by order of his Excellency Sir

George Prevost - Source: List of American Prisoners of War discharged at Quebec - Name of prize ship: Land forces.

Curtis, Morgan   Prisoner: 1376 - Rank: Private - By what ship or how taken: Troops - Time when: 19 Dec 1813 - Place where: Fort Niagara - Whether man of war, privateer, or merchant vessel: Taken on shore - When received: 29 Jan 1814 - From what ship or whence received: Montreal by land carriages. - Prisoner: 1376 - Rank: Private - Name of Prize: Land forces - By what ship or how taken: Taken on shore - Discharged: 9 Mar 1814 - By what order: Volunteered for the New Brunswick Fencibles - Source: List of American Prisoners of War discharged at Quebec - Name of prize ship: Land forces.

Daggett, Josiah   Prisoner: 38 - Rank: Private - Name of Prize: Land forces - By what ship or how taken: Taken on shore - Discharged: 31 Oct 1813 - By what order: HMS Malabar Transport by order of his Excellency Sir George Prevost - Source: List of American Prisoners of War discharged at Quebec - Name of prize ship: Land forces.

Daggett, Lewis   Prisoner: 31 - Rank: Corporal - Name of Prize: Land forces - By what ship or how taken: Taken on shore - Discharged: 31 Oct 1813 - By what order: HMS Malabar Transport by order of his Excellency Sir George Prevost - Source: List of American Prisoners of War discharged at Quebec - Name of prize ship: Land forces.

Dalloff, David   Prisoner: 1178 - Rank: Private - By what ship or how taken: Troops - Time when: 5 May 1813 - Place where: Rapids - Whether man of war, privateer, or merchant vessel: Taken on shore - When received: 25 Nov 1813 - From what ship or whence received: Town goal. - Prisoner: 1178 - Rank: Private - Name of Prize: Land forces - By what ship or how taken: Taken on shore - Discharged: 4 May 1814 - By what order: Returned to the United States - Source: List of American Prisoners of War discharged at Quebec - Name of prize ship: Land forces.

Dalyrumple, John   Prisoner: 1891 - Rank: Private - Name of Prize: Land forces - By what ship or how taken: Taken on shore - Discharged: 8 Nov 1814 - By what order: George No. 515 by Sir George Prevost - Source: List of American Prisoners of War discharged at Quebec - Name of prize ship: Land forces.

Dandridge, Richard   Prisoner: 674 - Rank: Corporal - Name of Prize: Land forces - By what ship or how taken: Taken on shore - Discharged: 10 Aug 1813 - By what order: HMS Regulus by order of his Excellency Sir George Prevost - Source: List of American Prisoners of War discharged at Quebec - Name of prize ship: Land forces.

Danforth, Joseph S.   Prisoner: 193 - Rank: Private - Name of Prize: Eagle - By what ship or how taken: Man of war - Discharged: 31 Oct 1813 - By what order: HMS Malabar Transport by order of his Excellency Sir George Prevost - Source: List of American Prisoners of War discharged at Quebec - Name of prize ship: Eagle.

Danickson, Benjamin   Prisoner: 1073 - Rank: Private - Name of Prize: Land forces - By what ship or how taken: Taken on shore - Discharged: 31 Oct 1813 - By what order: HMS Malabar Transport by order of his Excellency Sir George Prevost - Source: List of American Prisoners of War discharged at Quebec - Name of prize ship: Land forces.

Dannenburg, William   Prisoner: 1755 - Rank: Private - Name of Prize: Tigress - By what ship or how taken: Man of war - Discharged: 8 Nov 1814 - By what order: George No. 515 by Sir George Prevost - Source: List of American Prisoners of War discharged at Quebec - Name of prize ship: Tigress.

Darling, Gamaliel   Prisoner: 1568 - Rank: Sailing Master - Name of Prize: Somers - By what ship or how taken: Man of war - Discharged: 10 Nov 1814 - By what order: Lord Cathcart No. 161 for Halifax by order of Sir George Prevost - Source: List of American Prisoners of War discharged at Quebec - Name of prize ship: Somers.

Darling, Thomas   Prisoner: 1310 - Rank: Private - By what ship or how taken: Troops - Time when: 19 Dec 1813 - Place where: Fort Niagara - Whether man of war, privateer, or merchant vessel: Taken on shore - When received: 29 Jan 1814 - From what ship or whence received: Montreal by land carriages. - Prisoner: 1310 - Rank: Private - Name of Prize: Land forces - By what ship or how taken: Taken on shore - Discharged: 4 May 1814 - By what order: Returned to the United States - Source: List of American Prisoners of War discharged at Quebec - Name of prize ship: Land forces.

Davidson, John (1)   Prisoner: 481 - Rank: Private - Name of Prize: Land forces - By what ship or how taken: Taken on shore - Discharged: 10 Aug 1813 - By what order: HMS Regulus by order of his Excellency Sir George Prevost - Source: List of American Prisoners of War discharged at Quebec - Name of prize ship: Land forces.

Davidson, John (2)   Prisoner: 604 - Rank: Private - Name of Prize: Land forces - By what ship or how taken: Taken on shore - Discharged: 31 Oct 1813 - By what order: HMS Malabar Transport by order of his

Excellency Sir George Prevost - Source: List of American Prisoners of War discharged at Quebec - Name of prize ship: Land forces.

Davis, Benjamin   Prisoner: 572 - Rank: Private - Name of Prize: Land forces - By what ship or how taken: Taken on shore - Discharged: 10 Aug 1813 - By what order: HMS Regulus by order of his Excellency Sir George Prevost - Source: List of American Prisoners of War discharged at Quebec - Name of prize ship: Land forces.

Davis, Elnathan   Prisoner: 324 - Rank: Private - Name of Prize: Land forces - By what ship or how taken: Taken on shore - Discharged: 31 Oct 1813 - By what order: HMS Malabar Transport by order of his Excellency Sir George Prevost - Source: List of American Prisoners of War discharged at Quebec - Name of prize ship: Land forces.

Davis, Ezra   Prisoner: 596 - Rank: Private - Name of Prize: Land forces - By what ship or how taken: Taken on shore - Discharged: 10 Aug 1813 - By what order: HMS Regulus by order of his Excellency Sir George Prevost - Source: List of American Prisoners of War discharged at Quebec - Name of prize ship: Land forces.

Davis, John (1)   Prisoner: 675 - Rank: Private - Name of Prize: Land forces - By what ship or how taken: Taken on shore - Discharged: 10 Aug 1813 - By what order: HMS Regulus by order of his Excellency Sir George Prevost - Source: List of American Prisoners of War discharged at Quebec - Name of prize ship: Land forces.

Davis, John (2)   Prisoner: 497 - Rank: Private - Name of Prize: Land forces - By what ship or how taken: Taken on shore - Discharged: 10 Aug 1813 - By what order: HMS Regulus by order of his Excellency Sir George Prevost - Source: List of American Prisoners of War discharged at Quebec - Name of prize ship: Land forces.

Davis, John (3)   Prisoner: 1096 - Rank: Private - Name of Prize: Land forces - By what ship or how taken: Taken on shore - Discharged: 31 Oct 1813 - By what order: HMS Malabar Transport by order of his Excellency Sir George Prevost - Source: List of American Prisoners of War discharged at Quebec - Name of prize ship: Land forces.

Davis, Moses   Prisoner: 23 - Rank: Private - Name of Prize: Land forces - By what ship or how taken: Taken on shore - Discharged: 31 Oct 1813 - By what order: HMS Malabar Transport by order of his Excellency Sir George Prevost - Source: List of American Prisoners of War discharged at Quebec - Name of prize ship: Land forces.

Davis, Peter   Prisoner: 1214 - Rank: Ensign - By what ship or how taken: Troops - Time when: 19 Dec 1813 - Place where: Fort Niagara - Whether man of war, privateer, or merchant vessel: Taken on shore - When received: 28 Jan 1814 - From what ship or whence received: Montreal by land carriages. - Prisoner: 1214 - Rank: Ensign - Name of Prize: Land forces - By what ship or how taken: Taken on shore - Discharged: 6 May 1814 - By what order: Returned to the United States - Source: List of American Prisoners of War discharged at Quebec - Name of prize ship: Land forces.

Davis, Stephen   Prisoner: 81 - Rank: Private - Source: Account of American prisoners of war who died at Quebec in the Months of July, August & September 1813 - Ship or Corps: Land forces - Vessel: Taken on shore - Place born: Newberg, MA - Age: 47 - Where taken: Stoney Point - Date of death: 10 Aug 1813.

Davis, Theddock   Prisoner: 600 - Rank: Private - Name of Prize: Land forces - By what ship or how taken: Taken on shore - Discharged: 10 Aug 1813 - By what order: HMS Regulus by order of his Excellency Sir George Prevost - Source: List of American Prisoners of War discharged at Quebec - Name of prize ship: Land forces.

Davis, Thomas (1)   Prisoner: 475 - Rank: Private - Name of Prize: Land forces - By what ship or how taken: Taken on shore - Discharged: 10 Aug 1813 - By what order: HMS Regulus by order of his Excellency Sir George Prevost - Source: List of American Prisoners of War discharged at Quebec - Name of prize ship: Land forces.

Davis, Thomas (2)   Prisoner: 1048 - Rank: Private - Name of Prize: Growler - By what ship or how taken: Man of war - Discharged: 31 Oct 1813 - By what order: HMS Malabar Transport by order of his Excellency Sir George Prevost - Source: List of American Prisoners of War discharged at Quebec - Name of prize ship: Growler.

Davis, Thomas (3)   Prisoner: 1900 - Rank: Private - Name of Prize: Land forces - By what ship or how taken: Taken on shore - Discharged: 8 Nov 1814 - By what order: George No. 515 by Sir George Prevost - Source: List of American Prisoners of War discharged at Quebec - Name of prize ship: Land forces.

Day, Andrew D.   Prisoner: 1798 - Rank: Private - Name of Prize: Land forces - By what ship or how taken: Taken on shore - Discharged: 8 Nov 1814 - By what order: George No. 515 by Sir George Prevost - Source: List of American Prisoners of War discharged at Quebec - Name of prize ship: Land forces.

Day, John   Prisoner: 1251 - Rank: Blacksmith - By what ship or how taken: Troops - Time when: 19 Dec 1813 - Place where: Fort Niagara - Whether man of war, privateer, or merchant vessel: Taken on shore - When received: 29 Jan 1814 - From what ship or whence received: Montreal by land carriages. - Prisoner: 1251 - Rank: Blacksmith - Name of Prize: Land forces - By what ship or how taken: Taken on shore - Discharged: 4 May 1814 - By what order: Returned to the United States - Source: List of American Prisoners of War

discharged at Quebec - Name of prize ship: Land forces.

Deacon, David   Prisoner: 1067 - Rank: Lieutenant - Name of Prize: Growler - By what ship or how taken: Man of war - Discharged: 16 Nov 1813 - By what order: Returned to the United States - Source: List of American Prisoners of War discharged at Quebec - Name of prize ship: Growler.

Dearborn, Solomon   Prisoner: 60 - Rank: Private - Source: Account of American prisoners of war who died at Quebec in the Months of July, August & September 1813 - Ship or Corps: Land forces - Vessel: Taken on shore - Place born: Saco, MA - Age: 28 - Where taken: Stoney Point - Date of death: 23 Jul 1813.

Dearing, John   Prisoner: 82 - Rank: Private - Source: Account of American prisoners of war who died at Quebec in the Months of July, August & September 1813 - Ship or Corps: Land forces - Vessel: Taken on shore - Place born: Arundel, MA - Age: 25 - Where taken: Stoney Point - Date of death: 28 Sep 1813 - Disorder or casualty: Typhus fever.

Decker, Zeli   Prisoner: 1105 - Rank: Private - Name of Prize: Land forces - By what ship or how taken: Taken on shore - Discharged: 31 Oct 1813 - By what order: HMS Malabar Transport by order of his Excellency Sir George Prevost - Source: List of American Prisoners of War discharged at Quebec - Name of prize ship: Land forces.

DeFriend, John   Prisoner: 322 - Rank: Private - Source: Account of American prisoners of war who died at Quebec in the Months of July, August & September 1813 - Ship or Corps: Land forces - Vessel: Taken on shore - Place born: Merygo, PA - Age: 30 - Where taken: Stoney Point - Date of death: 17 Jul 1813 - Disorder or casualty: Dysentery.

Dellaghen, George   Prisoner: 709 - Rank: Private - Name of Prize: Land forces - By what ship or how taken: Taken on shore - Discharged: 10 Aug 1813 - By what order: HMS Regulus by order of his Excellency Sir George Prevost - Source: List of American Prisoners of War discharged at Quebec - Name of prize ship: Land forces.

Denison, Bebel   Prisoner: 1824 - Rank: Private - Name of Prize: Land forces - By what ship or how taken: Taken on shore - Discharged: 8 Nov 1814 - By what order: George No. 515 by Sir George Prevost - Source: List of American Prisoners of War discharged at Quebec - Name of prize ship: Land forces.

Denison, John   Prisoner: 1845 - Rank: Corporal - Name of Prize: Land forces - By what ship or how taken: Taken on shore - Discharged: 8 Nov 1814 - By what order: George No. 515 by Sir George Prevost - Source: List of American Prisoners of War discharged at Quebec - Name of prize ship: Land forces.

Denison, Luther   Prisoner: 1798 - Rank: Private - Name of Prize: Land forces - By what ship or how taken: Taken on shore - Discharged: 8 Nov 1814 - By what order: George No. 515 by Sir George Prevost - Source: List of American Prisoners of War discharged at Quebec - Name of prize ship: Land forces.

Diffenderffer, Frederick   Prisoner: 1391 - Rank: Private - By what ship or how taken: Troops - Time when: 19 Dec 1813 - Place where: Fort Niagara - Whether man of war, privateer, or merchant vessel: Taken on shore - When received: 29 Jan 1814 - From what ship or whence received: Montreal by land carriages. - Prisoner: 1391 - Rank: Private - Name of Prize: Land forces - By what ship or how taken: Taken on shore - Discharged: 4 May 1814 - By what order: Returned to the United States - Source: List of American Prisoners of War discharged at Quebec - Name of prize ship: Land forces.

Dill, Peter   Prisoner: 541 - Rank: Private - Name of Prize: Land forces - By what ship or how taken: Taken on shore - Discharged: 31 Oct 1813 - By what order: HMS Malabar Transport by order of his Excellency Sir George Prevost - Source: List of American Prisoners of War discharged at Quebec - Name of prize ship: Land forces.

Diller, Robert   Prisoner: 1258 - Rank: Private - By what ship or how taken: Troops - Time when: 19 Dec 1813 - Place where: Fort Niagara - Whether man of war, privateer, or merchant vessel: Taken on shore - When received: 29 Jan 1814 - From what ship or whence received: Montreal by land carriages. - Prisoner: 1258 - Rank: Private - Name of Prize: Land forces - By what ship or how taken: Taken on shore - Discharged: 4 May 1814 - By what order: Returned to the United States - Source: List of American Prisoners of War discharged at Quebec - Name of prize ship: Land forces.

Diver, David   Prisoner: 1063 - Rank: Private - Name of Prize: Land forces - By what ship or how taken: Taken on shore - Discharged: 24 Nov 1813 - By what order: Sent to HMS Aeolus - Source: List of American Prisoners of War discharged at Quebec - Name of prize ship: Land forces.

Dixon, James   Prisoner: 423 - Rank: Corporal - Name of Prize: Land forces - By what ship or how taken: Taken on shore - Discharged: 31 Oct 1813 - By what order: HMS Malabar Transport by order of his Excellency Sir George Prevost - Source: List of American Prisoners of War discharged at Quebec - Name of prize ship: Land forces.

Dodd, Moses   Prisoner: 1911 - Rank: Private - Name of Prize: Land forces - By what ship or how taken: Taken on shore - Discharged: 8 Nov 1814 - By what order: George No. 515 by Sir George Prevost - Source: List of

American Prisoners of War discharged at Quebec - Name of prize ship: Land forces.

Donaldson, Thomas   Prisoner: 714 - Rank: Private - Name of Prize: Land forces - By what ship or how taken: Taken on shore - Discharged: 31 Oct 1813 - By what order: HMS Malabar Transport by order of his Excellency Sir George Prevost - Source: List of American Prisoners of War discharged at Quebec - Name of prize ship: Land forces.

Doolittle, William   Prisoner: 1918 - Rank: Private - Name of Prize: Land forces - By what ship or how taken: Taken on shore - Discharged: 8 Nov 1814 - By what order: George No. 515 by Sir George Prevost - Source: List of American Prisoners of War discharged at Quebec - Name of prize ship: Land forces.

Dorens, William   Prisoner: 989 - Rank: Seaman - Name of Prize: Growler - By what ship or how taken: Man of war - Discharged: 31 Oct 1813 - By what order: HMS Malabar Transport by order of his Excellency Sir George Prevost - Source: List of American Prisoners of War discharged at Quebec - Name of prize ship: Growler.

Doty, Ambrose   Prisoner: 1847 - Rank: Citizen - Name of Prize: Land forces - By what ship or how taken: Taken on shore - Discharged: 8 Nov 1814 - By what order: George No. 515 by Sir George Prevost - Source: List of American Prisoners of War discharged at Quebec - Name of prize ship: Land forces.

Dougherty, Hamilton   Prisoner: 505 - Rank: Private - Name of Prize: Land forces - By what ship or how taken: Taken on shore - Discharged: 10 Aug 1813 - By what order: HMS Regulus by order of his Excellency Sir George Prevost - Source: List of American Prisoners of War discharged at Quebec - Name of prize ship: Land forces.

Dougherty, James   Prisoner: 1417 - Rank: Private - By what ship or how taken: Troops - Time when: 19 Dec 1813 - Place where: Fort Niagara - Whether man of war, privateer, or merchant vessel: Taken on shore - When received: 29 Jan 1814 - From what ship or whence received: Montreal by land carriages. - Prisoner: 1417 - Rank: Private - Name of Prize: Land forces - By what ship or how taken: Taken on shore - Discharged: 4 May 1814 - By what order: Returned to the United States - Source: List of American Prisoners of War discharged at Quebec - Name of prize ship: Land forces.

Dougherty, Jared   Prisoner: 1264 - Rank: Private - By what ship or how taken: Troops - Time when: 19 Dec 1813 - Place where: Fort Niagara - Whether man of war, privateer, or merchant vessel: Taken on shore - When received: 29 Jan 1814 - From what ship or whence received: Montreal by land carriages. - Prisoner: 1264 - Rank: Private - Name of Prize: Land forces - By what ship or how taken: Taken on shore - Discharged: 4 May 1814 - By what order: Returned to the United States - Source: List of American Prisoners of War discharged at Quebec - Name of prize ship: Land forces.

Dougherty, William   Prisoner: 737 - Rank: Private - Name of Prize: Land forces - By what ship or how taken: Taken on shore - Discharged: 31 Oct 1813 - By what order: HMS Malabar Transport by order of his Excellency Sir George Prevost - Source: List of American Prisoners of War discharged at Quebec - Name of prize ship: Land forces.

Doughty, Elias   Prisoner: 321 - Rank: Private - Name of Prize: Land forces - By what ship or how taken: Taken on shore - Discharged: 31 Oct 1813 - By what order: HMS Malabar Transport by order of his Excellency Sir George Prevost - Source: List of American Prisoners of War discharged at Quebec - Name of prize ship: Land forces.

Douglass, Luther   Prisoner: 1830 - Rank: Private - Name of Prize: Land forces - By what ship or how taken: Taken on shore - Discharged: 8 Nov 1814 - By what order: George No. 515 by Sir George Prevost - Source: List of American Prisoners of War discharged at Quebec - Name of prize ship: Land forces.

Drake, Elisha   Prisoner: 223 - Rank: Private - Name of Prize: Growler - By what ship or how taken: Man of war - Discharged: 31 Oct 1813 - By what order: HMS Malabar Transport by order of his Excellency Sir George Prevost - Source: List of American Prisoners of War discharged at Quebec - Name of prize ship: Growler.

Drake, George W.   Prisoner: 1374 - Rank: Private - By what ship or how taken: Troops - Time when: 19 Dec 1813 - Place where: Fort Niagara - Whether man of war, privateer, or merchant vessel: Taken on shore - When received: 29 Jan 1814 - From what ship or whence received: Montreal by land carriages. - Prisoner: 1374 - Rank: Private - Name of Prize: Land forces - By what ship or how taken: Taken on shore - Discharged: 4 May 1814 - By what order: Returned to the United States - Source: List of American Prisoners of War discharged at Quebec - Name of prize ship: Land forces.

Draper, Francis   Prisoner: 262 - Rank: Sergeant - Name of Prize: Land forces - By what ship or how taken: Taken on shore - Discharged: 3 Apr 1814 - By what order: Returned to the United States - Source: List of American Prisoners of War discharged at Quebec - Name of prize ship: Land forces.

Drayton, Joseph   Prisoner: 1311 - Rank: Private - By what ship or how taken: Troops - Time when: 19 Dec 1813 - Place where: Fort Niagara - Whether man of war, privateer, or merchant vessel: Taken on shore - When

received: 29 Jan 1814 - From what ship or whence received: Montreal by land carriages. - Prisoner: 1311 - Rank: Private - Name of Prize: Land forces - By what ship or how taken: Taken on shore - Discharged: 4 May 1814 - By what order: Returned to the United States - Source: List of American Prisoners of War discharged at Quebec - Name of prize ship: Land forces.

Dresser, Thomas Prisoner: 214 - Rank: Private - Name of Prize: Eagle - By what ship or how taken: Man of war - Discharged: 31 Oct 1813 - By what order: HMS Malabar Transport by order of his Excellency Sir George Prevost - Source: List of American Prisoners of War discharged at Quebec - Name of prize ship: Eagle.

Drew, Ira Prisoner: 140 - Rank: Lieutenant - Name of Prize: Land forces - By what ship or how taken: Taken on shore - Discharged: 10 Aug 1813 - By what order: HMS Regulus by order of his Excellency Sir George Prevost - Source: List of American Prisoners of War discharged at Quebec - Name of prize ship: Land forces.

Dubois, David Prisoner: 697 - Rank: Private - Name of Prize: Land forces - By what ship or how taken: Taken on shore - Discharged: 10 Aug 1813 - By what order: HMS Regulus by order of his Excellency Sir George Prevost - Source: List of American Prisoners of War discharged at Quebec - Name of prize ship: Land forces.

Duffy, Ebenezer Prisoner: 1013 - Rank: Seaman - Name of Prize: Juliet - By what ship or how taken: Man of war - Discharged: 31 Oct 1813 - By what order: HMS Malabar Transport by order of his Excellency Sir George Prevost - Source: List of American Prisoners of War discharged at Quebec - Name of prize ship: Juliet.

Dugan, James Prisoner: 913 - Rank: Private - Name of Prize: Land forces - By what ship or how taken: Taken on shore - Discharged: 31 Oct 1813 - By what order: HMS Malabar Transport by order of his Excellency Sir George Prevost - Source: List of American Prisoners of War discharged at Quebec - Name of prize ship: Land forces.

Duguinour, Charles Prisoner: 457 - Rank: Private - Name of Prize: Land forces - By what ship or how taken: Taken on shore - Discharged: 10 Aug 1813 - By what order: HMS Regulus by order of his Excellency Sir George Prevost - Source: List of American Prisoners of War discharged at Quebec - Name of prize ship: Land forces.

Dungan, Benjamin Prisoner: 363 - Rank: Private - Name of Prize: Land forces - By what ship or how taken: Taken on shore - Discharged: 31 Oct 1813 - By what order: HMS Malabar Transport by order of his Excellency Sir George Prevost - Source: List of American Prisoners of War discharged at Quebec - Name of prize ship: Land forces.

Dunn, Joel Prisoner: 1896 - Rank: Sergeant - Name of Prize: Land forces - By what ship or how taken: Taken on shore - Discharged: 8 Nov 1814 - By what order: George No. 515 by Sir George Prevost - Source: List of American Prisoners of War discharged at Quebec - Name of prize ship: Land forces.

Dunn, William Prisoner: 1029 - Rank: Seaman - Name of Prize: Growler - By what ship or how taken: Man of war - Discharged: 1 Nov 1813 - By what order: HMS Hero by order of his Excellency Sir George Prevost - Source: List of American prisoners sent to England on the HMS Hero - Name of prize ship: Growler.

Dunning, Jesse Prisoner: 415 - Rank: Private - Name of Prize: Land forces - By what ship or how taken: Taken on shore - Discharged: 31 Oct 1813 - By what order: HMS Malabar Transport by order of his Excellency Sir George Prevost - Source: List of American Prisoners of War discharged at Quebec - Name of prize ship: Land forces.

Dyer, Daniel Prisoner: 167 - Rank: Boy - Name of Prize: Eagle - By what ship or how taken: Man of war - Discharged: 31 Oct 1813 - By what order: HMS Malabar Transport by order of his Excellency Sir George Prevost - Source: List of American Prisoners of War discharged at Quebec - Name of prize ship: Eagle.

Dyer, Dyson Prisoner: 1151 - Rank: Private - By what ship or how taken: Troops - Time when: 5 May 1813 - Place where: Rapids, River Raisin - Whether man of war, privateer, or merchant vessel: Taken on shore - When received: 25 Nov 1813 - From what ship or whence received: Town goal. - Prisoner: 1151 - Rank: Private - Name of Prize: Land forces - By what ship or how taken: Taken on shore - Discharged: 4 May 1814 - By what order: Returned to the United States - Source: List of American Prisoners of War discharged at Quebec - Name of prize ship: Land forces.

Dyer, Isaac Prisoner: 165 - Rank: Seaman - Source: Account of American prisoners of war who died at Quebec in the Months of July, August & September 1813 - Ship or Corps: Eagle - Vessel: Man of war - Place born: Truro, MA - Age: 21 - Where taken: Lake Champlain - Date of death: 10 Sep 1813 - Disorder or casualty: Dysentery.

Dyke, Elijhua Prisoner: 1868 - Rank: Private - Name of Prize: Land forces - By what ship or how taken: Taken on shore - Discharged: 8 Nov 1814 - By what order: George No. 515 by Sir George Prevost - Source: List of American Prisoners of War discharged at Quebec - Name of prize ship: Land forces.

Eades, Thomas Prisoner: 1375 - Rank: Private - By what ship or how taken: Troops - Time when: 19 Dec 1813 - Place where: Fort Niagara - Whether man of war, privateer, or merchant vessel: Taken on shore - When

received: 29 Jan 1814 - From what ship or whence received: Montreal by land carriages. - Prisoner: 1375 - Rank: Private - Name of Prize: Land forces - By what ship or how taken: Taken on shore - Discharged: 4 May 1814 - By what order: Returned to the United States - Source: List of American Prisoners of War discharged at Quebec - Name of prize ship: Land forces.

Eastman, Henry   Prisoner: 1681 - Rank: Private - Name of Prize: Land forces - By what ship or how taken: Taken on shore - Discharged: 8 Nov 1814 - By what order: George No. 515 by Sir George Prevost - Source: List of American Prisoners of War discharged at Quebec - Name of prize ship: Land forces.

Eaton, Moses   Prisoner: 1168 - Rank: Private - By what ship or how taken: Troops - Time when: 5 May 1813 - Place where: Rapids - Whether man of war, privateer, or merchant vessel: Taken on shore - When received: 25 Nov 1813 - From what ship or whence received: Town goal. - Prisoner: 1168 - Rank: Private - Name of Prize: Land forces - By what ship or how taken: Taken on shore - Discharged: 4 May 1814 - By what order: Returned to the United States - Source: List of American Prisoners of War discharged at Quebec - Name of prize ship: Land forces.

Eaton, William (1)   Prisoner: 725 - Rank: Private - Name of Prize: Land forces - By what ship or how taken: Taken on shore - Discharged: 4 May 1814 - By what order: Returned to the United States - Source: List of American Prisoners of War discharged at Quebec - Name of prize ship: Land forces.

Eaton, William (2)   Prisoner: 576 - Rank: Private - Source: Account of American prisoners of war who died at Quebec in the Months of July, August & September 1813 - Ship or Corps: Land forces - Vessel: Taken on shore - Place born: New Jersey - Age: 17 - Where taken: Beaver Dams - Date of death: 23 Aug 1813.

Edget, Horan   Prisoner: 1850 - Rank: Private - Name of Prize: Land forces - By what ship or how taken: Taken on shore - Discharged: 8 Nov 1814 - By what order: George No. 515 by Sir George Prevost - Source: List of American Prisoners of War discharged at Quebec - Name of prize ship: Land forces.

Edson, Nathaniel   Prisoner: 1181 - Rank: Private - By what ship or how taken: Troops - Time when: 5 May 1813 - Place where: Rapids - Whether man of war, privateer, or merchant vessel: Taken on shore - When received: 25 Nov 1813 - From what ship or whence received: Town goal. - Prisoner: 1181 - Rank: Private - Name of Prize: Land forces - By what ship or how taken: Taken on shore - Discharged: 4 May 1814 - By what order: Returned to the United States - Source: List of American Prisoners of War discharged at Quebec - Name of prize ship: Land forces.

Edy, Charles   Prisoner: 1820 - Rank: Private - Name of Prize: Land forces - By what ship or how taken: Taken on shore - Discharged: 8 Nov 1814 - By what order: George No. 515 by Sir George Prevost - Source: List of American Prisoners of War discharged at Quebec - Name of prize ship: Land forces.

Ells, John   Prisoner: 33 - Rank: Private - Name of Prize: Land forces - By what ship or how taken: Taken on shore - Discharged: 31 Oct 1813 - By what order: HMS Malabar Transport by order of his Excellency Sir George Prevost - Source: List of American Prisoners of War discharged at Quebec - Name of prize ship: Land forces.

Elly, Daniel   Prisoner: 1742 - Rank: Seaman - Name of Prize: Tigress - By what ship or how taken: Man of war - Discharged: 7 Nov 1813 - By what order: HMS Freedom No. 582 by order of his Excellency Sir George Prevost - Source: List of American Prisoners of War discharged at Quebec - Name of prize ship: Tigress.

Elton, Moses   Prisoner: 1397 - Rank: Private - By what ship or how taken: Troops - Time when: 19 Dec 1813 - Place where: Fort Niagara - Whether man of war, privateer, or merchant vessel: Taken on shore - When received: 29 Jan 1814 - From what ship or whence received: Montreal by land carriages. - Prisoner: 1397 - Rank: Private - Name of Prize: Land forces - By what ship or how taken: Taken on shore - Discharged: 4 May 1814 - By what order: Returned to the United States - Source: List of American Prisoners of War discharged at Quebec - Name of prize ship: Land forces.

Emery, James   Prisoner: 229 - Rank: Private - Name of Prize: Eagle - By what ship or how taken: Man of war - Discharged: 31 Oct 1813 - By what order: HMS Malabar Transport by order of his Excellency Sir George Prevost - Source: List of American Prisoners of War discharged at Quebec - Name of prize ship: Eagle.

Emery, Stephen   Prisoner: 311 - Rank: Sergeant - Name of Prize: Land forces - By what ship or how taken: Taken on shore - Discharged: 31 Oct 1813 - By what order: HMS Malabar Transport by order of his Excellency Sir George Prevost - Source: List of American Prisoners of War discharged at Quebec - Name of prize ship: Land forces.

English, John   Prisoner: 575 - Rank: Private - Name of Prize: Land forces - By what ship or how taken: Taken on shore - Discharged: 31 Oct 1813 - By what order: HMS Malabar Transport by order of his Excellency Sir George Prevost - Source: List of American Prisoners of War discharged at Quebec - Name of prize ship: Land forces.

Enos, Abner   Prisoner: 1979 - Rank: Master's Mate - Name of Prize: Land forces - By what ship or how taken: Taken on shore - Discharged: 13 Mar 1815 - By what order: Returned to the United States - Source: List of

American Prisoners of War discharged at Quebec - Name of prize ship: Land forces.

Ervin, Lewis Prisoner: 625 - Rank: Private - Name of Prize: Land forces - By what ship or how taken: Taken on shore - Discharged: 2 Nov 1813 - Source: List of Prisoners received on board the Malabar, discharged from hospital - Name of prize ship: Land forces.

Erwin, James B. Prisoner: 268 - Rank: Sergeant - Name of Prize: Land forces - By what ship or how taken: Taken on shore - Discharged: 31 Oct 1813 - By what order: HMS Malabar Transport by order of his Excellency Sir George Prevost - Source: List of American Prisoners of War discharged at Quebec - Name of prize ship: Land forces.

Erwin, John Prisoner: 307 - Rank: Private - Name of Prize: Land forces - By what ship or how taken: Taken on shore - Discharged: 31 Oct 1813 - By what order: HMS Malabar Transport by order of his Excellency Sir George Prevost - Source: List of American Prisoners of War discharged at Quebec - Name of prize ship: Land forces.

Erwing, Patrick Prisoner: 1174 - Rank: Private - By what ship or how taken: Troops - Time when: 5 May 1813 - Place where: Rapids - Whether man of war, privateer, or merchant vessel: Taken on shore - When received: 25 Nov 1813 - From what ship or whence received: Town goal. - Prisoner: 1174 - Rank: Private - Name of Prize: Land forces - By what ship or how taken: Taken on shore - Discharged: 4 May 1814 - By what order: Returned to the United States - Source: List of American Prisoners of War discharged at Quebec - Name of prize ship: Land forces.

Estes, Edward Prisoner: 238 - Rank: Private - Name of Prize: Land forces - By what ship or how taken: Taken on shore - Discharged: 2 Nov 1813 - Source: List of Prisoners received on board the Malabar, discharged from hospital - Name of prize ship: Land forces.

Esty, Israel Prisoner: 1795 - Rank: Private - Name of Prize: Land forces - By what ship or how taken: Taken on shore - Discharged: 8 Nov 1814 - By what order: George No. 515 by Sir George Prevost - Source: List of American Prisoners of War discharged at Quebec - Name of prize ship: Land forces.

Evans, Thomas Prisoner: 53 - Rank: Private - Name of Prize: Land forces - By what ship or how taken: Taken on shore - Discharged: 31 Oct 1813 - By what order: HMS Malabar Transport by order of his Excellency Sir George Prevost - Source: List of American Prisoners of War discharged at Quebec - Name of prize ship: Land forces.

Evener, Christian Prisoner: 312 - Rank: Private - Name of Prize: Land forces - By what ship or how taken: Taken on shore - Discharged: 31 Oct 1813 - By what order: HMS Malabar Transport by order of his Excellency Sir George Prevost - Source: List of American Prisoners of War discharged at Quebec - Name of prize ship: Land forces.

Everton, Benjamin Prisoner: 710 - Rank: Private - Name of Prize: Land forces - By what ship or how taken: Taken on shore - Discharged: 31 Oct 1813 - By what order: HMS Malabar Transport by order of his Excellency Sir George Prevost - Source: List of American Prisoners of War discharged at Quebec - Name of prize ship: Land forces.

Ewings, James Prisoner: 1363 - Rank: Private - By what ship or how taken: Troops - Time when: 19 Dec 1813 - Place where: Fort Niagara - Whether man of war, privateer, or merchant vessel: Taken on shore - When received: 29 Jan 1814 - From what ship or whence received: Montreal by land carriages. - Prisoner: 1363 - Rank: Private - Name of Prize: Land forces - By what ship or how taken: Taken on shore - Discharged: 4 May 1814 - By what order: Returned to the United States - Source: List of American Prisoners of War discharged at Quebec - Name of prize ship: Land forces.

Fagan, Philip Prisoner: 1951 - Rank: Private - Name of Prize: Land forces - By what ship or how taken: Taken on shore - Discharged: 13 Mar 1815 - By what order: Returned to the United States - Source: List of American Prisoners of War discharged at Quebec - Name of prize ship: Land forces.

Fairchild, Cyrus Prisoner: 1112 - Rank: Private - Name of Prize: Land forces - By what ship or how taken: Taken on shore - Discharged: 31 Oct 1813 - By what order: HMS Malabar Transport by order of his Excellency Sir George Prevost - Source: List of American Prisoners of War discharged at Quebec - Name of prize ship: Land forces.

Falcon, John Prisoner: 1758 - Rank: Private - Name of Prize: Tigress - By what ship or how taken: Man of war - Discharged: 8 Nov 1814 - By what order: George No. 515 by Sir George Prevost - Source: List of American Prisoners of War discharged at Quebec - Name of prize ship: Tigress.

Farnham, Gaius Prisoner: 1275 - Rank: Sergeant - By what ship or how taken: Troops - Time when: 19 Dec 1813 - Place where: Fort Niagara - Whether man of war, privateer, or merchant vessel: Taken on shore - When received: 29 Jan 1814 - From what ship or whence received: Montreal by land carriages. - Prisoner: 1275 - Rank: Sergeant - Name of Prize: Land forces - By what ship or how taken: Taken on shore - Discharged: 28

Feb 1814 - By what order: Transferred to John Thomas No. 23 Transferred to Sovereign No. 28 Transport - Source: List of American Prisoners of War discharged at Quebec - Name of prize ship: Land forces.

Farr, Chester W. Prisoner: 1853 - Rank: Private - Name of Prize: Land forces - By what ship or how taken: Taken on shore - Discharged: 8 Nov 1814 - By what order: George No. 515 by Sir George Prevost - Source: List of American Prisoners of War discharged at Quebec - Name of prize ship: Land forces.

Farrard, Michael Prisoner: 1383 - Rank: Private - By what ship or how taken: Troops - Time when: 19 Dec 1813 - Place where: Fort Niagara - Whether man of war, privateer, or merchant vessel: Taken on shore - When received: 29 Jan 1814 - From what ship or whence received: Montreal by land carriages. - Prisoner: 1383 - Rank: Private - Name of Prize: Land forces - By what ship or how taken: Taken on shore - Discharged: 4 May 1814 - By what order: Returned to the United States - Source: List of American Prisoners of War discharged at Quebec - Name of prize ship: Land forces.

Farrell, Michael Prisoner: 835 - Rank: Private - Name of Prize: Land forces - By what ship or how taken: Taken on shore - Discharged: 31 Oct 1813 - By what order: HMS Malabar Transport by order of his Excellency Sir George Prevost - Source: List of American Prisoners of War discharged at Quebec - Name of prize ship: Land forces.

Farrell, Richard Prisoner: 1736 - Rank: Seaman - Name of Prize: Tigress - By what ship or how taken: Man of war - Discharged: 7 Nov 1813 - By what order: HMS Freedom No. 582 by order of his Excellency Sir George Prevost - Source: List of American Prisoners of War discharged at Quebec - Name of prize ship: Tigress.

Felton, John Prisoner: 1721 - Rank: Boatman's Mate - Name of Prize: Scorpion - By what ship or how taken: Man of war - Discharged: 7 Nov 1813 - By what order: HMS Freedom No. 582 by order of his Excellency Sir George Prevost - Source: List of American Prisoners of War discharged at Quebec - Name of prize ship: Scorpion.

Feney, John Prisoner: 252 - Rank: Private - Name of Prize: Land forces - By what ship or how taken: Taken on shore - Discharged: 10 Aug 1813 - By what order: HMS Regulus by order of his Excellency Sir George Prevost - Source: List of American Prisoners of War discharged at Quebec - Name of prize ship: Land forces - Comments: British subject, sent to England.

Fenning, Charles Prisoner: 1320 - Rank: Private - Source: Account of American prisoners of war who died at Quebec between 14 February 1814 and 23 December 1814 - Ship or Corps: Land forces - Vessel: Taken on shore - Place born: Pennsylvania - Age: 36 - Where taken: Fort Niagara - Date of death: 5 Jun 1814 - Disorder or casualty: Ascites.

Ferrish, Barney Prisoner: 1061 - Rank: Private - Name of Prize: Land forces - By what ship or how taken: Taken on shore - Discharged: 31 Oct 1813 - By what order: HMS Malabar Transport by order of his Excellency Sir George Prevost - Source: List of American Prisoners of War discharged at Quebec - Name of prize ship: Land forces.

Field, Eli Prisoner: 10 - Rank: Private - Name of Prize: Land forces - By what ship or how taken: Taken on shore - Discharged: 31 Oct 1813 - By what order: HMS Malabar Transport by order of his Excellency Sir George Prevost - Source: List of American Prisoners of War discharged at Quebec - Name of prize ship: Land forces.

Filkens, John Prisoner: 598 - Rank: Private - Name of Prize: Land forces - By what ship or how taken: Taken on shore - Discharged: 10 Aug 1813 - By what order: HMS Regulus by order of his Excellency Sir George Prevost - Source: List of American Prisoners of War discharged at Quebec - Name of prize ship: Land forces.

Fincher, Jesse Prisoner: 1297 - Rank: Private - By what ship or how taken: Troops - Time when: 19 Dec 1813 - Place where: Fort Niagara - Whether man of war, privateer, or merchant vessel: Taken on shore - When received: 29 Jan 1814 - From what ship or whence received: Montreal by land carriages. - Prisoner: 1297 - Rank: Private - Name of Prize: Land forces - By what ship or how taken: Taken on shore - Discharged: 4 May 1814 - By what order: Returned to the United States - Source: List of American Prisoners of War discharged at Quebec - Name of prize ship: Land forces.

Finegan, James Prisoner: 703 - Rank: Corporal - Name of Prize: Land forces - By what ship or how taken: Taken on shore - Discharged: 10 Aug 1813 - By what order: HMS Regulus by order of his Excellency Sir George Prevost - Source: List of American Prisoners of War discharged at Quebec - Name of prize ship: Land forces.

Finney, Elisha Prisoner: 384 - Rank: Private - Source: Account of American prisoners of war who died at Quebec in the Months of July, August & September 1813 - Ship or Corps: Land forces - Vessel: Taken on shore - Place born: Shanod - Age: 37 - Where taken: Stoney Point - Date of death: 28 Jul 1813.

Fisher, Jacob Prisoner: 624 - Rank: Private - Name of Prize: Land forces - By what ship or how taken: Taken on shore - Discharged: 10 Aug 1813 - By what order: HMS Regulus by order of his Excellency Sir George Prevost - Source: List of American Prisoners of War discharged at Quebec - Name of prize ship: Land forces.

Fisher, William   Prisoner: 1724 - Rank: Quartermaster - Name of Prize: Scorpion - By what ship or how taken: Man of war - Discharged: 7 Nov 1813 - By what order: HMS Freedom No. 582 by order of his Excellency Sir George Prevost - Source: List of American Prisoners of War discharged at Quebec - Name of prize ship: Scorpion.

Fistock, Thomas   Prisoner: 998 - Rank: Seaman - Name of Prize: Juliet - By what ship or how taken: Man of war - Discharged: 31 Oct 1813 - By what order: HMS Malabar Transport by order of his Excellency Sir George Prevost - Source: List of American Prisoners of War discharged at Quebec - Name of prize ship: Juliet.

Fitzgerald, Aaron   Prisoner: 109 - Rank: Private - Name of Prize: Land forces - By what ship or how taken: Taken on shore - Discharged: 4 May 1814 - By what order: Returned to the United States - Source: List of American Prisoners of War discharged at Quebec - Name of prize ship: Land forces.

Fitzgerald, James   Prisoner: 969 - Rank: Private - Name of Prize: Land forces - By what ship or how taken: Taken on shore - Discharged: 31 Oct 1813 - By what order: HMS Malabar Transport by order of his Excellency Sir George Prevost - Source: List of American Prisoners of War discharged at Quebec - Name of prize ship: Land forces.

Fleming, Joseph   Prisoner: 365 - Rank: Private - Name of Prize: Land forces - By what ship or how taken: Taken on shore - Discharged: 31 Oct 1813 - By what order: HMS Malabar Transport by order of his Excellency Sir George Prevost - Source: List of American Prisoners of War discharged at Quebec - Name of prize ship: Land forces.

Fleming, William   Prisoner: 1154 - Rank: Private - By what ship or how taken: Troops - Time when: 5 May 1813 - Place where: Rapids, River Raisin - Whether man of war, privateer, or merchant vessel: Taken on shore - When received: 25 Nov 1813 - From what ship or whence received: Town goal. - Prisoner: 1154 - Rank: Private - Name of Prize: Land forces - By what ship or how taken: Taken on shore - Discharged: 4 May 1814 - By what order: Returned to the United States - Source: List of American Prisoners of War discharged at Quebec - Name of prize ship: Land forces.

Flury, Francis   Prisoner: 1759 - Rank: Private - Name of Prize: Tigress - By what ship or how taken: Man of war - Discharged: 8 Nov 1814 - By what order: George No. 515 by Sir George Prevost - Source: List of American Prisoners of War discharged at Quebec - Name of prize ship: Tigress.

Fobes, Levin   Prisoner: 83 - Rank: Private - Name of Prize: Land forces - By what ship or how taken: Taken on shore - Discharged: 31 Oct 1813 - By what order: HMS Malabar Transport by order of his Excellency Sir George Prevost - Source: List of American Prisoners of War discharged at Quebec - Name of prize ship: Land forces.

Folson, John   Prisoner: 1952 - Rank: Private - Name of Prize: Land forces - By what ship or how taken: Taken on shore - Discharged: 13 Mar 1815 - By what order: Returned to the United States - Source: List of American Prisoners of War discharged at Quebec - Name of prize ship: Land forces.

Foot, Henry   Prisoner: 327 - Rank: Private - Name of Prize: Land forces - By what ship or how taken: Taken on shore - Discharged: 31 Oct 1813 - By what order: HMS Malabar Transport by order of his Excellency Sir George Prevost - Source: List of American Prisoners of War discharged at Quebec - Name of prize ship: Land forces.

Forrest, Arthur   Prisoner: 632 - Rank: Private - Name of Prize: Land forces - By what ship or how taken: Taken on shore - Discharged: 10 Aug 1813 - By what order: HMS Regulus by order of his Excellency Sir George Prevost - Source: List of American Prisoners of War discharged at Quebec - Name of prize ship: Land forces.

Forrester, Peter   Prisoner: 1227 - Rank: Private - By what ship or how taken: Troops - Time when: 19 Dec 1813 - Place where: Fort Niagara - Whether man of war, privateer, or merchant vessel: Taken on shore - When received: 29 Jan 1814 - From what ship or whence received: Montreal by land carriages. - Prisoner: 1227 - Rank: Private - Name of Prize: Land forces - By what ship or how taken: Taken on shore - Discharged: 4 May 1814 - By what order: Returned to the United States - Source: List of American Prisoners of War discharged at Quebec - Name of prize ship: Land forces.

Foster, George   Prisoner: 369 - Rank: Private - Name of Prize: Land forces - By what ship or how taken: Taken on shore - Discharged: 31 Oct 1813 - By what order: HMS Malabar Transport by order of his Excellency Sir George Prevost - Source: List of American Prisoners of War discharged at Quebec - Name of prize ship: Land forces.

Foster, Hulitt   Prisoner: 641 - Rank: Private - Source: Account of American prisoners of war who died at Quebec in the Months of July, August & September 1813 - Ship or Corps: Land forces - Vessel: Taken on shore - Place born: New Jersey - Age: 35 - Where taken: Beaver Dams - Date of death: 23 Sep 1813 - Disorder or casualty: Dysentery.

Foster, Nathaniel   Prisoner: 231 - Rank: Private - Source: Account of American prisoners of war who died at

Quebec in the Months of July, August & September 1813 - Ship or Corps: Growler - Vessel: Man of war - Place born: Freeport, MA - Age: 17 - Where taken: Lake Champlain - Date of death: 28 Aug 1813 - Disorder or casualty: Typhus fever.

Fover, John   Prisoner: 437 - Rank: Private - Name of Prize: Land forces - By what ship or how taken: Taken on shore - Discharged: 10 Aug 1813 - By what order: HMS Regulus by order of his Excellency Sir George Prevost - Source: List of American Prisoners of War discharged at Quebec - Name of prize ship: Land forces.

Francisco, John   Prisoner: 706 - Rank: Private - Name of Prize: Land forces - By what ship or how taken: Taken on shore - Discharged: 10 Aug 1813 - By what order: HMS Regulus by order of his Excellency Sir George Prevost - Source: List of American Prisoners of War discharged at Quebec - Name of prize ship: Land forces.

Frank, Christian F.   Prisoner: 699 - Rank: Private - Name of Prize: Land forces - By what ship or how taken: Taken on shore - Discharged: 10 Aug 1813 - By what order: HMS Regulus by order of his Excellency Sir George Prevost - Source: List of American Prisoners of War discharged at Quebec - Name of prize ship: Land forces.

Frank, James   Prisoner: 1068 - Rank: Sailing Master - Name of Prize: Juliet - By what ship or how taken: Man of war - Discharged: 4 May 1814 - By what order: Returned to the United States - Source: List of American Prisoners of War discharged at Quebec - Name of prize ship: Juliet.

Franklin, G.   Prisoner: 1828 - Rank: Private - Name of Prize: Land forces - By what ship or how taken: Taken on shore - Discharged: 8 Nov 1814 - By what order: George No. 515 by Sir George Prevost - Source: List of American Prisoners of War discharged at Quebec - Name of prize ship: Land forces.

Fraser, Hubbard   Prisoner: 436 - Rank: Private - Name of Prize: Land forces - By what ship or how taken: Taken on shore - Discharged: 10 Aug 1813 - By what order: HMS Regulus by order of his Excellency Sir George Prevost - Source: List of American Prisoners of War discharged at Quebec - Name of prize ship: Land forces.

Frederick, Henry   Prisoner: 1203 - Rank: Lieutenant - By what ship or how taken: Troops - Time when: 19 Dec 1813 - Place where: Fort Niagara - Whether man of war, privateer, or merchant vessel: Taken on shore - When received: 18 Jan 1814 - From what ship or whence received: Montreal by land carriages. - Prisoner: 1203 - Rank: Lieutenant - Name of Prize: Land forces - By what ship or how taken: Taken on shore - Discharged: 4 May 1814 - By what order: Returned to the United States - Source: List of American Prisoners of War discharged at Quebec - Name of prize ship: Land forces.

Fredericks, Peter D.   Prisoner: 1872 - Rank: Private - Name of Prize: Land forces - By what ship or how taken: Taken on shore - Discharged: 8 Nov 1814 - By what order: George No. 515 by Sir George Prevost - Source: List of American Prisoners of War discharged at Quebec - Name of prize ship: Land forces.

Freeborne, John   Prisoner: 144 - Rank: Master's Mate - Name of Prize: Eagle - By what ship or how taken: Man of war - Discharged: 6 May 1814 - By what order: Returned to the United States - Source: List of American Prisoners of War discharged at Quebec - Name of prize ship: Eagle.

Freeman, James   Prisoner: 315 - Rank: Private - Name of Prize: Land forces - By what ship or how taken: Taken on shore - Discharged: 4 May 1814 - By what order: Returned to the United States - Source: List of American Prisoners of War discharged at Quebec - Name of prize ship: Land forces.

French, Thomas   Prisoner: 1889 - Rank: Private - Name of Prize: Land forces - By what ship or how taken: Taken on shore - Discharged: 8 Nov 1814 - By what order: George No. 515 by Sir George Prevost - Source: List of American Prisoners of War discharged at Quebec - Name of prize ship: Land forces.

Fricks, John   Prisoner: 174 - Rank: Able Seaman - Name of Prize: Growler - By what ship or how taken: Man of war - Discharged: 4 May 1814 - By what order: Returned to the United States - Source: List of American Prisoners of War discharged at Quebec - Name of prize ship: Growler.

Frisk, Howard   Prisoner: 1125 - Rank: Private - Name of Prize: Land forces - By what ship or how taken: Taken on shore - Discharged: 31 Oct 1813 - By what order: HMS Malabar Transport by order of his Excellency Sir George Prevost - Source: List of American Prisoners of War discharged at Quebec - Name of prize ship: Land forces.

Fritz, Charles   Prisoner: 712 - Rank: Private - Name of Prize: Land forces - By what ship or how taken: Taken on shore - Discharged: 10 Aug 1813 - By what order: HMS Regulus by order of his Excellency Sir George Prevost - Source: List of American Prisoners of War discharged at Quebec - Name of prize ship: Land forces.

Fruhen, Edward   Prisoner: 1058 - Rank: Private - Name of Prize: Land forces - By what ship or how taken: Taken on shore - Discharged: 31 Oct 1813 - By what order: HMS Malabar Transport by order of his Excellency Sir George Prevost - Source: List of American Prisoners of War discharged at Quebec - Name of prize ship: Land forces.

Fuller, John B.   Prisoner: 1927 - Rank: Private - Name of Prize: Land forces - By what ship or how taken: Taken on shore - Discharged: 13 Mar 1815 - By what order: Returned to the United States - Source: List of

American Prisoners of War discharged at Quebec - Name of prize ship: Land forces.

Fullerton, John   Prisoner: 590 - Rank: Private - Name of Prize: Land forces - By what ship or how taken: Taken on shore - Discharged: 10 Aug 1813 - By what order: HMS Regulus by order of his Excellency Sir George Prevost - Source: List of American Prisoners of War discharged at Quebec - Name of prize ship: Land forces.

Fullerton, William   Prisoner: 593 - Rank: Private - Name of Prize: Land forces - By what ship or how taken: Taken on shore - Discharged: 10 Aug 1813 - By what order: HMS Regulus by order of his Excellency Sir George Prevost - Source: List of American Prisoners of War discharged at Quebec - Name of prize ship: Land forces.

Furbush, Joshua   Prisoner: 162 - Rank: Able Seaman - Name of Prize: Eagle - By what ship or how taken: Man of war - Discharged: 4 May 1814 - By what order: Returned to the United States - Source: List of American Prisoners of War discharged at Quebec - Name of prize ship: Eagle.

Gain, John   Prisoner: 1369 - Rank: Private - By what ship or how taken: Troops - Time when: 19 Dec 1813 - Place where: Fort Niagara - Whether man of war, privateer, or merchant vessel: Taken on shore - When received: 29 Jan 1814 - From what ship or whence received: Montreal by land carriages. - Prisoner: 1369 - Rank: Private - Name of Prize: Land forces - By what ship or how taken: Taken on shore - Discharged: 4 May 1814 - By what order: Returned to the United States - Source: List of American Prisoners of War discharged at Quebec - Name of prize ship: Land forces.

Galloway, Samuel   Prisoner: 1511 - Rank: Major - Name of Prize: Land forces - By what ship or how taken: Taken on shore - Discharged: 10 Nov 1814 - By what order: Stately No. 400 to Halifax by order of Sir George Prevost - Source: List of American Prisoners of War discharged at Quebec - Name of prize ship: Land forces.

Garbound, John   Prisoner: 1885 - Rank: Private - Name of Prize: Land forces - By what ship or how taken: Taken on shore - Discharged: 8 Nov 1814 - By what order: George No. 515 by Sir George Prevost - Source: List of American Prisoners of War discharged at Quebec - Name of prize ship: Land forces.

Garland, Levy   Prisoner: 440 - Rank: Private - Name of Prize: Land forces - By what ship or how taken: Taken on shore - Discharged: 10 Aug 1813 - By what order: HMS Regulus by order of his Excellency Sir George Prevost - Source: List of American Prisoners of War discharged at Quebec - Name of prize ship: Land forces.

Garner, Hiram   Prisoner: 1784 - Rank: Private - Name of Prize: Land forces - By what ship or how taken: Taken on shore - Discharged: 8 Nov 1814 - By what order: George No. 515 by Sir George Prevost - Source: List of American Prisoners of War discharged at Quebec - Name of prize ship: Land forces.

Gates, Horatio   Prisoner: 1304 - Rank: Private - By what ship or how taken: Troops - Time when: 19 Dec 1813 - Place where: Fort Niagara - Whether man of war, privateer, or merchant vessel: Taken on shore - When received: 29 Jan 1814 - From what ship or whence received: Montreal by land carriages. - Prisoner: 1304 - Rank: Private - Name of Prize: Land forces - By what ship or how taken: Taken on shore - Discharged: 4 May 1814 - By what order: Returned to the United States - Source: List of American Prisoners of War discharged at Quebec - Name of prize ship: Land forces.

Gazler, John   Prisoner: 1200 - Rank: Seaman - By what ship or how taken: Citizen - When received: 12 Dec 1813 - From what ship or whence received: Town goal. - Prisoner: 1200 - Rank: Seaman - Name of Prize: Merchant service - Discharged: 4 May 1814 - By what order: Returned to the United States - Source: List of American Prisoners of War discharged at Quebec - Name of Price: Merchant service.

Gentry, John   Prisoner: 1387 - Rank: Private - By what ship or how taken: Troops - Time when: 19 Dec 1813 - Place where: Fort Niagara - Whether man of war, privateer, or merchant vessel: Taken on shore - When received: 29 Jan 1814 - From what ship or whence received: Montreal by land carriages. - Prisoner: 1387 - Rank: Private - Name of Prize: Land forces - By what ship or how taken: Taken on shore - Discharged: 4 May 1814 - By what order: Returned to the United States - Source: List of American Prisoners of War discharged at Quebec - Name of prize ship: Land forces.

George, John   Prisoner: 1266 - Rank: Corporal - By what ship or how taken: Troops - Time when: 19 Dec 1813 - Place where: Fort Niagara - Whether man of war, privateer, or merchant vessel: Taken on shore - When received: 29 Jan 1814 - From what ship or whence received: Montreal by land carriages. - Prisoner: 1266 - Rank: Private - Name of Prize: Land forces - By what ship or how taken: Taken on shore - Discharged: 4 May 1814 - By what order: Returned to the United States - Source: List of American Prisoners of War discharged at Quebec - Name of prize ship: Land forces.

Gibbs, Erebus   Prisoner: 1240 - Rank: Civilian - By what ship or how taken: Troops - Time when: 19 Dec 1813 - Place where: Fort Niagara - Whether man of war, privateer, or merchant vessel: Taken on shore - When received: 29 Jan 1814 - From what ship or whence received: Montreal by land carriages. - Prisoner: 1240 - Rank: Civilian - Name of Prize: Land forces - By what ship or how taken: Taken on shore - Discharged: 4 May 1814 - By what order: Returned to the United States - Source: List of American Prisoners of War

discharged at Quebec - Name of prize ship: Land forces.

Gibson, Ebenezer   Prisoner: 232 - Rank: Private - Name of Prize: Eagle - By what ship or how taken: Man of war - Discharged: 31 Oct 1813 - By what order: HMS Malabar Transport by order of his Excellency Sir George Prevost - Source: List of American Prisoners of War discharged at Quebec - Name of prize ship: Eagle.

Gibson, Fortune   Prisoner: 1062 - Rank: Private - Name of Prize: Land forces - By what ship or how taken: Taken on shore - Discharged: 31 Oct 1813 - By what order: HMS Malabar Transport by order of his Excellency Sir George Prevost - Source: List of American Prisoners of War discharged at Quebec - Name of prize ship: Land forces.

Gibson, Samuel   Prisoner: 1990 - Rank: Seaman - Name of Prize: George - By what ship or how taken: Merchant Vessel - Discharged: 13 Mar 1815 - By what order: Returned to the United States - Source: List of American Prisoners of War discharged at Quebec - Name of prize ship: George.

Gifford, Francis   Prisoner: 1277 - Rank: Private - By what ship or how taken: Troops - Time when: 19 Dec 1813 - Place where: Fort Niagara - Whether man of war, privateer, or merchant vessel: Taken on shore - When received: 29 Jan 1814 - From what ship or whence received: Montreal by land carriages. - Prisoner: 1277 - Rank: Private - Name of Prize: Land forces - By what ship or how taken: Taken on shore - Discharged: 4 May 1814 - By what order: Returned to the United States - Source: List of American Prisoners of War discharged at Quebec - Name of prize ship: Land forces.

Gilbert, John   Prisoner: 1973 - Rank: Alien enemy - Name of Prize: Land forces - By what ship or how taken: Taken on shore - Discharged: 13 Mar 1815 - By what order: Returned to the United States - Source: List of American Prisoners of War discharged at Quebec - Name of prize ship: Land forces.

Gilbert, John C.   Prisoner: 1194 - By what ship or how taken: Citizen - When received: 12 Dec 1813 - From what ship or whence received: Town goal. - Prisoner: 1194 - Rank: Private - Name of Prize: Land forces - By what ship or how taken: Taken on shore - Discharged: 29 Mar 1814 - By what order: Returned to the United States - Source: List of American Prisoners of War discharged at Quebec - Name of prize ship: Land forces.

Gilbreath, John   Prisoner: 1207 - Rank: Lieutenant - By what ship or how taken: Troops - Time when: 19 Dec 1813 - Place where: Fort Niagara - Whether man of war, privateer, or merchant vessel: Taken on shore - When received: 18 Jan 1814 - From what ship or whence received: Montreal by land carriages. - Prisoner: 1207 - Rank: Lieutenant - Name of Prize: Land forces - By what ship or how taken: Taken on shore - Discharged: 6 May 1814 - By what order: Returned to the United States - Source: List of American Prisoners of War discharged at Quebec - Name of prize ship: Land forces.

Gilchrist, James   Prisoner: 1176 - Rank: Private - By what ship or how taken: Troops - Time when: 5 May 1813 - Place where: Rapids - Whether man of war, privateer, or merchant vessel: Taken on shore - When received: 25 Nov 1813 - From what ship or whence received: Town goal. - Prisoner: 1176 - Rank: Private - Name of Prize: Land forces - By what ship or how taken: Taken on shore - Discharged: 4 May 1814 - By what order: Returned to the United States - Source: List of American Prisoners of War discharged at Quebec - Name of prize ship: Land forces.

Gill, Emanuel   Prisoner: 1761 - Rank: Private - Name of Prize: Scorpion - By what ship or how taken: Man of war - Discharged: 8 Nov 1814 - By what order: George No. 515 by Sir George Prevost - Source: List of American Prisoners of War discharged at Quebec - Name of prize ship: Scorpion.

Gill, William   Prisoner: 1468 - Rank: Private - Name of Prize: Land forces - By what ship or how taken: Taken on shore - Discharged: 8 Nov 1814 - By what order: George No. 515 by Sir George Prevost - Source: List of American Prisoners of War discharged at Quebec - Name of prize ship: Land forces.

Gillespie, Martin   Prisoner: 1748 - Rank: Private - Name of Prize: Scorpion - By what ship or how taken: Man of war - Discharged: 8 Nov 1814 - By what order: George No. 515 by Sir George Prevost - Source: List of American Prisoners of War discharged at Quebec - Name of prize ship: Scorpion.

Gillespie, William   Prisoner: 1097 - Rank: Private - Name of Prize: Land forces - By what ship or how taken: Taken on shore - Discharged: 31 Oct 1813 - By what order: HMS Malabar Transport by order of his Excellency Sir George Prevost - Source: List of American Prisoners of War discharged at Quebec - Name of prize ship: Land forces.

Gillett, Eleazer   Prisoner: 1817 - Rank: Private - Name of Prize: Land forces - By what ship or how taken: Taken on shore - Discharged: 8 Nov 1814 - By what order: George No. 515 by Sir George Prevost - Source: List of American Prisoners of War discharged at Quebec - Name of prize ship: Land forces.

Gillett, Walker   Prisoner: 1679 - Rank: Master - Name of Prize: Jack - By what ship or how taken: Merchant Vessel - Discharged: 10 Nov 1814 - By what order: Lord Cathcart No. 161 for Halifax by order of Sir George Prevost - Source: List of American Prisoners of War discharged at Quebec - Name of prize ship: Jack.

Gilmore, John   Prisoner: 1640 - Rank: Private - Name of Prize: Land forces - By what ship or how taken: Taken on shore - Discharged: 13 Mar 1815 - By what order: Returned to the United States - Source: List of American Prisoners of War discharged at Quebec - Name of prize ship: Land forces.

Ginning, Stephen   Prisoner: 1813 - Rank: Private - Name of Prize: Land forces - By what ship or how taken: Taken on shore - Discharged: 8 Nov 1814 - By what order: George No. 515 by Sir George Prevost - Source: List of American Prisoners of War discharged at Quebec - Name of prize ship: Land forces.

Givin, Richard   Prisoner: 1341 - Rank: Private - By what ship or how taken: Troops - Time when: 19 Dec 1813 - Place where: Fort Niagara - Whether man of war, privateer, or merchant vessel: Taken on shore - When received: 29 Jan 1814 - From what ship or whence received: Montreal by land carriages. - Prisoner: 1341 - Rank: Private - Name of Prize: Land forces - By what ship or how taken: Taken on shore - Discharged: 4 May 1814 - By what order: Returned to the United States - Source: List of American Prisoners of War discharged at Quebec - Name of prize ship: Land forces.

Glenn, James   Prisoner: 1392 - Rank: Private - By what ship or how taken: Troops - Time when: 19 Dec 1813 - Place where: Fort Niagara - Whether man of war, privateer, or merchant vessel: Taken on shore - When received: 29 Jan 1814 - From what ship or whence received: Montreal by land carriages. - Prisoner: 1392 - Rank: Private - Name of Prize: Land forces - By what ship or how taken: Taken on shore - Discharged: 4 May 1814 - By what order: Returned to the United States - Source: List of American Prisoners of War discharged at Quebec - Name of prize ship: Land forces. - Prisoner: 1392 - Rank: Private - By what ship or how taken: Troops - Time when: 19 Dec 1813 - Place where: Fort Niagara - Whether man of war, privateer, or merchant vessel: Taken on shore - When received: 29 Jan 1814 - From what ship or whence received: Montreal by land carriages.

Goddard, Lewis   Prisoner: 250 - Rank: Lieutenant - Name of Prize: Land forces - By what ship or how taken: Taken on shore - Discharged: 10 Aug 1813 - By what order: HMS Regulus by order of his Excellency Sir George Prevost - Source: List of American Prisoners of War discharged at Quebec - Name of prize ship: Land forces.

Godwin, Henry   Prisoner: 531 - Rank: Lieutenant - Name of Prize: Land forces - By what ship or how taken: Taken on shore - Discharged: 10 Aug 1813 - By what order: HMS Regulus by order of his Excellency Sir George Prevost - Source: List of American Prisoners of War discharged at Quebec - Name of prize ship: Land forces.

Goldman, Thomas   Prisoner: 1982 - Rank: Musician - Name of Prize: Land forces - By what ship or how taken: Taken on shore - Discharged: 13 Mar 1815 - By what order: Returned to the United States - Source: List of American Prisoners of War discharged at Quebec - Name of prize ship: Land forces.

Gonsolty, Samuel   Prisoner: 1848 - Rank: Private - Name of Prize: Land forces - By what ship or how taken: Taken on shore - Discharged: 8 Nov 1814 - By what order: George No. 515 by Sir George Prevost - Source: List of American Prisoners of War discharged at Quebec - Name of prize ship: Land forces.

Good, Daniel   Prisoner: 1829 - Rank: Private - Name of Prize: Land forces - By what ship or how taken: Taken on shore - Discharged: 8 Nov 1814 - By what order: George No. 515 by Sir George Prevost - Source: List of American Prisoners of War discharged at Quebec - Name of prize ship: Land forces.

Goodman, Elisha   Prisoner: 13 - Rank: Private - Source: Account of American prisoners of war who died at Quebec between 14 February 1814 and 23 December 1814 - Ship or Corps: Land forces - Vessel: Taken on shore - Place born: Sudbury, MA - Age: 27 - Where taken: Stoney Point - Date of death: 13 May 1814 - Disorder or casualty: Debility.

Goodwin, Joseph   Prisoner: 679 - Rank: Private - Name of Prize: Land forces - By what ship or how taken: Taken on shore - Discharged: 10 Aug 1813 - By what order: HMS Regulus by order of his Excellency Sir George Prevost - Source: List of American Prisoners of War discharged at Quebec - Name of prize ship: Land forces.

Goodwin, Richard   Prisoner: 329 - Rank: Private - Name of Prize: Land forces - By what ship or how taken: Taken on shore - Discharged: 31 Oct 1813 - By what order: HMS Malabar Transport by order of his Excellency Sir George Prevost - Source: List of American Prisoners of War discharged at Quebec - Name of prize ship: Land forces.

Goodwin, Simeon   Prisoner: 1117 - Rank: Private - Name of Prize: Land forces - By what ship or how taken: Taken on shore - Discharged: 31 Oct 1813 - By what order: HMS Malabar Transport by order of his Excellency Sir George Prevost - Source: List of American Prisoners of War discharged at Quebec - Name of prize ship: Land forces.

Gossett, Stephen   Prisoner: 371 - Rank: Private - Name of Prize: Land forces - By what ship or how taken: Taken on shore - Discharged: 31 Oct 1813 - By what order: HMS Malabar Transport by order of his Excellency Sir George Prevost - Source: List of American Prisoners of War discharged at Quebec - Name of prize ship: Land forces.

Gray, Samuel Prisoner: 762 - Rank: Private - Name of Prize: Land forces - By what ship or how taken: Taken on shore - Discharged: 10 Aug 1813 - By what order: HMS Regulus by order of his Excellency Sir George Prevost - Source: List of American Prisoners of War discharged at Quebec - Name of prize ship: Land forces - Comments: British subject, sent to England.

Grayson, John Prisoner: 1319 - Rank: Corporal - By what ship or how taken: Troops - Time when: 19 Dec 1813 - Place where: Fort Niagara - Whether man of war, privateer, or merchant vessel: Taken on shore - When received: 29 Jan 1814 - From what ship or whence received: Montreal by land carriages. - Prisoner: 1319 - Rank: Private - Name of Prize: Land forces - By what ship or how taken: Taken on shore - Discharged: 27 Feb 1814 - By what order: Volunteered for the New Brunswick Fencibles - Source: List of American Prisoners of War discharged at Quebec - Name of prize ship: Land forces.

Gready, Martin Prisoner: 1075 - Rank: Private - Name of Prize: Land forces - By what ship or how taken: Taken on shore - Discharged: 31 Oct 1813 - By what order: HMS Malabar Transport by order of his Excellency Sir George Prevost - Source: List of American Prisoners of War discharged at Quebec - Name of prize ship: Land forces.

Greaves, Philander Prisoner: 1241 - Rank: Civilian - By what ship or how taken: Troops - Time when: 19 Dec 1813 - Place where: Fort Niagara - Whether man of war, privateer, or merchant vessel: Taken on shore - When received: 29 Jan 1814 - From what ship or whence received: Montreal by land carriages. - Prisoner: 1241 - Rank: Civilian - Name of Prize: Land forces - By what ship or how taken: Taken on shore - Discharged: 4 May 1814 - By what order: Returned to the United States - Source: List of American Prisoners of War discharged at Quebec - Name of prize ship: Land forces.

Green, Eli Prisoner: 55 - Rank: Private - Source: Account of American prisoners of war who died at Quebec in the Months of July, August & September 1813 - Ship or Corps: Land forces - Vessel: Taken on shore - Place born: Walpole, NH - Age: 16 - Where taken: Stoney Point - Date of death: 23 Jul 1813.

Green, Jeremiah N. Prisoner: 1309 - Rank: Private - By what ship or how taken: Troops - Time when: 19 Dec 1813 - Place where: Fort Niagara - Whether man of war, privateer, or merchant vessel: Taken on shore - When received: 29 Jan 1814 - From what ship or whence received: Montreal by land carriages. - Prisoner: 1309 - Rank: Private - Name of Prize: Land forces - By what ship or how taken: Taken on shore - Discharged: 4 May 1814 - By what order: Returned to the United States - Source: List of American Prisoners of War discharged at Quebec - Name of prize ship: Land forces.

Green, John (1) Prisoner: 295 - Rank: Private - Name of Prize: Land forces - By what ship or how taken: Taken on shore - Discharged: 31 Oct 1813 - By what order: HMS Malabar Transport by order of his Excellency Sir George Prevost - Source: List of American Prisoners of War discharged at Quebec - Name of prize ship: Land forces.

Green, John (2) Prisoner: 514 - Rank: Private - Name of Prize: Land forces - By what ship or how taken: Taken on shore - Discharged: 10 Aug 1813 - By what order: HMS Regulus by order of his Excellency Sir George Prevost - Source: List of American Prisoners of War discharged at Quebec - Name of prize ship: Land forces.

Green, Samuel Prisoner: 1754 - Rank: Private - Name of Prize: Tigress - By what ship or how taken: Man of war - Discharged: 8 Nov 1814 - By what order: George No. 515 by Sir George Prevost - Source: List of American Prisoners of War discharged at Quebec - Name of prize ship: Tigress.

Green, Thomas (1) Prisoner: 954 - Rank: Private - Name of Prize: Land forces - By what ship or how taken: Taken on shore - Discharged: 31 Oct 1813 - By what order: HMS Malabar Transport by order of his Excellency Sir George Prevost - Source: List of American Prisoners of War discharged at Quebec - Name of prize ship: Land forces.

Green, Thomas (2) Prisoner: 983 - Rank: Sergeant - Name of Prize: Land forces - By what ship or how taken: Taken on shore - Discharged: 31 Oct 1813 - By what order: HMS Malabar Transport by order of his Excellency Sir George Prevost - Source: List of American Prisoners of War discharged at Quebec - Name of prize ship: Land forces.

Greene, Paul Prisoner: 1147 - Rank: Private - By what ship or how taken: Troops - Time when: 15 Aug 1812 - Place where: Rapids, River Raisin - Whether man of war, privateer, or merchant vessel: Taken on shore - When received: 25 Nov 1813 - From what ship or whence received: Town goal. - Prisoner: 1147 - Rank: Private - Name of Prize: Land forces - By what ship or how taken: Taken on shore - Discharged: 4 May 1814 - By what order: Returned to the United States - Source: List of American Prisoners of War discharged at Quebec - Name of prize ship: Land forces.

Greenley, William Prisoner: 1359 - Rank: Private - By what ship or how taken: Troops - Time when: 19 Dec 1813 - Place where: Fort Niagara - Whether man of war, privateer, or merchant vessel: Taken on shore - When received: 29 Jan 1814 - From what ship or whence received: Montreal by land carriages. - Prisoner: 1359 -

Rank: Private - Name of Prize: Land forces - By what ship or how taken: Taken on shore - Discharged: 4 May 1814 - By what order: Returned to the United States - Source: List of American Prisoners of War discharged at Quebec - Name of prize ship: Land forces.

Gregory, Francis H.   Prisoner: 1715 - Rank: Lieutenant - Name of Prize: Scorpion - By what ship or how taken: Man of war - Discharged: 10 Nov 1814 - By what order: Lord Cathcart No. 161 for Halifax by order of Sir George Prevost - Source: List of American Prisoners of War discharged at Quebec - Name of prize ship: Scorpion.

Grey, James   Prisoner: 702 - Rank: Private - Name of Prize: Land forces - By what ship or how taken: Taken on shore - Discharged: 10 Aug 1813 - By what order: HMS Regulus by order of his Excellency Sir George Prevost - Source: List of American Prisoners of War discharged at Quebec - Name of prize ship: Land forces.

Griffin, John   Prisoner: 483 - Rank: Private - Name of Prize: Land forces - By what ship or how taken: Taken on shore - Discharged: 10 Aug 1813 - By what order: HMS Regulus by order of his Excellency Sir George Prevost - Source: List of American Prisoners of War discharged at Quebec - Name of prize ship: Land forces.

Griffin, William   Prisoner: 1745 - Rank: Seaman - Name of Prize: Tigress - By what ship or how taken: Man of war - Discharged: 7 Nov 1813 - By what order: HMS Freedom No. 582 by order of his Excellency Sir George Prevost - Source: List of American Prisoners of War discharged at Quebec - Name of prize ship: Tigress.

Grimes, Nicholas   Prisoner: 549 - Rank: Private - Name of Prize: Land forces - By what ship or how taken: Taken on shore - Discharged: 10 Aug 1813 - By what order: HMS Regulus by order of his Excellency Sir George Prevost - Source: List of American Prisoners of War discharged at Quebec - Name of prize ship: Land forces.

Grinder, John   Prisoner: 1787 - Rank: Private - Name of Prize: Land forces - By what ship or how taken: Taken on shore - Discharged: 8 Nov 1814 - By what order: George No. 515 by Sir George Prevost - Source: List of American Prisoners of War discharged at Quebec - Name of prize ship: Land forces.

Groomes, Richard   Prisoner: 1162 - Rank: Corporal - By what ship or how taken: Troops - Time when: 5 May 1813 - Place where: Fort Meigs - Whether man of war, privateer, or merchant vessel: Taken on shore - When received: 25 Nov 1813 - From what ship or whence received: Town goal. - Prisoner: 1162 - Rank: Private - Name of Prize: Land forces - By what ship or how taken: Taken on shore - Discharged: 4 May 1814 - By what order: Returned to the United States - Source: List of American Prisoners of War discharged at Quebec - Name of prize ship: Land forces.

Grouse, Frederick   Prisoner: 439 - Rank: Private - Name of Prize: Land forces - By what ship or how taken: Taken on shore - Discharged: 10 Aug 1813 - By what order: HMS Regulus by order of his Excellency Sir George Prevost - Source: List of American Prisoners of War discharged at Quebec - Name of prize ship: Land forces.

Groves, George   Prisoner: 1290 - Rank: Private - By what ship or how taken: Troops - Time when: 19 Dec 1813 - Place where: Fort Niagara - Whether man of war, privateer, or merchant vessel: Taken on shore - When received: 29 Jan 1814 - From what ship or whence received: Montreal by land carriages. - Prisoner: 1290 - Rank: Private - Name of Prize: Land forces - By what ship or how taken: Taken on shore - Discharged: 4 May 1814 - By what order: Returned to the United States - Source: List of American Prisoners of War discharged at Quebec - Name of prize ship: Land forces.

Guest, Charles   Prisoner: 1218 - Rank: Private - By what ship or how taken: Troops - Time when: 19 Dec 1813 - Place where: Fort Niagara - Whether man of war, privateer, or merchant vessel: Taken on shore - When received: 29 Jan 1814 - From what ship or whence received: Montreal by land carriages. - Prisoner: 1218 - Rank: Private - Name of Prize: Land forces - By what ship or how taken: Taken on shore - Discharged: 4 May 1814 - By what order: Returned to the United States - Source: List of American Prisoners of War discharged at Quebec - Name of prize ship: Land forces.

Gulintine, James   Prisoner: 1879 - Rank: Private - Name of Prize: Land forces - By what ship or how taken: Taken on shore - Discharged: 8 Nov 1814 - By what order: George No. 515 by Sir George Prevost - Source: List of American Prisoners of War discharged at Quebec - Name of prize ship: Land forces.

Gunison, James   Prisoner: 1118 - Rank: Private - Name of Prize: Land forces - By what ship or how taken: Taken on shore - Discharged: 31 Oct 1813 - By what order: HMS Malabar Transport by order of his Excellency Sir George Prevost - Source: List of American Prisoners of War discharged at Quebec - Name of prize ship: Land forces.

Gustavas, John   Prisoner: 1677 - Rank: Seaman - Name of Prize: Forsyth - By what ship or how taken: Merchant Vessel - Discharged: 7 Nov 1813 - By what order: HMS Freedom No. 582 by order of his Excellency Sir George Prevost - Source: List of American Prisoners of War discharged at Quebec - Name of prize ship: Forsyth.

Guynnup, John   Prisoner: 1055 - Rank: Private - Name of Prize: Growler - By what ship or how taken: Man of war - Discharged: 31 Oct 1813 - By what order: HMS Malabar Transport by order of his Excellency Sir George Prevost - Source: List of American Prisoners of War discharged at Quebec - Name of prize ship: Growler.

Hagan, Thomas   Prisoner: 1349 - Rank: Sergeant - By what ship or how taken: Troops - Time when: 19 Dec 1813 - Place where: Fort Niagara - Whether man of war, privateer, or merchant vessel: Taken on shore - When received: 29 Jan 1814 - From what ship or whence received: Montreal by land carriages. - Prisoner: 1349 - Rank: Sergeant - Name of Prize: Land forces - By what ship or how taken: Taken on shore - Discharged: 4 May 1814 - By what order: Returned to the United States - Source: List of American Prisoners of War discharged at Quebec - Name of prize ship: Land forces.

Hagar, Henry   Prisoner: 7 - Rank: Private - Name of Prize: Land forces - By what ship or how taken: Taken on shore - Discharged: 31 Oct 1813 - By what order: HMS Malabar Transport by order of his Excellency Sir George Prevost - Source: List of American Prisoners of War discharged at Quebec - Name of prize ship: Land forces.

Hagerty, Thomas   Prisoner: 1884 - Rank: Private - Name of Prize: Land forces - By what ship or how taken: Taken on shore - Discharged: 8 Nov 1814 - By what order: George No. 515 by Sir George Prevost - Source: List of American Prisoners of War discharged at Quebec - Name of prize ship: Land forces.

Haines, Daniel   Prisoner: 209 - Rank: Private - Name of Prize: Eagle - By what ship or how taken: Man of war - Discharged: 31 Oct 1813 - By what order: HMS Malabar Transport by order of his Excellency Sir George Prevost - Source: List of American Prisoners of War discharged at Quebec - Name of prize ship: Eagle.

Haines, Joel   Prisoner: 1307 - Rank: Private - By what ship or how taken: Troops - Time when: 19 Dec 1813 - Place where: Fort Niagara - Whether man of war, privateer, or merchant vessel: Taken on shore - When received: 29 Jan 1814 - From what ship or whence received: Montreal by land carriages. - Prisoner: 1307 - Rank: Private - Name of Prize: Land forces - By what ship or how taken: Taken on shore - Discharged: 4 May 1814 - By what order: Returned to the United States - Source: List of American Prisoners of War discharged at Quebec - Name of prize ship: Land forces.

Hale, William   Prisoner: 637 - Rank: Private - Name of Prize: Land forces - By what ship or how taken: Taken on shore - Discharged: 10 Aug 1813 - By what order: HMS Regulus by order of his Excellency Sir George Prevost - Source: List of American Prisoners of War discharged at Quebec - Name of prize ship: Land forces.

Halison, Jacob   Prisoner: 1252 - Rank: Private - By what ship or how taken: Troops - Time when: 19 Dec 1813 - Place where: Fort Niagara - Whether man of war, privateer, or merchant vessel: Taken on shore - When received: 29 Jan 1814 - From what ship or whence received: Montreal by land carriages.

Hall, Allen   Prisoner: 1171 - Rank: Private - Name of Prize: Land forces - By what ship or how taken: Taken on shore - Discharged: 4 May 1814 - By what order: Returned to the United States - Source: List of American Prisoners of War discharged at Quebec - Name of prize ship: Land forces. - Prisoner: 1171 - Rank: Private - By what ship or how taken: Troops - Time when: 5 May 1813 - Place where: Rapids - Whether man of war, privateer, or merchant vessel: Taken on shore - When received: 25 Nov 1813 - From what ship or whence received: Town goal.

Hall, Daniel   Prisoner: 1887 - Rank: Private - Name of Prize: Land forces - By what ship or how taken: Taken on shore - Discharged: 8 Nov 1814 - By what order: George No. 515 by Sir George Prevost - Source: List of American Prisoners of War discharged at Quebec - Name of prize ship: Land forces.

Hall, Lot   Prisoner: 85 - Rank: Private - Name of Prize: Land forces - By what ship or how taken: Taken on shore - Discharged: 31 Oct 1813 - By what order: HMS Malabar Transport by order of his Excellency Sir George Prevost - Source: List of American Prisoners of War discharged at Quebec - Name of prize ship: Land forces.

Hall, William   Prisoner: 1337 - Rank: Private - Name of Prize: Land forces - By what ship or how taken: Taken on shore - Discharged: 4 May 1814 - By what order: Returned to the United States - Source: List of American Prisoners of War discharged at Quebec - Name of prize ship: Land forces. - Prisoner: 1337 - Rank: Private - By what ship or how taken: Troops - Time when: 19 Dec 1813 - Place where: Fort Niagara - Whether man of war, privateer, or merchant vessel: Taken on shore - When received: 29 Jan 1814 - From what ship or whence received: Montreal by land carriages.

Halles, John   Prisoner: 486 - Rank: Private - Name of Prize: Land forces - By what ship or how taken: Taken on shore - Discharged: 10 Aug 1813 - By what order: HMS Regulus by order of his Excellency Sir George Prevost - Source: List of American Prisoners of War discharged at Quebec - Name of prize ship: Land forces. - Prisoner: 486 - Rank: Private - Source: Account of American prisoners of war who died at Quebec in the Months of July, August & September 1813 - Ship or Corps: Land forces - Vessel: Taken on shore - Place born: Holland - Age: 23 - Where taken: Beaver Dams - Date of death: 5 Jul 1813.

Ham, Robert   Prisoner: 225 - Rank: Private - Name of Prize: Eagle - By what ship or how taken: Man of war -

Discharged: 31 Oct 1813 - By what order: HMS Malabar Transport by order of his Excellency Sir George Prevost - Source: List of American Prisoners of War discharged at Quebec - Name of prize ship: Eagle.

Ham, Rufus Prisoner: 211 - Rank: Private - Name of Prize: Growler - By what ship or how taken: Man of war - Discharged: 31 Oct 1813 - By what order: HMS Malabar Transport by order of his Excellency Sir George Prevost - Source: List of American Prisoners of War discharged at Quebec - Name of prize ship: Growler.

Hamilton, John Prisoner: 1243 - Rank: Private - Name of Prize: Land forces - By what ship or how taken: Taken on shore - Discharged: 4 May 1814 - By what order: Returned to the United States - Source: List of American Prisoners of War discharged at Quebec - Name of prize ship: Land forces. - Prisoner: 1243 - Rank: Private - By what ship or how taken: Troops - Time when: 19 Dec 1813 - Place where: Fort Niagara - Whether man of war, privateer, or merchant vessel: Taken on shore - When received: 29 Jan 1814 - From what ship or whence received: Montreal by land carriages.

Hanadon, Elisha Prisoner: 42 - Rank: Private - Source: Account of American prisoners of war who died at Quebec in the Months of July, August & September 1813 - Ship or Corps: Land forces - Vessel: Taken on shore - Place born: Norton, MA - Age: 24 - Where taken: Beaver Dams - Date of death: 15 Jul 1813.

Hanes, James Prisoner: 175 - Rank: Seaman - Name of Prize: Growler - By what ship or how taken: Man of war - Discharged: 31 Oct 1813 - By what order: HMS Malabar Transport by order of his Excellency Sir George Prevost - Source: List of American Prisoners of War discharged at Quebec - Name of prize ship: Growler.

Hanes, Robert Prisoner: 1032 - Rank: Seaman - Name of Prize: Growler - By what ship or how taken: Man of war - Discharged: 31 Oct 1813 - By what order: HMS Malabar Transport by order of his Excellency Sir George Prevost - Source: List of American Prisoners of War discharged at Quebec - Name of prize ship: Growler.

Hansel, William Prisoner: 1336 - Rank: Private - Name of Prize: Land forces - By what ship or how taken: Taken on shore - Discharged: 4 May 1814 - By what order: Returned to the United States - Source: List of American Prisoners of War discharged at Quebec - Name of prize ship: Land forces. - Prisoner: 1336 - Rank: Private - By what ship or how taken: Troops - Time when: 19 Dec 1813 - Place where: Fort Niagara - Whether man of war, privateer, or merchant vessel: Taken on shore - When received: 29 Jan 1814 - From what ship or whence received: Montreal by land carriages.

Hard, Daniel Prisoner: 1108 - Rank: Corporal - Name of Prize: Land forces - By what ship or how taken: Taken on shore - Discharged: 31 Oct 1813 - By what order: HMS Malabar Transport by order of his Excellency Sir George Prevost - Source: List of American Prisoners of War discharged at Quebec - Name of prize ship: Land forces.

Harding, Amasa Prisoner: 1299 - Rank: Private - By what ship or how taken: Troops - Time when: 19 Dec 1813 - Place where: Fort Niagara - Whether man of war, privateer, or merchant vessel: Taken on shore - When received: 29 Jan 1814 - From what ship or whence received: Montreal by land carriages. - Prisoner: 1299 - Rank: Private - Name of Prize: Land forces - By what ship or how taken: Taken on shore - Discharged: 4 May 1814 - By what order: Returned to the United States - Source: List of American Prisoners of War discharged at Quebec - Name of prize ship: Land forces.

Hardy, Andrew H. Prisoner: 1519 - Rank: Private - Name of Prize: Land forces - By what ship or how taken: Taken on shore - Discharged: 10 Nov 1814 - By what order: Sovereign No. 628 to Halifax by order of Sir George Prevost - Source: List of American Prisoners of War discharged at Quebec - Name of prize ship: Land forces.

Hardy, Elisha Prisoner: 397 - Rank: Private - Name of Prize: Land forces - By what ship or how taken: Taken on shore - Discharged: 24 Nov 1813 - By what order: Sent to HMS Aeolus - Source: List of American Prisoners of War discharged at Quebec - Name of prize ship: Land forces.

Hargood, George Prisoner: 696 - Rank: Private - Name of Prize: Land forces - By what ship or how taken: Taken on shore - Discharged: 10 Aug 1813 - By what order: HMS Regulus by order of his Excellency Sir George Prevost - Source: List of American Prisoners of War discharged at Quebec - Name of prize ship: Land forces.

Harkness, James Prisoner: 655 - Rank: Private - Name of Prize: Land forces - By what ship or how taken: Taken on shore - Discharged: 10 Aug 1813 - By what order: HMS Regulus by order of his Excellency Sir George Prevost - Source: List of American Prisoners of War discharged at Quebec - Name of prize ship: Land forces.

Harley, George Prisoner: 1308 - Rank: Private - By what ship or how taken: Troops - Time when: 19 Dec 1813 - Place where: Fort Niagara - Whether man of war, privateer, or merchant vessel: Taken on shore - When received: 29 Jan 1814 - From what ship or whence received: Montreal by land carriages. - Prisoner: 1308 - Rank: Private - Name of Prize: Land forces - By what ship or how taken: Taken on shore - Discharged: 4 May 1814 - By what order: Returned to the United States - Source: List of American Prisoners of War discharged at Quebec - Name of prize ship: Land forces.

Harper, William Prisoner: 1225 - Rank: Private - By what ship or how taken: Troops - Time when: 19 Dec 1813 -

Place where: Fort Niagara - Whether man of war, privateer, or merchant vessel: Taken on shore - When received: 29 Jan 1814 - From what ship or whence received: Montreal by land carriages. - Prisoner: 1225 - Rank: Private - Name of Prize: Land forces - By what ship or how taken: Taken on shore - Discharged: 27 Feb 1814 - By what order: Volunteered for the New Brunswick Fencibles - Source: List of American Prisoners of War discharged at Quebec - Name of prize ship: Land forces.

Harrington, Estes Prisoner: 951 - Rank: Sergeant - Name of Prize: Land forces - By what ship or how taken: Taken on shore - Discharged: 31 Oct 1813 - By what order: HMS Malabar Transport by order of his Excellency Sir George Prevost - Source: List of American Prisoners of War discharged at Quebec - Name of prize ship: Land forces.

Harris, James (1) Prisoner: 1422 - Rank: Private - By what ship or how taken: Troops - Time when: 19 Dec 1813 - Place where: Fort Niagara - Whether man of war, privateer, or merchant vessel: Taken on shore - When received: 29 Jan 1814 - From what ship or whence received: Montreal by land carriages. - Prisoner: 1422 - Rank: Private - Name of Prize: Land forces - By what ship or how taken: Taken on shore - Discharged: 4 May 1814 - By what order: Returned to the United States - Source: List of American Prisoners of War discharged at Quebec - Name of prize ship: Land forces.

Harris, James (2) Prisoner: 1942 - Rank: Private - Name of Prize: Land forces - By what ship or how taken: Taken on shore - Discharged: 13 Mar 1815 - By what order: Returned to the United States - Source: List of American Prisoners of War discharged at Quebec - Name of prize ship: Land forces.

Harrison, Joseph Prisoner: 1504 - Rank: Private - Name of Prize: Land forces - By what ship or how taken: Taken on shore - Discharged: 13 Mar 1815 - By what order: Returned to the United States - Source: List of American Prisoners of War discharged at Quebec - Name of prize ship: Land forces.

Hartwell, Calvin Prisoner: 1929 - Rank: Private - Name of Prize: Land forces - By what ship or how taken: Taken on shore - Discharged: 13 Mar 1815 - By what order: Returned to the United States - Source: List of American Prisoners of War discharged at Quebec - Name of prize ship: Land forces.

Harvey, Charles Prisoner: 1326 - Rank: Sergeant - Name of Prize: Land forces - By what ship or how taken: Taken on shore - Discharged: 4 May 1814 - By what order: Returned to the United States - Source: List of American Prisoners of War discharged at Quebec - Name of prize ship: Land forces. - Prisoner: 1326 - Rank: Sergeant - By what ship or how taken: Troops - Time when: 19 Dec 1813 - Place where: Fort Niagara - Whether man of war, privateer, or merchant vessel: Taken on shore - When received: 29 Jan 1814 - From what ship or whence received: Montreal by land carriages.

Harvey, Luther Prisoner: 19 - Rank: Musician - Name of Prize: Land forces - By what ship or how taken: Taken on shore - Discharged: 31 Oct 1813 - By what order: HMS Malabar Transport by order of his Excellency Sir George Prevost - Source: List of American Prisoners of War discharged at Quebec - Name of prize ship: Land forces.

Harvey, William Prisoner: 195 - Rank: Private - Name of Prize: Eagle - By what ship or how taken: Man of war - Discharged: 31 Oct 1813 - By what order: HMS Malabar Transport by order of his Excellency Sir George Prevost - Source: List of American Prisoners of War discharged at Quebec - Name of prize ship: Eagle.

Hawkins, Gilbert Prisoner: 1371 - Rank: Sergeant - By what ship or how taken: Troops - Time when: 19 Dec 1813 - Place where: Fort Niagara - Whether man of war, privateer, or merchant vessel: Taken on shore - When received: 29 Jan 1814 - From what ship or whence received: Montreal by land carriages. - Prisoner: 1371 - Rank: Sergeant - Name of Prize: Land forces - By what ship or how taken: Taken on shore - Discharged: 4 May 1814 - By what order: Returned to the United States - Source: List of American Prisoners of War discharged at Quebec - Name of prize ship: Land forces.

Hawley, Comfort Prisoner: 1882 - Rank: Private - Name of Prize: Land forces - By what ship or how taken: Taken on shore - Discharged: 8 Nov 1814 - By what order: George No. 515 by Sir George Prevost - Source: List of American Prisoners of War discharged at Quebec - Name of prize ship: Land forces.

Hayes, Patrick Prisoner: 1321 - Rank: Private - By what ship or how taken: Troops - Time when: 19 Dec 1813 - Place where: Fort Niagara - Whether man of war, privateer, or merchant vessel: Taken on shore - When received: 29 Jan 1814 - From what ship or whence received: Montreal by land carriages. - Prisoner: 1321 - Rank: Private - Name of Prize: Land forces - By what ship or how taken: Taken on shore - Discharged: 4 May 1814 - By what order: Returned to the United States - Source: List of American Prisoners of War discharged at Quebec - Name of prize ship: Land forces.

Haynes, Clement Prisoner: 648 - Rank: Corporal - Name of Prize: Land forces - By what ship or how taken: Taken on shore - Discharged: 10 Aug 1813 - By what order: HMS Regulus by order of his Excellency Sir George Prevost - Source: List of American Prisoners of War discharged at Quebec - Name of prize ship: Land forces.

Hayway, Richard   Prisoner: 57 - Rank: Private - Name of Prize: Land forces - By what ship or how taken: Taken on shore - Discharged: 31 Oct 1813 - By what order: HMS Malabar Transport by order of his Excellency Sir George Prevost - Source: List of American Prisoners of War discharged at Quebec - Name of prize ship: Land forces.

Hazard, Ezekiel   Prisoner: 693 - Rank: Private - Source: Account of American prisoners of war who died at Quebec between 14 February 1814 and 23 December 1814 - Ship or Corps: Land forces - Vessel: Taken on shore - Place born: Rhode Island - Age: 24 - Where taken: Beaver Dams - Date of death: 25 Feb 1814 - Disorder or casualty: Catarrh.

Head, William   Prisoner: 1364 - Rank: Sergeant - By what ship or how taken: Troops - Time when: 19 Dec 1813 - Place where: Fort Niagara - Whether man of war, privateer, or merchant vessel: Taken on shore - When received: 29 Jan 1814 - From what ship or whence received: Montreal by land carriages. - Prisoner: 1364 - Rank: Sergeant - Name of Prize: Land forces - By what ship or how taken: Taken on shore - Discharged: 4 May 1814 - By what order: Returned to the United States - Source: List of American Prisoners of War discharged at Quebec - Name of prize ship: Land forces.

Headman, Charles   Prisoner: 1009 - Rank: Seaman - Name of Prize: Juliet - By what ship or how taken: Man of war - Discharged: 31 Oct 1813 - By what order: HMS Malabar Transport by order of his Excellency Sir George Prevost - Source: List of American Prisoners of War discharged at Quebec - Name of prize ship: Juliet.

Heath, John   Prisoner: 9 - Rank: Private - Name of Prize: Land forces - By what ship or how taken: Taken on shore - Discharged: 4 May 1814 - By what order: Returned to the United States - Source: List of American Prisoners of War discharged at Quebec - Name of prize ship: Land forces.

Heath, Peter   Prisoner: 1699 - Rank: Private - Name of Prize: Land forces - By what ship or how taken: Taken on shore - Discharged: 8 Nov 1814 - By what order: George No. 515 by Sir George Prevost - Source: List of American Prisoners of War discharged at Quebec - Name of prize ship: Land forces.

Heddericks, George   Prisoner: 285 - Rank: Private - Name of Prize: Land forces - By what ship or how taken: Taken on shore - Discharged: 31 Oct 1813 - By what order: HMS Malabar Transport by order of his Excellency Sir George Prevost - Source: List of American Prisoners of War discharged at Quebec - Name of prize ship: Land forces.

Heddon, Amos   Prisoner: 686 - Rank: Private - Name of Prize: Land forces - By what ship or how taken: Taken on shore - Discharged: 10 Aug 1813 - By what order: HMS Regulus by order of his Excellency Sir George Prevost - Source: List of American Prisoners of War discharged at Quebec - Name of prize ship: Land forces.

Heler, Peter   Prisoner: 1859 - Rank: Private - Name of Prize: Land forces - By what ship or how taken: Taken on shore - Discharged: 8 Nov 1814 - By what order: George No. 515 by Sir George Prevost - Source: List of American Prisoners of War discharged at Quebec - Name of prize ship: Land forces.

Helswath, John   Prisoner: 669 - Rank: Private - Name of Prize: Land forces - By what ship or how taken: Taken on shore - Discharged: 10 Aug 1813 - By what order: HMS Regulus by order of his Excellency Sir George Prevost - Source: List of American Prisoners of War discharged at Quebec - Name of prize ship: Land forces.

Hendericks, John   Prisoner: 1100 - Rank: Private - Name of Prize: Land forces - By what ship or how taken: Taken on shore - Discharged: 31 Oct 1813 - By what order: HMS Malabar Transport by order of his Excellency Sir George Prevost - Source: List of American Prisoners of War discharged at Quebec - Name of prize ship: Land forces.

Henderson, Amos   Prisoner: 1953 - Rank: Private - Name of Prize: Land forces - By what ship or how taken: Taken on shore - Discharged: 13 Mar 1815 - By what order: Returned to the United States - Source: List of American Prisoners of War discharged at Quebec - Name of prize ship: Land forces.

Henderson, George   Prisoner: 1925 - Rank: Private - Name of Prize: Land forces - By what ship or how taken: Taken on shore - Discharged: 10 Nov 1814 - By what order: Sovereign No. 628 to Halifax by order of Sir George Prevost - Source: List of American Prisoners of War discharged at Quebec - Name of prize ship: Land forces.

Henon, James   Prisoner: 966 - Rank: Private - Name of Prize: Land forces - By what ship or how taken: Taken on shore - Discharged: 31 Oct 1813 - By what order: HMS Malabar Transport by order of his Excellency Sir George Prevost - Source: List of American Prisoners of War discharged at Quebec - Name of prize ship: Land forces.

Henry, John   Prisoner: 1869 - Rank: Private - Name of Prize: Land forces - By what ship or how taken: Taken on shore - Discharged: 8 Nov 1814 - By what order: George No. 515 by Sir George Prevost - Source: List of American Prisoners of War discharged at Quebec - Name of prize ship: Land forces.

Henry, Samuel   Prisoner: 683 - Rank: Private - Name of Prize: Land forces - By what ship or how taken: Taken on

shore - Discharged: 10 Aug 1813 - By what order: HMS Regulus by order of his Excellency Sir George Prevost - Source: List of American Prisoners of War discharged at Quebec - Name of prize ship: Land forces.

Herley, John   Prisoner: 1842 - Rank: Private - Name of Prize: Land forces - By what ship or how taken: Taken on shore - Discharged: 8 Nov 1814 - By what order: George No. 515 by Sir George Prevost - Source: List of American Prisoners of War discharged at Quebec - Name of prize ship: Land forces.

Heron, James E.   Prisoner: 1210 - Rank: Asst. Comp. - By what ship or how taken: Troops - Time when: 19 Dec 1813 - Place where: Fort Niagara - Whether man of war, privateer, or merchant vessel: Taken on shore - When received: 18 Jan 1814 - From what ship or whence received: Montreal by land carriages. - Prisoner: 1210 - Rank: Asst. Com. - Name of Prize: Land forces - By what ship or how taken: Taken on shore - Discharged: 31 Jan 1814 - By what order: Returned to the United States - Source: List of American Prisoners of War discharged at Quebec - Name of prize ship: Land forces.

Herrick, Eli - Rank: Corporal - Source: Account of American prisoners of war who died at Quebec in the Months of July, August & September 1813 - Ship or Corps: Land forces - Vessel: Taken on shore - Place born: Green, MA - Age: 20 - Where taken: Lake Champlain - Date of death: 30 Jul 1813.

Herrick, Oliver   Prisoner: 147 - Rank: Captain - Name of Prize: Land forces - By what ship or how taken: Taken on shore - Discharged: 10 Aug 1813 - By what order: HMS Regulus by order of his Excellency Sir George Prevost - Source: List of American Prisoners of War discharged at Quebec - Name of prize ship: Land forces.

Herring, John   Prisoner: 492 - Rank: Private - Name of Prize: Land forces - By what ship or how taken: Taken on shore - Discharged: 10 Aug 1813 - By what order: HMS Regulus by order of his Excellency Sir George Prevost - Source: List of American Prisoners of War discharged at Quebec - Name of prize ship: Land forces.

Hewins, Thomas   Prisoner: 1165 - Rank: Sergeant - By what ship or how taken: Troops - Time when: 27 Oct 1812 - Place where: Rapids - Whether man of war, privateer, or merchant vessel: Taken on shore - When received: 25 Nov 1813 - From what ship or whence received: Town goal. - Prisoner: 1165 - Rank: Private - Name of Prize: Land forces - By what ship or how taken: Taken on shore - Discharged: 4 May 1814 - By what order: Returned to the United States - Source: List of American Prisoners of War discharged at Quebec - Name of prize ship: Land forces.

Hex, Comfort   Prisoner: 1776 - Rank: Private - Name of Prize: Land forces - By what ship or how taken: Taken on shore - Discharged: 8 Nov 1814 - By what order: George No. 515 by Sir George Prevost - Source: List of American Prisoners of War discharged at Quebec - Name of prize ship: Land forces.

Hickling, William   Prisoner: 1833 - Rank: Private - Name of Prize: Land forces - By what ship or how taken: Taken on shore - Discharged: 8 Nov 1814 - By what order: George No. 515 by Sir George Prevost - Source: List of American Prisoners of War discharged at Quebec - Name of prize ship: Land forces.

Hicks, Isaac   Prisoner: 1052 - Rank: Private - Name of Prize: Growler - By what ship or how taken: Man of war - Discharged: 31 Oct 1813 - By what order: HMS Malabar Transport by order of his Excellency Sir George Prevost - Source: List of American Prisoners of War discharged at Quebec - Name of prize ship: Growler.

Higgens, Hiram   Prisoner: 1864 - Rank: Corporal - Name of Prize: Land forces - By what ship or how taken: Taken on shore - Discharged: 8 Nov 1814 - By what order: George No. 515 by Sir George Prevost - Source: List of American Prisoners of War discharged at Quebec - Name of prize ship: Land forces.

Hill, Allen   Prisoner: 1373 - Rank: Private - By what ship or how taken: Troops - Time when: 19 Dec 1813 - Place where: Fort Niagara - Whether man of war, privateer, or merchant vessel: Taken on shore - When received: 29 Jan 1814 - From what ship or whence received: Montreal by land carriages. - Prisoner: 1373 - Rank: Private - Name of Prize: Land forces - By what ship or how taken: Taken on shore - Discharged: 4 May 1814 - By what order: Returned to the United States - Source: List of American Prisoners of War discharged at Quebec - Name of prize ship: Land forces.

Hill, Stephen   Prisoner: 695 - Rank: Corporal - Name of Prize: Land forces - By what ship or how taken: Taken on shore - Discharged: 10 Aug 1813 - By what order: HMS Regulus by order of his Excellency Sir George Prevost - Source: List of American Prisoners of War discharged at Quebec - Name of prize ship: Land forces.

Hill, Valentine   Prisoner: 1796 - Rank: Private - Name of Prize: Land forces - By what ship or how taken: Taken on shore - Discharged: 8 Nov 1814 - By what order: George No. 515 by Sir George Prevost - Source: List of American Prisoners of War discharged at Quebec - Name of prize ship: Land forces.

Hill, William   Prisoner: 1086 - Rank: Private - Name of Prize: Land forces - By what ship or how taken: Taken on shore - Discharged: 31 Oct 1813 - By what order: HMS Malabar Transport by order of his Excellency Sir George Prevost - Source: List of American Prisoners of War discharged at Quebec - Name of prize ship: Land forces.

Hince, John   Prisoner: 1301 - Rank: Private - By what ship or how taken: Troops - Time when: 19 Dec 1813 - Place where: Fort Niagara - Whether man of war, privateer, or merchant vessel: Taken on shore - When received: 29 Jan 1814 - From what ship or whence received: Montreal by land carriages. - Prisoner: 1301 - Rank: Private - Name of Prize: Land forces - By what ship or how taken: Taken on shore - Discharged: 11 Mar 1814 - By what order: Volunteered for the New Brunswick Fencibles - Source: List of American Prisoners of War discharged at Quebec - Name of prize ship: Land forces.

Hind, Nathaniel   Prisoner: 1298 - Rank: Private - Name of Prize: Land forces - By what ship or how taken: Taken on shore - Discharged: 27 Feb 1814 - By what order: Volunteered for the New Brunswick Fencibles - Source: List of American Prisoners of War discharged at Quebec - Name of prize ship: Land forces. - Prisoner: 1298 - Rank: Private - By what ship or how taken: Troops - Time when: 19 Dec 1813 - Place where: Fort Niagara - Whether man of war, privateer, or merchant vessel: Taken on shore - When received: 29 Jan 1814 - From what ship or whence received: Montreal by land carriages.

Hogg, George   Prisoner: 490 - Rank: Private - Name of Prize: Land forces - By what ship or how taken: Taken on shore - Discharged: 10 Aug 1813 - By what order: HMS Regulus by order of his Excellency Sir George Prevost - Source: List of American Prisoners of War discharged at Quebec - Name of prize ship: Land forces.

Holford, Elijah   Prisoner: 1477 - Rank: Private - Name of Prize: Land forces - By what ship or how taken: Taken on shore - Discharged: 10 Nov 1814 - By what order: Sovereign No. 628 to Halifax by order of Sir George Prevost - Source: List of American Prisoners of War discharged at Quebec - Name of prize ship: Land forces.

Hollaby, John   Prisoner: 1424 - Rank: Private - Name of Prize: Land forces - By what ship or how taken: Taken on shore - Discharged: 4 May 1814 - By what order: Returned to the United States - Source: List of American Prisoners of War discharged at Quebec - Name of prize ship: Land forces. - Prisoner: 1424 - Rank: Private - By what ship or how taken: Troops - Time when: 19 Dec 1813 - Place where: Fort Niagara - Whether man of war, privateer, or merchant vessel: Taken on shore - When received: 29 Jan 1814 - From what ship or whence received: Montreal by land carriages.

Hollaway, John   Prisoner: 557 - Rank: Private - Name of Prize: Land forces - By what ship or how taken: Taken on shore - Discharged: 31 Oct 1813 - By what order: HMS Malabar Transport by order of his Excellency Sir George Prevost - Source: List of American Prisoners of War discharged at Quebec - Name of prize ship: Land forces.

Holmes, Charles   Prisoner: 1398 - Rank: Private - By what ship or how taken: Troops - Time when: 19 Dec 1813 - Place where: Fort Niagara - Whether man of war, privateer, or merchant vessel: Taken on shore - When received: 29 Jan 1814 - From what ship or whence received: Montreal by land carriages. - Prisoner: 1398 - Rank: Private - Name of Prize: Land forces - By what ship or how taken: Taken on shore - Discharged: 4 May 1814 - By what order: Returned to the United States - Source: List of American Prisoners of War discharged at Quebec - Name of prize ship: Land forces.

Holmes, Rubin   Prisoner: 1799 - Rank: Private - Name of Prize: Land forces - By what ship or how taken: Taken on shore - Discharged: 8 Nov 1814 - By what order: George No. 515 by Sir George Prevost - Source: List of American Prisoners of War discharged at Quebec - Name of prize ship: Land forces.

Holmes, Thomas   Prisoner: 1325 - Rank: Private - Name of Prize: Land forces - By what ship or how taken: Taken on shore - Discharged: 4 May 1814 - By what order: Returned to the United States - Source: List of American Prisoners of War discharged at Quebec - Name of prize ship: Land forces. - Prisoner: 1325 - Rank: Private - By what ship or how taken: Troops - Time when: 19 Dec 1813 - Place where: Fort Niagara - Whether man of war, privateer, or merchant vessel: Taken on shore - When received: 29 Jan 1814 - From what ship or whence received: Montreal by land carriages.

Holson, James   Prisoner: 613 - Rank: Private - Name of Prize: Land forces - By what ship or how taken: Taken on shore - Discharged: 10 Aug 1813 - By what order: HMS Regulus by order of his Excellency Sir George Prevost - Source: List of American Prisoners of War discharged at Quebec - Name of prize ship: Land forces.

Holts, George   Prisoner: 1941 - Rank: Private - Name of Prize: Land forces - By what ship or how taken: Taken on shore - Discharged: 13 Mar 1815 - By what order: Returned to the United States - Source: List of American Prisoners of War discharged at Quebec - Name of prize ship: Land forces.

Honeywell, Enoch   Prisoner: 599 - Rank: Private - Name of Prize: Land forces - By what ship or how taken: Taken on shore - Discharged: 10 Aug 1813 - By what order: HMS Regulus by order of his Excellency Sir George Prevost - Source: List of American Prisoners of War discharged at Quebec - Name of prize ship: Land forces.

Hood, Frederick   Prisoner: 970 - Rank: Private - Name of Prize: Land forces - By what ship or how taken: Taken on shore - Discharged: 31 Oct 1813 - By what order: HMS Malabar Transport by order of his Excellency Sir George Prevost - Source: List of American Prisoners of War discharged at Quebec - Name of prize ship: Land forces.

Hooke, Thomas   Prisoner: 1429 - Rank: Able Seaman - Name of Prize: Gbe - By what ship or how taken: Letter of Marque - Discharged: 9 Jun 1814 - By what order: Mulgrave Transport No. 311 - Source: List of American

Prisoners of War discharged at Quebec - Name of prize ship: Gbe. - Prisoner: 1429 - Rank: Able seaman - By what ship or how taken: Nymph - Time when: 1 Feb 1814 - Place where: off Bermuda - Whether man of war, privateer, or merchant vessel: Letter of Marque - When received: 24 May 1814 - From what ship or whence received: Mary Transport No. 368.

Hooker, George   Prisoner: 498 - Rank: Private - Source: Account of American prisoners of war who died at Quebec in the Months of July, August & September 1813 - Ship or Corps: Land forces - Vessel: Taken on shore - Date of death: 26 Jul 1813.

Hooker, Horace   Prisoner: 342 - Rank: Private - Source: Account of American prisoners of war who died at Quebec in the Months of July, August & September 1813 - Ship or Corps: Land forces - Vessel: Taken on shore - Place born: Vermont - Age: 24 - Where taken: Hoxenburgh - Date of death: 9 Sep 1813 - Disorder or casualty: Diarrhea.

Hooper, John   Prisoner: 56 - Rank: Private - Name of Prize: Land forces - By what ship or how taken: Taken on shore - Discharged: 31 Oct 1813 - By what order: HMS Malabar Transport by order of his Excellency Sir George Prevost - Source: List of American Prisoners of War discharged at Quebec - Name of prize ship: Land forces.

Hope, Levi   Prisoner: 1069 - Rank: Steward - Name of Prize: Growler - By what ship or how taken: Man of war - Discharged: 4 May 1814 - By what order: Returned to the United States - Source: List of American Prisoners of War discharged at Quebec - Name of prize ship: Growler.

Hopkins, John   Prisoner: 1333 - Rank: Musician - Name of Prize: Land forces - By what ship or how taken: Taken on shore - Discharged: 27 Feb 1814 - By what order: Volunteered for the New Brunswick Fencibles - Source: List of American Prisoners of War discharged at Quebec - Name of prize ship: Land forces. - Prisoner: 1333 - Rank: Musician - By what ship or how taken: Troops - Time when: 19 Dec 1813 - Place where: Fort Niagara - Whether man of war, privateer, or merchant vessel: Taken on shore - When received: 29 Jan 1814 - From what ship or whence received: Montreal by land carriages.

Hopkinson, Caleb   Prisoner: 1873 - Rank: Private - Name of Prize: Land forces - By what ship or how taken: Taken on shore - Discharged: 8 Nov 1814 - By what order: George No. 515 by Sir George Prevost - Source: List of American Prisoners of War discharged at Quebec - Name of prize ship: Land forces.

Horn, Andrew   Prisoner: 73 - Rank: Private - Name of Prize: Land forces - By what ship or how taken: Taken on shore - Discharged: 31 Oct 1813 - By what order: HMS Malabar Transport by order of his Excellency Sir George Prevost - Source: List of American Prisoners of War discharged at Quebec - Name of prize ship: Land forces.

Horn, Wentworth   Prisoner: 70 - Rank: Drummer - Name of Prize: Land forces - By what ship or how taken: Taken on shore - Discharged: 31 Oct 1813 - By what order: HMS Malabar Transport by order of his Excellency Sir George Prevost - Source: List of American Prisoners of War discharged at Quebec - Name of prize ship: Land forces.

Horney, David   Prisoner: 387 - Rank: Private - Name of Prize: Land forces - By what ship or how taken: Taken on shore - Discharged: 31 Oct 1813 - By what order: HMS Malabar Transport by order of his Excellency Sir George Prevost - Source: List of American Prisoners of War discharged at Quebec - Name of prize ship: Land forces.

Horton, Cyrus   Prisoner: 1880 - Rank: Private - Name of Prize: Land forces - By what ship or how taken: Taken on shore - Discharged: 8 Nov 1814 - By what order: George No. 515 by Sir George Prevost - Source: List of American Prisoners of War discharged at Quebec - Name of prize ship: Land forces.

Hosea, Nathaniel   Prisoner: 993 - Rank: Seaman - Name of Prize: Juliet - By what ship or how taken: Man of war - Discharged: 1 Nov 1813 - By what order: HMS Hero by order of his Excellency Sir George Prevost - Source: List of American prisoners sent to England on the HMS Hero - Name of prize ship: Juliet.

Hosea, Nathaniel B.   Prisoner: 993 - Rank: Able Seaman - Name of Prize: Julia - By what ship or how taken: Man of war - Discharged: 4 May 1814 - By what order: Returned to the United States - Source: List of American Prisoners of War discharged at Quebec - Name of prize ship: Julia.

Hotchkess, Henry   Prisoner: 25 - Rank: Private - Name of Prize: Land forces - By what ship or how taken: Taken on shore - Discharged: 31 Oct 1813 - By what order: HMS Malabar Transport by order of his Excellency Sir George Prevost - Source: List of American Prisoners of War discharged at Quebec - Name of prize ship: Land forces.

Houndshell, John   Prisoner: 1338 - Rank: Private - By what ship or how taken: Troops - Time when: 19 Dec 1813 - Place where: Fort Niagara - Whether man of war, privateer, or merchant vessel: Taken on shore - When received: 29 Jan 1814 - From what ship or whence received: Montreal by land carriages. - Prisoner: 1338 - Rank: Private - Name of Prize: Land forces - By what ship or how taken: Taken on shore - Discharged: 22

Feb 1814 - By what order: Volunteered for the New Brunswick Fencibles - Source: List of American Prisoners of War discharged at Quebec - Name of prize ship: Land forces.

House, Frederick   Prisoner: 677 - Rank: Sergeant - Name of Prize: Land forces - By what ship or how taken: Taken on shore - Discharged: 10 Aug 1813 - By what order: HMS Regulus by order of his Excellency Sir George Prevost - Source: List of American Prisoners of War discharged at Quebec - Name of prize ship: Land forces.

Hovet, Nathaniel   Prisoner: 1187 - Rank: Private - Name of Prize: Land forces - By what ship or how taken: Taken on shore - Discharged: 4 May 1814 - By what order: Returned to the United States - Source: List of American Prisoners of War discharged at Quebec - Name of prize ship: Land forces. - Prisoner: 1187 - Rank: Private - By what ship or how taken: Troops - Time when: 5 May 1813 - Place where: Rapids - Whether man of war, privateer, or merchant vessel: Taken on shore - When received: 11 Dec 1813 - From what ship or whence received: Town goal.

Howard, Edward   Prisoner: 1305 - Rank: Private - By what ship or how taken: Troops - Time when: 19 Dec 1813 - Place where: Fort Niagara - Whether man of war, privateer, or merchant vessel: Taken on shore - When received: 29 Jan 1814 - From what ship or whence received: Montreal by land carriages. - Prisoner: 1305 - Rank: Private - Name of Prize: Land forces - By what ship or how taken: Taken on shore - Discharged: 4 May 1814 - By what order: Returned to the United States - Source: List of American Prisoners of War discharged at Quebec - Name of prize ship: Land forces.

Howard, Joseph   Prisoner: 89 - Rank: Private - Source: Account of American prisoners of war who died at Quebec in the Months of July, August & September 1813 - Ship or Corps: Land forces - Vessel: Taken on shore - Place born: Bridgetown, MA - Age: 15 - Where taken: Stoney Point - Date of death: 3 Jul 1813.

Howard, Josiah   Prisoner: 58 - Rank: Private - Name of Prize: Land forces - By what ship or how taken: Taken on shore - Discharged: 31 Oct 1813 - By what order: HMS Malabar Transport by order of his Excellency Sir George Prevost - Source: List of American Prisoners of War discharged at Quebec - Name of prize ship: Land forces.

Howard, Lewis   Prisoner: 87 - Rank: Private - Name of Prize: Land forces - By what ship or how taken: Taken on shore - Discharged: 2 Nov 1813 - Source: List of Prisoners received on board the Malabar, discharged from hospital - Name of prize ship: Land forces. - Prisoner: 87 - Rank: Private - Name of Prize: Land forces - By what ship or how taken: Taken on shore - Discharged: 4 May 1814 - By what order: Returned to the United States - Source: List of American Prisoners of War discharged at Quebec - Name of prize ship: Land forces.

Howard, Ralph   Prisoner: 1865 - Rank: Private - Name of Prize: Land forces - By what ship or how taken: Taken on shore - Discharged: 8 Nov 1814 - By what order: George No. 515 by Sir George Prevost - Source: List of American Prisoners of War discharged at Quebec - Name of prize ship: Land forces.

Howe, Calvin   Prisoner: 15 - Rank: Private - Name of Prize: Land forces - By what ship or how taken: Taken on shore - Discharged: 31 Oct 1813 - By what order: HMS Malabar Transport by order of his Excellency Sir George Prevost - Source: List of American Prisoners of War discharged at Quebec - Name of prize ship: Land forces.

Howe, John   Prisoner: 123 - Rank: Private - Name of Prize: Land forces - By what ship or how taken: Taken on shore - Discharged: 31 Oct 1813 - By what order: HMS Malabar Transport by order of his Excellency Sir George Prevost - Source: List of American Prisoners of War discharged at Quebec - Name of prize ship: Land forces.

Hubbard, Thomas   Prisoner: 84 - Rank: Private - Name of Prize: Land forces - By what ship or how taken: Taken on shore - Discharged: 31 Oct 1813 - By what order: HMS Malabar Transport by order of his Excellency Sir George Prevost - Source: List of American Prisoners of War discharged at Quebec - Name of prize ship: Land forces.

Hubbard, William   Prisoner: 1961 - Rank: Private - Name of Prize: Land forces - By what ship or how taken: Taken on shore - Discharged: 13 Mar 1815 - By what order: Returned to the United States - Source: List of American Prisoners of War discharged at Quebec - Name of prize ship: Land forces.

Hunt, John   Prisoner: 166 - Rank: Seaman - Name of Prize: Eagle - By what ship or how taken: Man of war - Discharged: 31 Oct 1813 - By what order: HMS Malabar Transport by order of his Excellency Sir George Prevost - Source: List of American Prisoners of War discharged at Quebec - Name of prize ship: Eagle.

Hunt, Solomon   Prisoner: 118 - Rank: Private - Source: Account of American prisoners of war who died at Quebec in the Months of July, August & September 1813 - Ship or Corps: Land forces - Vessel: Taken on shore - Place born: Tewksbury - Age: 41 - Where taken: Stoney Point - Date of death: 4 Aug 1813.

Hunter, James   Prisoner: 592 - Rank: Private - Name of Prize: Land forces - By what ship or how taken: Taken on shore - Discharged: 10 Aug 1813 - By what order: HMS Regulus by order of his Excellency Sir George

Prevost - Source: List of American Prisoners of War discharged at Quebec - Name of prize ship: Land forces.

Hunter, Joseph   Prisoner: 429 - Rank: Private - Name of Prize: Land forces - By what ship or how taken: Taken on shore - Discharged: 10 Aug 1813 - By what order: HMS Regulus by order of his Excellency Sir George Prevost - Source: List of American Prisoners of War discharged at Quebec - Name of prize ship: Land forces.

Hurd, John   Prisoner: 565 - Rank: Private - Name of Prize: Land forces - By what ship or how taken: Taken on shore - Discharged: 10 Aug 1813 - By what order: HMS Regulus by order of his Excellency Sir George Prevost - Source: List of American Prisoners of War discharged at Quebec - Name of prize ship: Land forces.

Hutchison, David   Prisoner: 1271 - Rank: Private - Name of Prize: Land forces - By what ship or how taken: Taken on shore - Discharged: 4 May 1814 - By what order: Returned to the United States - Source: List of American Prisoners of War discharged at Quebec - Name of prize ship: Land forces. - Rank: Private - By what ship or how taken: Troops - Time when: 19 Dec 1813 - Place where: Fort Niagara - Whether man of war, privateer, or merchant vessel: Taken on shore - When received: 29 Jan 1814 - From what ship or whence received: Montreal by land carriages.

Hutchison, Robert B.   Prisoner: 1856 - Rank: Private - Name of Prize: Land forces - By what ship or how taken: Taken on shore - Discharged: 8 Nov 1814 - By what order: George No. 515 by Sir George Prevost - Source: List of American Prisoners of War discharged at Quebec - Name of prize ship: Land forces.

Hyde, Nathan   Prisoner: 1146 - Rank: Private - Name of Prize: Land forces - By what ship or how taken: Taken on shore - Discharged: 4 May 1814 - By what order: Returned to the United States - Source: List of American Prisoners of War discharged at Quebec - Name of prize ship: Land forces. - Prisoner: 1146 - Rank: Private - By what ship or how taken: Troops - Time when: 27 Oct 1812 - Place where: Rapids, River Raisin - Whether man of war, privateer, or merchant vessel: Taken on shore - When received: 25 Nov 1813 - From what ship or whence received: Town goal.

Hydendry, Henry   Prisoner: 1094 - Rank: Private - Name of Prize: Land forces - By what ship or how taken: Taken on shore - Discharged: 31 Oct 1813 - By what order: HMS Malabar Transport by order of his Excellency Sir George Prevost - Source: List of American Prisoners of War discharged at Quebec - Name of prize ship: Land forces.

Ingalls, Jonathan   Prisoner: 133 - Rank: Private - Source: Account of American prisoners of war who died at Quebec in the Months of July, August & September 1813 - Ship or Corps: Land forces - Vessel: Taken on shore - Place born: Haverhill - Age: 38 - Where taken: Stoney Point - Date of death: 14 Aug 1813.

Inghram, Benjamin   Prisoner: 1076 - Rank: Private - Name of Prize: Land forces - By what ship or how taken: Taken on shore - Discharged: 31 Oct 1813 - By what order: HMS Malabar Transport by order of his Excellency Sir George Prevost - Source: List of American Prisoners of War discharged at Quebec - Name of prize ship: Land forces.

Inghram, Nathaniel   Prisoner: 1806 - Rank: Private - Name of Prize: Land forces - By what ship or how taken: Taken on shore - Discharged: 8 Nov 1814 - By what order: George No. 515 by Sir George Prevost - Source: List of American Prisoners of War discharged at Quebec - Name of prize ship: Land forces.

Ireland, Jonas   Prisoner: 74 - Rank: Private - Name of Prize: Land forces - By what ship or how taken: Taken on shore - Discharged: 31 Oct 1813 - By what order: HMS Malabar Transport by order of his Excellency Sir George Prevost - Source: List of American Prisoners of War discharged at Quebec - Name of prize ship: Land forces.

Ireland, Jonathan   Prisoner: 578 - Rank: Private - Name of Prize: Land forces - By what ship or how taken: Taken on shore - Discharged: 10 Aug 1813 - By what order: HMS Regulus by order of his Excellency Sir George Prevost - Source: List of American Prisoners of War discharged at Quebec - Name of prize ship: Land forces.

Jack, Andrew   Prisoner: 1148 - Rank: Private - By what ship or how taken: Troops - Time when: 5 May 1813 - Place where: Rapids, River Raisin - Whether man of war, privateer, or merchant vessel: Taken on shore - When received: 25 Nov 1813 - From what ship or whence received: Town goal. - Prisoner: 1148 - Rank: Private - Name of Prize: Land forces - By what ship or how taken: Taken on shore - Discharged: 4 May 1814 - By what order: Returned to the United States - Source: List of American Prisoners of War discharged at Quebec - Name of prize ship: Land forces.

Jackson, Barnaby   Prisoner: 1750 - Rank: Private - Name of Prize: Tigress - By what ship or how taken: Man of war - Discharged: 8 Nov 1814 - By what order: George No. 515 by Sir George Prevost - Source: List of American Prisoners of War discharged at Quebec - Name of prize ship: Tigress.

Jackson, Enoch   Prisoner: 122 - Rank: Private - Name of Prize: Land forces - By what ship or how taken: Taken on shore - Discharged: 31 Oct 1813 - By what order: HMS Malabar Transport by order of his Excellency Sir George Prevost - Source: List of American Prisoners of War discharged at Quebec - Name of prize ship: Land forces.

Jacobs, John   Prisoner: 615 - Rank: Private - Name of Prize: Land forces - By what ship or how taken: Taken on shore - Discharged: 10 Aug 1813 - By what order: HMS Regulus by order of his Excellency Sir George Prevost - Source: List of American Prisoners of War discharged at Quebec - Name of prize ship: Land forces.

Jamison, John   Prisoner: 271 - Rank: Private - Name of Prize: Land forces - By what ship or how taken: Taken on shore - Discharged: 31 Oct 1813 - By what order: HMS Malabar Transport by order of his Excellency Sir George Prevost - Source: List of American Prisoners of War discharged at Quebec - Name of prize ship: Land forces.

Jennings, Noah   Prisoner: 1300 - Rank: Private - By what ship or how taken: Troops - Time when: 19 Dec 1813 - Place where: Fort Niagara - Whether man of war, privateer, or merchant vessel: Taken on shore - When received: 29 Jan 1814 - From what ship or whence received: Montreal by land carriages. - Prisoner: 1300 - Rank: Private - Name of Prize: Land forces - By what ship or how taken: Taken on shore - Discharged: 4 May 1814 - By what order: Returned to the United States - Source: List of American Prisoners of War discharged at Quebec - Name of prize ship: Land forces.

Johnson, Daniel   Prisoner: 1688 - Rank: Private - Name of Prize: Land forces - By what ship or how taken: Taken on shore - Discharged: 8 Nov 1814 - By what order: George No. 515 by Sir George Prevost - Source: List of American Prisoners of War discharged at Quebec - Name of prize ship: Land forces.

Johnson, David   Prisoner: 60 - Rank: Private - Name of Prize: Land forces - By what ship or how taken: Taken on shore - Discharged: 31 Oct 1813 - By what order: HMS Malabar Transport by order of his Excellency Sir George Prevost - Source: List of American Prisoners of War discharged at Quebec - Name of prize ship: Land forces.

Johnson, Doctor   Prisoner: 1456 - Rank: Private - Name of Prize: Land forces - By what ship or how taken: Taken on shore - Discharged: 8 Nov 1814 - By what order: George No. 515 by Sir George Prevost - Source: List of American Prisoners of War discharged at Quebec - Name of prize ship: Land forces.

Johnson, Hugh   Prisoner: 634 - Rank: Private - Name of Prize: Land forces - By what ship or how taken: Taken on shore - Discharged: 10 Aug 1813 - By what order: HMS Regulus by order of his Excellency Sir George Prevost - Source: List of American Prisoners of War discharged at Quebec - Name of prize ship: Land forces.

Johnson, Isaac   Prisoner: 623 - Rank: Private - Name of Prize: Land forces - By what ship or how taken: Taken on shore - Discharged: 10 Aug 1813 - By what order: HMS Regulus by order of his Excellency Sir George Prevost - Source: List of American Prisoners of War discharged at Quebec - Name of prize ship: Land forces.

Johnson, James H.   Prisoner: 1912 - Rank: Private - Name of Prize: Land forces - By what ship or how taken: Taken on shore - Discharged: 16 Mar 1815 - By what order: Returned to the United States - Source: List of American Prisoners of War discharged at Quebec - Name of prize ship: Land forces.

Johnson, Jason   Prisoner: 585 - Rank: Private - Name of Prize: Land forces - By what ship or how taken: Taken on shore - Discharged: 31 Oct 1813 - By what order: HMS Malabar Transport by order of his Excellency Sir George Prevost - Source: List of American Prisoners of War discharged at Quebec - Name of prize ship: Land forces.

Johnson, John   Prisoner: 59 - Rank: Private - Name of Prize: Land forces - By what ship or how taken: Taken on shore - Discharged: 31 Oct 1813 - By what order: HMS Malabar Transport by order of his Excellency Sir George Prevost - Source: List of American Prisoners of War discharged at Quebec - Name of prize ship: Land forces.

Johnson, Noble   Prisoner: 652 - Rank: Private - Name of Prize: Land forces - By what ship or how taken: Taken on shore - Discharged: 31 Oct 1813 - By what order: HMS Malabar Transport by order of his Excellency Sir George Prevost - Source: List of American Prisoners of War discharged at Quebec - Name of prize ship: Land forces.

Johnson, Ross   Prisoner: 1197 - By what ship or how taken: Citizen - When received: 12 Dec 1813 - From what ship or whence received: Town goal. - Prisoner: 1197 - Rank: Private - Name of Prize: Land forces - By what ship or how taken: Taken on shore - Discharged: 4 May 1814 - By what order: Returned to the United States - Source: List of American Prisoners of War discharged at Quebec - Name of prize ship: Land forces.

Johnson, Thomas   Prisoner: 1137 - Rank: Private - Name of Prize: Land forces - By what ship or how taken: Taken on shore - Discharged: 4 May 1814 - By what order: Returned to the United States - Source: List of American Prisoners of War discharged at Quebec - Name of prize ship: Land forces. - Prisoner: 1137 - Rank: Private - By what ship or how taken: Troops - Time when: 22 Jan 1813 - Place where: Rapids, River Raisin - Whether man of war, privateer, or merchant vessel: Taken on shore - When received: 25 Nov 1813 - From what ship or whence received: Town goal.

Johnson, Truman   Prisoner: 282 - Rank: Private - Name of Prize: Land forces - By what ship or how taken: Taken on shore - Discharged: 31 Oct 1813 - By what order: HMS Malabar Transport by order of his Excellency Sir

George Prevost - Source: List of American Prisoners of War discharged at Quebec - Name of prize ship: Land forces.

Johnson, William (1)   Prisoner: 558 - Rank: Private - Name of Prize: Land forces - By what ship or how taken: Taken on shore - Discharged: 10 Aug 1813 - By what order: HMS Regulus by order of his Excellency Sir George Prevost - Source: List of American Prisoners of War discharged at Quebec - Name of prize ship: Land forces.

Johnson, William (2)   Prisoner: 1208 - Rank: Ensign - By what ship or how taken: Troops - Time when: 19 Dec 1813 - Place where: Fort Niagara - Whether man of war, privateer, or merchant vessel: Taken on shore - When received: 18 Jan 1814 - From what ship or whence received: Montreal by land carriages.

Johnson, William (3)   Prisoner: 1510 - Rank: Cornet - Name of Prize: Land forces - By what ship or how taken: Taken on shore - Discharged: 10 Nov 1814 - By what order: Stately No. 400 to Halifax by order of Sir George Prevost - Source: List of American Prisoners of War discharged at Quebec - Name of prize ship: Land forces.

Johnson, William (4)   Prisoner: 1854 - Rank: Private - Name of Prize: Land forces - By what ship or how taken: Taken on shore - Discharged: 8 Nov 1814 - By what order: George No. 515 by Sir George Prevost - Source: List of American Prisoners of War discharged at Quebec - Name of prize ship: Land forces.

Johnston, Asa   Prisoner: 1289 - Rank: Private - Name of Prize: Land forces - By what ship or how taken: Taken on shore - Discharged: 4 May 1814 - By what order: Returned to the United States - Source: List of American Prisoners of War discharged at Quebec - Name of prize ship: Land forces. - Prisoner: 1289 - Rank: Private - By what ship or how taken: Troops - Time when: 19 Dec 1813 - Place where: Fort Niagara - Whether man of war, privateer, or merchant vessel: Taken on shore - When received: 29 Jan 1814 - From what ship or whence received: Montreal by land carriages.

Johnston, James   Prisoner: 1287 - Rank: Private - Name of Prize: Land forces - By what ship or how taken: Taken on shore - Discharged: 4 May 1814 - By what order: Returned to the United States - Source: List of American Prisoners of War discharged at Quebec - Name of prize ship: Land forces. - Prisoner: 1287 - Rank: Private - By what ship or how taken: Troops - Time when: 19 Dec 1813 - Place where: Fort Niagara - Whether man of war, privateer, or merchant vessel: Taken on shore - When received: 29 Jan 1814 - From what ship or whence received: Montreal by land carriages.

Johnston, Littleton   Prisoner: 1205 - Rank: Lieutenant - By what ship or how taken: Troops - Time when: 19 Dec 1813 - Place where: Fort Niagara - Whether man of war, privateer, or merchant vessel: Taken on shore - When received: 18 Jan 1814 - From what ship or whence received: Montreal by land carriages. - Prisoner: 1205 - Rank: Lieutenant - Name of Prize: Land forces - By what ship or how taken: Taken on shore - Discharged: 4 May 1814 - By what order: Returned to the United States - Source: List of American Prisoners of War discharged at Quebec - Name of prize ship: Land forces.

Johnston, Richard   Prisoner: 1352 - Rank: Private - By what ship or how taken: Troops - Time when: 19 Dec 1813 - Place where: Fort Niagara - Whether man of war, privateer, or merchant vessel: Taken on shore - When received: 29 Jan 1814 - From what ship or whence received: Montreal by land carriages. - Prisoner: 1352 - Rank: Private - Name of Prize: Land forces - By what ship or how taken: Taken on shore - Discharged: 4 May 1814 - By what order: Returned to the United States - Source: List of American Prisoners of War discharged at Quebec - Name of prize ship: Land forces.

Johnston, William (1)   Prisoner: 1208 - Rank: Ensign - Name of Prize: Land forces - By what ship or how taken: Taken on shore - Discharged: 6 May 1814 - By what order: Returned to the United States - Source: List of American Prisoners of War discharged at Quebec - Name of prize ship: Land forces.

Johnston, William (2)   Prisoner: 1354 - Rank: Sergeant - By what ship or how taken: Troops - Time when: 19 Dec 1813 - Place where: Fort Niagara - Whether man of war, privateer, or merchant vessel: Taken on shore - When received: 29 Jan 1814 - From what ship or whence received: Montreal by land carriages. - Prisoner: 1354 - Rank: Sergeant - Name of Prize: Land forces - By what ship or how taken: Taken on shore - Discharged: 25 Feb 1814 - By what order: Volunteered for the New Brunswick Fencibles - Source: List of American Prisoners of War discharged at Quebec - Name of prize ship: Land forces.

Jones, Enoch   Prisoner: 368 - Rank: Private - Name of Prize: Land forces - By what ship or how taken: Taken on shore - Discharged: 31 Oct 1813 - By what order: HMS Malabar Transport by order of his Excellency Sir George Prevost - Source: List of American Prisoners of War discharged at Quebec - Name of prize ship: Land forces.

Jones, Henry   Prisoner: 340 - Rank: Private - Name of Prize: Land forces - By what ship or how taken: Taken on shore - Discharged: 31 Oct 1813 - By what order: HMS Malabar Transport by order of his Excellency Sir George Prevost - Source: List of American Prisoners of War discharged at Quebec - Name of prize ship:

Land forces.

Jones, John   Prisoner: 1136 - Rank: Private - Name of Prize: Land forces - By what ship or how taken: Taken on shore - Discharged: 4 May 1814 - By what order: Returned to the United States - Source: List of American Prisoners of War discharged at Quebec - Name of prize ship: Land forces. - Prisoner: 1136 - Rank: Private - By what ship or how taken: Troops - Time when: 5 May 1813 - Place where: Rapids, River Raisin - Whether man of war, privateer, or merchant vessel: Taken on shore - When received: 25 Nov 1813 - From what ship or whence received: Town goal.

Jones, Leroy   Prisoner: 1139 - Rank: Private - By what ship or how taken: Troops - Time when: 22 Jan 1813 - Place where: Rapids, River Raisin - Whether man of war, privateer, or merchant vessel: Taken on shore - When received: 25 Nov 1813 - From what ship or whence received: Town goal. - Prisoner: 1139 - Rank: Private - Name of Prize: Land forces - By what ship or how taken: Taken on shore - Discharged: 4 May 1814 - By what order: Returned to the United States - Source: List of American Prisoners of War discharged at Quebec - Name of prize ship: Land forces.

Jones, Philander   Prisoner: 344 - Rank: Private - Name of Prize: Land forces - By what ship or how taken: Taken on shore - Discharged: 31 Oct 1813 - By what order: HMS Malabar Transport by order of his Excellency Sir George Prevost - Source: List of American Prisoners of War discharged at Quebec - Name of prize ship: Land forces.

Jones, Samuel   Prisoner: 1254 - Rank: Private - By what ship or how taken: Troops - Time when: 19 Dec 1813 - Place where: Fort Niagara - Whether man of war, privateer, or merchant vessel: Taken on shore - When received: 29 Jan 1814 - From what ship or whence received: Montreal by land carriages. - Prisoner: 1254 - Rank: Private - Name of Prize: Land forces - By what ship or how taken: Taken on shore - Discharged: 4 May 1814 - By what order: Returned to the United States - Source: List of American Prisoners of War discharged at Quebec - Name of prize ship: Land forces.

Jones, Thomas   Prisoner: 926 - Rank: Private - Name of Prize: Land forces - By what ship or how taken: Taken on shore - Discharged: 31 Oct 1813 - By what order: HMS Malabar Transport by order of his Excellency Sir George Prevost - Source: List of American Prisoners of War discharged at Quebec - Name of prize ship: Land forces.

Jones, William (1)   Prisoner: 284 - Rank: Private - Name of Prize: Land forces - By what ship or how taken: Taken on shore - Discharged: 31 Oct 1813 - By what order: HMS Malabar Transport by order of his Excellency Sir George Prevost - Source: List of American Prisoners of War discharged at Quebec - Name of prize ship: Land forces.

Jones, William (2)   Prisoner: 573 - Rank: Private - Name of Prize: Land forces - By what ship or how taken: Taken on shore - Discharged: 10 Aug 1813 - By what order: HMS Regulus by order of his Excellency Sir George Prevost - Source: List of American Prisoners of War discharged at Quebec - Name of prize ship: Land forces.

Jones, William (2)   Prisoner: 1698 - Rank: Private - Name of Prize: Land forces - By what ship or how taken: Taken on shore - Discharged: 8 Nov 1814 - By what order: George No. 515 by Sir George Prevost - Source: List of American Prisoners of War discharged at Quebec - Name of prize ship: Land forces.

Joseph, John   Prisoner: 1016 - Rank: Private - Name of Prize: Juliet - By what ship or how taken: Man of war - Discharged: 31 Oct 1813 - By what order: HMS Malabar Transport by order of his Excellency Sir George Prevost - Source: List of American Prisoners of War discharged at Quebec - Name of prize ship: Juliet.

Joy, Bennett   Prisoner: 1975 - Rank: Private - Name of Prize: Land forces - By what ship or how taken: Taken on shore - Discharged: 13 Mar 1815 - By what order: Returned to the United States - Source: List of American Prisoners of War discharged at Quebec - Name of prize ship: Land forces.

Judd, William   Prisoner: 1935 - Rank: Private - Source: Account of American prisoners of war who died at Quebec between 14 February 1814 and 23 December 1814 - Ship or Corps: Land forces - Vessel: Taken on shore - Place born: Vermont - Age: 20 - Where taken: Fort Erie - Date of death: 7 Nov 1814 - Disorder or casualty: Dysentery.

Kail, Horace   Prisoner: 1982 - Rank: Private - Source: Account of American prisoners of war who died at Quebec between 14 February 1814 and 23 December 1814 - Ship or Corps: Land forces - Vessel: Taken on shore - Place born: Connecticut - Age: 23 - Where taken: Fort George - Date of death: 28 Mar 1814 - Disorder or casualty: phthisis.

Kain, John   Prisoner: 862 - Rank: Private - Name of Prize: Land forces - By what ship or how taken: Taken on shore - Discharged: 31 Oct 1813 - By what order: HMS Malabar Transport by order of his Excellency Sir George Prevost - Source: List of American Prisoners of War discharged at Quebec - Name of prize ship: Land forces.

Kawkenbroke, Henry   Prisoner: 477 - Rank: Private - Name of Prize: Land forces - By what ship or how taken:

Taken on shore - Discharged: 10 Aug 1813 - By what order: HMS Regulus by order of his Excellency Sir George Prevost - Source: List of American Prisoners of War discharged at Quebec - Name of prize ship: Land forces.

Kehae, John   Prisoner: 1772 - Rank: Corporal - Name of Prize: Land forces - By what ship or how taken: Taken on shore - Discharged: 8 Nov 1814 - By what order: George No. 515 by Sir George Prevost - Source: List of American Prisoners of War discharged at Quebec - Name of prize ship: Land forces.

Keller, John   Prisoner: 1098 - Rank: Private - Name of Prize: Land forces - By what ship or how taken: Taken on shore - Discharged: 31 Oct 1813 - By what order: HMS Malabar Transport by order of his Excellency Sir George Prevost - Source: List of American Prisoners of War discharged at Quebec - Name of prize ship: Land forces.

Kelley, Charles   Prisoner: 758 - Rank: Private - Name of Prize: Land forces - By what ship or how taken: Taken on shore - Discharged: 10 Aug 1813 - By what order: HMS Regulus by order of his Excellency Sir George Prevost - Source: List of American Prisoners of War discharged at Quebec - Name of prize ship: Land forces - Comments: British subject, sent to England.

Kelley, James   Prisoner: 1085 - Rank: Private - Name of Prize: Land forces - By what ship or how taken: Taken on shore - Discharged: 31 Oct 1813 - By what order: HMS Malabar Transport by order of his Excellency Sir George Prevost - Source: List of American Prisoners of War discharged at Quebec - Name of prize ship: Land forces.

Kellogg, Isar   Prisoner: 726 - Rank: Corporal - Name of Prize: Land forces - By what ship or how taken: Taken on shore - Discharged: 10 Aug 1813 - By what order: HMS Regulus by order of his Excellency Sir George Prevost - Source: List of American Prisoners of War discharged at Quebec - Name of prize ship: Land forces.

Kelly, William   Prisoner: 388 - Rank: Private - Name of Prize: Land forces - By what ship or how taken: Taken on shore - Discharged: 31 Oct 1813 - By what order: HMS Malabar Transport by order of his Excellency Sir George Prevost - Source: List of American Prisoners of War discharged at Quebec - Name of prize ship: Land forces.

Kennedy, William   Prisoner: 1409 - Rank: Corporal - Name of Prize: Land forces - By what ship or how taken: Taken on shore - Discharged: 4 May 1814 - By what order: Returned to the United States - Source: List of American Prisoners of War discharged at Quebec - Name of prize ship: Land forces. - Prisoner: 1409 - Rank: Corporal - By what ship or how taken: Troops - Time when: 19 Dec 1813 - Place where: Fort Niagara - Whether man of war, privateer, or merchant vessel: Taken on shore - When received: 29 Jan 1814 - From what ship or whence received: Montreal by land carriages.

Kimball, Benjamin   Prisoner: 35 - Rank: Private - Source: Account of American prisoners of war who died at Quebec in the Months of July, August & September 1813 - Ship or Corps: Land forces - Vessel: Taken on shore - Place born: Topsfield, MA - Age: 35 - Where taken: Stoney Point - Date of death: 6 Aug 1813.

Kimball, Hannibal   Prisoner: 88 - Rank: Private - Name of Prize: Land forces - By what ship or how taken: Taken on shore - Discharged: 4 May 1814 - By what order: Returned to the United States - Source: List of American Prisoners of War discharged at Quebec - Name of prize ship: Land forces.

Kimball, Nathaniel   Prisoner: 90 - Rank: Private - Name of Prize: Land forces - By what ship or how taken: Taken on shore - Discharged: 31 Oct 1813 - By what order: HMS Malabar Transport by order of his Excellency Sir George Prevost - Source: List of American Prisoners of War discharged at Quebec - Name of prize ship: Land forces.

Kimbell, Abel   Prisoner: 5 - Rank: Private - Name of Prize: Land forces - By what ship or how taken: Taken on shore - Discharged: 4 May 1814 - By what order: Returned to the United States - Source: List of American Prisoners of War discharged at Quebec - Name of prize ship: Land forces.

Kimble, Caleb   Prisoner: 1874 - Rank: Private - Name of Prize: Land forces - By what ship or how taken: Taken on shore - Discharged: 8 Nov 1814 - By what order: George No. 515 by Sir George Prevost - Source: List of American Prisoners of War discharged at Quebec - Name of prize ship: Land forces.

Kindle, Rezin   Prisoner: 1142 - Rank: Private - By what ship or how taken: Troops - Time when: 22 Jan 1813 - Place where: Rapids, River Raisin - Whether man of war, privateer, or merchant vessel: Taken on shore - When received: 25 Nov 1813 - From what ship or whence received: Town goal. - Prisoner: 1142 - Rank: Private - Name of Prize: Land forces - By what ship or how taken: Taken on shore - Discharged: 4 May 1814 - By what order: Returned to the United States - Source: List of American Prisoners of War discharged at Quebec - Name of prize ship: Land forces.

King, Elijah   Prisoner: 1892 - Rank: Corporal - Name of Prize: Land forces - By what ship or how taken: Taken on shore - Discharged: 8 Nov 1814 - By what order: George No. 515 by Sir George Prevost - Source: List of American Prisoners of War discharged at Quebec - Name of prize ship: Land forces.

King, Robert   Prisoner: 1943 - Rank: Private - Name of Prize: Land forces - By what ship or how taken: Taken on shore - Discharged: 13 Mar 1815 - By what order: Returned to the United States - Source: List of American Prisoners of War discharged at Quebec - Name of prize ship: Land forces.

King, William   Prisoner: 449 - Rank: Private - Name of Prize: Land forces - By what ship or how taken: Taken on shore - Discharged: 10 Aug 1813 - By what order: HMS Regulus by order of his Excellency Sir George Prevost - Source: List of American Prisoners of War discharged at Quebec - Name of prize ship: Land forces.

Kingman, Ebenezer   Prisoner: 91 - Rank: Private - Name of Prize: Land forces - By what ship or how taken: Taken on shore - Discharged: 31 Oct 1813 - By what order: HMS Malabar Transport by order of his Excellency Sir George Prevost - Source: List of American Prisoners of War discharged at Quebec - Name of prize ship: Land forces.

Kingsland, Joseph   Prisoner: 556 - Rank: Private - Name of Prize: Land forces - By what ship or how taken: Taken on shore - Discharged: 31 Oct 1813 - By what order: HMS Malabar Transport by order of his Excellency Sir George Prevost - Source: List of American Prisoners of War discharged at Quebec - Name of prize ship: Land forces.

Knags, Witmore   Prisoner: 1191 - By what ship or how taken: Citizen - When received: 12 Dec 1813 - From what ship or whence received: Town goal. - Prisoner: 1191 - Rank: Private - Name of Prize: Land forces - By what ship or how taken: Taken on shore - Discharged: 4 May 1814 - By what order: Returned to the United States - Source: List of American Prisoners of War discharged at Quebec - Name of prize ship: Land forces.

Knight, Andrew   Prisoner: 92 - Rank: Private - Source: Account of American prisoners of war who died at Quebec in the Months of July, August & September 1813 - Ship or Corps: Land forces - Vessel: Taken on shore - Place born: Waterboro, MA - Age: 17 - Where taken: Stoney Point - Date of death: 27 Aug 1813 - Disorder or casualty: Typhus fever.

Knight, Hudson   Prisoner: 71 - Rank: Fifer - Name of Prize: Land forces - By what ship or how taken: Taken on shore - Discharged: 31 Oct 1813 - By what order: HMS Malabar Transport by order of his Excellency Sir George Prevost - Source: List of American Prisoners of War discharged at Quebec - Name of prize ship: Land forces.

Knight, William   Prisoner: 277 - Rank: Boy - Name of Prize: Land forces - By what ship or how taken: Taken on shore - Discharged: 31 Oct 1813 - By what order: HMS Malabar Transport by order of his Excellency Sir George Prevost - Source: List of American Prisoners of War discharged at Quebec - Name of prize ship: Land forces.

Knowles, Joseph   Prisoner: 1159 - Rank: Corporal - By what ship or how taken: Troops - Time when: 5 May 1813 - Place where: Rapids, River Raisin - Whether man of war, privateer, or merchant vessel: Taken on shore - When received: 25 Nov 1813 - From what ship or whence received: Town goal. - Prisoner: 1159 - Rank: Private - Name of Prize: Land forces - By what ship or how taken: Taken on shore - Discharged: 4 May 1814 - By what order: Returned to the United States - Source: List of American Prisoners of War discharged at Quebec - Name of prize ship: Land forces.

Knowles, Seth   Prisoner: 975 - Rank: Private - Name of Prize: Land forces - By what ship or how taken: Taken on shore - Discharged: 31 Oct 1813 - By what order: HMS Malabar Transport by order of his Excellency Sir George Prevost - Source: List of American Prisoners of War discharged at Quebec - Name of prize ship: Land forces.

Knowlton, Ebenezer   Prisoner: 707 - Rank: Private - Name of Prize: Land forces - By what ship or how taken: Taken on shore - Discharged: 10 Aug 1813 - By what order: HMS Regulus by order of his Excellency Sir George Prevost - Source: List of American Prisoners of War discharged at Quebec - Name of prize ship: Land forces.

Koontz, Jacob   Prisoner: 1228 - Rank: Private - By what ship or how taken: Troops - Time when: 19 Dec 1813 - Place where: Fort Niagara - Whether man of war, privateer, or merchant vessel: Taken on shore - When received: 29 Jan 1814 - From what ship or whence received: Montreal by land carriages. - Prisoner: 1228 - Rank: Private - Name of Prize: Land forces - By what ship or how taken: Taken on shore - Discharged: 4 May 1814 - By what order: Returned to the United States - Source: List of American Prisoners of War discharged at Quebec - Name of prize ship: Land forces.

Kowited, Aaron   Prisoner: 1937 - Rank: Private - Name of Prize: Land forces - By what ship or how taken: Taken on shore - Discharged: 13 Mar 1815 - By what order: Returned to the United States - Source: List of American Prisoners of War discharged at Quebec - Name of prize ship: Land forces.

Kronneger, John   Prisoner: 279 - Rank: Private - Name of Prize: Land forces - By what ship or how taken: Taken on shore - Discharged: 31 Oct 1813 - By what order: HMS Malabar Transport by order of his Excellency Sir George Prevost - Source: List of American Prisoners of War discharged at Quebec - Name of prize ship:

Land forces.

La Bonte, Francis   Prisoner: 1198 - By what ship or how taken: Citizen - When received: 12 Dec 1813 - From what ship or whence received: Town goal. - Prisoner: 1198 - Rank: Private - Name of Prize: Came in from the American Lines - Discharged: 3 Jan 1814 - By what order: Volunteered for the New Brunswick Fencibles - Source: List of American Prisoners of War discharged at Quebec - Name of prize ship: Came in from the American Lines.

Labrey, Ephraim   Prisoner: 63 - Rank: Private - Name of Prize: Land forces - By what ship or how taken: Taken on shore - Discharged: 31 Oct 1813 - By what order: HMS Malabar Transport by order of his Excellency Sir George Prevost - Source: List of American Prisoners of War discharged at Quebec - Name of prize ship: Land forces.

Labrey, Stephen   Prisoner: 1809 - Rank: Private - Name of Prize: Land forces - By what ship or how taken: Taken on shore - Discharged: 8 Nov 1814 - By what order: George No. 515 by Sir George Prevost - Source: List of American Prisoners of War discharged at Quebec - Name of prize ship: Land forces.

Lackey, Amasa   Prisoner: 366 - Rank: Private - Source: Account of American prisoners of war who died at Quebec between 14 February 1814 and 23 December 1814 - Ship or Corps: Land forces - Vessel: Taken on shore - Place born: Brookfield - Age: 26 - Where taken: Stoney Point - Date of death: 2 Apr 1814 - Disorder or casualty: Debility.

Lackey, Hugh   Prisoner: 1246 - Rank: Sergeant - By what ship or how taken: Troops - Time when: 19 Dec 1813 - Place where: Fort Niagara - Whether man of war, privateer, or merchant vessel: Taken on shore - When received: 29 Jan 1814 - From what ship or whence received: Montreal by land carriages. - Prisoner: 1246 - Rank: Sergeant - Name of Prize: Land forces - By what ship or how taken: Taken on shore - Discharged: 4 May 1814 - By what order: Returned to the United States - Source: List of American Prisoners of War discharged at Quebec - Name of prize ship: Land forces.

Laforge, Charles   Prisoner: 1047 - Rank: Private - Name of Prize: Growler - By what ship or how taken: Man of war - Discharged: 31 Oct 1813 - By what order: HMS Malabar Transport by order of his Excellency Sir George Prevost - Source: List of American Prisoners of War discharged at Quebec - Name of prize ship: Growler.

Lake, Elishua   Prisoner: 1867 - Rank: Private - Name of Prize: Land forces - By what ship or how taken: Taken on shore - Discharged: 8 Nov 1814 - By what order: George No. 515 by Sir George Prevost - Source: List of American Prisoners of War discharged at Quebec - Name of prize ship: Land forces.

Lamb, Joshua F.   Prisoner: 68 - Rank: Corporal - Source: Account of American prisoners of war who died at Quebec between 14 February 1814 and 23 December 1814 - Ship or Corps: Land forces - Vessel: Taken on shore - Place born: Oxford, MA - Age: 23 - Where taken: Stoney Point - Date of death: 14 Feb 1814 - Disorder or casualty: Dysentery.

Lander, Charles   Prisoner: 119 - Rank: Private - Source: Account of American prisoners of war who died at Quebec in the Months of July, August & September 1813 - Ship or Corps: Land forces - Vessel: Taken on shore - Place born: Boston, MA - Age: 52 - Where taken: Stoney Point - Date of death: 22 Jul 1813 - Disorder or casualty: Diarrhea.

Landers, John   Prisoner: 1950 - Rank: Private - Name of Prize: Land forces - By what ship or how taken: Taken on shore - Discharged: 13 Mar 1815 - By what order: Returned to the United States - Source: List of American Prisoners of War discharged at Quebec - Name of prize ship: Land forces.

Landsdale, James B.   Prisoner: 1394 - Rank: Private - By what ship or how taken: Troops - Time when: 19 Dec 1813 - Place where: Fort Niagara - Whether man of war, privateer, or merchant vessel: Taken on shore - When received: 29 Jan 1814 - From what ship or whence received: Montreal by land carriages. - Prisoner: 1394 - Rank: Private - Name of Prize: Land forces - By what ship or how taken: Taken on shore - Discharged: 4 May 1814 - By what order: Returned to the United States - Source: List of American Prisoners of War discharged at Quebec - Name of prize ship: Land forces.

Lane, Benjamin   Prisoner: 513 - Rank: Private - Source: Account of American prisoners of war who died at Quebec in the Months of July, August & September 1813 - Ship or Corps: Land forces - Vessel: Taken on shore - Place born: York States - Age: 29 - Where taken: Beaver Dams - Date of death: 23 Jul 1813.

Lane, Jesse   Prisoner: 974 - Rank: Private - Name of Prize: Land forces - By what ship or how taken: Taken on shore - Discharged: 31 Oct 1813 - By what order: HMS Malabar Transport by order of his Excellency Sir George Prevost - Source: List of American Prisoners of War discharged at Quebec - Name of prize ship: Land forces.

Lark, Joseph   Prisoner: 1367 - Rank: Private - By what ship or how taken: Troops - Time when: 19 Dec 1813 - Place where: Fort Niagara - Whether man of war, privateer, or merchant vessel: Taken on shore - When received: 29 Jan 1814 - From what ship or whence received: Montreal by land carriages.

Larkins, Thomas   Prisoner: 1316 - Rank: Private - Name of Prize: Land forces - By what ship or how taken: Taken on shore - Discharged: 22 Feb 1814 - By what order: Volunteered for the New Brunswick Fencibles - Source: List of American Prisoners of War discharged at Quebec - Name of prize ship: Land forces. - Prisoner: 1316 - Rank: Private - By what ship or how taken: Troops - Time when: 19 Dec 1813 - Place where: Fort Niagara - Whether man of war, privateer, or merchant vessel: Taken on shore - When received: 29 Jan 1814 - From what ship or whence received: Montreal by land carriages.

Larney, Joseph R.   Prisoner: 1090 - Rank: Private - Name of Prize: Land forces - By what ship or how taken: Taken on shore - Discharged: 31 Oct 1813 - By what order: HMS Malabar Transport by order of his Excellency Sir George Prevost - Source: List of American Prisoners of War discharged at Quebec - Name of prize ship: Land forces.

Larue, Thomas   Prisoner: 1532 - Rank: Private - Name of Prize: Land forces - By what ship or how taken: Taken on shore - Discharged: 8 Nov 1814 - By what order: George No. 515 by Sir George Prevost - Source: List of American Prisoners of War discharged at Quebec - Name of prize ship: Land forces.

Lash, Jeremiah   Prisoner: 684 - Rank: Private - Name of Prize: Land forces - By what ship or how taken: Taken on shore - Discharged: 10 Aug 1813 - By what order: HMS Regulus by order of his Excellency Sir George Prevost - Source: List of American Prisoners of War discharged at Quebec - Name of prize ship: Land forces.

Latham, Edward   Prisoner: 471 - Rank: Private - Name of Prize: Land forces - By what ship or how taken: Taken on shore - Discharged: 10 Aug 1813 - By what order: HMS Regulus by order of his Excellency Sir George Prevost - Source: List of American Prisoners of War discharged at Quebec - Name of prize ship: Land forces.

Latimer. Arthur   Prisoner: 1708 - Rank: Midshipman - By what ship or how taken: Man of war - Discharged: 10 Nov 1814 - By what order: Lord Cathcart No. 161 for Halifax by order of Sir George Prevost - Source: List of American Prisoners of War discharged at Quebec.

Laundrough, Andrew   Prisoner: 1756 - Rank: Private - Name of Prize: Scorpion - By what ship or how taken: Man of war - Discharged: 8 Nov 1814 - By what order: George No. 515 by Sir George Prevost - Source: List of American Prisoners of War discharged at Quebec - Name of prize ship: Scorpion.

Law, Samuel   Prisoner: 678 - Rank: Private - Name of Prize: Land forces - By what ship or how taken: Taken on shore - Discharged: 31 Oct 1813 - By what order: HMS Malabar Transport by order of his Excellency Sir George Prevost - Source: List of American Prisoners of War discharged at Quebec - Name of prize ship: Land forces.

Lawood, William   Prisoner: 443 - Rank: Private - Name of Prize: Land forces - By what ship or how taken: Taken on shore - Discharged: 31 Oct 1813 - By what order: HMS Malabar Transport by order of his Excellency Sir George Prevost - Source: List of American Prisoners of War discharged at Quebec - Name of prize ship: Land forces.

Lawton, John (1)   Prisoner: 1006 - Rank: Seaman - Name of Prize: Juliet - By what ship or how taken: Man of war - Discharged: 31 Oct 1813 - By what order: HMS Malabar Transport by order of his Excellency Sir George Prevost - Source: List of American Prisoners of War discharged at Quebec - Name of prize ship: Juliet.

Lawton, John (2)   Prisoner: 1722 - Rank: Carpenter's mate - Name of Prize: Scorpion - By what ship or how taken: Man of war - Discharged: 7 Nov 1813 - By what order: HMS Freedom No. 582 by order of his Excellency Sir George Prevost - Source: List of American Prisoners of War discharged at Quebec - Name of prize ship: Scorpion.

Lawton, Perry   Prisoner: 21 - Rank: Private - Source: Account of American prisoners of war who died at Quebec in the Months of July, August & September 1813 - Ship or Corps: Land forces - Vessel: Taken on shore - Place born: Swansea - Age: 19 - Where taken: Stoney Point - Date of death: 20 Jul 1813 - Disorder or casualty: Synochus.

Leach, George W.   Prisoner: 1800 - Rank: Private - Name of Prize: Land forces - By what ship or how taken: Taken on shore - Discharged: 8 Nov 1814 - By what order: George No. 515 by Sir George Prevost - Source: List of American Prisoners of War discharged at Quebec - Name of prize ship: Land forces.

Learned, Henry   Prisoner: 666 - Rank: Private - Name of Prize: Land forces - By what ship or how taken: Taken on shore - Discharged: 10 Aug 1813 - By what order: HMS Regulus by order of his Excellency Sir George Prevost - Source: List of American Prisoners of War discharged at Quebec - Name of prize ship: Land forces.

Leazer, Elisha   Prisoner: 550 - Rank: Corporal - Name of Prize: Land forces - By what ship or how taken: Taken on shore - Discharged: 10 Aug 1813 - By what order: HMS Regulus by order of his Excellency Sir George Prevost - Source: List of American Prisoners of War discharged at Quebec - Name of prize ship: Land forces.

Ledman, Francis   Prisoner: 310 - Rank: Private - Name of Prize: Land forces - By what ship or how taken: Taken on shore - Discharged: 31 Oct 1813 - By what order: HMS Malabar Transport by order of his Excellency Sir

George Prevost - Source: List of American Prisoners of War discharged at Quebec - Name of prize ship: Land forces.

Ledrew, Amable   Prisoner: 1702 - Rank: Private - Name of Prize: Land forces - By what ship or how taken: Taken on shore - Discharged: 8 Nov 1814 - By what order: George No. 515 by Sir George Prevost - Source: List of American Prisoners of War discharged at Quebec - Name of prize ship: Land forces.

Lee, Daniel   Prisoner: 325 - Rank: Private - Name of Prize: Land forces - By what ship or how taken: Taken on shore - Discharged: 31 Oct 1813 - By what order: HMS Malabar Transport by order of his Excellency Sir George Prevost - Source: List of American Prisoners of War discharged at Quebec - Name of prize ship: Land forces.

Legg, David   Prisoner: 304 - Rank: Private - Name of Prize: Land forces - By what ship or how taken: Taken on shore - Discharged: 31 Oct 1813 - By what order: HMS Malabar Transport by order of his Excellency Sir George Prevost - Source: List of American Prisoners of War discharged at Quebec - Name of prize ship: Land forces.

Leonard, Isaac   Prisoner: 1158 - Rank: Corporal - By what ship or how taken: Troops - Time when: 5 May 1813 - Place where: Rapids, River Raisin - Whether man of war, privateer, or merchant vessel: Taken on shore - When received: 25 Nov 1813 - From what ship or whence received: Town goal. - Prisoner: 1158 - Rank: Corporal - Name of Prize: Land forces - By what ship or how taken: Taken on shore - Discharged: 4 May 1814 - By what order: Returned to the United States - Source: List of American Prisoners of War discharged at Quebec - Name of prize ship: Land forces.

Leonard, Nathaniel (1)   Prisoner: 1212 - Rank: Captain - By what ship or how taken: Troops - Time when: 19 Dec 1813 - Place where: Fort Niagara - Whether man of war, privateer, or merchant vessel: Taken on shore - When received: 28 Jan 1814 - From what ship or whence received: Montreal by land carriages. - Prisoner: 1212 - Rank: Captain - Name of Prize: Land forces - By what ship or how taken: Taken on shore - Discharged: 6 May 1814 - By what order: Returned to the United States - Source: List of American Prisoners of War discharged at Quebec - Name of prize ship: Land forces.

Leonard, Nathaniel (2)   Prisoner: 1215 - Rank: Non-combatant - By what ship or how taken: Troops - Time when: 19 Dec 1813 - Place where: Fort Niagara - Whether man of war, privateer, or merchant vessel: Taken on shore - When received: 28 Jan 1814 - From what ship or whence received: Montreal by land carriages. - Prisoner: 1215 - Rank: Non-combatant - Name of Prize: Land forces - By what ship or how taken: Taken on shore - Discharged: 6 May 1814 - By what order: Returned to the United States - Source: List of American Prisoners of War discharged at Quebec - Name of prize ship: Land forces.

Leping, Anthony   Prisoner: 1901 - Rank: Private - Name of Prize: Land forces - By what ship or how taken: Taken on shore - Discharged: 13 Mar 1815 - By what order: Returned to the United States - Source: List of American Prisoners of War discharged at Quebec - Name of prize ship: Land forces.

Leping, Noel   Prisoner: 1909 - Rank: Private - Name of Prize: Land forces - By what ship or how taken: Taken on shore - Discharged: 8 Nov 1814 - By what order: George No. 515 by Sir George Prevost - Source: List of American Prisoners of War discharged at Quebec - Name of prize ship: Land forces.

Leverton, John   Prisoner: 444 - Rank: Private - Name of Prize: Land forces - By what ship or how taken: Taken on shore - Discharged: 10 Aug 1813 - By what order: HMS Regulus by order of his Excellency Sir George Prevost - Source: List of American Prisoners of War discharged at Quebec - Name of prize ship: Land forces.

Levi, Henry   Prisoner: 716 - Rank: Corporal - Name of Prize: Land forces - By what ship or how taken: Taken on shore - Discharged: 10 Aug 1813 - By what order: HMS Regulus by order of his Excellency Sir George Prevost - Source: List of American Prisoners of War discharged at Quebec - Name of prize ship: Land forces.

Lewes, William   Prisoner: 1567 - Rank: Servant - Name of Prize: Land forces - By what ship or how taken: Taken on shore - Discharged: 8 Nov 1814 - By what order: George No. 515 by Sir George Prevost - Source: List of American Prisoners of War discharged at Quebec - Name of prize ship: Land forces.

Lewis, Dudley   Prisoner: 586 - Rank: Private - Name of Prize: Land forces - By what ship or how taken: Taken on shore - Discharged: 10 Aug 1813 - By what order: HMS Regulus by order of his Excellency Sir George Prevost - Source: List of American Prisoners of War discharged at Quebec - Name of prize ship: Land forces.

Lewis, John   Prisoner: 30 - Rank: Private - Source: Account of American prisoners of war who died at Quebec in the Months of July, August & September 1813 - Ship or Corps: Land forces - Vessel: Taken on shore - Place born: Temple, NH - Age: 34 - Where taken: Stoney Point - Date of death: 1 Sep 1813 - Disorder or casualty: Diarrhea.

Lewis, Leonard   Prisoner: 1008 - Rank: Seaman - Name of Prize: Juliet - By what ship or how taken: Man of war - Discharged: 31 Oct 1813 - By what order: HMS Malabar Transport by order of his Excellency Sir George Prevost - Source: List of American Prisoners of War discharged at Quebec - Name of prize ship: Juliet.

Lewis, Samuel   Prisoner: 1890 - Rank: Private - Name of Prize: Land forces - By what ship or how taken: Taken on shore - Discharged: 8 Nov 1814 - By what order: George No. 515 by Sir George Prevost - Source: List of American Prisoners of War discharged at Quebec - Name of prize ship: Land forces.

Lewis, William   Prisoner: 247 - Rank: Lieutenant Colonel - Name of Prize: Land forces - By what ship or how taken: Taken on shore - Discharged: 29 Mar 1814 - By what order: Returned to the United States - Source: List of American Prisoners of War discharged at Quebec - Name of prize ship: Land forces.

Libby, Thomas   Prisoner: 1188 - Rank: Private - Source: Account of American prisoners of war who died at Quebec between 14 February 1814 and 23 December 1814 - Ship or Corps: Land forces - Vessel: Taken on shore - Place born: Rhode Island - Age: 20 - Where taken: Beaver Dams - Date of death: 25 Feb 1814 - Disorder or casualty: From shot wounds in the head.

Light, Jacob   Prisoner: 408 - Rank: Private - Name of Prize: Land forces - By what ship or how taken: Taken on shore - Discharged: 31 Oct 1813 - By what order: HMS Malabar Transport by order of his Excellency Sir George Prevost - Source: List of American Prisoners of War discharged at Quebec - Name of prize ship: Land forces.

Liles, James   Prisoner: 1904 - Rank: Private - Name of Prize: Land forces - By what ship or how taken: Taken on shore - Discharged: 8 Nov 1814 - By what order: George No. 515 by Sir George Prevost - Source: List of American Prisoners of War discharged at Quebec - Name of prize ship: Land forces.

Limmer, Peter D.   Prisoner: 1057 - Rank: Private - Name of Prize: Land forces - By what ship or how taken: Taken on shore - Discharged: 31 Oct 1813 - By what order: HMS Malabar Transport by order of his Excellency Sir George Prevost - Source: List of American Prisoners of War discharged at Quebec - Name of prize ship: Land forces.

Lines, John   Prisoner: 1189 - Rank: Private - By what ship or how taken: Troops - Time when: 5 May 1813 - Place where: Rapids - Whether man of war, privateer, or merchant vessel: Taken on shore - When received: 12 Dec 1813 - From what ship or whence received: Town goal. - Prisoner: 1189 - Rank: Private - Name of Prize: Land forces - By what ship or how taken: Taken on shore - Discharged: 4 May 1814 - By what order: Returned to the United States - Source: List of American Prisoners of War discharged at Quebec - Name of prize ship: Land forces.

Linet, Samuel   Prisoner: 136 - Rank: Private - Name of Prize: Land forces - By what ship or how taken: Taken on shore - Discharged: 31 Oct 1813 - By what order: HMS Malabar Transport by order of his Excellency Sir George Prevost - Source: List of American Prisoners of War discharged at Quebec - Name of prize ship: Land forces.

Linger, John   Prisoner: 1123 - Rank: Private - Name of Prize: Land forces - By what ship or how taken: Taken on shore - Discharged: 31 Oct 1813 - By what order: HMS Malabar Transport by order of his Excellency Sir George Prevost - Source: List of American Prisoners of War discharged at Quebec - Name of prize ship: Land forces.

Linnerd, Alfred   Prisoner: 607 - Rank: Private - Name of Prize: Land forces - By what ship or how taken: Taken on shore - Discharged: 10 Aug 1813 - By what order: HMS Regulus by order of his Excellency Sir George Prevost - Source: List of American Prisoners of War discharged at Quebec - Name of prize ship: Land forces.

Little, Peter   Prisoner: 733 - Rank: Private - Name of Prize: Land forces - By what ship or how taken: Taken on shore - Discharged: 10 Aug 1813 - By what order: HMS Regulus by order of his Excellency Sir George Prevost - Source: List of American Prisoners of War discharged at Quebec - Name of prize ship: Land forces.

Lloyd, Thompson C.   Prisoner: 1343 - Rank: Sergeant - By what ship or how taken: Troops - Time when: 19 Dec 1813 - Place where: Fort Niagara - Whether man of war, privateer, or merchant vessel: Taken on shore - When received: 29 Jan 1814 - From what ship or whence received: Montreal by land carriages. - Prisoner: 1343 - Rank: Sergeant - Name of Prize: Land forces - By what ship or how taken: Taken on shore - Discharged: 4 May 1814 - By what order: Returned to the United States - Source: List of American Prisoners of War discharged at Quebec - Name of prize ship: Land forces.

Lloyd, William   Prisoner: 958 - Rank: Private - Name of Prize: Land forces - By what ship or how taken: Taken on shore - Discharged: 31 Oct 1813 - By what order: HMS Malabar Transport by order of his Excellency Sir George Prevost - Source: List of American Prisoners of War discharged at Quebec - Name of prize ship: Land forces.

Lockard, Thomas   Prisoner: 1402 - Rank: Private - By what ship or how taken: Troops - Time when: 19 Dec 1813 - Place where: Fort Niagara - Whether man of war, privateer, or merchant vessel: Taken on shore - When received: 29 Jan 1814 - From what ship or whence received: Montreal by land carriages. - Prisoner: 1402 - Rank: Private - Name of Prize: Land forces - By what ship or how taken: Taken on shore - Discharged: 4 May 1814 - By what order: Returned to the United States - Source: List of American Prisoners of War

discharged at Quebec - Name of prize ship: Land forces.

Logan, Philip   Prisoner: 1948 - Rank: Private - Name of Prize: Land forces - By what ship or how taken: Taken on shore - Discharged: 13 Mar 1815 - By what order: Returned to the United States - Source: List of American Prisoners of War discharged at Quebec - Name of prize ship: Land forces.

Logan, Timothy   Prisoner: 633 - Rank: Private - Name of Prize: Land forces - By what ship or how taken: Taken on shore - Discharged: 10 Aug 1813 - By what order: HMS Regulus by order of his Excellency Sir George Prevost - Source: List of American Prisoners of War discharged at Quebec - Name of prize ship: Land forces.

Long, Peter W.   Prisoner: 1682 - Rank: Private - Name of Prize: Land forces - By what ship or how taken: Taken on shore - Discharged: 8 Nov 1814 - By what order: George No. 515 by Sir George Prevost - Source: List of American Prisoners of War discharged at Quebec - Name of prize ship: Land forces.

Lonumsbery, Lemuel   Prisoner: 1104 - Rank: Private - Name of Prize: Land forces - By what ship or how taken: Taken on shore - Discharged: 31 Oct 1813 - By what order: HMS Malabar Transport by order of his Excellency Sir George Prevost - Source: List of American Prisoners of War discharged at Quebec - Name of prize ship: Land forces.

Loomis, Gustavus   Prisoner: 1202 - Rank: Lieutenant - By what ship or how taken: Troops - Time when: 19 Dec 1813 - Place where: Fort Niagara - Whether man of war, privateer, or merchant vessel: Taken on shore - When received: 18 Jan 1814 - From what ship or whence received: Montreal by land carriages. - Prisoner: 1202 - Rank: Lieutenant - Name of Prize: Land forces - By what ship or how taken: Taken on shore - Discharged: 4 May 1814 - By what order: Returned to the United States - Source: List of American Prisoners of War discharged at Quebec - Name of prize ship: Land forces.

Loomis, Jarius   Prisoner: 143 - Rank: Sailing Master - Name of Prize: Eagle - By what ship or how taken: Man of war - Discharged: 4 May 1814 - By what order: Returned to the United States - Source: List of American Prisoners of War discharged at Quebec - Name of prize ship: Eagle.

Lord, Horatio   Prisoner: 1255 - Rank: Private - By what ship or how taken: Troops - Time when: 19 Dec 1813 - Place where: Fort Niagara - Whether man of war, privateer, or merchant vessel: Taken on shore - When received: 29 Jan 1814 - From what ship or whence received: Montreal by land carriages. - Prisoner: 1255 - Rank: Private - Name of Prize: Land forces - By what ship or how taken: Taken on shore - Discharged: 4 May 1814 - By what order: Returned to the United States - Source: List of American Prisoners of War discharged at Quebec - Name of prize ship: Land forces.

Lord, Samuel   Prisoner: 1732 - Rank: Seaman - Name of Prize: Scorpion - By what ship or how taken: Man of war - Discharged: 7 Nov 1813 - By what order: HMS Freedom No. 582 by order of his Excellency Sir George Prevost - Source: List of American Prisoners of War discharged at Quebec - Name of prize ship: Scorpion.

Loren, Thomas   Prisoner: 393 - Rank: Private - Name of Prize: Land forces - By what ship or how taken: Taken on shore - Discharged: 31 Oct 1813 - By what order: HMS Malabar Transport by order of his Excellency Sir George Prevost - Source: List of American Prisoners of War discharged at Quebec - Name of prize ship: Land forces.

Lothrop, Abijah   Prisoner: 1696 - Rank: Private - Name of Prize: Land forces - By what ship or how taken: Taken on shore - Discharged: 8 Nov 1814 - By what order: George No. 515 by Sir George Prevost - Source: List of American Prisoners of War discharged at Quebec - Name of prize ship: Land forces.

Lounge, Isaac   Prisoner: 1404 - Rank: Private - By what ship or how taken: Troops - Time when: 19 Dec 1813 - Place where: Fort Niagara - Whether man of war, privateer, or merchant vessel: Taken on shore - When received: 29 Jan 1814 - From what ship or whence received: Montreal by land carriages. - Prisoner: 1404 - Rank: Private - Name of Prize: Land forces - By what ship or how taken: Taken on shore - Discharged: 4 May 1814 - By what order: Returned to the United States - Source: List of American Prisoners of War discharged at Quebec - Name of prize ship: Land forces.

Love, Thomas C.   Prisoner: 1945 - Rank: Sergeant - Name of Prize: Land forces - By what ship or how taken: Taken on shore - Discharged: 13 Mar 1815 - By what order: Returned to the United States - Source: List of American Prisoners of War discharged at Quebec - Name of prize ship: Land forces.

Lovejoy, Jacob   Prisoner: 210 - Rank: Private - Name of Prize: Growler - By what ship or how taken: Man of war - Discharged: 31 Oct 1813 - By what order: HMS Malabar Transport by order of his Excellency Sir George Prevost - Source: List of American Prisoners of War discharged at Quebec - Name of prize ship: Growler.

Lowell, Nicholas   Prisoner: 1834 - Rank: Private - Name of Prize: Land forces - By what ship or how taken: Taken on shore - Discharged: 8 Nov 1814 - By what order: George No. 515 by Sir George Prevost - Source: List of American Prisoners of War discharged at Quebec - Name of prize ship: Land forces.

Lucas, Ephraim   Prisoner: 113 - Rank: Private - Name of Prize: Land forces - By what ship or how taken: Taken on shore - Discharged: 31 Oct 1813 - By what order: HMS Malabar Transport by order of his Excellency Sir

George Prevost - Source: List of American Prisoners of War discharged at Quebec - Name of prize ship: Land forces.

Luce, Aaron   Prisoner: 1284 - Rank: Private - By what ship or how taken: Troops - Time when: 19 Dec 1813 - Place where: Fort Niagara - Whether man of war, privateer, or merchant vessel: Taken on shore - When received: 29 Jan 1814 - From what ship or whence received: Montreal by land carriages. - Prisoner: 1284 - Rank: Private - Name of Prize: Land forces - By what ship or how taken: Taken on shore - Discharged: 4 May 1814 - By what order: Returned to the United States - Source: List of American Prisoners of War discharged at Quebec - Name of prize ship: Land forces.

Luce, John   Prisoner: 1706 - Rank: Captain - Name of Prize: Land forces - By what ship or how taken: Taken on shore - Discharged: 13 Mar 1815 - By what order: Returned to the United States - Source: List of American Prisoners of War discharged at Quebec - Name of prize ship: Land forces.

Luce, Robert   Prisoner: 1815 - Rank: Private - Name of Prize: Land forces - By what ship or how taken: Taken on shore - Discharged: 8 Nov 1814 - By what order: George No. 515 by Sir George Prevost - Source: List of American Prisoners of War discharged at Quebec - Name of prize ship: Land forces.

Lytle, Daniel   Prisoner: 1092 - Rank: Private - Name of Prize: Land forces - By what ship or how taken: Taken on shore - Discharged: 31 Oct 1813 - By what order: HMS Malabar Transport by order of his Excellency Sir George Prevost - Source: List of American Prisoners of War discharged at Quebec - Name of prize ship: Land forces.

Mack, Abner   Prisoner: 132 - Rank: Private - Name of Prize: Land forces - By what ship or how taken: Taken on shore - Discharged: 31 Oct 1813 - By what order: HMS Malabar Transport by order of his Excellency Sir George Prevost - Source: List of American Prisoners of War discharged at Quebec - Name of prize ship: Land forces.

MacNalley, John   Prisoner: 1306 - Rank: Private - By what ship or how taken: Troops - Time when: 19 Dec 1813 - Place where: Fort Niagara - Whether man of war, privateer, or merchant vessel: Taken on shore - When received: 29 Jan 1814 - From what ship or whence received: Montreal by land carriages. - Prisoner: 1306 - Rank: Private - Name of Prize: Land forces - By what ship or how taken: Taken on shore - Discharged: 24 Feb 1814 - By what order: Volunteered for the New Brunswick Fencibles - Source: List of American Prisoners of War discharged at Quebec - Name of prize ship: Land forces.

Madden, Thomas   Prisoner: 191 - Rank: Private - Name of Prize: Growler - By what ship or how taken: Man of war - Discharged: 31 Oct 1813 - By what order: HMS Malabar Transport by order of his Excellency Sir George Prevost - Source: List of American Prisoners of War discharged at Quebec - Name of prize ship: Growler.

Madison, George   Prisoner: 248 - Rank: Major - Name of Prize: Land forces - By what ship or how taken: Taken on shore - Discharged: 29 Mar 1814 - By what order: Returned to the United States - Source: List of American Prisoners of War discharged at Quebec - Name of prize ship: Land forces.

Mahan, Francis   Prisoner: 1138 - Rank: Private - By what ship or how taken: Troops - Time when: 22 Jan 1813 - Place where: Rapids, River Raisin - Whether man of war, privateer, or merchant vessel: Taken on shore - When received: 25 Nov 1813 - From what ship or whence received: Town goal. - Prisoner: 1138 - Rank: Private - Name of Prize: Land forces - By what ship or how taken: Taken on shore - Discharged: 4 May 1814 - By what order: Returned to the United States - Source: List of American Prisoners of War discharged at Quebec - Name of prize ship: Land forces.

Makle, Francis   Prisoner: 1757 - Rank: Private - Name of Prize: Scorpion - By what ship or how taken: Man of war - Discharged: 8 Nov 1814 - By what order: George No. 515 by Sir George Prevost - Source: List of American Prisoners of War discharged at Quebec - Name of prize ship: Scorpion.

Malone, John   Prisoner: 1412 - Rank: Private - By what ship or how taken: Troops - Time when: 19 Dec 1813 - Place where: Fort Niagara - Whether man of war, privateer, or merchant vessel: Taken on shore - When received: 29 Jan 1814 - From what ship or whence received: Montreal by land carriages. - Prisoner: 1412 - Rank: Private - Name of Prize: Land forces - By what ship or how taken: Taken on shore - Discharged: 4 May 1814 - By what order: Returned to the United States - Source: List of American Prisoners of War discharged at Quebec - Name of prize ship: Land forces.

Manchester, Noah   Prisoner: 1281 - Rank: Private - By what ship or how taken: Troops - Time when: 19 Dec 1813 - Place where: Fort Niagara - Whether man of war, privateer, or merchant vessel: Taken on shore - When received: 29 Jan 1814 - From what ship or whence received: Montreal by land carriages. - Prisoner: 1281 - Rank: Private - Name of Prize: Land forces - By what ship or how taken: Taken on shore - Discharged: 11 Mar 1814 - By what order: Volunteered for the New Brunswick Fencibles - Source: List of American Prisoners of War discharged at Quebec - Name of prize ship: Land forces.

Mandeville, Peter   Prisoner: 1119 - Rank: Private - Name of Prize: Land forces - By what ship or how taken: Taken on shore - Discharged: 31 Oct 1813 - By what order: HMS Malabar Transport by order of his Excellency Sir George Prevost - Source: List of American Prisoners of War discharged at Quebec - Name of prize ship: Land forces.

Mann, Charles   Prisoner: 1673 - Rank: Seaman - Name of Prize: Taken on a gig (a ship's long boat) - By what ship or how taken: Man of war - Discharged: 10 Nov 1814 - By what order: Lord Cathcart No. 161 for Halifax by order of Sir George Prevost - Source: List of American Prisoners of War discharged at Quebec - Name of prize ship: Taken on a gig (a ship's long boat).

Maples, Burton   Prisoner: 454 - Rank: Private - Name of Prize: Land forces - By what ship or how taken: Taken on shore - Discharged: 10 Aug 1813 - By what order: HMS Regulus by order of his Excellency Sir George Prevost - Source: List of American Prisoners of War discharged at Quebec - Name of prize ship: Land forces.

March, William   Prisoner: 701 - Rank: Private - Name of Prize: Land forces - By what ship or how taken: Taken on shore - Discharged: 10 Aug 1813 - By what order: HMS Regulus by order of his Excellency Sir George Prevost - Source: List of American Prisoners of War discharged at Quebec - Name of prize ship: Land forces.

Marker, Benjamin   Prisoner: 1345 - Rank: Private - By what ship or how taken: Troops - Time when: 19 Dec 1813 - Place where: Fort Niagara - Whether man of war, privateer, or merchant vessel: Taken on shore - When received: 29 Jan 1814 - From what ship or whence received: Montreal by land carriages. - Prisoner: 1345 - Rank: Private - Name of Prize: Land forces - By what ship or how taken: Taken on shore - Discharged: 4 May 1814 - By what order: Returned to the United States - Source: List of American Prisoners of War discharged at Quebec - Name of prize ship: Land forces.

Marks, Henry   Prisoner: 1244 - Rank: Private - By what ship or how taken: Troops - Time when: 19 Dec 1813 - Place where: Fort Niagara - Whether man of war, privateer, or merchant vessel: Taken on shore - When received: 29 Jan 1814 - From what ship or whence received: Montreal by land carriages. - Prisoner: 1244 - Rank: Private - Name of Prize: Land forces - By what ship or how taken: Taken on shore - Discharged: 4 May 1814 - By what order: Returned to the United States - Source: List of American Prisoners of War discharged at Quebec - Name of prize ship: Land forces.

Marsh, Hosea   Prisoner: 1860 - Rank: Private - Name of Prize: Land forces - By what ship or how taken: Taken on shore - Discharged: 8 Nov 1814 - By what order: George No. 515 by Sir George Prevost - Source: List of American Prisoners of War discharged at Quebec - Name of prize ship: Land forces.

Marshall, Joseph   Prisoner: 523 - Rank: Lieutenant - Name of Prize: Land forces - By what ship or how taken: Taken on shore - Discharged: 10 Aug 1813 - By what order: HMS Regulus by order of his Excellency Sir George Prevost - Source: List of American Prisoners of War discharged at Quebec - Name of prize ship: Land forces.

Marshall, William   Prisoner: 673 - Rank: Private - Name of Prize: Land forces - By what ship or how taken: Taken on shore - Discharged: 10 Aug 1813 - By what order: HMS Regulus by order of his Excellency Sir George Prevost - Source: List of American Prisoners of War discharged at Quebec - Name of prize ship: Land forces.

Martin, Bryan   Prisoner: 658 - Rank: Private - Name of Prize: Land forces - By what ship or how taken: Taken on shore - Discharged: 10 Aug 1813 - By what order: HMS Regulus by order of his Excellency Sir George Prevost - Source: List of American Prisoners of War discharged at Quebec - Name of prize ship: Land forces.

Martin, James (1)   Prisoner: 274 - Rank: Private - Name of Prize: Land forces - By what ship or how taken: Taken on shore - Discharged: 4 May 1814 - By what order: Returned to the United States - Source: List of American Prisoners of War discharged at Quebec - Name of prize ship: Land forces.

Martin, James (2)   Prisoner: 1739 - Rank: Seaman - Name of Prize: Tigress - By what ship or how taken: Man of war - Discharged: 7 Nov 1813 - By what order: HMS Freedom No. 582 by order of his Excellency Sir George Prevost - Source: List of American Prisoners of War discharged at Quebec - Name of prize ship: Tigress.

Martin, Sylvanus   Prisoner: 46 - Rank: Private - Source: Account of American prisoners of war who died at Quebec in the Months of July, August & September 1813 - Ship or Corps: Land forces - Vessel: Taken on shore - Place born: Swansea - Age: 28 - Where taken: Stoney Point - Date of death: 3 Aug 1813.

Martin, William   Prisoner: 622 - Rank: Private - Name of Prize: Land forces - By what ship or how taken: Taken on shore - Discharged: 10 Aug 1813 - By what order: HMS Regulus by order of his Excellency Sir George Prevost - Source: List of American Prisoners of War discharged at Quebec - Name of prize ship: Land forces.

Marvel, Joseph   Prisoner: 1010 - Rank: Seaman - Name of Prize: Juliet - By what ship or how taken: Man of war - Discharged: 31 Oct 1813 - By what order: HMS Malabar Transport by order of his Excellency Sir George Prevost - Source: List of American Prisoners of War discharged at Quebec - Name of prize ship: Juliet.

Masters, John   Prisoner: 1172 - Rank: Private - By what ship or how taken: Troops - Time when: 5 May 1813 -

Place where: Rapids - Whether man of war, privateer, or merchant vessel: Taken on shore - When received: 25 Nov 1813 - From what ship or whence received: Town goal. - Prisoner: 1172 - Rank: Private - Name of Prize: Land forces - By what ship or how taken: Taken on shore - Discharged: 4 May 1814 - By what order: Returned to the United States - Source: List of American Prisoners of War discharged at Quebec - Name of prize ship: Land forces.

Mathews, Daniel   Prisoner: 720 - Rank: Private - Name of Prize: Land forces - By what ship or how taken: Taken on shore - Discharged: 10 Aug 1813 - By what order: HMS Regulus by order of his Excellency Sir George Prevost - Source: List of American Prisoners of War discharged at Quebec - Name of prize ship: Land forces.

Mathews, John   Prisoner: 651 - Rank: Private - Name of Prize: Land forces - By what ship or how taken: Taken on shore - Discharged: 10 Aug 1813 - By what order: HMS Regulus by order of his Excellency Sir George Prevost - Source: List of American Prisoners of War discharged at Quebec - Name of prize ship: Land forces.

Matlock, Joseph   Prisoner: 478 - Rank: Private - Name of Prize: Land forces - By what ship or how taken: Taken on shore - Discharged: 10 Aug 1813 - By what order: HMS Regulus by order of his Excellency Sir George Prevost - Source: List of American Prisoners of War discharged at Quebec - Name of prize ship: Land forces.

Maxwell, Thompson   Prisoner: 1956 - Rank: Forage master - Name of Prize: Land forces - By what ship or how taken: Taken on shore - Discharged: 13 Mar 1815 - By what order: Returned to the United States - Source: List of American Prisoners of War discharged at Quebec - Name of prize ship: Land forces.

McCallen, Benjamin   Prisoner: 724 - Rank: Private - Name of Prize: Land forces - By what ship or how taken: Taken on shore - Discharged: 10 Aug 1813 - By what order: HMS Regulus by order of his Excellency Sir George Prevost - Source: List of American Prisoners of War discharged at Quebec - Name of prize ship: Land forces.

McCann, Edward   Prisoner: 1099 - Rank: Private - Name of Prize: Land forces - By what ship or how taken: Taken on shore - Discharged: 31 Oct 1813 - By what order: HMS Malabar Transport by order of his Excellency Sir George Prevost - Source: List of American Prisoners of War discharged at Quebec - Name of prize ship: Land forces.

McCardall, Jacob   Prisoner: 1423 - Rank: Private - By what ship or how taken: Troops - Time when: 19 Dec 1813 - Place where: Fort Niagara - Whether man of war, privateer, or merchant vessel: Taken on shore - When received: 29 Jan 1814 - From what ship or whence received: Montreal by land carriages. - Prisoner: 1423 - Rank: Private - Name of Prize: Land forces - By what ship or how taken: Taken on shore - Discharged: 4 May 1814 - By what order: Returned to the United States - Source: List of American Prisoners of War discharged at Quebec - Name of prize ship: Land forces.

McCarthy, Charles   Prisoner: 1059 - Rank: Private - Name of Prize: Land forces - By what ship or how taken: Taken on shore - Discharged: 31 Oct 1813 - By what order: HMS Malabar Transport by order of his Excellency Sir George Prevost - Source: List of American Prisoners of War discharged at Quebec - Name of prize ship: Land forces.

McClary, James   Prisoner: 1804 - Rank: Private - Name of Prize: Land forces - By what ship or how taken: Taken on shore - Discharged: 8 Nov 1814 - By what order: George No. 515 by Sir George Prevost - Source: List of American Prisoners of War discharged at Quebec - Name of prize ship: Land forces.

McConaghey, Benjamin   Prisoner: 670 - Rank: Private - Name of Prize: Land forces - By what ship or how taken: Taken on shore - Discharged: 10 Aug 1813 - By what order: HMS Regulus by order of his Excellency Sir George Prevost - Source: List of American Prisoners of War discharged at Quebec - Name of prize ship: Land forces - Comments: British subject, sent to England.

McCorkhill, James   Prisoner: 540 - Rank: Private - Name of Prize: Land forces - By what ship or how taken: Taken on shore - Discharged: 10 Aug 1813 - By what order: HMS Regulus by order of his Excellency Sir George Prevost - Source: List of American Prisoners of War discharged at Quebec - Name of prize ship: Land forces.

McCouhen, Stephen   Prisoner: 431 - Rank: Private - Name of Prize: Land forces - By what ship or how taken: Taken on shore - Discharged: 10 Aug 1813 - By what order: HMS Regulus by order of his Excellency Sir George Prevost - Source: List of American Prisoners of War discharged at Quebec - Name of prize ship: Land forces.

McCrackin, Hiram   Prisoner: 1849 - Rank: Private - Name of Prize: Land forces - By what ship or how taken: Taken on shore - Discharged: 8 Nov 1814 - By what order: George No. 515 by Sir George Prevost - Source: List of American Prisoners of War discharged at Quebec - Name of prize ship: Land forces.

McCrory, James   Prisoner: 520 - Rank: Private - Name of Prize: Land forces - By what ship or how taken: Taken on shore - Discharged: 10 Aug 1813 - By what order: HMS Regulus by order of his Excellency Sir George Prevost - Source: List of American Prisoners of War discharged at Quebec - Name of prize ship: Land forces.

McCrory, Thomas Prisoner: 1362 - Rank: Sergeant - By what ship or how taken: Troops - Time when: 19 Dec 1813 - Place where: Fort Niagara - Whether man of war, privateer, or merchant vessel: Taken on shore - When received: 29 Jan 1814 - From what ship or whence received: Montreal by land carriages. - Prisoner: 1362 - Rank: Sergeant - Name of Prize: Land forces - By what ship or how taken: Taken on shore - Discharged: 4 May 1814 - By what order: Returned to the United States - Source: List of American Prisoners of War discharged at Quebec - Name of prize ship: Land forces.

McCurdy, Robert Prisoner: 1182 - Rank: Private - By what ship or how taken: Troops - Time when: 5 May 1813 - Place where: Rapids - Whether man of war, privateer, or merchant vessel: Taken on shore - When received: 25 Nov 1813 - From what ship or whence received: Town goal. - Prisoner: 1182 - Rank: Private - Name of Prize: Land forces - By what ship or how taken: Taken on shore - Discharged: 4 May 1814 - By what order: Returned to the United States - Source: List of American Prisoners of War discharged at Quebec - Name of prize ship: Land forces.

McCurl, Isaac Prisoner: 1295 - Rank: Private - By what ship or how taken: Troops - Time when: 19 Dec 1813 - Place where: Fort Niagara - Whether man of war, privateer, or merchant vessel: Taken on shore - When received: 29 Jan 1814 - From what ship or whence received: Montreal by land carriages. - Prisoner: 1295 - Rank: Private - Name of Prize: Land forces - By what ship or how taken: Taken on shore - Discharged: 4 May 1814 - By what order: Returned to the United States - Source: List of American Prisoners of War discharged at Quebec - Name of prize ship: Land forces.

McDonald, Francis Prisoner: 1089 - Rank: Private - Name of Prize: Land forces - By what ship or how taken: Taken on shore - Discharged: 31 Oct 1813 - By what order: HMS Malabar Transport by order of his Excellency Sir George Prevost - Source: List of American Prisoners of War discharged at Quebec - Name of prize ship: Land forces.

McDonald, Peter Prisoner: 403 - Rank: Private - Name of Prize: Land forces - By what ship or how taken: Taken on shore - Discharged: 31 Oct 1813 - By what order: HMS Malabar Transport by order of his Excellency Sir George Prevost - Source: List of American Prisoners of War discharged at Quebec - Name of prize ship: Land forces.

McDonald, Theophilus Prisoner: 574 - Rank: Private - Name of Prize: Land forces - By what ship or how taken: Taken on shore - Discharged: 10 Aug 1813 - By what order: HMS Regulus by order of his Excellency Sir George Prevost - Source: List of American Prisoners of War discharged at Quebec - Name of prize ship: Land forces.

McEver, William Prisoner: 687 - Rank: Private - Name of Prize: Land forces - By what ship or how taken: Taken on shore - Discharged: 10 Aug 1813 - By what order: HMS Regulus by order of his Excellency Sir George Prevost - Source: List of American Prisoners of War discharged at Quebec - Name of prize ship: Land forces - Comments: British subject, sent to England.

McGalthary, Thomas Prisoner: 1433 - Rank: Passenger - Name of Prize: Lezare - By what ship or how taken: Privateer - Discharged: 24 May 1813 - By what order: Mulgrave Transport No. 311 - Source: List of American Prisoners of War discharged at Quebec - Name of prize ship: Lezare. - Prisoner: 1433 - Rank: Able seaman - By what ship or how taken: Prometheus - Time when: 5 May 1814 - Place where: off Halifax - Whether man of war, privateer, or merchant vessel: Privateer - When received: 24 May 1814 - From what ship or whence received: Mary Transport No. 368.

McGee, George Prisoner: 1115 - Rank: Private - Name of Prize: Land forces - By what ship or how taken: Taken on shore - Discharged: 31 Oct 1813 - By what order: HMS Malabar Transport by order of his Excellency Sir George Prevost - Source: List of American Prisoners of War discharged at Quebec - Name of prize ship: Land forces.

McGee, Truman Prisoner: 181 - Rank: Private - Name of Prize: Growler - By what ship or how taken: Man of war - Discharged: 4 May 1814 - By what order: Returned to the United States - Source: List of American Prisoners of War discharged at Quebec - Name of prize ship: Growler.

McGee, William Prisoner: 1046 - Rank: Private - Name of Prize: Growler - By what ship or how taken: Man of war - Discharged: 31 Oct 1813 - By what order: HMS Malabar Transport by order of his Excellency Sir George Prevost - Source: List of American Prisoners of War discharged at Quebec - Name of prize ship: Growler.

McGowens, Patrick Prisoner: 1920 - Rank: Private - Name of Prize: Land forces - By what ship or how taken: Taken on shore - Discharged: 10 Nov 1814 - By what order: Sovereign No. 628 to Halifax by order of Sir George Prevost - Source: List of American Prisoners of War discharged at Quebec - Name of prize ship: Land forces.

McGunnell, Michael Prisoner: 1242 - Rank: Private - By what ship or how taken: Troops - Time when: 19 Dec

1813 - Place where: Fort Niagara - Whether man of war, privateer, or merchant vessel: Taken on shore - When received: 29 Jan 1814 - From what ship or whence received: Montreal by land carriages. - Prisoner: 1242 - Rank: Private - Name of Prize: Land forces - By what ship or how taken: Taken on shore - Discharged: 4 May 1814 - By what order: Returned to the United States - Source: List of American Prisoners of War discharged at Quebec - Name of prize ship: Land forces.

McIlroy, James   Prisoner: 1130 - Rank: Private - By what ship or how taken: Troops - Time when: 5 May 1813 - Place where: Rapids, River Raisin - Whether man of war, privateer, or merchant vessel: Taken on shore - When received: 25 Nov 1813 - From what ship or whence received: Town goal. - Prisoner: 1130 - Rank: Private - Name of Prize: Land forces - By what ship or how taken: Taken on shore - Discharged: 4 May 1814 - By what order: Returned to the United States - Source: List of American Prisoners of War discharged at Quebec - Name of prize ship: Land forces.

McIntire, Tedrick   Prisoner: 362 - Rank: Private - Name of Prize: Land forces - By what ship or how taken: Taken on shore - Discharged: 31 Oct 1813 - By what order: HMS Malabar Transport by order of his Excellency Sir George Prevost - Source: List of American Prisoners of War discharged at Quebec - Name of prize ship: Land forces.

McIntruff, William   Prisoner: 1368 - Rank: Private - By what ship or how taken: Troops - Time when: 19 Dec 1813 - Place where: Fort Niagara - Whether man of war, privateer, or merchant vessel: Taken on shore - When received: 29 Jan 1814 - From what ship or whence received: Montreal by land carriages. - Prisoner: 1368 - Rank: Private - Name of Prize: Land forces - By what ship or how taken: Taken on shore - Discharged: 4 May 1814 - By what order: Returned to the United States - Source: List of American Prisoners of War discharged at Quebec - Name of prize ship: Land forces.

McIntyre, James   Prisoner: 1932 - Rank: Private - Source: Account of American prisoners of war who died at Quebec between 14 February 1814 and 23 December 1814 - Ship or Corps: Land forces - Vessel: Taken on shore - Place born: Connecticut - Age: 62 - Where taken: Fort Erie - Date of death: 23 Dec 1814 - Disorder or casualty: Dysentery.

McKenzie, Kenneth   Prisoner: 399 - Rank: Captain - Name of Prize: Land forces - By what ship or how taken: Taken on shore - Discharged: 10 Aug 1813 - By what order: HMS Regulus by order of his Excellency Sir George Prevost - Source: List of American Prisoners of War discharged at Quebec - Name of prize ship: Land forces.

McKenzie, Thomas   Prisoner: 1083 - Rank: Private - Name of Prize: Land forces - By what ship or how taken: Taken on shore - Discharged: 31 Oct 1813 - By what order: HMS Malabar Transport by order of his Excellency Sir George Prevost - Source: List of American Prisoners of War discharged at Quebec - Name of prize ship: Land forces.

McLoghlan, Mark   Prisoner: 1291 - Rank: Private - By what ship or how taken: Troops - Time when: 19 Dec 1813 - Place where: Fort Niagara - Whether man of war, privateer, or merchant vessel: Taken on shore - When received: 29 Jan 1814 - From what ship or whence received: Montreal by land carriages. - Prisoner: 1291 - Rank: Private - Name of Prize: Land forces - By what ship or how taken: Taken on shore - Discharged: 4 May 1814 - By what order: Returned to the United States - Source: List of American Prisoners of War discharged at Quebec - Name of prize ship: Land forces.

McManers, John   Prisoner: 1366 - Rank: Corporal - By what ship or how taken: Troops - Time when: 19 Dec 1813 - Place where: Fort Niagara - Whether man of war, privateer, or merchant vessel: Taken on shore - When received: 29 Jan 1814 - From what ship or whence received: Montreal by land carriages. - Prisoner: 1366 - Rank: Corporal - Name of Prize: Land forces - By what ship or how taken: Taken on shore - Discharged: 4 May 1814 - By what order: Returned to the United States - Source: List of American Prisoners of War discharged at Quebec - Name of prize ship: Land forces.

McMillen, Archibald   Prisoner: 48 - Rank: Private - Source: Account of American prisoners of war who died at Quebec in the Months of July, August & September 1813 - Ship or Corps: Land forces - Vessel: Taken on shore - Place born: New Hampshire - Age: 25 - Where taken: Stoney Point - Date of death: 12 Aug 1813.

McMullin, George   Prisoner: 743 - Rank: Private - Name of Prize: Land forces - By what ship or how taken: Taken on shore - Discharged: 10 Aug 1813 - By what order: HMS Regulus by order of his Excellency Sir George Prevost - Source: List of American Prisoners of War discharged at Quebec - Name of prize ship: Land forces - Comments: British subject, sent to England.

McMullin, William   Prisoner: 1132 - Rank: Private - By what ship or how taken: Troops - Time when: 5 May 1813 - Place where: Rapids, River Raisin - Whether man of war, privateer, or merchant vessel: Taken on shore - When received: 25 Nov 1813 - From what ship or whence received: Town goal. - Prisoner: 1132 - Rank: Private - Name of Prize: Land forces - By what ship or how taken: Taken on shore - Discharged: 4 May 1814

- By what order: Returned to the United States - Source: List of American Prisoners of War discharged at Quebec - Name of prize ship: Land forces.

McQuaid, Edward   Prisoner: 1351 - Rank: Private - By what ship or how taken: Troops - Time when: 19 Dec 1813 - Place where: Fort Niagara - Whether man of war, privateer, or merchant vessel: Taken on shore - When received: 29 Jan 1814 - From what ship or whence received: Montreal by land carriages. - Prisoner: 1351 - Rank: Private - Name of Prize: Land forces - By what ship or how taken: Taken on shore - Discharged: 4 May 1814 - By what order: Returned to the United States - Source: List of American Prisoners of War discharged at Quebec - Name of prize ship: Land forces.

McWilliams, William   Prisoner: 1342 - Rank: Private - By what ship or how taken: Troops - Time when: 19 Dec 1813 - Place where: Fort Niagara - Whether man of war, privateer, or merchant vessel: Taken on shore - When received: 29 Jan 1814 - From what ship or whence received: Montreal by land carriages. - Prisoner: 1342 - Rank: Private - Name of Prize: Land forces - By what ship or how taken: Taken on shore - Discharged: 4 May 1814 - By what order: Returned to the United States - Source: List of American Prisoners of War discharged at Quebec - Name of prize ship: Land forces.

Mead, William   Prisoner: 1969 - Rank: Private - Name of Prize: Land forces - By what ship or how taken: Taken on shore - Discharged: 16 Mar 1815 - By what order: Returned to the United States - Source: List of American Prisoners of War discharged at Quebec - Name of prize ship: Land forces.

Mecham, Jesse   Prisoner: 976 - Rank: Private - Name of Prize: Land forces - By what ship or how taken: Taken on shore - Discharged: 31 Oct 1813 - By what order: HMS Malabar Transport by order of his Excellency Sir George Prevost - Source: List of American Prisoners of War discharged at Quebec - Name of prize ship: Land forces.

Meloney, Simeon   Prisoner: 1893 - Rank: Private - Name of Prize: Land forces - By what ship or how taken: Taken on shore - Discharged: 8 Nov 1814 - By what order: George No. 515 by Sir George Prevost - Source: List of American Prisoners of War discharged at Quebec - Name of prize ship: Land forces.

Merrill, Abraham   Prisoner: 1180 - Rank: Private - By what ship or how taken: Troops - Time when: 5 May 1813 - Place where: Rapids - Whether man of war, privateer, or merchant vessel: Taken on shore - When received: 25 Nov 1813 - From what ship or whence received: Town goal. - Prisoner: 1180 - Rank: Private - Name of Prize: Land forces - By what ship or how taken: Taken on shore - Discharged: 4 May 1814 - By what order: Returned to the United States - Source: List of American Prisoners of War discharged at Quebec - Name of prize ship: Land forces.

Merrill, Charles   Prisoner: 1843 - Rank: Private - Name of Prize: Land forces - By what ship or how taken: Taken on shore - Discharged: 8 Nov 1814 - By what order: George No. 515 by Sir George Prevost - Source: List of American Prisoners of War discharged at Quebec - Name of prize ship: Land forces.

Merrill, Elijah   Prisoner: 12 - Rank: Private - Source: Account of American prisoners of war who died at Quebec in the Months of July, August & September 1813 - Ship or Corps: Land forces - Vessel: Taken on shore - Place born: Conway, NH - Age: 23 - Where taken: Stoney Point - Date of death: 26 Sep 1813 - Disorder or casualty: Dysentery.

Merrill, Jacob   Prisoner: 93 - Rank: Private - Name of Prize: Land forces - By what ship or how taken: Taken on shore - Discharged: 31 Oct 1813 - By what order: HMS Malabar Transport by order of his Excellency Sir George Prevost - Source: List of American Prisoners of War discharged at Quebec - Name of prize ship: Land forces.

Merrill, Malachi   Prisoner: 1313 - Rank: Private - By what ship or how taken: Troops - Time when: 19 Dec 1813 - Place where: Fort Niagara - Whether man of war, privateer, or merchant vessel: Taken on shore - When received: 29 Jan 1814 - From what ship or whence received: Montreal by land carriages. - Prisoner: 1313 - Rank: Private - Name of Prize: Land forces - By what ship or how taken: Taken on shore - Discharged: 4 May 1814 - By what order: Returned to the United States - Source: List of American Prisoners of War discharged at Quebec - Name of prize ship: Land forces.

Merrill, Nathaniel   Prisoner: 1978 - Rank: Private - Name of Prize: Land forces - By what ship or how taken: Taken on shore - Discharged: 13 Mar 1815 - By what order: Returned to the United States - Source: List of American Prisoners of War discharged at Quebec - Name of prize ship: Land forces.

Merrill, Theodosius   Prisoner: 221 - Rank: Private - Name of Prize: Growler - By what ship or how taken: Man of war - Discharged: 31 Oct 1813 - By what order: HMS Malabar Transport by order of his Excellency Sir George Prevost - Source: List of American Prisoners of War discharged at Quebec - Name of prize ship: Growler.

Merritt, Jacob   Prisoner: 215 - Rank: Private - Name of Prize: Growler - By what ship or how taken: Man of war - Discharged: 31 Oct 1813 - By what order: HMS Malabar Transport by order of his Excellency Sir George

Prevost - Source: List of American Prisoners of War discharged at Quebec - Name of prize ship: Growler.

Merritt, John   Prisoner: 187 - Rank: Private - Name of Prize: Growler - By what ship or how taken: Man of war - Discharged: 31 Oct 1813 - By what order: HMS Malabar Transport by order of his Excellency Sir George Prevost - Source: List of American Prisoners of War discharged at Quebec - Name of prize ship: Growler.

Miles, Elias   Prisoner: 1160 - Rank: Private - Name of Prize: Land forces - By what ship or how taken: Taken on shore - Discharged: 4 May 1814 - By what order: Returned to the United States - Source: List of American Prisoners of War discharged at Quebec - Name of prize ship: Land forces.

Miles, John   Prisoner: 731 - Rank: Private - Name of Prize: Land forces - By what ship or how taken: Taken on shore - Discharged: 10 Aug 1813 - By what order: HMS Regulus by order of his Excellency Sir George Prevost - Source: List of American Prisoners of War discharged at Quebec - Name of prize ship: Land forces.

Millan, George   Prisoner: 1944 - Rank: Private - Name of Prize: Land forces - By what ship or how taken: Taken on shore - Discharged: 13 Mar 1815 - By what order: Returned to the United States - Source: List of American Prisoners of War discharged at Quebec - Name of prize ship: Land forces.

Miller, Garrett   Prisoner: 473 - Rank: Private - Name of Prize: Land forces - By what ship or how taken: Taken on shore - Discharged: 10 Aug 1813 - By what order: HMS Regulus by order of his Excellency Sir George Prevost - Source: List of American Prisoners of War discharged at Quebec - Name of prize ship: Land forces.

Miller, James (1)   Prisoner: 1332 - Rank: Private - By what ship or how taken: Troops - Time when: 19 Dec 1813 - Place where: Fort Niagara - Whether man of war, privateer, or merchant vessel: Taken on shore - When received: 29 Jan 1814 - From what ship or whence received: Montreal by land carriages. - Prisoner: 1332 - Rank: Private - Name of Prize: Land forces - By what ship or how taken: Taken on shore - Discharged: 4 May 1814 - By what order: Returned to the United States - Source: List of American Prisoners of War discharged at Quebec - Name of prize ship: Land forces.

Miller, James (2)   Prisoner: 1753 - Rank: Private - Name of Prize: Scorpion - By what ship or how taken: Man of war - Discharged: 8 Nov 1814 - By what order: George No. 515 by Sir George Prevost - Source: List of American Prisoners of War discharged at Quebec - Name of prize ship: Scorpion.

Miller, Rubin   Prisoner: 1294 - Rank: Private - By what ship or how taken: Troops - Time when: 19 Dec 1813 - Place where: Fort Niagara - Whether man of war, privateer, or merchant vessel: Taken on shore - When received: 29 Jan 1814 - From what ship or whence received: Montreal by land carriages. - Prisoner: 1294 - Rank: Private - Name of Prize: Land forces - By what ship or how taken: Taken on shore - Discharged: 4 May 1814 - By what order: Returned to the United States - Source: List of American Prisoners of War discharged at Quebec - Name of prize ship: Land forces.

Milless, Stephen   Prisoner: 554 - Rank: Private - Name of Prize: Land forces - By what ship or how taken: Taken on shore - Discharged: 10 Aug 1813 - By what order: HMS Regulus by order of his Excellency Sir George Prevost - Source: List of American Prisoners of War discharged at Quebec - Name of prize ship: Land forces.

Millhanks, David   Prisoner: 1910 - Rank: Private - Name of Prize: Land forces - By what ship or how taken: Taken on shore - Discharged: 8 Nov 1814 - By what order: George No. 515 by Sir George Prevost - Source: List of American Prisoners of War discharged at Quebec - Name of prize ship: Land forces.

Million, Rodney   Prisoner: 1141 - Rank: Private - By what ship or how taken: Troops - Time when: 22 Jan 1813 - Place where: Rapids, River Raisin - Whether man of war, privateer, or merchant vessel: Taken on shore - When received: 25 Nov 1813 - From what ship or whence received: Town goal. - Prisoner: 1141 - Rank: Private - Name of Prize: Land forces - By what ship or how taken: Taken on shore - Discharged: 4 May 1814 - By what order: Returned to the United States - Source: List of American Prisoners of War discharged at Quebec - Name of prize ship: Land forces.

Mills, Elias   Prisoner: 1160 - Rank: Corporal - By what ship or how taken: Troops - Time when: 5 May 1813 - Place where: Rapids, River Raisin - Whether man of war, privateer, or merchant vessel: Taken on shore - When received: 25 Nov 1813 - From what ship or whence received: Town goal.

Minn, Lewis   Prisoner: 336 - Rank: Private - Name of Prize: Land forces - By what ship or how taken: Taken on shore - Discharged: 31 Oct 1813 - By what order: HMS Malabar Transport by order of his Excellency Sir George Prevost - Source: List of American Prisoners of War discharged at Quebec - Name of prize ship: Land forces.

Mitchell, Charles   Prisoner: 661 - Rank: Private - Name of Prize: Land forces - By what ship or how taken: Taken on shore - Discharged: 10 Aug 1813 - By what order: HMS Regulus by order of his Excellency Sir George Prevost - Source: List of American Prisoners of War discharged at Quebec - Name of prize ship: Land forces.

Mitchell, William   Prisoner: 95 - Rank: Private - Source: Account of American prisoners of war who died at Quebec in the Months of July, August & September 1813 - Ship or Corps: Land forces - Vessel: Taken on shore - Place born: Freeport, MA - Age: 45 - Where taken: Stoney Point - Date of death: 4 Aug 1813.

Monteath, Walter N. Prisoner: 147 - Rank: Midshipman - Name of Prize: Growler - By what ship or how taken: Man of war - Discharged: 4 May 1814 - By what order: Returned to the United States - Source: List of American Prisoners of War discharged at Quebec - Name of prize ship: Growler.

Moones, Green Prisoner: 1156 - Rank: Private - By what ship or how taken: Troops - Time when: 5 May 1813 - Place where: Rapids, River Raisin - Whether man of war, privateer, or merchant vessel: Taken on shore - When received: 25 Nov 1813 - From what ship or whence received: Town goal. - Prisoner: 1156 - Rank: Private - Name of Prize: Land forces - By what ship or how taken: Taken on shore - Discharged: 12 Mar 1814 - By what order: Volunteered for the New Brunswick Fencibles - Source: List of American Prisoners of War discharged at Quebec - Name of prize ship: Land forces.

Moore, Abel Prisoner: 1224 - Rank: Private - By what ship or how taken: Troops - Time when: 19 Dec 1813 - Place where: Fort Niagara - Whether man of war, privateer, or merchant vessel: Taken on shore - When received: 29 Jan 1814 - From what ship or whence received: Montreal by land carriages. - Prisoner: 1224 - Rank: Private - Name of Prize: Land forces - By what ship or how taken: Taken on shore - Discharged: 4 May 1814 - By what order: Returned to the United States - Source: List of American Prisoners of War discharged at Quebec - Name of prize ship: Land forces.

Moore, Abraham Prisoner: 1897 - Rank: Private - Name of Prize: Land forces - By what ship or how taken: Taken on shore - Discharged: 8 Nov 1814 - By what order: George No. 515 by Sir George Prevost - Source: List of American Prisoners of War discharged at Quebec - Name of prize ship: Land forces.

Moore, John Prisoner: 559 - Rank: Private - Name of Prize: Land forces - By what ship or how taken: Taken on shore - Discharged: 10 Aug 1813 - By what order: HMS Regulus by order of his Excellency Sir George Prevost - Source: List of American Prisoners of War discharged at Quebec - Name of prize ship: Land forces.

Moore, Joshua Prisoner: 334 - Rank: Private - Source: Account of American prisoners of war who died at Quebec in the Months of July, August & September 1813 - Ship or Corps: Land forces - Vessel: Taken on shore - Place born: Morris County - Age: 35 - Where taken: Stoney Point - Date of death: 11 Sep 1813 - Disorder or casualty: Diarrhea.

Moore, Nathaniel Prisoner: 1808 - Rank: Private - Name of Prize: Land forces - By what ship or how taken: Taken on shore - Discharged: 8 Nov 1814 - By what order: George No. 515 by Sir George Prevost - Source: List of American Prisoners of War discharged at Quebec - Name of prize ship: Land forces.

Morgan, William Prisoner: 1726 - Rank: Seaman - Name of Prize: Scorpion - By what ship or how taken: Man of war - Discharged: 7 Nov 1813 - By what order: HMS Freedom No. 582 by order of his Excellency Sir George Prevost - Source: List of American Prisoners of War discharged at Quebec - Name of prize ship: Scorpion.

Morres, Morris Prisoner: 395 - Rank: Private - Name of Prize: Land forces - By what ship or how taken: Taken on shore - Discharged: 31 Oct 1813 - By what order: HMS Malabar Transport by order of his Excellency Sir George Prevost - Source: List of American Prisoners of War discharged at Quebec - Name of prize ship: Land forces.

Morrice, Samuel H. Prisoner: 1432 - Rank: Passenger - Name of Prize: Cossack - By what ship or how taken: Privateer - Discharged: 24 May 1813 - By what order: Mulgrave Transport No. 311 - Source: List of American Prisoners of War discharged at Quebec - Name of prize ship: Cossack. - Prisoner: 1432 - Rank: Able seaman - By what ship or how taken: Embles - Time when: 15 Dec 1813 - Place where: St. Johns - Whether man of war, privateer, or merchant vessel: Privateer - When received: 24 May 1814 - From what ship or whence received: Mary Transport No. 368.

Morris, George N. Prisoner: 539 - Rank: Lieutenant - Name of Prize: Land forces - By what ship or how taken: Taken on shore - Discharged: 10 Aug 1813 - By what order: HMS Regulus by order of his Excellency Sir George Prevost - Source: List of American Prisoners of War discharged at Quebec - Name of prize ship: Land forces.

Morris, James Prisoner: 1405 - Rank: Private - Name of Prize: Land forces - By what ship or how taken: Taken on shore - Discharged: 4 May 1814 - By what order: Returned to the United States - Source: List of American Prisoners of War discharged at Quebec - Name of prize ship: Land forces.

Morris, James Prisoner: 1405 - Rank: Private - By what ship or how taken: Troops - Time when: 19 Dec 1813 - Place where: Fort Niagara - Whether man of war, privateer, or merchant vessel: Taken on shore - When received: 29 Jan 1814 - From what ship or whence received: Montreal by land carriages.

Morrison, Alexander Prisoner: 1968 - Rank: Private - Name of Prize: Land forces - By what ship or how taken: Taken on shore - Discharged: 13 Mar 1815 - By what order: Returned to the United States - Source: List of American Prisoners of War discharged at Quebec - Name of prize ship: Land forces.

Morrison, William Prisoner: 1339 - Rank: Private - By what ship or how taken: Troops - Time when: 19 Dec

1813 - Place where: Fort Niagara - Whether man of war, privateer, or merchant vessel: Taken on shore - When received: 29 Jan 1814 - From what ship or whence received: Montreal by land carriages. - Prisoner: 1339 - Rank: Private - Name of Prize: Land forces - By what ship or how taken: Taken on shore - Discharged: 4 May 1814 - By what order: Returned to the United States - Source: List of American Prisoners of War discharged at Quebec - Name of prize ship: Land forces.

Morse, Jacob   Prisoner: 155 - Rank: Seaman - Name of Prize: Growler - By what ship or how taken: Man of war - Discharged: 31 Oct 1813 - By what order: HMS Malabar Transport by order of his Excellency Sir George Prevost - Source: List of American Prisoners of War discharged at Quebec - Name of prize ship: Growler.

Morse, Joshua   Prisoner: 237 - Rank: Private - Name of Prize: Growler - By what ship or how taken: Man of war - Discharged: 31 Oct 1813 - By what order: HMS Malabar Transport by order of his Excellency Sir George Prevost - Source: List of American Prisoners of War discharged at Quebec - Name of prize ship: Growler.

Morse, Lemond   Prisoner: 420 - Rank: Corporal - Name of Prize: Land forces - By what ship or how taken: Taken on shore - Discharged: 31 Oct 1813 - By what order: HMS Malabar Transport by order of his Excellency Sir George Prevost - Source: List of American Prisoners of War discharged at Quebec - Name of prize ship: Land forces.

Mortimore, Thomas   Prisoner: 1035 - Rank: Seaman - Name of Prize: Growler - By what ship or how taken: Man of war - Discharged: 1 Nov 1813 - By what order: HMS Hero by order of his Excellency Sir George Prevost - Source: List of American prisoners sent to England on the HMS Hero - Name of prize ship: Growler. - Prisoner: 1035 - Rank: Able Seaman - Name of Prize: Growler - By what ship or how taken: Man of war - Discharged: 4 May 1814 - By what order: Returned to the United States - Source: List of American Prisoners of War discharged at Quebec - Name of prize ship: Growler.

Morton, Seth   Prisoner: 1781 - Rank: Private - Name of Prize: Land forces - By what ship or how taken: Taken on shore - Discharged: 8 Nov 1814 - By what order: George No. 515 by Sir George Prevost - Source: List of American Prisoners of War discharged at Quebec - Name of prize ship: Land forces.

Mount, James   Prisoner: 1922 - Rank: Private - Name of Prize: Land forces - By what ship or how taken: Taken on shore - Discharged: 10 Nov 1814 - By what order: Sovereign No. 628 to Halifax by order of Sir George Prevost - Source: List of American Prisoners of War discharged at Quebec - Name of prize ship: Land forces.

Mudge, Ebenezer   Prisoner: 185 - Rank: Private - Name of Prize: Growler - By what ship or how taken: Man of war - Discharged: 31 Oct 1813 - By what order: HMS Malabar Transport by order of his Excellency Sir George Prevost - Source: List of American Prisoners of War discharged at Quebec - Name of prize ship: Growler.

Muller, Jesse   Prisoner: 1940 - Rank: Private - Name of Prize: Land forces - By what ship or how taken: Taken on shore - Discharged: 13 Mar 1815 - By what order: Returned to the United States - Source: List of American Prisoners of War discharged at Quebec - Name of prize ship: Land forces.

Mullett, William   Prisoner: 1038 - Rank: Seaman - Name of Prize: Growler - By what ship or how taken: Man of war - Discharged: 31 Oct 1813 - By what order: HMS Malabar Transport by order of his Excellency Sir George Prevost - Source: List of American Prisoners of War discharged at Quebec - Name of prize ship: Growler.

Mullinex, Samuel   Prisoner: 910 - Rank: Private - Name of Prize: Land forces - By what ship or how taken: Taken on shore - Discharged: 31 Oct 1813 - By what order: HMS Malabar Transport by order of his Excellency Sir George Prevost - Source: List of American Prisoners of War discharged at Quebec - Name of prize ship: Land forces.

Mullins, Owen   Prisoner: 616 - Rank: Private - Name of Prize: Land forces - By what ship or how taken: Taken on shore - Discharged: 10 Aug 1813 - By what order: HMS Regulus by order of his Excellency Sir George Prevost - Source: List of American Prisoners of War discharged at Quebec - Name of prize ship: Land forces.

Munger, Horace   Prisoner: 959 - Rank: Private - Name of Prize: Land forces - By what ship or how taken: Taken on shore - Discharged: 31 Oct 1813 - By what order: HMS Malabar Transport by order of his Excellency Sir George Prevost - Source: List of American Prisoners of War discharged at Quebec - Name of prize ship: Land forces.

Munroe, John   Prisoner: 11 - Rank: Private - Name of Prize: Land forces - By what ship or how taken: Taken on shore - Discharged: 31 Oct 1813 - By what order: HMS Malabar Transport by order of his Excellency Sir George Prevost - Source: List of American Prisoners of War discharged at Quebec - Name of prize ship: Land forces.

Munroe, William   Prisoner: 1019 - Rank: Private - Name of Prize: Batteaux - By what ship or how taken: Man of war - Discharged: 31 Oct 1813 - By what order: HMS Malabar Transport by order of his Excellency Sir George Prevost - Source: List of American Prisoners of War discharged at Quebec - Name of prize ship:

Batteaux.

Murphy, George   Prisoner: 672 - Rank: Corporal - Name of Prize: Land forces - By what ship or how taken: Taken on shore - Discharged: 10 Aug 1813 - By what order: HMS Regulus by order of his Excellency Sir George Prevost - Source: List of American Prisoners of War discharged at Quebec - Name of prize ship: Land forces.

Murphy, William   Prisoner: 1886 - Rank: Private - Name of Prize: Land forces - By what ship or how taken: Taken on shore - Discharged: 8 Nov 1814 - By what order: George No. 515 by Sir George Prevost - Source: List of American Prisoners of War discharged at Quebec - Name of prize ship: Land forces.

Murry, James   Prisoner: 234 - Rank: Private - Name of Prize: Eagle - By what ship or how taken: Man of war - Discharged: 31 Oct 1813 - By what order: HMS Malabar Transport by order of his Excellency Sir George Prevost - Source: List of American Prisoners of War discharged at Quebec - Name of prize ship: Eagle.

Murtain, Lewis   Prisoner: 1379 - Rank: Sergeant - By what ship or how taken: Troops - Time when: 19 Dec 1813 - Place where: Fort Niagara - Whether man of war, privateer, or merchant vessel: Taken on shore - When received: 29 Jan 1814 - From what ship or whence received: Montreal by land carriages. - Prisoner: 1379 - Rank: Sergeant - Name of Prize: Land forces - By what ship or how taken: Taken on shore - Discharged: 4 May 1814 - By what order: Returned to the United States - Source: List of American Prisoners of War discharged at Quebec - Name of prize ship: Land forces.

Myer, Michael   Prisoner: 1908 - Rank: Private - Name of Prize: Land forces - By what ship or how taken: Taken on shore - Discharged: 8 Nov 1814 - By what order: George No. 515 by Sir George Prevost - Source: List of American Prisoners of War discharged at Quebec - Name of prize ship: Land forces.

Myers, Godfred   Prisoner: 594 - Rank: Private - Name of Prize: Land forces - By what ship or how taken: Taken on shore - Discharged: 10 Aug 1813 - By what order: HMS Regulus by order of his Excellency Sir George Prevost - Source: List of American Prisoners of War discharged at Quebec - Name of prize ship: Land forces.

Neighbours, John   Prisoner: 1335 - Rank: Private - By what ship or how taken: Troops - Time when: 19 Dec 1813 - Place where: Fort Niagara - Whether man of war, privateer, or merchant vessel: Taken on shore - When received: 29 Jan 1814 - From what ship or whence received: Montreal by land carriages. - Prisoner: 1335 - Rank: Private - Name of Prize: Land forces - By what ship or how taken: Taken on shore - Discharged: 4 May 1814 - By what order: Returned to the United States - Source: List of American Prisoners of War discharged at Quebec - Name of prize ship: Land forces.

Nelson, James   Prisoner: 1110 - Rank: Private - Name of Prize: Land forces - By what ship or how taken: Taken on shore - Discharged: 31 Oct 1813 - By what order: HMS Malabar Transport by order of his Excellency Sir George Prevost - Source: List of American Prisoners of War discharged at Quebec - Name of prize ship: Land forces.

Nelson, Timothy   Prisoner: 1947 - Rank: Private - Name of Prize: Land forces - By what ship or how taken: Taken on shore - Discharged: 13 Mar 1815 - By what order: Returned to the United States - Source: List of American Prisoners of War discharged at Quebec - Name of prize ship: Land forces.

Nesbit, Shedderick   Prisoner: 417 - Rank: Corporal - Name of Prize: Land forces - By what ship or how taken: Taken on shore - Discharged: 31 Oct 1813 - By what order: HMS Malabar Transport by order of his Excellency Sir George Prevost - Source: List of American Prisoners of War discharged at Quebec - Name of prize ship: Land forces.

Nesbitt, John   Prisoner: 1419 - Rank: Sergeant - By what ship or how taken: Troops - Time when: 19 Dec 1813 - Place where: Fort Niagara - Whether man of war, privateer, or merchant vessel: Taken on shore - When received: 29 Jan 1814 - From what ship or whence received: Montreal by land carriages. - Prisoner: 1419 - Rank: Sergeant - Name of Prize: Land forces - By what ship or how taken: Taken on shore - Discharged: 4 May 1814 - By what order: Returned to the United States - Source: List of American Prisoners of War discharged at Quebec - Name of prize ship: Land forces.

Neuman, Henry   Prisoner: 328 - Rank: Private - Name of Prize: Land forces - By what ship or how taken: Taken on shore - Discharged: 4 May 1814 - By what order: Returned to the United States - Source: List of American Prisoners of War discharged at Quebec - Name of prize ship: Land forces.

Newman, Stokely   Prisoner: 962 - Rank: Private - Name of Prize: Land forces - By what ship or how taken: Taken on shore - Discharged: 31 Oct 1813 - By what order: HMS Malabar Transport by order of his Excellency Sir George Prevost - Source: List of American Prisoners of War discharged at Quebec - Name of prize ship: Land forces.

Newton, John   Prisoner: 646 - Rank: Private - Name of Prize: Land forces - By what ship or how taken: Taken on shore - Discharged: 10 Aug 1813 - By what order: HMS Regulus by order of his Excellency Sir George Prevost - Source: List of American Prisoners of War discharged at Quebec - Name of prize ship: Land forces.

Nicholson, John   Prisoner: 1312 - Rank: Private - By what ship or how taken: Troops - Time when: 19 Dec 1813 -

Place where: Fort Niagara - Whether man of war, privateer, or merchant vessel: Taken on shore - When received: 29 Jan 1814 - From what ship or whence received: Montreal by land carriages. - Prisoner: 1312 - Rank: Private - Name of Prize: Land forces - By what ship or how taken: Taken on shore - Discharged: 4 May 1814 - By what order: Returned to the United States - Source: List of American Prisoners of War discharged at Quebec - Name of prize ship: Land forces.

Nicholson, Solomon Prisoner: 114 - Rank: Private - Name of Prize: Land forces - By what ship or how taken: Taken on shore - Discharged: 31 Oct 1813 - By what order: HMS Malabar Transport by order of his Excellency Sir George Prevost - Source: List of American Prisoners of War discharged at Quebec - Name of prize ship: Land forces.

Nicholson, William Prisoner: 163 - Rank: Seaman - Name of Prize: Eagle - By what ship or how taken: Man of war - Discharged: 31 Oct 1813 - By what order: HMS Malabar Transport by order of his Excellency Sir George Prevost - Source: List of American Prisoners of War discharged at Quebec - Name of prize ship: Eagle.

Nixon, William Prisoner: 587 - Rank: Private - Name of Prize: Land forces - By what ship or how taken: Taken on shore - Discharged: 10 Aug 1813 - By what order: HMS Regulus by order of his Excellency Sir George Prevost - Source: List of American Prisoners of War discharged at Quebec - Name of prize ship: Land forces.

Northup, Thomas Prisoner: 1812 - Rank: Private - Name of Prize: Land forces - By what ship or how taken: Taken on shore - Discharged: 8 Nov 1814 - By what order: George No. 515 by Sir George Prevost - Source: List of American Prisoners of War discharged at Quebec - Name of prize ship: Land forces.

Norton, Andrew Prisoner: 1744 - Rank: Seaman - Name of Prize: Tigress - By what ship or how taken: Man of war - Discharged: 7 Nov 1813 - By what order: HMS Freedom No. 582 by order of his Excellency Sir George Prevost - Source: List of American Prisoners of War discharged at Quebec - Name of prize ship: Tigress.

Norton, Lewis Prisoner: 1718 - Rank: Private - Name of Prize: Land forces - By what ship or how taken: Taken on shore - Discharged: 10 Nov 1814 - By what order: Stately No. 400 to Halifax by order of Sir George Prevost - Source: List of American Prisoners of War discharged at Quebec - Name of prize ship: Land forces.

Nose, Jacob Prisoner: 713 - Rank: Private - Name of Prize: Land forces - By what ship or how taken: Taken on shore - Discharged: 10 Aug 1813 - By what order: HMS Regulus by order of his Excellency Sir George Prevost - Source: List of American Prisoners of War discharged at Quebec - Name of prize ship: Land forces.

Nourse, Thomas B. W. Prisoner: 1175 - Rank: Private - By what ship or how taken: Troops - Time when: 5 May 1813 - Place where: Rapids - Whether man of war, privateer, or merchant vessel: Taken on shore - When received: 25 Nov 1813 - From what ship or whence received: Town goal. - Prisoner: 1175 - Rank: Private - Name of Prize: Land forces - By what ship or how taken: Taken on shore - Discharged: 4 May 1814 - By what order: Returned to the United States - Source: List of American Prisoners of War discharged at Quebec - Name of prize ship: Land forces.

Nunn, John Prisoner: 1386 - Rank: Private - By what ship or how taken: Troops - Time when: 19 Dec 1813 - Place where: Fort Niagara - Whether man of war, privateer, or merchant vessel: Taken on shore - When received: 29 Jan 1814 - From what ship or whence received: Montreal by land carriages. - Prisoner: 1386 - Rank: Private - Name of Prize: Land forces - By what ship or how taken: Taken on shore - Discharged: 4 May 1814 - By what order: Returned to the United States - Source: List of American Prisoners of War discharged at Quebec - Name of prize ship: Land forces.

Nute, John Prisoner: 96 - Rank: Private - Name of Prize: Land forces - By what ship or how taken: Taken on shore - Discharged: 4 May 1814 - By what order: Returned to the United States - Source: List of American Prisoners of War discharged at Quebec - Name of prize ship: Land forces.

Nutter, John Prisoner: 1780 - Rank: Private - Name of Prize: Land forces - By what ship or how taken: Taken on shore - Discharged: 8 Nov 1814 - By what order: George No. 515 by Sir George Prevost - Source: List of American Prisoners of War discharged at Quebec - Name of prize ship: Land forces.

Nye, James Prisoner: 1988 - Rank: Seaman - Name of Prize: George - By what ship or how taken: Merchant Vessel - Discharged: 13 Mar 1815 - By what order: Returned to the United States - Source: List of American Prisoners of War discharged at Quebec - Name of prize ship: George.

Oates, John Prisoner: 455 - Rank: Private - Name of Prize: Land forces - By what ship or how taken: Taken on shore - Discharged: 10 Aug 1813 - By what order: HMS Regulus by order of his Excellency Sir George Prevost - Source: List of American Prisoners of War discharged at Quebec - Name of prize ship: Land forces.

O'Conner, Michael Prisoner: 1247 - Rank: Private - By what ship or how taken: Troops - Time when: 19 Dec 1813 - Place where: Fort Niagara - Whether man of war, privateer, or merchant vessel: Taken on shore - When received: 29 Jan 1814 - From what ship or whence received: Montreal by land carriages. - Prisoner:

1247 - Rank: Private - Name of Prize: Land forces - By what ship or how taken: Taken on shore - Discharged: 4 May 1814 - By what order: Returned to the United States - Source: List of American Prisoners of War discharged at Quebec - Name of prize ship: Land forces.

Ogle, Howard   Prisoner: 1122 - Rank: Private - Name of Prize: Land forces - By what ship or how taken: Taken on shore - Discharged: 31 Oct 1813 - By what order: HMS Malabar Transport by order of his Excellency Sir George Prevost - Source: List of American Prisoners of War discharged at Quebec - Name of prize ship: Land forces.

Oiler, George   Prisoner: 563 - Rank: Private - Name of Prize: Land forces - By what ship or how taken: Taken on shore - Discharged: 10 Aug 1813 - By what order: HMS Regulus by order of his Excellency Sir George Prevost - Source: List of American Prisoners of War discharged at Quebec - Name of prize ship: Land forces.

Oitest, Con.   Prisoner: 665 - Rank: Private - Name of Prize: Land forces - By what ship or how taken: Taken on shore - Discharged: 10 Aug 1813 - By what order: HMS Regulus by order of his Excellency Sir George Prevost - Source: List of American Prisoners of War discharged at Quebec - Name of prize ship: Land forces - Comments: British subject, sent to England.

Oliver, Griffin   Prisoner: 1671 - Rank: Seaman - Name of Prize: Taken in a gig (a ship's long boat) - By what ship or how taken: Man of war - Discharged: 7 Nov 1813 - By what order: HMS Freedom No. 582 by order of his Excellency Sir George Prevost - Source: List of American Prisoners of War discharged at Quebec - Name of prize ship: Taken in a gig (a ship's long boat).

Olley, Nathan   Prisoner: 131 - Rank: Private - Name of Prize: Land forces - By what ship or how taken: Taken on shore - Discharged: 31 Oct 1813 - By what order: HMS Malabar Transport by order of his Excellency Sir George Prevost - Source: List of American Prisoners of War discharged at Quebec - Name of prize ship: Land forces.

Orcutt, Rufus   Prisoner: 1765 - Rank: Sergeant - Name of Prize: Land forces - By what ship or how taken: Taken on shore - Discharged: 8 Nov 1814 - By what order: George No. 515 by Sir George Prevost - Source: List of American Prisoners of War discharged at Quebec - Name of prize ship: Land forces.

Orn, Ebenezer   Prisoner: 1260 - Rank: Private - By what ship or how taken: Troops - Time when: 19 Dec 1813 - Place where: Fort Niagara - Whether man of war, privateer, or merchant vessel: Taken on shore - When received: 29 Jan 1814 - From what ship or whence received: Montreal by land carriages. - Prisoner: 1260 - Rank: Private - Name of Prize: Land forces - By what ship or how taken: Taken on shore - Discharged: 4 May 1814 - By what order: Returned to the United States - Source: List of American Prisoners of War discharged at Quebec - Name of prize ship: Land forces.

Orn, Joseph   Prisoner: 1259 - Rank: Private - By what ship or how taken: Troops - Time when: 19 Dec 1813 - Place where: Fort Niagara - Whether man of war, privateer, or merchant vessel: Taken on shore - When received: 29 Jan 1814 - From what ship or whence received: Montreal by land carriages.

Orn, Joshua   Prisoner: 1259 - Rank: Private - Name of Prize: Land forces - By what ship or how taken: Taken on shore - Discharged: 4 May 1814 - By what order: Returned to the United States - Source: List of American Prisoners of War discharged at Quebec - Name of prize ship: Land forces.

Osgood, Richard   Prisoner: 245 - Rank: Private - Name of Prize: Land forces - By what ship or how taken: Taken on shore - Discharged: 31 Oct 1813 - By what order: HMS Malabar Transport by order of his Excellency Sir George Prevost - Source: List of American Prisoners of War discharged at Quebec - Name of prize ship: Land forces.

Osgood, Samuel W.   Prisoner: 1021 - Rank: Master's Mate - Name of Prize: Growler - By what ship or how taken: Man of war - Discharged: 4 May 1814 - By what order: Returned to the United States - Source: List of American Prisoners of War discharged at Quebec - Name of prize ship: Growler.

Ostunder, Jones   Prisoner: 358 - Rank: Private - Name of Prize: Land forces - By what ship or how taken: Taken on shore - Discharged: 31 Oct 1813 - By what order: HMS Malabar Transport by order of his Excellency Sir George Prevost - Source: List of American Prisoners of War discharged at Quebec - Name of prize ship: Land forces.

Owen, Amasa   Prisoner: 1265 - Rank: Corporal - By what ship or how taken: Troops - Time when: 19 Dec 1813 - Place where: Fort Niagara - Whether man of war, privateer, or merchant vessel: Taken on shore - When received: 29 Jan 1814 - From what ship or whence received: Montreal by land carriages. - Prisoner: 1265 - Rank: Corporal - Name of Prize: Land forces - By what ship or how taken: Taken on shore - Discharged: 12 Mar 1814 - By what order: Volunteered for the New Brunswick Fencibles - Source: List of American Prisoners of War discharged at Quebec - Name of prize ship: Land forces.

Owen, Frederick   Prisoner: 1785 - Rank: Private - Name of Prize: Land forces - By what ship or how taken: Taken on shore - Discharged: 8 Nov 1814 - By what order: George No. 515 by Sir George Prevost - Source: List of

American Prisoners of War discharged at Quebec - Name of prize ship: Land forces.

Owen, Jeremiah Prisoner: 1358 - Rank: Private - By what ship or how taken: Troops - Time when: 19 Dec 1813 - Place where: Fort Niagara - Whether man of war, privateer, or merchant vessel: Taken on shore - When received: 29 Jan 1814 - From what ship or whence received: Montreal by land carriages. - Prisoner: 1358 - Rank: Private - Name of Prize: Land forces - By what ship or how taken: Taken on shore - Discharged: 4 May 1814 - By what order: Returned to the United States - Source: List of American Prisoners of War discharged at Quebec - Name of prize ship: Land forces.

Owens John Prisoner: 727 - Rank: Private - Name of Prize: Land forces - By what ship or how taken: Taken on shore - Discharged: 10 Aug 1813 - By what order: HMS Regulus by order of his Excellency Sir George Prevost - Source: List of American Prisoners of War discharged at Quebec - Name of prize ship: Land forces.

Packard, Joseph Prisoner: 1977 - Rank: Private - Name of Prize: Land forces - By what ship or how taken: Taken on shore - Discharged: 13 Mar 1815 - By what order: Returned to the United States - Source: List of American Prisoners of War discharged at Quebec - Name of prize ship: Land forces.

Palmer, Gordon Prisoner: 1014 - Rank: Boatman - Name of Prize: Batteaux - By what ship or how taken: Man of war - Discharged: 31 Oct 1813 - By what order: HMS Malabar Transport by order of his Excellency Sir George Prevost - Source: List of American Prisoners of War discharged at Quebec - Name of prize ship: Batteaux.

Palmer, John W. Prisoner: 1666 - Rank: Master's Mate - Name of Prize: Scorpion - By what ship or how taken: Man of war - Discharged: 10 Nov 1814 - By what order: Lord Cathcart No. 161 for Halifax by order of Sir George Prevost - Source: List of American Prisoners of War discharged at Quebec - Name of prize ship: Scorpion.

Palmer, Nicholas Prisoner: 717 - Rank: Private - Name of Prize: Land forces - By what ship or how taken: Taken on shore - Discharged: 4 May 1814 - By what order: Returned to the United States - Source: List of American Prisoners of War discharged at Quebec - Name of prize ship: Land forces.

Palmer, Thomas Prisoner: 1741 - Rank: Seaman - Name of Prize: Tigress - By what ship or how taken: Man of war - Discharged: 7 Nov 1813 - By what order: HMS Freedom No. 582 by order of his Excellency Sir George Prevost - Source: List of American Prisoners of War discharged at Quebec - Name of prize ship: Tigress.

Palmer, William Prisoner: 1012 - Rank: Seaman - Name of Prize: Juliet - By what ship or how taken: Man of war - Discharged: 31 Oct 1813 - By what order: HMS Malabar Transport by order of his Excellency Sir George Prevost - Source: List of American Prisoners of War discharged at Quebec - Name of prize ship: Juliet.

Pangburn, Edward Prisoner: 643 - Rank: Private - Name of Prize: Land forces - By what ship or how taken: Taken on shore - Discharged: 10 Aug 1813 - By what order: HMS Regulus by order of his Excellency Sir George Prevost - Source: List of American Prisoners of War discharged at Quebec - Name of prize ship: Land forces.

Parbolt, William Prisoner: 1017 - Rank: Private - Name of Prize: Juliet - By what ship or how taken: Man of war - Discharged: 31 Oct 1813 - By what order: HMS Malabar Transport by order of his Excellency Sir George Prevost - Source: List of American Prisoners of War discharged at Quebec - Name of prize ship: Juliet.

Parcel, James H. Prisoner: 1317 - Rank: Sergeant - By what ship or how taken: Troops - Time when: 19 Dec 1813 - Place where: Fort Niagara - Whether man of war, privateer, or merchant vessel: Taken on shore - When received: 29 Jan 1814 - From what ship or whence received: Montreal by land carriages. - Prisoner: 1317 - Rank: Sergeant - Name of Prize: Land forces - By what ship or how taken: Taken on shore - Discharged: 4 May 1814 - By what order: Returned to the United States - Source: List of American Prisoners of War discharged at Quebec - Name of prize ship: Land forces.

Park, Luther Prisoner: 183 - Rank: Corporal - Name of Prize: Growler - By what ship or how taken: Man of war - Discharged: 31 Oct 1813 - By what order: HMS Malabar Transport by order of his Excellency Sir George Prevost - Source: List of American Prisoners of War discharged at Quebec - Name of prize ship: Growler.

Parker, Edward Prisoner: 224 - Rank: Private - Source: Account of American prisoners of war who died at Quebec in the Months of July, August & September 1813 - Ship or Corps: Growler - Vessel: Man of war - Place born: Freeport, MA - Age: 21 - Where taken: Lake Champlain - Date of death: 19 Sep 1813 - Disorder or casualty: Typhus fever.

Parker, John Prisoner: 1740 - Rank: Seaman - Name of Prize: Tigress - By what ship or how taken: Man of war - Discharged: 7 Nov 1813 - By what order: HMS Freedom No. 582 by order of his Excellency Sir George Prevost - Source: List of American Prisoners of War discharged at Quebec - Name of prize ship: Tigress.

Parkinson, James Prisoner: 1876 - Rank: Private - Name of Prize: Land forces - By what ship or how taken: Taken on shore - Discharged: 8 Nov 1814 - By what order: George No. 515 by Sir George Prevost - Source:

List of American Prisoners of War discharged at Quebec - Name of prize ship: Land forces.

Parks, Henry   Prisoner: 1939 - Rank: Private - Name of Prize: Land forces - By what ship or how taken: Taken on shore - Discharged: 13 Mar 1815 - By what order: Returned to the United States - Source: List of American Prisoners of War discharged at Quebec - Name of prize ship: Land forces.

Parks, Selvey   Prisoner: 484 - Rank: Private - Name of Prize: Land forces - By what ship or how taken: Taken on shore - Discharged: 10 Aug 1813 - By what order: HMS Regulus by order of his Excellency Sir George Prevost - Source: List of American Prisoners of War discharged at Quebec - Name of prize ship: Land forces.

Parsons, Samuel   Prisoner: 386 - Rank: Private - Name of Prize: Land forces - By what ship or how taken: Taken on shore - Discharged: 31 Oct 1813 - By what order: HMS Malabar Transport by order of his Excellency Sir George Prevost - Source: List of American Prisoners of War discharged at Quebec - Name of prize ship: Land forces.

Parth, James E.   Prisoner: 1928 - Rank: Private - Name of Prize: Land forces - By what ship or how taken: Taken on shore - Discharged: 13 Mar 1815 - By what order: Returned to the United States - Source: List of American Prisoners of War discharged at Quebec - Name of prize ship: Land forces.

Patterson, John   Prisoner: 1248 - Rank: Private - By what ship or how taken: Troops - Time when: 19 Dec 1813 - Place where: Fort Niagara - Whether man of war, privateer, or merchant vessel: Taken on shore - When received: 29 Jan 1814 - From what ship or whence received: Montreal by land carriages. - Prisoner: 1248 - Rank: Private - Name of Prize: Land forces - By what ship or how taken: Taken on shore - Discharged: 4 May 1814 - By what order: Returned to the United States - Source: List of American Prisoners of War discharged at Quebec - Name of prize ship: Land forces.

Patterson, Thomas   Prisoner: 1793 - Rank: Private - Name of Prize: Land forces - By what ship or how taken: Taken on shore - Discharged: 8 Nov 1814 - By what order: George No. 515 by Sir George Prevost - Source: List of American Prisoners of War discharged at Quebec - Name of prize ship: Land forces.

Patton, David   Prisoner: 595 - Rank: Private - Name of Prize: Land forces - By what ship or how taken: Taken on shore - Discharged: 10 Aug 1813 - By what order: HMS Regulus by order of his Excellency Sir George Prevost - Source: List of American Prisoners of War discharged at Quebec - Name of prize ship: Land forces.

Paul, Simeon   Prisoner: 227 - Rank: Private - Source: Account of American prisoners of war who died at Quebec in the Months of July, August & September 1813 - Ship or Corps: Eagle - Vessel: Man of war - Place born: New Gloucester, MA - Age: 17 - Where taken: Lake Champlain - Date of death: 25 Aug 1813 - Disorder or casualty: Synochus.

Paulding, Philip   Prisoner: 1923 - Rank: Private - Name of Prize: Land forces - By what ship or how taken: Taken on shore - Discharged: 10 Nov 1814 - By what order: Sovereign No. 628 to Halifax by order of Sir George Prevost - Source: List of American Prisoners of War discharged at Quebec - Name of prize ship: Land forces.

Pauling, William K.   Prisoner: 1209 - Rank: Ensign - By what ship or how taken: Troops - Time when: 19 Dec 1813 - Place where: Fort Niagara - Whether man of war, privateer, or merchant vessel: Taken on shore - When received: 18 Jan 1814 - From what ship or whence received: Montreal by land carriages. - Prisoner: 1209 - Rank: Ensign - Name of Prize: Land forces - By what ship or how taken: Taken on shore - Discharged: 6 May 1814 - By what order: Returned to the United States - Source: List of American Prisoners of War discharged at Quebec - Name of prize ship: Land forces.

Payne, Rubin   Prisoner: 186 - Rank: Private - Name of Prize: Eagle - By what ship or how taken: Man of war - Discharged: 31 Oct 1813 - By what order: HMS Malabar Transport by order of his Excellency Sir George Prevost - Source: List of American Prisoners of War discharged at Quebec - Name of prize ship: Eagle.

Pearl, John   Prisoner: 28 - Rank: Private - Name of Prize: Land forces - By what ship or how taken: Taken on shore - Discharged: 31 Oct 1813 - By what order: HMS Malabar Transport by order of his Excellency Sir George Prevost - Source: List of American Prisoners of War discharged at Quebec - Name of prize ship: Land forces.

Pearson, John   Prisoner: 1037 - Rank: Seaman - Name of Prize: Growler - By what ship or how taken: Man of war - Discharged: 31 Oct 1813 - By what order: HMS Malabar Transport by order of his Excellency Sir George Prevost - Source: List of American Prisoners of War discharged at Quebec - Name of prize ship: Growler.

Peck, Adam   Prisoner: 1204 - Rank: Lieutenant - By what ship or how taken: Troops - Time when: 19 Dec 1813 - Place where: Fort Niagara - Whether man of war, privateer, or merchant vessel: Taken on shore - When received: 18 Jan 1814 - From what ship or whence received: Montreal by land carriages.
Prisoner: 1204 - Rank: Private - Name of Prize: Land forces - By what ship or how taken: Taken on shore - Discharged: 4 May 1814 - By what order: Returned to the United States - Source: List of American Prisoners of War discharged at Quebec - Name of prize ship: Land forces.

Peck, Otis   Prisoner: 1288 - Rank: Private - By what ship or how taken: Troops - Time when: 19 Dec 1813 - Place where: Fort Niagara - Whether man of war, privateer, or merchant vessel: Taken on shore - When received: 29 Jan 1814 - From what ship or whence received: Montreal by land carriages. - Prisoner: 1288 - Rank: Private - Name of Prize: Land forces - By what ship or how taken: Taken on shore - Discharged: 4 May 1814 - By what order: Returned to the United States - Source: List of American Prisoners of War discharged at Quebec - Name of prize ship: Land forces.

Penby, Joseph   Prisoner: 212 - Rank: Private - Name of Prize: Growler - By what ship or how taken: Man of war - Discharged: 31 Oct 1813 - By what order: HMS Malabar Transport by order of his Excellency Sir George Prevost - Source: List of American Prisoners of War discharged at Quebec - Name of prize ship: Growler.

Pennell, Samuel   Prisoner: 97 - Rank: Private - Name of Prize: Land forces - By what ship or how taken: Taken on shore - Discharged: 31 Oct 1813 - By what order: HMS Malabar Transport by order of his Excellency Sir George Prevost - Source: List of American Prisoners of War discharged at Quebec - Name of prize ship: Land forces.

Perham, John   Prisoner: 345 - Rank: Private - Name of Prize: Land forces - By what ship or how taken: Taken on shore - Discharged: 31 Oct 1813 - By what order: HMS Malabar Transport by order of his Excellency Sir George Prevost - Source: List of American Prisoners of War discharged at Quebec - Name of prize ship: Land forces.

Perkins, John   Prisoner: 1143 - Rank: Private - By what ship or how taken: Troops - Time when: 5 May 1813 - Place where: Rapids, River Raisin - Whether man of war, privateer, or merchant vessel: Taken on shore - When received: 25 Nov 1813 - From what ship or whence received: Town goal. - Prisoner: 1143 - Rank: Private - Name of Prize: Land forces - By what ship or how taken: Taken on shore - Discharged: 4 May 1814 - By what order: Returned to the United States - Source: List of American Prisoners of War discharged at Quebec - Name of prize ship: Land forces.

Perry, David   Prisoner: 1306 - Rank: Lieutenant - Name of Prize: Land forces - By what ship or how taken: Taken on shore - Discharged: 14 Nov 1814 - By what order: Sovereign No. 628 to Halifax by order of Sir George Prevost - Source: List of American Prisoners of War discharged at Quebec - Name of prize ship: Land forces.

Petare, John   Prisoner: 823 - Rank: Private - Name of Prize: Land forces - By what ship or how taken: Taken on shore - Discharged: 4 May 1814 - By what order: Returned to the United States - Source: List of American Prisoners of War discharged at Quebec - Name of prize ship: Land forces.

Peterson, Lemuel   Prisoner: 1966 - Rank: Private - Name of Prize: Land forces - By what ship or how taken: Taken on shore - Discharged: 13 Mar 1815 - By what order: Returned to the United States - Source: List of American Prisoners of War discharged at Quebec - Name of prize ship: Land forces.

Peterson, Peter   Prisoner: 61 - Rank: Private - Name of Prize: Land forces - By what ship or how taken: Taken on shore - Discharged: 31 Oct 1813 - By what order: HMS Malabar Transport by order of his Excellency Sir George Prevost - Source: List of American Prisoners of War discharged at Quebec - Name of prize ship: Land forces.

Pettis, John   Prisoner: 1917 - Rank: Private - Name of Prize: Land forces - By what ship or how taken: Taken on shore - Discharged: 16 Mar 1815 - By what order: Returned to the United States - Source: List of American Prisoners of War discharged at Quebec - Name of prize ship: Land forces.

Phelps, John   Prisoner: 204 - Rank: Private - Name of Prize: Growler - By what ship or how taken: Man of war - Discharged: 31 Oct 1813 - By what order: HMS Malabar Transport by order of his Excellency Sir George Prevost - Source: List of American Prisoners of War discharged at Quebec - Name of prize ship: Growler.

Phillips, Augustus   Prisoner: 1747 - Rank: Seaman - Name of Prize: Tigress - By what ship or how taken: Man of war - Discharged: 7 Nov 1813 - By what order: HMS Freedom No. 582 by order of his Excellency Sir George Prevost - Source: List of American Prisoners of War discharged at Quebec - Name of prize ship: Tigress.

Phillips, John C.   Prisoner: 1 - Rank: Private - Name of Prize: Land forces - By what ship or how taken: Taken on shore - Discharged: 31 Oct 1813 - By what order: HMS Malabar Transport by order of his Excellency Sir George Prevost - Source: List of American Prisoners of War discharged at Quebec - Name of prize ship: Land forces.

Phillips, Joseph   Prisoner: 1825 - Rank: Private - Name of Prize: Land forces - By what ship or how taken: Taken on shore - Discharged: 8 Nov 1814 - By what order: George No. 515 by Sir George Prevost - Source: List of American Prisoners of War discharged at Quebec - Name of prize ship: Land forces.

Phillips, Samuel   Prisoner: 435 - Rank: Private - Name of Prize: Land forces - By what ship or how taken: Taken on shore - Discharged: 10 Aug 1813 - By what order: HMS Regulus by order of his Excellency Sir George Prevost - Source: List of American Prisoners of War discharged at Quebec - Name of prize ship: Land forces.

Phoenix, John   Prisoner: 1004 - Rank: Cabin Boy - Name of Prize: Juliet - By what ship or how taken: Man of war

- Discharged: 31 Oct 1813 - By what order: HMS Malabar Transport by order of his Excellency Sir George Prevost - Source: List of American Prisoners of War discharged at Quebec - Name of prize ship: Juliet.

Pier, Henry   Prisoner: 1857 - Rank: Private - Name of Prize: Land forces - By what ship or how taken: Taken on shore - Discharged: 8 Nov 1814 - By what order: George No. 515 by Sir George Prevost - Source: List of American Prisoners of War discharged at Quebec - Name of prize ship: Land forces.

Pierce, Henry   Prisoner: 1926 - Rank: Private - Name of Prize: Land forces - By what ship or how taken: Taken on shore - Discharged: 10 Nov 1814 - By what order: Sovereign No. 628 to Halifax by order of Sir George Prevost - Source: List of American Prisoners of War discharged at Quebec - Name of prize ship: Land forces.

Pierce, Thomas   Prisoner: 1219 - Rank: Private - By what ship or how taken: Troops - Time when: 19 Dec 1813 - Place where: Fort Niagara - Whether man of war, privateer, or merchant vessel: Taken on shore - When received: 29 Jan 1814 - From what ship or whence received: Montreal by land carriages. - Prisoner: 1219 - Rank: Private - Name of Prize: Land forces - By what ship or how taken: Taken on shore - Discharged: 4 May 1814 - By what order: Returned to the United States - Source: List of American Prisoners of War discharged at Quebec - Name of prize ship: Land forces.

Pitcher, Jacob   Prisoner: 1858 - Rank: Private - Name of Prize: Land forces - By what ship or how taken: Taken on shore - Discharged: 8 Nov 1814 - By what order: George No. 515 by Sir George Prevost - Source: List of American Prisoners of War discharged at Quebec - Name of prize ship: Land forces.

Plants, Edward T.   Prisoner: 300 - Rank: Private - Name of Prize: Land forces - By what ship or how taken: Taken on shore - Discharged: 31 Oct 1813 - By what order: HMS Malabar Transport by order of his Excellency Sir George Prevost - Source: List of American Prisoners of War discharged at Quebec - Name of prize ship: Land forces.

Platenburgh, Jacob   Prisoner: 1078 - Rank: Private - Name of Prize: Land forces - By what ship or how taken: Taken on shore - Discharged: 31 Oct 1813 - By what order: HMS Malabar Transport by order of his Excellency Sir George Prevost - Source: List of American Prisoners of War discharged at Quebec - Name of prize ship: Land forces.

Plott, John   Prisoner: 1087 - Rank: Private - Name of Prize: Land forces - By what ship or how taken: Taken on shore - Discharged: 31 Oct 1813 - By what order: HMS Malabar Transport by order of his Excellency Sir George Prevost - Source: List of American Prisoners of War discharged at Quebec - Name of prize ship: Land forces.

Plummer, Isaac   Prisoner: 207 - Rank: Private - Name of Prize: Growler - By what ship or how taken: Man of war - Discharged: 31 Oct 1813 - By what order: HMS Malabar Transport by order of his Excellency Sir George Prevost - Source: List of American Prisoners of War discharged at Quebec - Name of prize ship: Growler.

Poff, Peter   Prisoner: 1217 - Rank: Private - By what ship or how taken: Troops - Time when: 19 Dec 1813 - Place where: Fort Niagara - Whether man of war, privateer, or merchant vessel: Taken on shore - When received: 29 Jan 1814 - From what ship or whence received: Montreal by land carriages. - Prisoner: 1217 - Rank: Private - Name of Prize: Land forces - By what ship or how taken: Taken on shore - Discharged: 27 Feb 1814 - By what order: Volunteered for the New Brunswick Fencibles - Source: List of American Prisoners of War discharged at Quebec - Name of prize ship: Land forces.

Pollard, Martin   Prisoner: 538 - Rank: Private - Name of Prize: Land forces - By what ship or how taken: Taken on shore - Discharged: 10 Aug 1813 - By what order: HMS Regulus by order of his Excellency Sir George Prevost - Source: List of American Prisoners of War discharged at Quebec - Name of prize ship: Land forces.

Post, John L.   Prisoner: 1774 - Rank: Private - Name of Prize: Land forces - By what ship or how taken: Taken on shore - Discharged: 8 Nov 1814 - By what order: George No. 515 by Sir George Prevost - Source: List of American Prisoners of War discharged at Quebec - Name of prize ship: Land forces.

Potter, John   Prisoner: 1934 - Rank: Private - Source: Account of American prisoners of war who died at Quebec between 14 February 1814 and 23 December 1814 - Ship or Corps: Land forces - Vessel: Taken on shore - Place born: Vermont - Age: 16 - Where taken: Fort Erie - Date of death: 7 Dec 1814 - Disorder or casualty: Phthisis (pulmonary tuberculosis).

Potts, Jeremiah   Prisoner: 1388 - Rank: Private - By what ship or how taken: Troops - Time when: 19 Dec 1813 - Place where: Fort Niagara - Whether man of war, privateer, or merchant vessel: Taken on shore - When received: 29 Jan 1814 - From what ship or whence received: Montreal by land carriages. - Prisoner: 1388 - Rank: Private - Name of Prize: Land forces - By what ship or how taken: Taken on shore - Discharged: 4 May 1814 - By what order: Returned to the United States - Source: List of American Prisoners of War discharged at Quebec - Name of prize ship: Land forces.

Powell, Perley   Prisoner: 1528 - Rank: Private - Name of Prize: Land forces - By what ship or how taken: Taken on shore - Discharged: 8 Nov 1814 - By what order: George No. 515 by Sir George Prevost - Source: List of

American Prisoners of War discharged at Quebec - Name of prize ship: Land forces.

Powers, Joseph   Prisoner: 474 - Rank: Private - Name of Prize: Land forces - By what ship or how taken: Taken on shore - Discharged: 10 Aug 1813 - By what order: HMS Regulus by order of his Excellency Sir George Prevost - Source: List of American Prisoners of War discharged at Quebec - Name of prize ship: Land forces.

Powers, William   Prisoner: 1901 - Rank: Private - Name of Prize: Land forces - By what ship or how taken: Taken on shore - Discharged: 8 Nov 1814 - By what order: George No. 515 by Sir George Prevost - Source: List of American Prisoners of War discharged at Quebec - Name of prize ship: Land forces.

Prater, Smith   Prisoner: 1924 - Rank: Private - Name of Prize: Land forces - By what ship or how taken: Taken on shore - Discharged: 10 Nov 1814 - By what order: Sovereign No. 628 to Halifax by order of Sir George Prevost - Source: List of American Prisoners of War discharged at Quebec - Name of prize ship: Land forces.

Pratt, Charles   Prisoner: 226 - Rank: Private - Name of Prize: Eagle - By what ship or how taken: Man of war - Discharged: 31 Oct 1813 - By what order: HMS Malabar Transport by order of his Excellency Sir George Prevost - Source: List of American Prisoners of War discharged at Quebec - Name of prize ship: Eagle.

Pratt, Nathaniel   Prisoner: 117 - Rank: Private - Source: Account of American prisoners of war who died at Quebec in the Months of July, August & September 1813 - Ship or Corps: Land forces - Vessel: Taken on shore - Place born: Halifax, MA - Age: 31 - Where taken: Stoney Point - Date of death: 23 Jul 1813.

Pratt, Walter   Prisoner: 220 - Rank: Private - Source: Account of American prisoners of war who died at Quebec in the Months of July, August & September 1813 - Ship or Corps: Eagle - Vessel: Man of war - Place born: Leeds, MA - Age: 17 - Where taken: Lake Champlain - Date of death: 15 Sep 1813 - Disorder or casualty: Typhus fever.

Prentice, James   Prisoner: 1237 - Rank: Private - By what ship or how taken: Troops - Time when: 19 Dec 1813 - Place where: Fort Niagara - Whether man of war, privateer, or merchant vessel: Taken on shore - When received: 29 Jan 1814 - From what ship or whence received: Montreal by land carriages. - Prisoner: 1237 - Rank: Private - Name of Prize: Land forces - By what ship or how taken: Taken on shore - Discharged: 27 Feb 1814 - By what order: Volunteered for the New Brunswick Fencibles - Source: List of American Prisoners of War discharged at Quebec - Name of prize ship: Land forces.

Price, George   Prisoner: 650 - Rank: Private - Name of Prize: Land forces - By what ship or how taken: Taken on shore - Discharged: 10 Aug 1813 - By what order: HMS Regulus by order of his Excellency Sir George Prevost - Source: List of American Prisoners of War discharged at Quebec - Name of prize ship: Land forces.

Price, Job   Prisoner: 654 - Rank: Private - Name of Prize: Land forces - By what ship or how taken: Taken on shore - Discharged: 10 Aug 1813 - By what order: HMS Regulus by order of his Excellency Sir George Prevost - Source: List of American Prisoners of War discharged at Quebec - Name of prize ship: Land forces.

Price, John   Prisoner: 603 - Rank: Private - Name of Prize: Land forces - By what ship or how taken: Taken on shore - Discharged: 31 Oct 1813 - By what order: HMS Malabar Transport by order of his Excellency Sir George Prevost - Source: List of American Prisoners of War discharged at Quebec - Name of prize ship: Land forces.

Price, Merritt   Prisoner: 507 - Rank: Private - Name of Prize: Land forces - By what ship or how taken: Taken on shore - Discharged: 10 Aug 1813 - By what order: HMS Regulus by order of his Excellency Sir George Prevost - Source: List of American Prisoners of War discharged at Quebec - Name of prize ship: Land forces.

Price, Robert   Prisoner: 317 - Rank: Private - Name of Prize: Land forces - By what ship or how taken: Taken on shore - Discharged: 31 Oct 1813 - By what order: HMS Malabar Transport by order of his Excellency Sir George Prevost - Source: List of American Prisoners of War discharged at Quebec - Name of prize ship: Land forces.

Pruitt, Gabriel   Prisoner: 1414 - Rank: Private - By what ship or how taken: Troops - Time when: 19 Dec 1813 - Place where: Fort Niagara - Whether man of war, privateer, or merchant vessel: Taken on shore - When received: 29 Jan 1814 - From what ship or whence received: Montreal by land carriages. - Prisoner: 1414 - Rank: Private - Name of Prize: Land forces - By what ship or how taken: Taken on shore - Discharged: 4 May 1814 - By what order: Returned to the United States - Source: List of American Prisoners of War discharged at Quebec - Name of prize ship: Land forces.

Quinn, Patrick   Prisoner: 1292 - Rank: Private - By what ship or how taken: Troops - Time when: 19 Dec 1813 - Place where: Fort Niagara - Whether man of war, privateer, or merchant vessel: Taken on shore - When received: 29 Jan 1814 - From what ship or whence received: Montreal by land carriages. - Prisoner: 1292 - Rank: Private - Name of Prize: Land forces - By what ship or how taken: Taken on shore - Discharged: 22 Feb 1814 - By what order: Volunteered for the New Brunswick Fencibles - Source: List of American Prisoners of War discharged at Quebec - Name of prize ship: Land forces.

Race, Jonathan   Prisoner: 352 - Rank: Private - Name of Prize: Land forces - By what ship or how taken: Taken on

shore - Discharged: 31 Oct 1813 - By what order: HMS Malabar Transport by order of his Excellency Sir George Prevost - Source: List of American Prisoners of War discharged at Quebec - Name of prize ship: Land forces.

Rambo, Peter   Prisoner: 1286 - Rank: Corporal - By what ship or how taken: Troops - Time when: 19 Dec 1813 - Place where: Fort Niagara - Whether man of war, privateer, or merchant vessel: Taken on shore - When received: 29 Jan 1814 - From what ship or whence received: Montreal by land carriages. - Prisoner: 1286 - Rank: Corporal - Name of Prize: Land forces - By what ship or how taken: Taken on shore - Discharged: 4 May 1814 - By what order: Returned to the United States - Source: List of American Prisoners of War discharged at Quebec - Name of prize ship: Land forces.

Ramsdell, Samuel   Prisoner: 26 - Rank: Private - Name of Prize: Land forces - By what ship or how taken: Taken on shore - Discharged: 2 Nov 1813 - Source: List of Prisoners received on board the Malabar, discharged from hospital - Name of prize ship: Land forces.

Ramsey, Joseph   Prisoner: 561 - Rank: Private - Name of Prize: Land forces - By what ship or how taken: Taken on shore - Discharged: 10 Aug 1813 - By what order: HMS Regulus by order of his Excellency Sir George Prevost - Source: List of American Prisoners of War discharged at Quebec - Name of prize ship: Land forces.

Randall, Grief   Prisoner: 1382 - Rank: Private - By what ship or how taken: Troops - Time when: 19 Dec 1813 - Place where: Fort Niagara - Whether man of war, privateer, or merchant vessel: Taken on shore - When received: 29 Jan 1814 - From what ship or whence received: Montreal by land carriages. - Prisoner: 1382 - Rank: Private - Name of Prize: Land forces - By what ship or how taken: Taken on shore - Discharged: 6 May 1814 - By what order: Returned to the United States - Source: List of American Prisoners of War discharged at Quebec - Name of prize ship: Land forces.

Randall, Isaac   Prisoner: 1905 - Rank: Private - Name of Prize: Land forces - By what ship or how taken: Taken on shore - Discharged: 8 Nov 1814 - By what order: George No. 515 by Sir George Prevost - Source: List of American Prisoners of War discharged at Quebec - Name of prize ship: Land forces.

Ranger, Benjamin   Prisoner: 1686 - Rank: Private - Name of Prize: Land forces - By what ship or how taken: Taken on shore - Discharged: 8 Nov 1814 - By what order: George No. 515 by Sir George Prevost - Source: List of American Prisoners of War discharged at Quebec - Name of prize ship: Land forces.

Ranney, Julius   Prisoner: 1695 - Rank: Corporal - Name of Prize: Land forces - By what ship or how taken: Taken on shore - Discharged: 8 Nov 1814 - By what order: George No. 515 by Sir George Prevost - Source: List of American Prisoners of War discharged at Quebec - Name of prize ship: Land forces.

Ranson, Given   Prisoner: 1106 - Rank: Lieutenant - Name of Prize: Land forces - By what ship or how taken: Taken on shore - Discharged: 6 May 1814 - By what order: Returned to the United States - Source: List of American Prisoners of War discharged at Quebec - Name of prize ship: Land forces.

Rathborn, Jeremiah   Prisoner: 233 - Rank: Private - Name of Prize: Land forces - By what ship or how taken: Taken on shore - Discharged: 31 Oct 1813 - By what order: HMS Malabar Transport by order of his Excellency Sir George Prevost - Source: List of American Prisoners of War discharged at Quebec - Name of prize ship: Land forces.

Rathburn, Jeremiah   Prisoner: 1844 - Rank: Private - Name of Prize: Land forces - By what ship or how taken: Taken on shore - Discharged: 8 Nov 1814 - By what order: George No. 515 by Sir George Prevost - Source: List of American Prisoners of War discharged at Quebec - Name of prize ship: Land forces.

Ray, George   Prisoner: 1801 - Rank: Private - Name of Prize: Land forces - By what ship or how taken: Taken on shore - Discharged: 8 Nov 1814 - By what order: George No. 515 by Sir George Prevost - Source: List of American Prisoners of War discharged at Quebec - Name of prize ship: Land forces.

Ray, John   Prisoner: 230 - Rank: Private - Name of Prize: Growler - By what ship or how taken: Man of war - Discharged: 31 Oct 1813 - By what order: HMS Malabar Transport by order of his Excellency Sir George Prevost - Source: List of American Prisoners of War discharged at Quebec - Name of prize ship: Growler.

Ray, Joseph   Prisoner: 1340 - Rank: Sergeant - By what ship or how taken: Troops - Time when: 19 Dec 1813 - Place where: Fort Niagara - Whether man of war, privateer, or merchant vessel: Taken on shore - When received: 29 Jan 1814 - From what ship or whence received: Montreal by land carriages. - Prisoner: 1340 - Rank: Sergeant - Name of Prize: Land forces - By what ship or how taken: Taken on shore - Discharged: 4 May 1814 - By what order: Returned to the United States - Source: List of American Prisoners of War discharged at Quebec - Name of prize ship: Land forces.

Rea, Charles   Prisoner: 1729 - Rank: Seaman - Name of Prize: Scorpion - By what ship or how taken: Man of war - Discharged: 7 Nov 1813 - By what order: HMS Freedom No. 582 by order of his Excellency Sir George Prevost - Source: List of American Prisoners of War discharged at Quebec - Name of prize ship: Scorpion.

Rea, John   Prisoner: 502 - Rank: Private - Name of Prize: Land forces - By what ship or how taken: Taken on

shore - Discharged: 10 Aug 1813 - By what order: HMS Regulus by order of his Excellency Sir George Prevost - Source: List of American Prisoners of War discharged at Quebec - Name of prize ship: Land forces.

Read, James   Prisoner: 354 - Rank: Private - Name of Prize: Land forces - By what ship or how taken: Taken on shore - Discharged: 31 Oct 1813 - By what order: HMS Malabar Transport by order of his Excellency Sir George Prevost - Source: List of American Prisoners of War discharged at Quebec - Name of prize ship: Land forces.

Read, Samuel R.   Prisoner: 201 - Rank: Corporal - Name of Prize: Growler - By what ship or how taken: Man of war - Discharged: 31 Oct 1813 - By what order: HMS Malabar Transport by order of his Excellency Sir George Prevost - Source: List of American Prisoners of War discharged at Quebec - Name of prize ship: Growler.

Reade, Thomas   Prisoner: 1730 - Rank: Seaman - Name of Prize: Scorpion - By what ship or how taken: Man of war - Discharged: 7 Nov 1813 - By what order: HMS Freedom No. 582 by order of his Excellency Sir George Prevost - Source: List of American Prisoners of War discharged at Quebec - Name of prize ship: Scorpion.

Reagan, James   Prisoner: 1963 - Rank: Sergeant - Name of Prize: Land forces - By what ship or how taken: Taken on shore - Discharged: 13 Mar 1815 - By what order: Returned to the United States - Source: List of American Prisoners of War discharged at Quebec - Name of prize ship: Land forces.

Redehouse, Conduit   Prisoner: 971 - Rank: Private - Name of Prize: Land forces - By what ship or how taken: Taken on shore - Discharged: 31 Oct 1813 - By what order: HMS Malabar Transport by order of his Excellency Sir George Prevost - Source: List of American Prisoners of War discharged at Quebec - Name of prize ship: Land forces.

Redfield, Anthony C.   Prisoner: 1245 - Rank: Private - By what ship or how taken: Troops - Time when: 19 Dec 1813 - Place where: Fort Niagara - Whether man of war, privateer, or merchant vessel: Taken on shore - When received: 29 Jan 1814 - From what ship or whence received: Montreal by land carriages. - Prisoner: 1245 - Rank: Private - Name of Prize: Land forces - By what ship or how taken: Taken on shore - Discharged: 4 May 1814 - By what order: Returned to the United States - Source: List of American Prisoners of War discharged at Quebec - Name of prize ship: Land forces.

Redman, Martin   Prisoner: 465 - Rank: Private - Name of Prize: Land forces - By what ship or how taken: Taken on shore - Discharged: 10 Aug 1813 - By what order: HMS Regulus by order of his Excellency Sir George Prevost - Source: List of American Prisoners of War discharged at Quebec - Name of prize ship: Land forces.

Reed, Isaac   Prisoner: 43 - Rank: Private - Source: Account of American prisoners of war who died at Quebec in the Months of July, August & September 1813 - Ship or Corps: Land forces - Vessel: Taken on shore - Place born: Dawiss, MA - Age: 16 - Where taken: Stoney Point - Date of death: 4 Aug 1813.

Reed, William   Prisoner: 1011 - Rank: Seaman - Name of Prize: Juliet - By what ship or how taken: Man of war - Discharged: 31 Oct 1813 - By what order: HMS Malabar Transport by order of his Excellency Sir George Prevost - Source: List of American Prisoners of War discharged at Quebec - Name of prize ship: Juliet.

Rehuhard, Thomas   Prisoner: 289 - Rank: Private - Name of Prize: Land forces - By what ship or how taken: Taken on shore - Discharged: 31 Oct 1813 - By what order: HMS Malabar Transport by order of his Excellency Sir George Prevost - Source: List of American Prisoners of War discharged at Quebec - Name of prize ship: Land forces.

Reyner, John   Prisoner: 1257 - Rank: Private - By what ship or how taken: Troops - Time when: 19 Dec 1813 - Place where: Fort Niagara - Whether man of war, privateer, or merchant vessel: Taken on shore - When received: 29 Jan 1814 - From what ship or whence received: Montreal by land carriages. - Prisoner: 1257 - Rank: Private - Name of Prize: Land forces - By what ship or how taken: Taken on shore - Discharged: 4 May 1814 - By what order: Returned to the United States - Source: List of American Prisoners of War discharged at Quebec - Name of prize ship: Land forces.

Reynolds, Gilbert   Prisoner: 1064 - Rank: Private - Name of Prize: Land forces - By what ship or how taken: Taken on shore - Discharged: 31 Oct 1813 - By what order: HMS Malabar Transport by order of his Excellency Sir George Prevost - Source: List of American Prisoners of War discharged at Quebec - Name of prize ship: Land forces.

Reynolds, John C.   Prisoner: 263 - Rank: Sergeant - Name of Prize: Land forces - By what ship or how taken: Taken on shore - Discharged: 26 Feb 1814 - By what order: Volunteered for the New Brunswick Fencibles - Source: List of American Prisoners of War discharged at Quebec - Name of prize ship: Land forces.

Reynolds, William   Prisoner: 1389 - Rank: Private - By what ship or how taken: Troops - Time when: 19 Dec 1813 - Place where: Fort Niagara - Whether man of war, privateer, or merchant vessel: Taken on shore - When received: 29 Jan 1814 - From what ship or whence received: Montreal by land carriages. - Prisoner: 1389 -

Rank: Private - Name of Prize: Land forces - By what ship or how taken: Taken on shore - Discharged: 4 May 1814 - By what order: Returned to the United States - Source: List of American Prisoners of War discharged at Quebec - Name of prize ship: Land forces.

Rhodes, Henry   Prisoner: 1894 - Rank: Private - Name of Prize: Land forces - By what ship or how taken: Taken on shore - Discharged: 8 Nov 1814 - By what order: George No. 515 by Sir George Prevost - Source: List of American Prisoners of War discharged at Quebec - Name of prize ship: Land forces.

Rice, John   Prisoner: 1269 - Rank: Private - By what ship or how taken: Troops - Time when: 19 Dec 1813 - Place where: Fort Niagara - Whether man of war, privateer, or merchant vessel: Taken on shore - When received: 29 Jan 1814 - From what ship or whence received: Montreal by land carriages. - Prisoner: 1269 - Rank: Private - Name of Prize: Land forces - By what ship or how taken: Taken on shore - Discharged: 4 May 1814 - By what order: Returned to the United States - Source: List of American Prisoners of War discharged at Quebec - Name of prize ship: Land forces.

Rice, Nathaniel (1)   Prisoner: 239 - Rank: Private - Name of Prize: Eagle - By what ship or how taken: Man of war - Discharged: 31 Oct 1813 - By what order: HMS Malabar Transport by order of his Excellency Sir George Prevost - Source: List of American Prisoners of War discharged at Quebec - Name of prize ship: Eagle.

Rice, Nathaniel (2)   Prisoner: 1861 - Rank: Private - Name of Prize: Land forces - By what ship or how taken: Taken on shore - Discharged: 8 Nov 1814 - By what order: George No. 515 by Sir George Prevost - Source: List of American Prisoners of War discharged at Quebec - Name of prize ship: Land forces.

Rice, Samuel   Prisoner: 190 - Rank: Private - Name of Prize: Growler - By what ship or how taken: Man of war - Discharged: 31 Oct 1813 - By what order: HMS Malabar Transport by order of his Excellency Sir George Prevost - Source: List of American Prisoners of War discharged at Quebec - Name of prize ship: Growler.

Richardson, Simeon   Prisoner: 236 - Rank: Private - Name of Prize: Growler - By what ship or how taken: Man of war - Discharged: 4 May 1814 - By what order: Returned to the United States - Source: List of American Prisoners of War discharged at Quebec - Name of prize ship: Growler.

Richards, Stephen   Prisoner: 1070 - Rank: Private - Name of Prize: Land forces - By what ship or how taken: Taken on shore - Discharged: 31 Oct 1813 - By what order: HMS Malabar Transport by order of his Excellency Sir George Prevost - Source: List of American Prisoners of War discharged at Quebec - Name of prize ship: Land forces.

Richardson, Jason   Prisoner: 1328 - Rank: Sergeant - By what ship or how taken: Troops - Time when: 19 Dec 1813 - Place where: Fort Niagara - Whether man of war, privateer, or merchant vessel: Taken on shore - When received: 29 Jan 1814 - From what ship or whence received: Montreal by land carriages. - Prisoner: 1328 - Rank: Sergeant - Name of Prize: Land forces - By what ship or how taken: Taken on shore - Discharged: 4 May 1814 - By what order: Returned to the United States - Source: List of American Prisoners of War discharged at Quebec - Name of prize ship: Land forces.

Richardson, John   Prisoner: 1054 - Rank: Private - Name of Prize: Growler - By what ship or how taken: Man of war - Discharged: 31 Oct 1813 - By what order: HMS Malabar Transport by order of his Excellency Sir George Prevost - Source: List of American Prisoners of War discharged at Quebec - Name of prize ship: Growler.

Richardson, William   Prisoner: 1280 - Rank: Private - By what ship or how taken: Troops - Time when: 19 Dec 1813 - Place where: Fort Niagara - Whether man of war, privateer, or merchant vessel: Taken on shore - When received: 29 Jan 1814 - From what ship or whence received: Montreal by land carriages. - Prisoner: 1280 - Rank: Private - Name of Prize: Land forces - By what ship or how taken: Taken on shore - Discharged: 4 May 1814 - By what order: Returned to the United States - Source: List of American Prisoners of War discharged at Quebec - Name of prize ship: Land forces.

Richie, Allen   Prisoner: 647 - Rank: Private - Name of Prize: Land forces - By what ship or how taken: Taken on shore - Discharged: 10 Aug 1813 - By what order: HMS Regulus by order of his Excellency Sir George Prevost - Source: List of American Prisoners of War discharged at Quebec - Name of prize ship: Land forces.

Ridden, John   Prisoner: 1675 - Rank: Seaman - Name of Prize: Taken in a gig (a ship's long boat) - By what ship or how taken: Man of war - Discharged: 7 Nov 1813 - By what order: HMS Freedom No. 582 by order of his Excellency Sir George Prevost - Source: List of American Prisoners of War discharged at Quebec - Name of prize ship: Taken in a gig (a ship's long boat).

Ridge, William   Prisoner: 1408 - Rank: Private - By what ship or how taken: Troops - Time when: 19 Dec 1813 - Place where: Fort Niagara - Whether man of war, privateer, or merchant vessel: Taken on shore - When received: 29 Jan 1814 - From what ship or whence received: Montreal by land carriages. - Prisoner: 1408 - Rank: Private - Name of Prize: Land forces - By what ship or how taken: Taken on shore - Discharged: 4 May 1814 - By what order: Returned to the United States - Source: List of American Prisoners of War

discharged at Quebec - Name of prize ship: Land forces.

Ridgen, James   Prisoner: 1199 - By what ship or how taken: Citizen - When received: 1 Dec 1813 - From what ship or whence received: Town goal. - Prisoner: 1199 - Rank: Private - Name of Prize: Came in from the American Lines - Discharged: 1 Dec 1813 - By what order: Town goal - Source: List of American Prisoners of War discharged at Quebec - Name of Price: Came in from the American Lines.

Riley, Pursey   Prisoner: 1855 - Rank: Private - Name of Prize: Land forces - By what ship or how taken: Taken on shore - Discharged: 8 Nov 1814 - By what order: George No. 515 by Sir George Prevost - Source: List of American Prisoners of War discharged at Quebec - Name of prize ship: Land forces.

Robb, James   Prisoner: 1881 - Rank: Private - Name of Prize: Land forces - By what ship or how taken: Taken on shore - Discharged: 8 Nov 1814 - By what order: George No. 515 by Sir George Prevost - Source: List of American Prisoners of War discharged at Quebec - Name of prize ship: Land forces.

Robb, Samuel   Prisoner: 392 - Rank: Private - Name of Prize: Land forces - By what ship or how taken: Taken on shore - Discharged: 31 Oct 1813 - By what order: HMS Malabar Transport by order of his Excellency Sir George Prevost - Source: List of American Prisoners of War discharged at Quebec - Name of prize ship: Land forces.

Roberts, Aaron   Prisoner: 1399 - Rank: Sergeant - By what ship or how taken: Troops - Time when: 19 Dec 1813 - Place where: Fort Niagara - Whether man of war, privateer, or merchant vessel: Taken on shore - When received: 29 Jan 1814 - From what ship or whence received: Montreal by land carriages.

Roberts, Aaron   Prisoner: 1399 - Rank: Sergeant - Name of Prize: Land forces - By what ship or how taken: Taken on shore - Discharged: 4 May 1814 - By what order: Returned to the United States - Source: List of American Prisoners of War discharged at Quebec - Name of prize ship: Land forces.

Roberts, Henry   Prisoner: 512 - Rank: Private - Name of Prize: Land forces - By what ship or how taken: Taken on shore - Discharged: 10 Aug 1813 - By what order: HMS Regulus by order of his Excellency Sir George Prevost - Source: List of American Prisoners of War discharged at Quebec - Name of prize ship: Land forces.

Roberts, Joel   Prisoner: 1025 - Rank: Seaman - Name of Prize: Growler - By what ship or how taken: Man of war - Discharged: 1 Nov 1813 - By what order: HMS Hero by order of his Excellency Sir George Prevost - Source: List of American prisoners sent to England on the HMS Hero - Name of prize ship: Growler.

Roberts, John   Prisoner: 1509 - Rank: Captain - Name of Prize: Land forces - By what ship or how taken: Taken on shore - Discharged: 10 Nov 1814 - By what order: Stately No. 400 to Halifax by order of Sir George Prevost - Source: List of American Prisoners of War discharged at Quebec - Name of prize ship: Land forces.

Roberts, William   Prisoner: 719 - Rank: Private - Name of Prize: Land forces - By what ship or how taken: Taken on shore - Discharged: 10 Aug 1813 - By what order: HMS Regulus by order of his Excellency Sir George Prevost - Source: List of American Prisoners of War discharged at Quebec - Name of prize ship: Land forces.

Robins, Joram (alias Roberts)   Prisoner: 812 - Rank: Drummer - Name of Prize: Land forces - By what ship or how taken: Taken on shore - Discharged: 31 Oct 1813 - By what order: HMS Malabar Transport by order of his Excellency Sir George Prevost - Source: List of American Prisoners of War discharged at Quebec - Name of prize ship: Land forces.

Robinson, Daniel   Prisoner: 680 - Rank: Private - Name of Prize: Land forces - By what ship or how taken: Taken on shore - Discharged: 10 Aug 1813 - By what order: HMS Regulus by order of his Excellency Sir George Prevost - Source: List of American Prisoners of War discharged at Quebec - Name of prize ship: Land forces.

Robinson, James   Prisoner: 1273 - Rank: Private - By what ship or how taken: Troops - Time when: 19 Dec 1813 - Place where: Fort Niagara - Whether man of war, privateer, or merchant vessel: Taken on shore - When received: 29 Jan 1814 - From what ship or whence received: Montreal by land carriages. - Prisoner: 1273 - Rank: Private - Name of Prize: Land forces - By what ship or how taken: Taken on shore - Discharged: 26 Feb 1814 - By what order: Volunteered for the New Brunswick Fencibles - Source: List of American Prisoners of War discharged at Quebec - Name of prize ship: Land forces.

Roderick, John   Prisoner: 1743 - Rank: Seaman - Name of Prize: Tigress - By what ship or how taken: Man of war - Discharged: 7 Nov 1813 - By what order: HMS Freedom No. 582 by order of his Excellency Sir George Prevost - Source: List of American Prisoners of War discharged at Quebec - Name of prize ship: Tigress.

Rodgers, George   Prisoner: 694 - Rank: Private - Name of Prize: Land forces - By what ship or how taken: Taken on shore - Discharged: 10 Aug 1813 - By what order: HMS Regulus by order of his Excellency Sir George Prevost - Source: List of American Prisoners of War discharged at Quebec - Name of prize ship: Land forces.

Rogers, Clement S.   Prisoner: 1569 - Rank: Midshipman - Name of Prize: Somers - By what ship or how taken: Man of war - Discharged: 10 Nov 1814 - By what order: Lord Cathcart No. 161 for Halifax by order of Sir George Prevost - Source: List of American Prisoners of War discharged at Quebec - Name of prize ship: Somers.

Rogers, Robert Prisoner: 1330 - Rank: Private - By what ship or how taken: Troops - Time when: 19 Dec 1813 - Place where: Fort Niagara - Whether man of war, privateer, or merchant vessel: Taken on shore - When received: 29 Jan 1814 - From what ship or whence received: Montreal by land carriages. - Prisoner: 1330 - Rank: Private - Name of Prize: Land forces - By what ship or how taken: Taken on shore - Discharged: 4 May 1814 - By what order: Returned to the United States - Source: List of American Prisoners of War discharged at Quebec - Name of prize ship: Land forces.

Rogers, Harrison G. Prisoner: 543 - Rank: QM Sgt - Name of Prize: Land forces - By what ship or how taken: Taken on shore - Discharged: 10 Aug 1813 - By what order: HMS Regulus by order of his Excellency Sir George Prevost - Source: List of American Prisoners of War discharged at Quebec - Name of prize ship: Land forces.

Roles, Rezin Prisoner: 426 - Rank: Private - Name of Prize: Land forces - By what ship or how taken: Taken on shore - Discharged: 31 Oct 1813 - By what order: HMS Malabar Transport by order of his Excellency Sir George Prevost - Source: List of American Prisoners of War discharged at Quebec - Name of prize ship: Land forces.

Rollins, Thomas Prisoner: 628 - Rank: Private - Name of Prize: Land forces - By what ship or how taken: Taken on shore - Discharged: 4 May 1814 - By what order: Returned to the United States - Source: List of American Prisoners of War discharged eagle at Quebec - Name of prize ship: Land forces.

Root, A. L. Prisoner: 1783 - Rank: Private - Name of Prize: Land forces - By what ship or how taken: Taken on shore - Discharged: 8 Nov 1814 - By what order: George No. 515 by Sir George Prevost - Source: List of American Prisoners of War discharged at Quebec - Name of prize ship: Land forces.

Root, John Prisoner: 427 - Rank: Private - Source: Account of American prisoners of war who died at Quebec in the Months of July, August & September 1813 - Ship or Corps: Land forces - Vessel: Taken on shore - Place born: Vermont - Age: 25 - Where taken: Beaver Dams - Date of death: 23 Aug 1813.

Rose, John Prisoner: 514 - Rank: Private - Name of Prize: Land forces - By what ship or how taken: Taken on shore - Discharged: 31 Oct 1813 - By what order: HMS Malabar Transport by order of his Excellency Sir George Prevost - Source: List of American Prisoners of War discharged at Quebec - Name of prize ship: Land forces.

Rose, Nathaniel Prisoner: 453 - Rank: Private - Name of Prize: Land forces - By what ship or how taken: Taken on shore - Discharged: 10 Aug 1813 - By what order: HMS Regulus by order of his Excellency Sir George Prevost - Source: List of American Prisoners of War discharged at Quebec - Name of prize ship: Land forces.

Ross, David Prisoner: 620 - Rank: Private - Name of Prize: Land forces - By what ship or how taken: Taken on shore - Discharged: 10 Aug 1813 - By what order: HMS Regulus by order of his Excellency Sir George Prevost - Source: List of American Prisoners of War discharged at Quebec - Name of prize ship: Land forces.

Ross, Ely H. Prisoner: 1803 - Rank: Private - Name of Prize: Land forces - By what ship or how taken: Taken on shore - Discharged: 8 Nov 1814 - By what order: George No. 515 by Sir George Prevost - Source: List of American Prisoners of War discharged at Quebec - Name of prize ship: Land forces.

Ross, Balman Prisoner: 1777 - Rank: Private - Name of Prize: Land forces - By what ship or how taken: Taken on shore - Discharged: 8 Nov 1814 - By what order: George No. 515 by Sir George Prevost - Source: List of American Prisoners of War discharged at Quebec - Name of prize ship: Land forces.

Rothworth, John Prisoner: 1693 - Rank: Private - Name of Prize: Land forces - By what ship or how taken: Taken on shore - Discharged: 8 Nov 1814 - By what order: George No. 515 by Sir George Prevost - Source: List of American Prisoners of War discharged at Quebec - Name of prize ship: Land forces.

Round, Rubin Prisoner: 493 - Rank: Private - Name of Prize: Land forces - By what ship or how taken: Taken on shore - Discharged: 10 Aug 1813 - By what order: HMS Regulus by order of his Excellency Sir George Prevost - Source: List of American Prisoners of War discharged at Quebec - Name of prize ship: Land forces.

Rowe, Benjamin (1) Prisoner: 100 - Rank: Private - Name of Prize: Land forces - By what ship or how taken: Taken on shore - Discharged: 31 Oct 1813 - By what order: HMS Malabar Transport by order of his Excellency Sir George Prevost - Source: List of American Prisoners of War discharged at Quebec - Name of prize ship: Land forces.

Rowe, Benjamin (2) Prisoner: 197 - Rank: Private - Name of Prize: Growler - By what ship or how taken: Man of war - Discharged: 4 May 1814 - By what order: Returned to the United States - Source: List of American Prisoners of War discharged at Quebec - Name of prize ship: Growler. - Prisoner: 197 - Rank: Private - Source: Account of American prisoners of war who died at Quebec in the Months of July, August & September 1813 - Ship or Corps: Eagle - Vessel: Man of war - Place born: Elimmorton, NH - Age: 18 - Where taken: Lake Champlain - Date of death: 14 Aug 1813.

Rowe, Jonathan Prisoner: 20 - Rank: Private - Name of Prize: Land forces - By what ship or how taken: Taken on

shore - Discharged: 31 Oct 1813 - By what order: HMS Malabar Transport by order of his Excellency Sir George Prevost - Source: List of American Prisoners of War discharged at Quebec - Name of prize ship: Land forces.

Rowe, Michael   Prisoner: 373 - Rank: Private - Name of Prize: Land forces - By what ship or how taken: Taken on shore - Discharged: 31 Oct 1813 - By what order: HMS Malabar Transport by order of his Excellency Sir George Prevost - Source: List of American Prisoners of War discharged at Quebec - Name of prize ship: Land forces.

Rowe, William   Prisoner: 1727 - Rank: Seaman - Name of Prize: Scorpion - By what ship or how taken: Man of war - Discharged: 7 Nov 1813 - By what order: HMS Freedom No. 582 by order of his Excellency Sir George Prevost - Source: List of American Prisoners of War discharged at Quebec - Name of prize ship: Scorpion.

Rowland, Alexander   Prisoner: 1114 - Rank: QM Sergeant - Name of Prize: Land forces - By what ship or how taken: Taken on shore - Discharged: 31 Oct 1813 - By what order: HMS Malabar Transport by order of his Excellency Sir George Prevost - Source: List of American Prisoners of War discharged at Quebec - Name of prize ship: Land forces.

Rowley, Charles   Prisoner: 1852 - Rank: Private - Name of Prize: Land forces - By what ship or how taken: Taken on shore - Discharged: 8 Nov 1814 - By what order: George No. 515 by Sir George Prevost - Source: List of American Prisoners of War discharged at Quebec - Name of prize ship: Land forces.

Rowley, Nathan   Prisoner: 629 - Rank: Private - Name of Prize: Land forces - By what ship or how taken: Taken on shore - Discharged: 10 Aug 1813 - By what order: HMS Regulus by order of his Excellency Sir George Prevost - Source: List of American Prisoners of War discharged at Quebec - Name of prize ship: Land forces.

Rowsey, Ralph   Prisoner: 1485 - Rank: Private - Name of Prize: Land forces - By what ship or how taken: Taken on shore - Discharged: 8 Nov 1814 - By what order: George No. 515 by Sir George Prevost - Source: List of American Prisoners of War discharged at Quebec - Name of prize ship: Land forces.

Runyan, Francis   Prisoner: 1163 - Rank: Corporal - By what ship or how taken: Troops - Time when: 5 May 1813 - Place where: Fort Meigs - Whether man of war, privateer, or merchant vessel: Taken on shore - When received: 25 Nov 1813 - From what ship or whence received: Town goal. - Prisoner: 1163 - Rank: Private - Name of Prize: Land forces - By what ship or how taken: Taken on shore - Discharged: 4 May 1814 - By what order: Returned to the United States - Source: List of American Prisoners of War discharged at Quebec - Name of prize ship: Land forces.

Runyan, Thomas   Prisoner: 1344 - Rank: Private - By what ship or how taken: Troops - Time when: 19 Dec 1813 - Place where: Fort Niagara - Whether man of war, privateer, or merchant vessel: Taken on shore - When received: 29 Jan 1814 - From what ship or whence received: Montreal by land carriages. - Prisoner: 1344 - Rank: Private - Name of Prize: Land forces - By what ship or how taken: Taken on shore - Discharged: 4 May 1814 - By what order: Returned to the United States - Source: List of American Prisoners of War discharged at Quebec - Name of prize ship: Land forces.

Russell, Benjamin   Prisoner: 1431 - Rank: Passenger - Name of Prize: Alfred - By what ship or how taken: Privateer - Discharged: 24 May 1813 - By what order: Mulgrave Transport No. 311 - Source: List of American Prisoners of War discharged at Quebec - Name of prize ship: Alfred. - Prisoner: 1431 - Rank: Able seaman - By what ship or how taken: Purveyor - Time when: 15 Feb 1814 - Place where: Brown Brook - Whether man of war, privateer, or merchant vessel: Privateer - When received: 24 May 1814 - From what ship or whence received: Mary Transport No. 368.

Rust, Richard H.   Prisoner: 1233 - Rank: Sergeant - By what ship or how taken: Troops - Time when: 19 Dec 1813 - Place where: Fort Niagara - Whether man of war, privateer, or merchant vessel: Taken on shore - When received: 29 Jan 1814 - From what ship or whence received: Montreal by land carriages. - Prisoner: 1233 - Rank: Sergeant - Name of Prize: Land forces - By what ship or how taken: Taken on shore - Discharged: 24 Feb 1814 - By what order: Volunteered for the New Brunswick Fencibles - Source: List of American Prisoners of War discharged at Quebec - Name of prize ship: Land forces.

Rutter, Thomas   Prisoner: 1665 - Rank: Sailing Master - Name of Prize: Scorpion - By what ship or how taken: Man of war - Discharged: 10 Nov 1814 - By what order: Lord Cathcart No. 161 for Halifax by order of Sir George Prevost - Source: List of American Prisoners of War discharged at Quebec - Name of prize ship: Scorpion.

Rutter, William   Prisoner: 1728 - Rank: Seaman - Name of Prize: Scorpion - By what ship or how taken: Man of war - Discharged: 7 Nov 1813 - By what order: HMS Freedom No. 582 by order of his Excellency Sir George Prevost - Source: List of American Prisoners of War discharged at Quebec - Name of prize ship: Scorpion.

Ryley, James   Prisoner: 1124 - Rank: Private - Name of Prize: Land forces - By what ship or how taken: Taken on shore - Discharged: 31 Oct 1813 - By what order: HMS Malabar Transport by order of his Excellency Sir George Prevost - Source: List of American Prisoners of War discharged at Quebec - Name of prize ship: Land forces.

Sage, Hartley   Prisoner: 1878 - Rank: Private - Name of Prize: Land forces - By what ship or how taken: Taken on shore - Discharged: 8 Nov 1814 - By what order: George No. 515 by Sir George Prevost - Source: List of American Prisoners of War discharged at Quebec - Name of prize ship: Land forces.

Sanborn, John L.   Prisoner: 179 - Rank: Sergeant - Source: Account of American prisoners of war who died at Quebec in the Months of July, August & September 1813 - Ship or Corps: Land forces - Vessel: Taken on shore - Place born: New Hampton, NH - Age: 22 - Where taken: Lake Champlain - Date of death: 23 Jul 1813.

Saunders, W. G.   Prisoner: 534 - Rank: Lieutenant - Name of Prize: Land forces - By what ship or how taken: Taken on shore - Discharged: 10 Aug 1813 - By what order: HMS Regulus by order of his Excellency Sir George Prevost - Source: List of American Prisoners of War discharged at Quebec - Name of prize ship: Land forces.

Sawyer, Charles W.   Prisoner: 1101 - Rank: Private - Name of Prize: Land forces - By what ship or how taken: Taken on shore - Discharged: 31 Oct 1813 - By what order: HMS Malabar Transport by order of his Excellency Sir George Prevost - Source: List of American Prisoners of War discharged at Quebec - Name of prize ship: Land forces.

Sawyer, Horace B.   Prisoner: 145 - Rank: Midshipman - Name of Prize: Eagle - By what ship or how taken: Man of war - Discharged: 10 Aug 1813 - By what order: HMS Regulus by order of his Excellency Sir George Prevost - Source: List of American Prisoners of War discharged at Quebec - Name of prize ship: Eagle.

Scerving, Joel   Prisoner: 1272 - Rank: Private - By what ship or how taken: Troops - Time when: 19 Dec 1813 - Place where: Fort Niagara - Whether man of war, privateer, or merchant vessel: Taken on shore - When received: 29 Jan 1814 - From what ship or whence received: Montreal by land carriages. - Prisoner: 1272 - Rank: Private - Name of Prize: Land forces - By what ship or how taken: Taken on shore - Discharged: 4 May 1814 - By what order: Returned to the United States - Source: List of American Prisoners of War discharged at Quebec - Name of prize ship: Land forces.

Schooley, William   Prisoner: 1084 - Rank: Private - Name of Prize: Land forces - By what ship or how taken: Taken on shore - Discharged: 31 Oct 1813 - By what order: HMS Malabar Transport by order of his Excellency Sir George Prevost - Source: List of American Prisoners of War discharged at Quebec - Name of prize ship: Land forces.

Schoolman, William   Prisoner: 715 - Rank: Private - Name of Prize: Land forces - By what ship or how taken: Taken on shore - Discharged: 10 Aug 1813 - By what order: HMS Regulus by order of his Excellency Sir George Prevost - Source: List of American Prisoners of War discharged at Quebec - Name of prize ship: Land forces.

Scisse, John   Prisoner: 1018 - Rank: Private - Name of Prize: Growler - By what ship or how taken: Man of war - Discharged: 31 Oct 1813 - By what order: HMS Malabar Transport by order of his Excellency Sir George Prevost - Source: List of American Prisoners of War discharged at Quebec - Name of prize ship: Growler.

Scisse, Thomas   Prisoner: 173 - Rank: Seaman - Name of Prize: Growler - By what ship or how taken: Man of war - Discharged: 31 Oct 1813 - By what order: HMS Malabar Transport by order of his Excellency Sir George Prevost - Source: List of American Prisoners of War discharged at Quebec - Name of prize ship: Growler.

Scott, Abraham   Prisoner: 125 - Rank: Private - Name of Prize: Land forces - By what ship or how taken: Taken on shore - Discharged: 31 Oct 1813 - By what order: HMS Malabar Transport by order of his Excellency Sir George Prevost - Source: List of American Prisoners of War discharged at Quebec - Name of prize ship: Land forces.

Scott, John   Prisoner: 480 - Rank: Private - Name of Prize: Land forces - By what ship or how taken: Taken on shore - Discharged: 10 Aug 1813 - By what order: HMS Regulus by order of his Excellency Sir George Prevost - Source: List of American Prisoners of War discharged at Quebec - Name of prize ship: Land forces.

Scott, Joseph M.   Prisoner: 1416 - Rank: Private - By what ship or how taken: Troops - Time when: 19 Dec 1813 - Place where: Fort Niagara - Whether man of war, privateer, or merchant vessel: Taken on shore - When received: 29 Jan 1814 - From what ship or whence received: Montreal by land carriages. - Prisoner: 1416 - Rank: Private - Name of Prize: Land forces - By what ship or how taken: Taken on shore - Discharged: 4 May 1814 - By what order: Returned to the United States - Source: List of American Prisoners of War discharged at Quebec - Name of prize ship: Land forces.

Scott, Silas   Prisoner: 982 - Rank: Private - Name of Prize: Land forces - By what ship or how taken: Taken on

shore - Discharged: 31 Oct 1813 - By what order: HMS Malabar Transport by order of his Excellency Sir George Prevost - Source: List of American Prisoners of War discharged at Quebec - Name of prize ship: Land forces.

Scott, Solomon   Prisoner: 389 - Rank: Private - Name of Prize: Land forces - By what ship or how taken: Taken on shore - Discharged: 4 May 1814 - By what order: Returned to the United States - Source: List of American Prisoners of War discharged at Quebec - Name of prize ship: Land forces.

Scott, William   Prisoner: 1190 - By what ship or how taken: Citizen - When received: 12 Dec 1813 - From what ship or whence received: Town goal. - Prisoner: 1190 - Rank: Private - Name of Prize: Land forces - By what ship or how taken: Taken on shore - Discharged: 4 May 1814 - By what order: Returned to the United States - Source: List of American Prisoners of War discharged at Quebec - Name of prize ship: Land forces.

Scott, William MD   Prisoner: 1186 - Rank: Doctor - By what ship or how taken: Troops - Time when: 5 May 1813 - Place where: Rapids - Whether man of war, privateer, or merchant vessel: Taken on shore - When received: 30 Nov 1813 - From what ship or whence received: Town goal. - Prisoner: 1186 - Rank: Doctor - Name of Prize: Taken in his own boat - Discharged: 31 Jan 1814 - By what order: Returned to the United States - Source: List of American Prisoners of War discharged at Quebec - Name of prize ship: Taken in his own boat.

Scrader, Anthony   Prisoner: 700 - Rank: Private - Name of Prize: Land forces - By what ship or how taken: Taken on shore - Discharged: 31 Oct 1813 - By what order: HMS Malabar Transport by order of his Excellency Sir George Prevost - Source: List of American Prisoners of War discharged at Quebec - Name of prize ship: Land forces.

Scruen, Richard   Prisoner: 545 - Rank: Private - Name of Prize: Land forces - By what ship or how taken: Taken on shore - Discharged: 10 Aug 1813 - By what order: HMS Regulus by order of his Excellency Sir George Prevost - Source: List of American Prisoners of War discharged at Quebec - Name of prize ship: Land forces.

Scudder, Stephen   Prisoner: 331 - Rank: Private - Name of Prize: Land forces - By what ship or how taken: Taken on shore - Discharged: 31 Oct 1813 - By what order: HMS Malabar Transport by order of his Excellency Sir George Prevost - Source: List of American Prisoners of War discharged at Quebec - Name of prize ship: Land forces.

Serviss, William G.   Prisoner: 1648 - Rank: Lieutenant - Name of Prize: Land forces - By what ship or how taken: Taken on shore - Discharged: 13 Mar 1815 - By what order: Returned to the United States - Source: List of American Prisoners of War discharged at Quebec - Name of prize ship: Land forces.

Shaddock, John   Prisoner: 120 - Rank: Private - Name of Prize: Land forces - By what ship or how taken: Taken on shore - Discharged: 31 Oct 1813 - By what order: HMS Malabar Transport by order of his Excellency Sir George Prevost - Source: List of American Prisoners of War discharged at Quebec - Name of prize ship: Land forces.

Shaffer, Valentine   Prisoner: 698 - Rank: Private - Name of Prize: Land forces - By what ship or how taken: Taken on shore - Discharged: 10 Aug 1813 - By what order: HMS Regulus by order of his Excellency Sir George Prevost - Source: List of American Prisoners of War discharged at Quebec - Name of prize ship: Land forces.

Sharp, Solomon   Prisoner: 192 - Rank: Private - Name of Prize: Growler - By what ship or how taken: Man of war - Discharged: 4 May 1814 - By what order: Returned to the United States - Source: List of American Prisoners of War discharged at Quebec - Name of prize ship: Growler.

Shasten, Jacob   Prisoner: 1216 - Rank: Private - By what ship or how taken: Troops - Time when: 19 Dec 1813 - Place where: Fort Niagara - Whether man of war, privateer, or merchant vessel: Taken on shore - When received: 28 Jan 1814 - From what ship or whence received: Montreal by land carriages. - Prisoner: 1216 - Rank: Private - Name of Prize: Land forces - By what ship or how taken: Taken on shore - Discharged: 6 May 1814 - By what order: Returned to the United States - Source: List of American Prisoners of War discharged at Quebec - Name of prize ship: Land forces.

Shaver, Frederick   Prisoner: 1983 - Rank: Citizen - Discharged: 13 Mar 1815 - By what order: Returned to the United States - Source: List of American Prisoners of War discharged at Quebec.

Shaver, George   Prisoner: 137 - Rank: Private - Source: Account of American prisoners of war who died at Quebec in the Months of July, August & September 1813 - Ship or Corps: Land forces - Vessel: Taken on shore - Place born: Canajoharie, NY - Age: 33 - Where taken: Stoney Point - Date of death: 26 Jul 1813.

Shell, Henry   Prisoner: 526 - Rank: Lieutenant - Name of Prize: Land forces - By what ship or how taken: Taken on shore - Discharged: 10 Aug 1813 - By what order: HMS Regulus by order of his Excellency Sir George Prevost - Source: List of American Prisoners of War discharged at Quebec - Name of prize ship: Land forces.

Shepheard, Christopher   Prisoner: 1826 - Rank: Private - Name of Prize: Land forces - By what ship or how taken: Taken on shore - Discharged: 8 Nov 1814 - By what order: George No. 515 by Sir George Prevost -

Source: List of American Prisoners of War discharged at Quebec - Name of prize ship: Land forces.

Shepheard, Samuel   Prisoner: 1170 - Rank: Private - By what ship or how taken: Troops - Time when: 5 May 1813 - Place where: Rapids - Whether man of war, privateer, or merchant vessel: Taken on shore - When received: 25 Nov 1813 - From what ship or whence received: Town goal. - Prisoner: 1170 - Rank: Private - Name of Prize: Land forces - By what ship or how taken: Taken on shore - Discharged: 4 May 1814 - By what order: Returned to the United States - Source: List of American Prisoners of War discharged at Quebec - Name of prize ship: Land forces.

Shoemaker, Henry   Prisoner: 1020 - Rank: Boatman - Name of Prize: Batteaux - By what ship or how taken: Man of war - Discharged: 31 Oct 1813 - By what order: HMS Malabar Transport by order of his Excellency Sir George Prevost - Source: List of American Prisoners of War discharged at Quebec - Name of prize ship: Batteaux.

Shups, David   Prisoner: 376 - Rank: Private - Name of Prize: Land forces - By what ship or how taken: Taken on shore - Discharged: 31 Oct 1813 - By what order: HMS Malabar Transport by order of his Excellency Sir George Prevost - Source: List of American Prisoners of War discharged at Quebec - Name of prize ship: Land forces.

Shute, John   Prisoner: 8 - Rank: Private - Name of Prize: Land forces - By what ship or how taken: Taken on shore - Discharged: 4 May 1814 - By what order: Returned to the United States - Source: List of American Prisoners of War discharged at Quebec - Name of prize ship: Land forces.

Shutt, Henry   Prisoner: 1390 - Rank: Corporal - By what ship or how taken: Troops - Time when: 19 Dec 1813 - Place where: Fort Niagara - Whether man of war, privateer, or merchant vessel: Taken on shore - When received: 29 Jan 1814 - From what ship or whence received: Montreal by land carriages. - Prisoner: 1390 - Rank: Corporal - Name of Prize: Land forces - By what ship or how taken: Taken on shore - Discharged: 4 May 1814 - By what order: Returned to the United States - Source: List of American Prisoners of War discharged at Quebec - Name of prize ship: Land forces.

Sias, Nathaniel   Prisoner: 1239 - Rank: Private - By what ship or how taken: Troops - Time when: 19 Dec 1813 - Place where: Fort Niagara - Whether man of war, privateer, or merchant vessel: Taken on shore - When received: 29 Jan 1814 - From what ship or whence received: Montreal by land carriages. - Prisoner: 1239 - Rank: Private - Name of Prize: Land forces - By what ship or how taken: Taken on shore - Discharged: 4 May 1814 - By what order: Returned to the United States - Source: List of American Prisoners of War discharged at Quebec - Name of prize ship: Land forces.

Sickles, James   Prisoner: 1871 - Rank: Private - Name of Prize: Land forces - By what ship or how taken: Taken on shore - Discharged: 8 Nov 1814 - By what order: George No. 515 by Sir George Prevost - Source: List of American Prisoners of War discharged at Quebec - Name of prize ship: Land forces.

Sickless, Michael   Prisoner: 555 - Rank: Private - Name of Prize: Land forces - By what ship or how taken: Taken on shore - Discharged: 10 Aug 1813 - By what order: HMS Regulus by order of his Excellency Sir George Prevost - Source: List of American Prisoners of War discharged at Quebec - Name of prize ship: Land forces.

Silence, Nicholas   Prisoner: 690 - Rank: Private - Name of Prize: Land forces - By what ship or how taken: Taken on shore - Discharged: 10 Aug 1813 - By what order: HMS Regulus by order of his Excellency Sir George Prevost - Source: List of American Prisoners of War discharged at Quebec - Name of prize ship: Land forces.

Simpson, Mark   Prisoner: 546 - Rank: Private - Name of Prize: Land forces - By what ship or how taken: Taken on shore - Discharged: 10 Aug 1813 - By what order: HMS Regulus by order of his Excellency Sir George Prevost - Source: List of American Prisoners of War discharged at Quebec - Name of prize ship: Land forces.

Sinclair, Jacob   Prisoner: 219 - Rank: Private - Source: Account of American prisoners of war who died at Quebec in the Months of July, August & September 1813 - Ship or Corps: Growler - Vessel: Man of war - Place born: Erey, MA - Age: 20 - Where taken: Lake Champlain - Date of death: 19 Sep 1813 - Disorder or casualty: Typhus fever.

Sloan, Ebenezer   Prisoner: 1193 - By what ship or how taken: Citizen - When received: 12 Dec 1813 - From what ship or whence received: Town goal. - Prisoner: 1193 - Rank: Private - Name of Prize: Land forces - By what ship or how taken: Taken on shore - Discharged: 4 May 1814 - By what order: Returned to the United States - Source: List of American Prisoners of War discharged at Quebec - Name of prize ship: Land forces.

Sly, Thomas   Prisoner: 711 - Rank: Private - Name of Prize: Land forces - By what ship or how taken: Taken on shore - Discharged: 10 Aug 1813 - By what order: HMS Regulus by order of his Excellency Sir George Prevost - Source: List of American Prisoners of War discharged at Quebec - Name of prize ship: Land forces.

Smelly, Thomas   Prisoner: 705 - Rank: Private - Name of Prize: Land forces - By what ship or how taken: Taken on shore - Discharged: 31 Oct 1813 - By what order: HMS Malabar Transport by order of his Excellency Sir George Prevost - Source: List of American Prisoners of War discharged at Quebec - Name of prize ship:

Land forces.

Smiles, Abraham Prisoner: 496 - Rank: Private - Name of Prize: Land forces - By what ship or how taken: Taken on shore - Discharged: 10 Aug 1813 - By what order: HMS Regulus by order of his Excellency Sir George Prevost - Source: List of American Prisoners of War discharged at Quebec - Name of prize ship: Land forces.

Smiley, John Prisoner: 739 - Rank: Private - Name of Prize: Land forces - By what ship or how taken: Taken on shore - Discharged: 10 Aug 1813 - By what order: HMS Regulus by order of his Excellency Sir George Prevost - Source: List of American Prisoners of War discharged at Quebec - Name of prize ship: Land forces - Comments: British subject, sent to England.

Smith, Benjamin Prisoner: 747 - Rank: Private - Name of Prize: Land forces - By what ship or how taken: Taken on shore - Discharged: 31 Oct 1813 - By what order: HMS Malabar Transport by order of his Excellency Sir George Prevost - Source: List of American Prisoners of War discharged at Quebec - Name of prize ship: Land forces.

Smith, Cornelius Prisoner: 126 - Rank: Private - Name of Prize: Land forces - By what ship or how taken: Taken on shore - Discharged: 31 Oct 1813 - By what order: HMS Malabar Transport by order of his Excellency Sir George Prevost - Source: List of American Prisoners of War discharged at Quebec - Name of prize ship: Land forces.

Smith, Daniel Prisoner: 208 - Rank: Boy - Name of Prize: Eagle - By what ship or how taken: Man of war - Discharged: 31 Oct 1813 - By what order: HMS Malabar Transport by order of his Excellency Sir George Prevost - Source: List of American Prisoners of War discharged at Quebec - Name of prize ship: Eagle.

Smith, Elijah Prisoner: 272 - Rank: Private - Name of Prize: Land forces - By what ship or how taken: Taken on shore - Discharged: 31 Oct 1813 - By what order: HMS Malabar Transport by order of his Excellency Sir George Prevost - Source: List of American Prisoners of War discharged at Quebec - Name of prize ship: Land forces.

Smith, Frederick Prisoner: 1091 - Rank: Private - Name of Prize: Land forces - By what ship or how taken: Taken on shore - Discharged: 31 Oct 1813 - By what order: HMS Malabar Transport by order of his Excellency Sir George Prevost - Source: List of American Prisoners of War discharged at Quebec - Name of prize ship: Land forces.

Smith, Henry (1) Prisoner: 721 - Rank: Private - Name of Prize: Land forces - By what ship or how taken: Taken on shore - Discharged: 10 Aug 1813 - By what order: HMS Regulus by order of his Excellency Sir George Prevost - Source: List of American Prisoners of War discharged at Quebec - Name of prize ship: Land forces.

Smith, Henry (2) Prisoner: 1689 - Rank: Private - Name of Prize: Land forces - By what ship or how taken: Taken on shore - Discharged: 8 Nov 1814 - By what order: George No. 515 by Sir George Prevost - Source: List of American Prisoners of War discharged at Quebec - Name of prize ship: Land forces.

Smith, Ira Prisoner: 1683 - Rank: Private - Name of Prize: Land forces - By what ship or how taken: Taken on shore - Discharged: 8 Nov 1814 - By what order: George No. 515 by Sir George Prevost - Source: List of American Prisoners of War discharged at Quebec - Name of prize ship: Land forces.

Smith, Jacob Prisoner: 609 - Rank: Private - Name of Prize: Land forces - By what ship or how taken: Taken on shore - Discharged: 10 Aug 1813 - By what order: HMS Regulus by order of his Excellency Sir George Prevost - Source: List of American Prisoners of War discharged at Quebec - Name of prize ship: Land forces.

Smith, John (1) Prisoner: 740 - Rank: Private - Name of Prize: Land forces - By what ship or how taken: Taken on shore - Discharged: 10 Aug 1813 - By what order: HMS Regulus by order of his Excellency Sir George Prevost - Source: List of American Prisoners of War discharged at Quebec - Name of prize ship: Land forces - Comments: British subject, sent to England.

Smith, John (2) Prisoner: 1184 - Rank: Private - Source: Account of American prisoners of war who died at Quebec between 14 February 1814 and 23 December 1814 - Ship or Corps: Land forces - Vessel: Taken on shore - Place born: Massachusetts - Age: 44 - Where taken: Fort Niagara - Date of death: 28 Apr 1814 - Disorder or casualty: Hemoptysis.

Smith, John (3) Prisoner: 1421 - Rank: Private - By what ship or how taken: Troops - Time when: 19 Dec 1813 - Place where: Fort Niagara - Whether man of war, privateer, or merchant vessel: Taken on shore - When received: 29 Jan 1814 - From what ship or whence received: Montreal by land carriages. - Prisoner: 1421 - Rank: Private - Name of Prize: Land forces - By what ship or how taken: Taken on shore - Discharged: 4 May 1814 - By what order: Returned to the United States - Source: List of American Prisoners of War discharged at Quebec - Name of prize ship: Land forces.

Smith, John (4) Prisoner: 1912 - Rank: Private - Name of Prize: Land forces - By what ship or how taken: Taken on shore - Discharged: 8 Nov 1814 - By what order: George No. 515 by Sir George Prevost - Source: List of American Prisoners of War discharged at Quebec - Name of prize ship: Land forces.

Smith, John C. Prisoner: 1987 - Rank: Citizen - Discharged: 13 Mar 1815 - By what order: Returned to the United States - Source: List of American Prisoners of War discharged at Quebec.

Smith, Joseph Prisoner: 62 - Rank: Private - Name of Prize: Land forces - By what ship or how taken: Taken on shore - Discharged: 31 Oct 1813 - By what order: HMS Malabar Transport by order of his Excellency Sir George Prevost - Source: List of American Prisoners of War discharged at Quebec - Name of prize ship: Land forces.

Smith, Richard Prisoner: 98 - Rank: Private - Name of Prize: Land forces - By what ship or how taken: Taken on shore - Discharged: 31 Oct 1813 - By what order: HMS Malabar Transport by order of his Excellency Sir George Prevost - Source: List of American Prisoners of War discharged at Quebec - Name of prize ship: Land forces.

Smith, Stephen Prisoner: 36 - Rank: Private - Source: Account of American prisoners of war who died at Quebec in the Months of July, August & September 1813 - Ship or Corps: Land forces - Vessel: Taken on shore - Place born: Taunton, MA - Age: 27 - Where taken: Stoney Point - Date of death: 5 Sep 1813 - Disorder or casualty: Paralysis of typhus.

Smith, Thomas Prisoner: 1690 - Rank: Private - Name of Prize: Land forces - By what ship or how taken: Taken on shore - Discharged: 8 Nov 1814 - By what order: George No. 515 by Sir George Prevost - Source: List of American Prisoners of War discharged at Quebec - Name of prize ship: Land forces.

Smith, William (1) Prisoner: 500 - Rank: Private - Source: Account of American prisoners of war who died at Quebec in the Months of July, August & September 1813 - Ship or Corps: Land forces - Vessel: Taken on shore - Place born: Maryland - Age: 24 - Where taken: Beaver Dams - Date of death: 17 Jul 1813.

Smith, William (2) Prisoner: 1044 - Rank: Seaman - Name of Prize: Juliet - By what ship or how taken: Man of war - Discharged: 31 Oct 1813 - By what order: HMS Malabar Transport by order of his Excellency Sir George Prevost - Source: List of American Prisoners of War discharged at Quebec - Name of prize ship: Juliet.

Smith, William (3) Prisoner: 1862 - Rank: Private - Name of Prize: Land forces - By what ship or how taken: Taken on shore - Discharged: 8 Nov 1814 - By what order: George No. 515 by Sir George Prevost - Source: List of American Prisoners of War discharged at Quebec - Name of prize ship: Land forces.

Smith, William H. Prisoner: 1763 - Rank: Sergeant - Name of Prize: Land forces - By what ship or how taken: Taken on shore - Discharged: 8 Nov 1814 - By what order: George No. 515 by Sir George Prevost - Source: List of American Prisoners of War discharged at Quebec - Name of prize ship: Land forces.

Smith, William Henry Prisoner: 1283 - Rank: Sergeant - By what ship or how taken: Troops - Time when: 19 Dec 1813 - Place where: Fort Niagara - Whether man of war, privateer, or merchant vessel: Taken on shore - When received: 29 Jan 1814 - From what ship or whence received: Montreal by land carriages. - Prisoner: 1283 - Rank: Private - Name of Prize: Land forces - By what ship or how taken: Taken on shore - Discharged: 4 May 1814 - By what order: Returned to the United States - Source: List of American Prisoners of War discharged at Quebec - Name of prize ship: Land forces.

Snell, Shedrick Prisoner: 1691 - Rank: Musician - Name of Prize: Land forces - By what ship or how taken: Taken on shore - Discharged: 10 Nov 1814 - By what order: Sovereign No. 628 to Halifax by order of Sir George Prevost - Source: List of American Prisoners of War discharged at Quebec - Name of prize ship: Land forces.

Snow, Asa Prisoner: 667 - Rank: Private - Name of Prize: Land forces - By what ship or how taken: Taken on shore - Discharged: 10 Aug 1813 - By what order: HMS Regulus by order of his Excellency Sir George Prevost - Source: List of American Prisoners of War discharged at Quebec - Name of prize ship: Land forces.

Snyder, George Prisoner: 692 - Rank: Private - Name of Prize: Land forces - By what ship or how taken: Taken on shore - Discharged: 10 Aug 1813 - By what order: HMS Regulus by order of his Excellency Sir George Prevost - Source: List of American Prisoners of War discharged at Quebec - Name of prize ship: Land forces.

Southard, William Prisoner: 1377 - Rank: Private - By what ship or how taken: Troops - Time when: 19 Dec 1813 - Place where: Fort Niagara - Whether man of war, privateer, or merchant vessel: Taken on shore - When received: 29 Jan 1814 - From what ship or whence received: Montreal by land carriages. - Prisoner: 1377 - Rank: Private - Name of Prize: Land forces - By what ship or how taken: Taken on shore - Discharged: 4 May 1814 - By what order: Returned to the United States - Source: List of American Prisoners of War discharged at Quebec - Name of prize ship: Land forces.

Sowder, Jacob Prisoner: 682 - Rank: Private - Name of Prize: Land forces - By what ship or how taken: Taken on shore - Discharged: 10 Aug 1813 - By what order: HMS Regulus by order of his Excellency Sir George Prevost - Source: List of American Prisoners of War discharged at Quebec - Name of prize ship: Land forces.

Spalding, William Prisoner: 495 - Rank: Private - Name of Prize: Land forces - By what ship or how taken: Taken on shore - Discharged: 10 Aug 1813 - By what order: HMS Regulus by order of his Excellency Sir George

Prevost - Source: List of American Prisoners of War discharged at Quebec - Name of prize ship: Land forces.

Sparks, William   Prisoner: 1196 - By what ship or how taken: Citizen - When received: 12 Dec 1813 - From what ship or whence received: Town goal. - Prisoner: 1196 - Rank: Private - Name of Prize: Land forces - By what ship or how taken: Taken on shore - Discharged: 4 May 1814 - By what order: Returned to the United States - Source: List of American Prisoners of War discharged at Quebec - Name of prize ship: Land forces.

Spencer, Andrew   Prisoner: 99 - Rank: Private - Name of Prize: Land forces - By what ship or how taken: Taken on shore - Discharged: 31 Oct 1813 - By what order: HMS Malabar Transport by order of his Excellency Sir George Prevost - Source: List of American Prisoners of War discharged at Quebec - Name of prize ship: Land forces.

Spencer, Nathaniel   Prisoner: 306 - Rank: Private - Name of Prize: Land forces - By what ship or how taken: Taken on shore - Discharged: 31 Oct 1813 - By what order: HMS Malabar Transport by order of his Excellency Sir George Prevost - Source: List of American Prisoners of War discharged at Quebec - Name of prize ship: Land forces.

Sperry, Jacob   Prisoner: 189 - Rank: Private - Name of Prize: Eagle - By what ship or how taken: Man of war - Discharged: 31 Oct 1813 - By what order: HMS Malabar Transport by order of his Excellency Sir George Prevost - Source: List of American Prisoners of War discharged at Quebec - Name of prize ship: Eagle.

Spink, Anthony   Prisoner: 375 - Rank: Private - Name of Prize: Land forces - By what ship or how taken: Taken on shore - Discharged: 31 Oct 1813 - By what order: HMS Malabar Transport by order of his Excellency Sir George Prevost - Source: List of American Prisoners of War discharged at Quebec - Name of prize ship: Land forces.

Spurgeon, Nathaniel   Prisoner: 1762 - Rank: Private - Name of Prize: Scorpion - By what ship or how taken: Man of war - Discharged: 8 Nov 1814 - By what order: George No. 515 by Sir George Prevost - Source: List of American Prisoners of War discharged at Quebec - Name of prize ship: Scorpion.

Spurrier, Lott   Prisoner: 547 - Rank: Private - Name of Prize: Land forces - By what ship or how taken: Taken on shore - Discharged: 10 Aug 1813 - By what order: HMS Regulus by order of his Excellency Sir George Prevost - Source: List of American Prisoners of War discharged at Quebec - Name of prize ship: Land forces.

Stanbury, John   Prisoner: 1685 - Rank: Private - Name of Prize: Land forces - By what ship or how taken: Taken on shore - Discharged: 8 Nov 1814 - By what order: George No. 515 by Sir George Prevost - Source: List of American Prisoners of War discharged at Quebec - Name of prize ship: Land forces.

Stanford, Nathaniel   Prisoner: 1737 - Rank: Seaman - Name of Prize: Tigress - By what ship or how taken: Man of war - Discharged: 7 Nov 1813 - By what order: HMS Freedom No. 582 by order of his Excellency Sir George Prevost - Source: List of American Prisoners of War discharged at Quebec - Name of prize ship: Tigress.

Stanhope, Curtis L.   Prisoner: 267 - Rank: Private - Name of Prize: Land forces - By what ship or how taken: Taken on shore - Discharged: 31 Oct 1813 - By what order: HMS Malabar Transport by order of his Excellency Sir George Prevost - Source: List of American Prisoners of War discharged at Quebec - Name of prize ship: Land forces.

Stansbury, Samuel   Prisoner: 283 - Rank: Private - Name of Prize: Land forces - By what ship or how taken: Taken on shore - Discharged: 31 Oct 1813 - By what order: HMS Malabar Transport by order of his Excellency Sir George Prevost - Source: List of American Prisoners of War discharged at Quebec - Name of prize ship: Land forces.

Stanton, Phineas   Prisoner: 1507 - Rank: Major - Name of Prize: Land forces - By what ship or how taken: Taken on shore - Discharged: 14 Nov 1814 - By what order: Sovereign No. 628 to Halifax by order of Sir George Prevost - Source: List of American Prisoners of War discharged at Quebec - Name of prize ship: Land forces.

Steans, Nathan   Prisoner: 194 - Rank: Private - Name of Prize: Eagle - By what ship or how taken: Man of war - Discharged: 31 Oct 1813 - By what order: HMS Malabar Transport by order of his Excellency Sir George Prevost - Source: List of American Prisoners of War discharged at Quebec - Name of prize ship: Eagle.

Stephens, Samuel   Prisoner: 1749 - Rank: Private - Name of Prize: Scorpion - By what ship or how taken: Man of war - Discharged: 8 Nov 1814 - By what order: George No. 515 by Sir George Prevost - Source: List of American Prisoners of War discharged at Quebec - Name of prize ship: Scorpion.

Stevens, Jeptha (1)   Prisoner: 1357 - Rank: Private - By what ship or how taken: Troops - Time when: 19 Dec 1813 - Place where: Fort Niagara - Whether man of war, privateer, or merchant vessel: Taken on shore - When received: 29 Jan 1814 - From what ship or whence received: Montreal by land carriages. - Prisoner: 1357 - Rank: Private - Name of Prize: Land forces - By what ship or how taken: Taken on shore - Discharged: 4 May 1814 - By what order: Returned to the United States - Source: List of American Prisoners of War discharged at Quebec - Name of prize ship: Land forces.

Stevens, Jephta (2) Prisoner: 1959 - Rank: Private - Name of Prize: Land forces - By what ship or how taken: Taken on shore - Discharged: 13 Mar 1815 - By what order: Returned to the United States - Source: List of American Prisoners of War discharged at Quebec - Name of prize ship: Land forces.

Stevens, John Prisoner: 1930 - Rank: Private - Name of Prize: Land forces - By what ship or how taken: Taken on shore - Discharged: 13 Mar 1815 - By what order: Returned to the United States - Source: List of American Prisoners of War discharged at Quebec - Name of prize ship: Land forces.

Stevens, Josiah Prisoner: 1353 - Rank: Private - By what ship or how taken: Troops - Time when: 19 Dec 1813 - Place where: Fort Niagara - Whether man of war, privateer, or merchant vessel: Taken on shore - When received: 29 Jan 1814 - From what ship or whence received: Montreal by land carriages. - Prisoner: 1353 - Rank: Private - Name of Prize: Land forces - By what ship or how taken: Taken on shore - Discharged: 4 May 1814 - By what order: Returned to the United States - Source: List of American Prisoners of War discharged at Quebec - Name of prize ship: Land forces.

Stevens, William Prisoner: 66 - Rank: Private - Name of Prize: Land forces - By what ship or how taken: Taken on shore - Discharged: 31 Oct 1813 - By what order: HMS Malabar Transport by order of his Excellency Sir George Prevost - Source: List of American Prisoners of War discharged at Quebec - Name of prize ship: Land forces.

Stewart, James (1) Prisoner: 1201 - Rank: Lieutenant - By what ship or how taken: Troops - Time when: 19 Dec 1813 - Place where: Fort Niagara - Whether man of war, privateer, or merchant vessel: Taken on shore - When received: 18 Jan 1814 - From what ship or whence received: Montreal by land carriages. - Prisoner: 1201 - Rank: Lieutenant - Name of Prize: Land forces - By what ship or how taken: Taken on shore - Discharged: 4 May 1814 - By what order: Returned to the United States - Source: List of American Prisoners of War discharged at Quebec - Name of prize ship: Land forces.

Stewart, James (2) Prisoner: 1185 - Rank: Ensign - By what ship or how taken: Troops - Time when: 5 May 1813 - Place where: Rapids - Whether man of war, privateer, or merchant vessel: Taken on shore - When received: 9 Nov 1813 - From what ship or whence received: Town goal. - Prisoner: 1185 - Rank: Ensign - Name of Prize: Land forces - By what ship or how taken: Taken on shore - Discharged: 6 May 1814 - By what order: Returned to the United States - Source: List of American Prisoners of War discharged at Quebec - Name of prize ship: Land forces.

Stickney, Abijah Prisoner: 1418 - Rank: Private - By what ship or how taken: Troops - Time when: 19 Dec 1813 - Place where: Fort Niagara - Whether man of war, privateer, or merchant vessel: Taken on shore - When received: 29 Jan 1814 - From what ship or whence received: Montreal by land carriages. - Prisoner: 1418 - Rank: Private - Name of Prize: Land forces - By what ship or how taken: Taken on shore - Discharged: 4 May 1814 - By what order: Returned to the United States - Source: List of American Prisoners of War discharged at Quebec - Name of prize ship: Land forces.

Stiles, William Prisoner: 367 - Rank: Private - Name of Prize: Land forces - By what ship or how taken: Taken on shore - Discharged: 31 Oct 1813 - By what order: HMS Malabar Transport by order of his Excellency Sir George Prevost - Source: List of American Prisoners of War discharged at Quebec - Name of prize ship: Land forces.

Stoddard, Whitman Prisoner: 1805 - Rank: Private - Name of Prize: Land forces - By what ship or how taken: Taken on shore - Discharged: 8 Nov 1814 - By what order: George No. 515 by Sir George Prevost - Source: List of American Prisoners of War discharged at Quebec - Name of prize ship: Land forces.

Stone, Stephen Prisoner: 1279 - Rank: Private - By what ship or how taken: Troops - Time when: 19 Dec 1813 - Place where: Fort Niagara - Whether man of war, privateer, or merchant vessel: Taken on shore - When received: 29 Jan 1814 - From what ship or whence received: Montreal by land carriages. - Prisoner: 1279 - Rank: Private - Name of Prize: Land forces - By what ship or how taken: Taken on shore - Discharged: 4 May 1814 - By what order: Returned to the United States - Source: List of American Prisoners of War discharged at Quebec - Name of prize ship: Land forces.

Stonner, Henry Prisoner: 1303 - Rank: Private - By what ship or how taken: Troops - Time when: 19 Dec 1813 - Place where: Fort Niagara - Whether man of war, privateer, or merchant vessel: Taken on shore - When received: 29 Jan 1814 - From what ship or whence received: Montreal by land carriages. - Prisoner: 1303 - Rank: Private - Name of Prize: Land forces - By what ship or how taken: Taken on shore - Discharged: 24 Feb 1814 - By what order: Volunteered for the New Brunswick Fencibles - Source: List of American Prisoners of War discharged at Quebec - Name of prize ship: Land forces.

Storey, Pliny Prisoner: 269 - Rank: Private - Name of Prize: Land forces - By what ship or how taken: Taken on shore - Discharged: 31 Oct 1813 - By what order: HMS Malabar Transport by order of his Excellency Sir George Prevost - Source: List of American Prisoners of War discharged at Quebec - Name of prize ship:

Land forces.

Stout, John Prisoner: 1870 - Rank: Private - Name of Prize: Land forces - By what ship or how taken: Taken on shore - Discharged: 8 Nov 1814 - By what order: George No. 515 by Sir George Prevost - Source: List of American Prisoners of War discharged at Quebec - Name of prize ship: Land forces.

Street, Ishmael Prisoner: 422 - Rank: Corporal - Name of Prize: Land forces - By what ship or how taken: Taken on shore - Discharged: 31 Oct 1813 - By what order: HMS Malabar Transport by order of his Excellency Sir George Prevost - Source: List of American Prisoners of War discharged at Quebec - Name of prize ship: Land forces.

Strickland, Richard Prisoner: 980 - Rank: Private - Name of Prize: Land forces - By what ship or how taken: Taken on shore - Discharged: 31 Oct 1813 - By what order: HMS Malabar Transport by order of his Excellency Sir George Prevost - Source: List of American Prisoners of War discharged at Quebec - Name of prize ship: Land forces.

Stroud, John Prisoner: 428 - Rank: Private - Name of Prize: Land forces - By what ship or how taken: Taken on shore - Discharged: 10 Aug 1813 - By what order: HMS Regulus by order of his Excellency Sir George Prevost - Source: List of American Prisoners of War discharged at Quebec - Name of prize ship: Land forces.

Stuart, David Prisoner: 591 - Rank: Private - Name of Prize: Land forces - By what ship or how taken: Taken on shore - Discharged: 10 Aug 1813 - By what order: HMS Regulus by order of his Excellency Sir George Prevost - Source: List of American Prisoners of War discharged at Quebec - Name of prize ship: Land forces.

Sullivan, David Prisoner: 1331 - Rank: Private - By what ship or how taken: Troops - Time when: 19 Dec 1813 - Place where: Fort Niagara - Whether man of war, privateer, or merchant vessel: Taken on shore - When received: 29 Jan 1814 - From what ship or whence received: Montreal by land carriages. - Prisoner: 1331 - Rank: Private - Name of Prize: Land forces - By what ship or how taken: Taken on shore - Discharged: 4 May 1814 - By what order: Returned to the United States - Source: List of American Prisoners of War discharged at Quebec - Name of prize ship: Land forces.

Summers, William Prisoner: 270 - Rank: Private - Name of Prize: Land forces - By what ship or how taken: Taken on shore - Discharged: 4 May 1814 - By what order: Returned to the United States - Source: List of American Prisoners of War discharged at Quebec - Name of prize ship: Land forces.

Swan, Samuel Prisoner: 515 - Rank: Private - Name of Prize: Land forces - By what ship or how taken: Taken on shore - Discharged: 10 Aug 1813 - By what order: HMS Regulus by order of his Excellency Sir George Prevost - Source: List of American Prisoners of War discharged at Quebec - Name of prize ship: Land forces.

Swartwout, Augustus Prisoner: 1708 - Rank: Midshipman - By what ship or how taken: Man of war - Discharged: 10 Nov 1814 - By what order: Lord Cathcart No. 161 for Halifax by order of Sir George Prevost - Source: List of American Prisoners of War discharged at Quebec.

Sydston, Roby Prisoner: 1597 - Rank: Private - Name of Prize: Land forces - By what ship or how taken: Taken on shore - Discharged: 8 Nov 1814 - By what order: George No. 515 by Sir George Prevost - Source: List of American Prisoners of War discharged at Quebec - Name of prize ship: Land forces.

Taggert, Thomas Prisoner: 1863 - Rank: Corporal - Name of Prize: Land forces - By what ship or how taken: Taken on shore - Discharged: 8 Nov 1814 - By what order: George No. 515 by Sir George Prevost - Source: List of American Prisoners of War discharged at Quebec - Name of prize ship: Land forces.

Talbott, Benjamin Prisoner: 605 - Rank: Private - Name of Prize: Land forces - By what ship or how taken: Taken on shore - Discharged: 10 Aug 1813 - By what order: HMS Regulus by order of his Excellency Sir George Prevost - Source: List of American Prisoners of War discharged at Quebec - Name of prize ship: Land forces.

Talbott, Elijah Prisoner: 488 - Rank: Private - Name of Prize: Land forces - By what ship or how taken: Taken on shore - Discharged: 10 Aug 1813 - By what order: HMS Regulus by order of his Excellency Sir George Prevost - Source: List of American Prisoners of War discharged at Quebec - Name of prize ship: Land forces.

Talbott, John H. Prisoner: 487 - Rank: Private - Name of Prize: Land forces - By what ship or how taken: Taken on shore - Discharged: 10 Aug 1813 - By what order: HMS Regulus by order of his Excellency Sir George Prevost - Source: List of American Prisoners of War discharged at Quebec - Name of prize ship: Land forces.

Talishan, Mathew Prisoner: 1927 - Rank: Private - Name of Prize: Land forces - By what ship or how taken: Taken on shore - Discharged: 10 Nov 1814 - By what order: Stately No. 400 to Halifax by order of Sir George Prevost - Source: List of American Prisoners of War discharged at Quebec - Name of prize ship: Land forces.

Tarrhill, Zem'h. Prisoner: 1407 - Rank: Private - By what ship or how taken: Troops - Time when: 19 Dec 1813 - Place where: Fort Niagara - Whether man of war, privateer, or merchant vessel: Taken on shore - When received: 29 Jan 1814 - From what ship or whence received: Montreal by land carriages. - Prisoner: 1407 - Rank: Private - Name of Prize: Land forces - By what ship or how taken: Taken on shore - Discharged: 4

May 1814 - By what order: Returned to the United States - Source: List of American Prisoners of War discharged at Quebec - Name of prize ship: Land forces.

Taylor, Isaac W. Prisoner: 1144 - Rank: Private - By what ship or how taken: Troops - Time when: 5 May 1813 - Place where: Rapids, River Raisin - Whether man of war, privateer, or merchant vessel: Taken on shore - When received: 25 Nov 1813 - From what ship or whence received: Town goal. - Prisoner: 1144 - Rank: Private - Name of Prize: Land forces - By what ship or how taken: Taken on shore - Discharged: 4 May 1814 - By what order: Returned to the United States - Source: List of American Prisoners of War discharged at Quebec - Name of prize ship: Land forces.

Taylor, John (1) Prisoner: 722 - Rank: Private - Name of Prize: Land forces - By what ship or how taken: Taken on shore - Discharged: 10 Aug 1813 - By what order: HMS Regulus by order of his Excellency Sir George Prevost - Source: List of American Prisoners of War discharged at Quebec - Name of prize ship: Land forces.

Taylor, John (2) Prisoner: 1039 - Rank: Seaman - Name of Prize: Growler - By what ship or how taken: Man of war - Discharged: 31 Oct 1813 - By what order: HMS Malabar Transport by order of his Excellency Sir George Prevost - Source: List of American Prisoners of War discharged at Quebec - Name of prize ship: Growler.

Taylor, Lewis L. Prisoner: 390 - Rank: Major - Name of Prize: Land forces - By what ship or how taken: Taken on shore - Discharged: 10 Aug 1813 - By what order: HMS Regulus by order of his Excellency Sir George Prevost - Source: List of American Prisoners of War discharged at Quebec - Name of prize ship: Land forces.

Taylor, Richard Prisoner: 425 - Rank: Private - Name of Prize: Land forces - By what ship or how taken: Taken on shore - Discharged: 4 May 1814 - By what order: Returned to the United States - Source: List of American Prisoners of War discharged at Quebec - Name of prize ship: Land forces.

Taylor, Samuel Prisoner: 1687 - Rank: Private - Name of Prize: Somers - By what ship or how taken: Man of war - Discharged: 8 Nov 1814 - By what order: George No. 515 by Sir George Prevost - Source: List of American Prisoners of War discharged at Quebec - Name of prize ship: Somers.

Taylor, Thomas (1) Prisoner: 216 - Rank: Private - Name of Prize: Eagle - By what ship or how taken: Man of war - Discharged: 31 Oct 1813 - By what order: HMS Malabar Transport by order of his Excellency Sir George Prevost - Source: List of American Prisoners of War discharged at Quebec - Name of prize ship: Eagle.

Taylor, Thomas (2) Prisoner: 1270 - Rank: Private - By what ship or how taken: Troops - Time when: 19 Dec 1813 - Place where: Fort Niagara - Whether man of war, privateer, or merchant vessel: Taken on shore - When received: 29 Jan 1814 - From what ship or whence received: Montreal by land carriages. - Prisoner: 1270 - Rank: Private - Name of Prize: Land forces - By what ship or how taken: Taken on shore - Discharged: 4 May 1814 - By what order: Returned to the United States - Source: List of American Prisoners of War discharged at Quebec - Name of prize ship: Land forces.

Taylor, William (1) Prisoner: 290 - Rank: Private - Name of Prize: Land forces - By what ship or how taken: Taken on shore - Discharged: 31 Oct 1813 - By what order: HMS Malabar Transport by order of his Excellency Sir George Prevost - Source: List of American Prisoners of War discharged at Quebec - Name of prize ship: Land forces.

Taylor, William (2) Prisoner: 1415 - Rank: Private - By what ship or how taken: Troops - Time when: 19 Dec 1813 - Place where: Fort Niagara - Whether man of war, privateer, or merchant vessel: Taken on shore - When received: 29 Jan 1814 - From what ship or whence received: Montreal by land carriages. - Prisoner: 1415 - Rank: Private - Name of Prize: Land forces - By what ship or how taken: Taken on shore - Discharged: 4 May 1814 - By what order: Returned to the United States - Source: List of American Prisoners of War discharged at Quebec - Name of prize ship: Land forces.

Temple, Loren Prisoner: 182 - Rank: Private - Name of Prize: Eagle - By what ship or how taken: Man of war - Discharged: 31 Oct 1813 - By what order: HMS Malabar Transport by order of his Excellency Sir George Prevost - Source: List of American Prisoners of War discharged at Quebec - Name of prize ship: Eagle.

Temple, William Prisoner: 1111 - Rank: Private - Name of Prize: Land forces - By what ship or how taken: Taken on shore - Discharged: 31 Oct 1813 - By what order: HMS Malabar Transport by order of his Excellency Sir George Prevost - Source: List of American Prisoners of War discharged at Quebec - Name of prize ship: Land forces.

Templin, John Prisoner: 1109 - Rank: Private - Name of Prize: Land forces - By what ship or how taken: Taken on shore - Discharged: 31 Oct 1813 - By what order: HMS Malabar Transport by order of his Excellency Sir George Prevost - Source: List of American Prisoners of War discharged at Quebec - Name of prize ship: Land forces.

Tenney, John Prisoner: 458 - Rank: Private - Name of Prize: Land forces - By what ship or how taken: Taken on

shore - Discharged: 10 Aug 1813 - By what order: HMS Regulus by order of his Excellency Sir George Prevost - Source: List of American Prisoners of War discharged at Quebec - Name of prize ship: Land forces.

Thead, Isaac Prisoner: 14 - Rank: Private - Name of Prize: Land forces - By what ship or how taken: Taken on shore - Discharged: 31 Oct 1813 - By what order: HMS Malabar Transport by order of his Excellency Sir George Prevost - Source: List of American Prisoners of War discharged at Quebec - Name of prize ship: Land forces.

Thebben, David Prisoner: 1314 - Rank: Private - By what ship or how taken: Troops - Time when: 19 Dec 1813 - Place where: Fort Niagara - Whether man of war, privateer, or merchant vessel: Taken on shore - When received: 29 Jan 1814 - From what ship or whence received: Montreal by land carriages. - Prisoner: 1314 - Rank: Private - Name of Prize: Land forces - By what ship or how taken: Taken on shore - Discharged: 4 May 1814 - By what order: Returned to the United States - Source: List of American Prisoners of War discharged at Quebec - Name of prize ship: Land forces.

Thisselwood, Charles Prisoner: 570 - Rank: Private - Name of Prize: Land forces - By what ship or how taken: Taken on shore - Discharged: 10 Aug 1813 - By what order: HMS Regulus by order of his Excellency Sir George Prevost - Source: List of American Prisoners of War discharged at Quebec - Name of prize ship: Land forces.

Thomas, John Prisoner: 1678 - Rank: Seaman - Name of Prize: Jack - By what ship or how taken: Merchant Vessel - Discharged: 7 Nov 1813 - By what order: HMS Freedom No. 582 by order of his Excellency Sir George Prevost - Source: List of American Prisoners of War discharged at Quebec - Name of prize ship: Jack.

Thomas, Samuel Prisoner: 730 - Rank: Private - Name of Prize: Land forces - By what ship or how taken: Taken on shore - Discharged: 10 Aug 1813 - By what order: HMS Regulus by order of his Excellency Sir George Prevost - Source: List of American Prisoners of War discharged at Quebec - Name of prize ship: Land forces.

Thompson, John Prisoner: 1103 - Rank: Private - Name of Prize: Land forces - By what ship or how taken: Taken on shore - Discharged: 31 Oct 1813 - By what order: HMS Malabar Transport by order of his Excellency Sir George Prevost - Source: List of American Prisoners of War discharged at Quebec - Name of prize ship: Land forces.

Thompson, William Prisoner: 1810 - Rank: Private - Name of Prize: Land forces - By what ship or how taken: Taken on shore - Discharged: 8 Nov 1814 - By what order: George No. 515 by Sir George Prevost - Source: List of American Prisoners of War discharged at Quebec - Name of prize ship: Land forces.

Thompson, John J. Prisoner: 1153 - Rank: Private - Name of Prize: Land forces - By what ship or how taken: Taken on shore - Discharged: 4 May 1814 - By what order: Returned to the United States - Source: List of American Prisoners of War discharged at Quebec - Name of prize ship: Land forces. - Prisoner: 1153 - Rank: Private - By what ship or how taken: Troops - Time when: 5 May 1813 - Place where: Rapids, River Raisin - Whether man of war, privateer, or merchant vessel: Taken on shore - When received: 25 Nov 1813 - From what ship or whence received: Town goal.

Thorn, John Prisoner: 1779 - Rank: Private - Name of Prize: Land forces - By what ship or how taken: Taken on shore - Discharged: 8 Nov 1814 - By what order: George No. 515 by Sir George Prevost - Source: List of American Prisoners of War discharged at Quebec - Name of prize ship: Land forces.

Thorn, William Prisoner: 1935 - Rank: Sergeant - Name of Prize: Land forces - By what ship or how taken: Taken on shore - Discharged: 13 Mar 1815 - By what order: Returned to the United States - Source: List of American Prisoners of War discharged at Quebec - Name of prize ship: Land forces.

Thornbery, Christopher Prisoner: 1981 - Rank: Private - Name of Prize: Land forces - By what ship or how taken: Taken on shore - Discharged: 13 Mar 1815 - By what order: Returned to the United States - Source: List of American Prisoners of War discharged at Quebec - Name of prize ship: Land forces.

Thornburgh, John Prisoner: 1334 - Rank: Sergeant - By what ship or how taken: Troops - Time when: 19 Dec 1813 - Place where: Fort Niagara - Whether man of war, privateer, or merchant vessel: Taken on shore - When received: 29 Jan 1814 - From what ship or whence received: Montreal by land carriages. - Prisoner: 1334 - Rank: Sergeant - Name of Prize: Land forces - By what ship or how taken: Taken on shore - Discharged: 4 May 1814 - By what order: Returned to the United States - Source: List of American Prisoners of War discharged at Quebec - Name of prize ship: Land forces.

Thornton, William Prisoner: 1016 - Rank: Seaman - Name of Prize: Growler - By what ship or how taken: Man of war - Discharged: 1 Nov 1813 - By what order: HMS Hero by order of his Excellency Sir George Prevost - Source: List of American prisoners sent to England on the HMS Hero - Name of prize ship: Growler.

Thristy, Joel Prisoner: 718 - Rank: Private - Name of Prize: Land forces - By what ship or how taken: Taken on shore - Discharged: 10 Aug 1813 - By what order: HMS Regulus by order of his Excellency Sir George

Prevost - Source: List of American Prisoners of War discharged at Quebec - Name of prize ship: Land forces.

Thunderville, John   Prisoner: 723 - Rank: Private - Name of Prize: Land forces - By what ship or how taken: Taken on shore - Discharged: 10 Aug 1813 - By what order: HMS Regulus by order of his Excellency Sir George Prevost - Source: List of American Prisoners of War discharged at Quebec - Name of prize ship: Land forces.

Tilden, Lemuel   Prisoner: 1179 - Rank: Private - By what ship or how taken: Troops - Time when: 5 May 1813 - Place where: Rapids - Whether man of war, privateer, or merchant vessel: Taken on shore - When received: 25 Nov 1813 - From what ship or whence received: Town goal. - Prisoner: 1179 - Rank: Private - Name of Prize: Land forces - By what ship or how taken: Taken on shore - Discharged: 4 May 1814 - By what order: Returned to the United States - Source: List of American Prisoners of War discharged at Quebec - Name of prize ship: Land forces.

Till, James   Prisoner: 571 - Rank: Private - Source: Account of American prisoners of war who died at Quebec in the Months of July, August & September 1813 - Ship or Corps: Land forces - Vessel: Taken on shore - Place born: New Jersey - Age: 33 - Where taken: Beaver Dams - Date of death: 31 Aug 1813 - Disorder or casualty: Typhus fever.

Timson, Peter   Prisoner: 1768 - Rank: Corporal - Name of Prize: Land forces - By what ship or how taken: Taken on shore - Discharged: 8 Nov 1814 - By what order: George No. 515 by Sir George Prevost - Source: List of American Prisoners of War discharged at Quebec - Name of prize ship: Land forces.

Tinker, Clark   Prisoner: 668 - Rank: Private - Name of Prize: Land forces - By what ship or how taken: Taken on shore - Discharged: 10 Aug 1813 - By what order: HMS Regulus by order of his Excellency Sir George Prevost - Source: List of American Prisoners of War discharged at Quebec - Name of prize ship: Land forces.

Tinny, Samuel   Prisoner: 107 - Rank: Private - Name of Prize: Land forces - By what ship or how taken: Taken on shore - Discharged: 31 Oct 1813 - By what order: HMS Malabar Transport by order of his Excellency Sir George Prevost - Source: List of American Prisoners of War discharged at Quebec - Name of prize ship: Land forces.

Titus, George   Prisoner: 24 - Rank: Private - Name of Prize: Land forces - By what ship or how taken: Taken on shore - Discharged: 4 May 1814 - By what order: Returned to the United States - Source: List of American Prisoners of War discharged at Quebec - Name of prize ship: Land forces.

Todd, John   Prisoner: 511 - Rank: Private - Name of Prize: Land forces - By what ship or how taken: Taken on shore - Discharged: 10 Aug 1813 - By what order: HMS Regulus by order of his Excellency Sir George Prevost - Source: List of American Prisoners of War discharged at Quebec - Name of prize ship: Land forces - Comments: British subject, sent to England.

Tone, Christopher   Prisoner: 1230 - Rank: Private - By what ship or how taken: Troops - Time when: 19 Dec 1813 - Place where: Fort Niagara - Whether man of war, privateer, or merchant vessel: Taken on shore - When received: 29 Jan 1814 - From what ship or whence received: Montreal by land carriages. - Prisoner: 1230 - Rank: Private - Name of Prize: Land forces - By what ship or how taken: Taken on shore - Discharged: 4 May 1814 - By what order: Returned to the United States - Source: List of American Prisoners of War discharged at Quebec - Name of prize ship: Land forces.

Toney, Joseph   Prisoner: 1050 - Rank: Private - Name of Prize: Growler - By what ship or how taken: Man of war - Discharged: 4 May 1814 - By what order: Returned to the United States - Source: List of American Prisoners of War discharged at Quebec - Name of prize ship: Growler. - Prisoner: 1050 - Rank: Private - Name of Prize: Land forces - By what ship or how taken: Taken on shore - Discharged: 2 Nov 1813 - Source: List of Prisoners received on board the Malabar, discharged from hospital - Name of prize ship: Land forces.

Townsend, Jeremiah   Prisoner: 1851 - Rank: Private - Name of Prize: Land forces - By what ship or how taken: Taken on shore - Discharged: 10 Nov 1814 - By what order: Sovereign No. 628 to Halifax by order of Sir George Prevost - Source: List of American Prisoners of War discharged at Quebec - Name of prize ship: Land forces.

Tracey, William   Prisoner: 491 - Rank: Private - Name of Prize: Land forces - By what ship or how taken: Taken on shore - Discharged: 10 Aug 1813 - By what order: HMS Regulus by order of his Excellency Sir George Prevost - Source: List of American Prisoners of War discharged at Quebec - Name of prize ship: Land forces.

Traymour, James   Prisoner: 275 - Rank: Private - Name of Prize: Land forces - By what ship or how taken: Taken on shore - Discharged: 31 Oct 1813 - By what order: HMS Malabar Transport by order of his Excellency Sir George Prevost - Source: List of American Prisoners of War discharged at Quebec - Name of prize ship: Land forces.

Tree, Almond   Prisoner: 1077 - Rank: Private - Name of Prize: Land forces - By what ship or how taken: Taken on shore - Discharged: 31 Oct 1813 - By what order: HMS Malabar Transport by order of his Excellency Sir

George Prevost - Source: List of American Prisoners of War discharged at Quebec - Name of prize ship: Land forces.

Trezell, Jacob   Prisoner: 1102 - Rank: Private - Name of Prize: Land forces - By what ship or how taken: Taken on shore - Discharged: 31 Oct 1813 - By what order: HMS Malabar Transport by order of his Excellency Sir George Prevost - Source: List of American Prisoners of War discharged at Quebec - Name of prize ship: Land forces.

Trimble, Carey A.   Prisoner: 1425 - Rank: Lieutenant - By what ship or how taken: Troops - Time when: 19 Dec 1813 - Place where: Fort Niagara - Whether man of war, privateer, or merchant vessel: Taken on shore - When received: 29 Jan 1814 - From what ship or whence received: Montreal by land carriages. - Prisoner: 1425 - Rank: Lieutenant - Name of Prize: Land forces - By what ship or how taken: Taken on shore - Discharged: 6 May 1814 - By what order: Returned to the United States - Source: List of American Prisoners of War discharged at Quebec - Name of prize ship: Land forces.

Troop, James   Prisoner: 1220 - Rank: Private - Name of Prize: Land forces - By what ship or how taken: Taken on shore - Discharged: 4 May 1814 - By what order: Returned to the United States - Source: List of American Prisoners of War discharged at Quebec - Name of prize ship: Land forces. - Prisoner: 1220 - Rank: Private - By what ship or how taken: Troops - Time when: 19 Dec 1813 - Place where: Fort Niagara - Whether man of war, privateer, or merchant vessel: Taken on shore - When received: 29 Jan 1814 - From what ship or whence received: Montreal by land carriages.

Trott, Thomas   Prisoner: 461 - Rank: Sergeant - Name of Prize: Land forces - By what ship or how taken: Taken on shore - Discharged: 3 Apr 1814 - By what order: Returned to the United States - Source: List of American Prisoners of War discharged at Quebec - Name of prize ship: Land forces.

Truby, Samuel   Prisoner: 1980 - Rank: Private - Name of Prize: Land forces - By what ship or how taken: Taken on shore - Discharged: 13 Mar 1815 - By what order: Returned to the United States - Source: List of American Prisoners of War discharged at Quebec - Name of prize ship: Land forces.

Truebridge, J.   Prisoner: 581 - Rank: Private - Name of Prize: Land forces - By what ship or how taken: Taken on shore - Discharged: 10 Aug 1813 - By what order: HMS Regulus by order of his Excellency Sir George Prevost - Source: List of American Prisoners of War discharged at Quebec - Name of prize ship: Land forces.

Trumball, John   Prisoner: 146 - Rank: Master's Mate - Name of Prize: Eagle - By what ship or how taken: Man of war - Discharged: 6 May 1814 - By what order: Returned to the United States - Source: List of American Prisoners of War discharged at Quebec - Name of prize ship: Eagle.

Trusry, Joel   Prisoner: 1672 - Rank: Seaman - Name of Prize: Taken in a gig (a ship's long boat) - By what ship or how taken: Man of war - Discharged: 7 Nov 1813 - By what order: HMS Freedom No. 582 by order of his Excellency Sir George Prevost - Source: List of American Prisoners of War discharged at Quebec - Name of prize ship: Taken in a gig (a ship's long boat).

Tubbs, Samuel F.   Prisoner: 1839 - Rank: Private - Name of Prize: Land forces - By what ship or how taken: Taken on shore - Discharged: 8 Nov 1814 - By what order: George No. 515 by Sir George Prevost - Source: List of American Prisoners of War discharged at Quebec - Name of prize ship: Land forces.

Tucker, Benjamin   Prisoner: 468 - Rank: Private - Name of Prize: Land forces - By what ship or how taken: Taken on shore - Discharged: 10 Aug 1813 - By what order: HMS Regulus by order of his Excellency Sir George Prevost - Source: List of American Prisoners of War discharged at Quebec - Name of prize ship: Land forces.

Tucker, Joseph   Prisoner: 728 - Rank: Private - Name of Prize: Land forces - By what ship or how taken: Taken on shore - Discharged: 10 Aug 1813 - By what order: HMS Regulus by order of his Excellency Sir George Prevost - Source: List of American Prisoners of War discharged at Quebec - Name of prize ship: Land forces.

Tuffs, William   Prisoner: 382 - Rank: Private - Name of Prize: Land forces - By what ship or how taken: Taken on shore - Discharged: 31 Oct 1813 - By what order: HMS Malabar Transport by order of his Excellency Sir George Prevost - Source: List of American Prisoners of War discharged at Quebec - Name of prize ship: Land forces.

Tully, Thomas   Prisoner: 1113 - Rank: Private - Name of Prize: Land forces - By what ship or how taken: Taken on shore - Discharged: 31 Oct 1813 - By what order: HMS Malabar Transport by order of his Excellency Sir George Prevost - Source: List of American Prisoners of War discharged at Quebec - Name of prize ship: Land forces.

Turner, Daniel   Prisoner: 1664 - Rank: Lieutenant - Name of Prize: Scorpion - By what ship or how taken: Man of war - Discharged: 10 Nov 1814 - By what order: Lord Cathcart No. 161 for Halifax by order of Sir George Prevost - Source: List of American Prisoners of War discharged at Quebec - Name of prize ship: Scorpion. - Prisoner: 1664 - Rank: Lieutenant - Name of Prize: Scorpion - By what ship or how taken: Man of war - Discharged: 14 Nov 1814 - By what order: Sovereign No. 628 to Halifax by order of Sir George Prevost -

Source: List of American Prisoners of War discharged at Quebec - Name of prize ship: Scorpion.

Turner, Henry   Prisoner: 169 - Rank: Cook - Name of Prize: Growler - By what ship or how taken: Man of war - Discharged: 31 Oct 1813 - By what order: HMS Malabar Transport by order of his Excellency Sir George Prevost - Source: List of American Prisoners of War discharged at Quebec - Name of prize ship: Growler.

Turner, Isaac   Prisoner: 1384 - Rank: Private - By what ship or how taken: Troops - Time when: 19 Dec 1813 - Place where: Fort Niagara - Whether man of war, privateer, or merchant vessel: Taken on shore - When received: 29 Jan 1814 - From what ship or whence received: Montreal by land carriages. - Prisoner: 1384 - Rank: Private - Name of Prize: Land forces - By what ship or how taken: Taken on shore - Discharged: 4 May 1814 - By what order: Returned to the United States - Source: List of American Prisoners of War discharged at Quebec - Name of prize ship: Land forces.

Turner, John   Prisoner: 1135 - Rank: Private - By what ship or how taken: Troops - Time when: 5 May 1813 - Place where: Rapids, River Raisin - Whether man of war, privateer, or merchant vessel: Taken on shore - When received: 25 Nov 1813 - From what ship or whence received: Town goal. - Prisoner: 1135 - Rank: Private - Name of Prize: Land forces - By what ship or how taken: Taken on shore - Discharged: 4 May 1814 - By what order: Returned to the United States - Source: List of American Prisoners of War discharged at Quebec - Name of prize ship: Land forces.

Updegrass, Jesse   Prisoner: 552 - Rank: Corporal - Name of Prize: Land forces - By what ship or how taken: Taken on shore - Discharged: 10 Aug 1813 - By what order: HMS Regulus by order of his Excellency Sir George Prevost - Source: List of American Prisoners of War discharged at Quebec - Name of prize ship: Land forces.

Usher, Edward   Prisoner: 466 - Rank: Private - Name of Prize: Land forces - By what ship or how taken: Taken on shore - Discharged: 10 Aug 1813 - By what order: HMS Regulus by order of his Excellency Sir George Prevost - Source: List of American Prisoners of War discharged at Quebec - Name of prize ship: Land forces.

Vail, William W.   Prisoner: 1965 - Rank: Private - Name of Prize: Land forces - By what ship or how taken: Taken on shore - Discharged: 13 Mar 1815 - By what order: Returned to the United States - Source: List of American Prisoners of War discharged at Quebec - Name of prize ship: Land forces.

Valentine, Elisha   Prisoner: 1385 - Rank: Private - By what ship or how taken: Troops - Time when: 19 Dec 1813 - Place where: Fort Niagara - Whether man of war, privateer, or merchant vessel: Taken on shore - When received: 29 Jan 1814 - From what ship or whence received: Montreal by land carriages. - Prisoner: 1385 - Rank: Private - Name of Prize: Land forces - By what ship or how taken: Taken on shore - Discharged: 25 Feb 1814 - By what order: Volunteered for the New Brunswick Fencibles - Source: List of American Prisoners of War discharged at Quebec - Name of prize ship: Land forces.

Valient, William   Prisoner: 649 - Rank: Private - Name of Prize: Land forces - By what ship or how taken: Taken on shore - Discharged: 10 Aug 1813 - By what order: HMS Regulus by order of his Excellency Sir George Prevost - Source: List of American Prisoners of War discharged at Quebec - Name of prize ship: Land forces.

Van Bibber, Isaac   Prisoner: 689 - Rank: Private - Name of Prize: Land forces - By what ship or how taken: Taken on shore - Discharged: 10 Aug 1813 - By what order: HMS Regulus by order of his Excellency Sir George Prevost - Source: List of American Prisoners of War discharged at Quebec - Name of prize ship: Land forces.

Van Frankling, Isaac   Prisoner: 1846 - Rank: Private - Name of Prize: Land forces - By what ship or how taken: Taken on shore - Discharged: 8 Nov 1814 - By what order: George No. 515 by Sir George Prevost - Source: List of American Prisoners of War discharged at Quebec - Name of prize ship: Land forces.

Van Kerven, Abraham   Prisoner: 1807 - Rank: Citizen - Name of Prize: Land forces - By what ship or how taken: Taken on shore - Discharged: 8 Nov 1814 - By what order: George No. 515 by Sir George Prevost - Source: List of American Prisoners of War discharged at Quebec - Name of prize ship: Land forces.

Vanderhull, Samuel   Prisoner: 639 - Rank: Private - Name of Prize: Land forces - By what ship or how taken: Taken on shore - Discharged: 10 Aug 1813 - By what order: HMS Regulus by order of his Excellency Sir George Prevost - Source: List of American Prisoners of War discharged at Quebec - Name of prize ship: Land forces.

Vanhorn, James   Prisoner: 1149 - Rank: Private - By what ship or how taken: Troops - Time when: 5 May 1813 - Place where: Rapids, River Raisin - Whether man of war, privateer, or merchant vessel: Taken on shore - When received: 25 Nov 1813 - From what ship or whence received: Town goal. - Prisoner: 1149 - Rank: Private - Name of Prize: Land forces - By what ship or how taken: Taken on shore - Discharged: 4 May 1814 - By what order: Returned to the United States - Source: List of American Prisoners of War discharged at Quebec - Name of prize ship: Land forces.

Vanhouten, Garrett   Prisoner: 1877 - Rank: Private - Name of Prize: Land forces - By what ship or how taken: Taken on shore - Discharged: 8 Nov 1814 - By what order: George No. 515 by Sir George Prevost - Source: List of American Prisoners of War discharged at Quebec - Name of prize ship: Land forces.

American Prisoners of War held at Montreal and Quebec during the War of 1812

Vanseeker, Cornelius Prisoner: 1223 - Rank: Private - By what ship or how taken: Troops - Time when: 19 Dec 1813 - Place where: Fort Niagara - Whether man of war, privateer, or merchant vessel: Taken on shore - When received: 29 Jan 1814 - From what ship or whence received: Montreal by land carriages. - Prisoner: 1223 - Rank: Private - Name of Prize: Land forces - By what ship or how taken: Taken on shore - Discharged: 26 Feb 1814 - By what order: Volunteered for the New Brunswick Fencibles - Source: List of American Prisoners of War discharged at Quebec - Name of prize ship: Land forces.

Vanslyck, Cornelius A. Prisoner: 1166 - Rank: Private - By what ship or how taken: Troops - Time when: 5 May 1813 - Place where: Rapids - Whether man of war, privateer, or merchant vessel: Taken on shore - When received: 25 Nov 1813 - From what ship or whence received: Town goal. - Prisoner: 1166 - Rank: Private - Name of Prize: Land forces - By what ship or how taken: Taken on shore - Discharged: 4 May 1814 - By what order: Returned to the United States - Source: List of American Prisoners of War discharged at Quebec - Name of prize ship: Land forces.

Vinton, Ezekiel Prisoner: 957 - Rank: Private - Name of Prize: Land forces - By what ship or how taken: Taken on shore - Discharged: 31 Oct 1813 - By what order: HMS Malabar Transport by order of his Excellency Sir George Prevost - Source: List of American Prisoners of War discharged at Quebec - Name of prize ship: Land forces.

Virgin, Levit Prisoner: 101 - Rank: Private - Name of Prize: Land forces - By what ship or how taken: Taken on shore - Discharged: 31 Oct 1813 - By what order: HMS Malabar Transport by order of his Excellency Sir George Prevost - Source: List of American Prisoners of War discharged at Quebec - Name of prize ship: Land forces.

Voight, Thomas Prisoner: 1274 - Rank: Private - Name of Prize: Land forces - By what ship or how taken: Taken on shore - Discharged: 27 Feb 1814 - By what order: Volunteered for the New Brunswick Fencibles - Source: List of American Prisoners of War discharged at Quebec - Name of prize ship: Land forces. - Prisoner: 1274 - Rank: Private - By what ship or how taken: Troops - Time when: 19 Dec 1813 - Place where: Fort Niagara - Whether man of war, privateer, or merchant vessel: Taken on shore - When received: 29 Jan 1814 - From what ship or whence received: Montreal by land carriages.

Von, Samuel Prisoner: 314 - Rank: Private - Name of Prize: Land forces - By what ship or how taken: Taken on shore - Discharged: 31 Oct 1813 - By what order: HMS Malabar Transport by order of his Excellency Sir George Prevost - Source: List of American Prisoners of War discharged at Quebec - Name of prize ship: Land forces.

Wade, Melvin Prisoner: 27 - Rank: Private - Name of Prize: Land forces - By what ship or how taken: Taken on shore - Discharged: 31 Oct 1813 - By what order: HMS Malabar Transport by order of his Excellency Sir George Prevost - Source: List of American Prisoners of War discharged at Quebec - Name of prize ship: Land forces.

Wade, Nathan Prisoner: 1738 - Rank: Seaman - Name of Prize: Tigress - By what ship or how taken: Man of war - Discharged: 7 Nov 1813 - By what order: HMS Freedom No. 582 by order of his Excellency Sir George Prevost - Source: List of American Prisoners of War discharged at Quebec - Name of prize ship: Tigress.

Wager, Joseph Prisoner: 1814 - Rank: Private - Name of Prize: Land forces - By what ship or how taken: Taken on shore - Discharged: 8 Nov 1814 - By what order: George No. 515 by Sir George Prevost - Source: List of American Prisoners of War discharged at Quebec - Name of prize ship: Land forces.

Wagerman, Jeremiah Prisoner: 588 - Rank: Private - Name of Prize: Land forces - By what ship or how taken: Taken on shore - Discharged: 10 Aug 1813 - By what order: HMS Regulus by order of his Excellency Sir George Prevost - Source: List of American Prisoners of War discharged at Quebec - Name of prize ship: Land forces.

Waite, Brunsey Prisoner: 1985 - Rank: Citizen - Discharged: 13 Mar 1815 - By what order: Returned to the United States - Source: List of American Prisoners of War discharged at Quebec.

Wakeman, Bradley Prisoner: 1970 - Rank: Private - Name of Prize: Land forces - By what ship or how taken: Taken on shore - Discharged: 13 Mar 1815 - By what order: Returned to the United States - Source: List of American Prisoners of War discharged at Quebec - Name of prize ship: Land forces.

Walker, Colman Prisoner: 1131 - Rank: Private - By what ship or how taken: Troops - Time when: 5 May 1813 - Place where: Rapids, River Raisin - Whether man of war, privateer, or merchant vessel: Taken on shore - When received: 25 Nov 1813 - From what ship or whence received: Town goal. - Prisoner: 1131 - Rank: Private - Name of Prize: Land forces - By what ship or how taken: Taken on shore - Discharged: 4 May 1814 - By what order: Returned to the United States - Source: List of American Prisoners of War discharged at Quebec - Name of prize ship: Land forces.

Walker, Simeon Prisoner: 638 - Rank: Private - Name of Prize: Land forces - By what ship or how taken: Taken on shore - Discharged: 10 Aug 1813 - By what order: HMS Regulus by order of his Excellency Sir George Prevost - Source: List of American Prisoners of War discharged at Quebec - Name of prize ship: Land forces.

Walker, William (1)   Prisoner: 3 - Rank: Private - Name of Prize: Land forces - By what ship or how taken: Taken on shore - Discharged: 31 Oct 1813 - By what order: HMS Malabar Transport by order of his Excellency Sir George Prevost - Source: List of American Prisoners of War discharged at Quebec - Name of prize ship: Land forces. - Prisoner: 3 - Rank: Private - Name of Prize: Land forces - By what ship or how taken: Taken on shore - Discharged: 31 Oct 1813 - By what order: HMS Malabar Transport by order of his Excellency Sir George Prevost - Source: List of American Prisoners of War discharged at Quebec - Name of prize ship: Land forces.

Walker, William (2)   Prisoner: 1234 - Rank: Private - By what ship or how taken: Troops - Time when: 19 Dec 1813 - Place where: Fort Niagara - Whether man of war, privateer, or merchant vessel: Taken on shore - When received: 29 Jan 1814 - From what ship or whence received: Montreal by land carriages. Prisoner: 1234 - Rank: Private - Name of Prize: Land forces - By what ship or how taken: Taken on shore - Discharged: 4 May 1814 - By what order: Returned to the United States - Source: List of American Prisoners of War discharged at Quebec - Name of prize ship: Land forces.

Wallace, Abel   Prisoner: 1836 - Rank: Private - Name of Prize: Land forces - By what ship or how taken: Taken on shore - Discharged: 8 Nov 1814 - By what order: George No. 515 by Sir George Prevost - Source: List of American Prisoners of War discharged at Quebec - Name of prize ship: Land forces.

Wallace, Samuel   Prisoner: 1410 - Rank: Private - By what ship or how taken: Troops - Time when: 19 Dec 1813 - Place where: Fort Niagara - Whether man of war, privateer, or merchant vessel: Taken on shore - When received: 29 Jan 1814 - From what ship or whence received: Montreal by land carriages. - Prisoner: 1410 - Rank: Private - Name of Prize: Land forces - By what ship or how taken: Taken on shore - Discharged: 4 May 1814 - By what order: Returned to the United States - Source: List of American Prisoners of War discharged at Quebec - Name of prize ship: Land forces.

Wallis, James   Prisoner: 1161 - Rank: Corporal - By what ship or how taken: Troops - Time when: 5 May 1813 - Place where: Fort Meigs - Whether man of war, privateer, or merchant vessel: Taken on shore - When received: 25 Nov 1813 - From what ship or whence received: Town goal. - Prisoner: 1161 - Rank: Private - Name of Prize: Land forces - By what ship or how taken: Taken on shore - Discharged: 4 May 1814 - By what order: Returned to the United States - Source: List of American Prisoners of War discharged at Quebec - Name of prize ship: Land forces.

Walton, Edward   Prisoner: 729 - Rank: Private - Name of Prize: Land forces - By what ship or how taken: Taken on shore - Discharged: 31 Oct 1813 - By what order: HMS Malabar Transport by order of his Excellency Sir George Prevost - Source: List of American Prisoners of War discharged at Quebec - Name of prize ship: Land forces.

Ward, John   Prisoner: 1127 - Rank: Private - By what ship or how taken: Troops - Time when: 5 May 1813 - Place where: Rapids, River Raisin - Whether man of war, privateer, or merchant vessel: Taken on shore - When received: 25 Nov 1813 - From what ship or whence received: Town goal. - Prisoner: 1127 - Rank: Private - Name of Prize: Land forces - By what ship or how taken: Taken on shore - Discharged: 4 May 1814 - By what order: Returned to the United States - Source: List of American Prisoners of War discharged at Quebec - Name of prize ship: Land forces.

Waring, Jonathan   Prisoner: 1121 - Rank: Private - Name of Prize: Land forces - By what ship or how taken: Taken on shore - Discharged: 31 Oct 1813 - By what order: HMS Malabar Transport by order of his Excellency Sir George Prevost - Source: List of American Prisoners of War discharged at Quebec - Name of prize ship: Land forces.

Warley, Joseph   Prisoner: 1120 - Rank: Private - Name of Prize: Land forces - By what ship or how taken: Taken on shore - Discharged: 31 Oct 1813 - By what order: HMS Malabar Transport by order of his Excellency Sir George Prevost - Source: List of American Prisoners of War discharged at Quebec - Name of prize ship: Land forces.

Warren, William G.   Prisoner: 1984 - Rank: Citizen - Discharged: 13 Mar 1815 - By what order: Returned to the United States - Source: List of American Prisoners of War discharged at Quebec.

Waterman, Elisha   Prisoner: 1381 - Rank: Private - By what ship or how taken: Troops - Time when: 19 Dec 1813 - Place where: Fort Niagara - Whether man of war, privateer, or merchant vessel: Taken on shore - When received: 29 Jan 1814 - From what ship or whence received: Montreal by land carriages. - Prisoner: 1381 - Rank: Private - Name of Prize: Land forces - By what ship or how taken: Taken on shore - Discharged: 4 May 1814 - By what order: Returned to the United States - Source: List of American Prisoners of War discharged at Quebec - Name of prize ship: Land forces.

Waughan, James Prisoner: 734 - Rank: Private - Name of Prize: Land forces - By what ship or how taken: Taken on shore - Discharged: 10 Aug 1813 - By what order: HMS Regulus by order of his Excellency Sir George Prevost - Source: List of American Prisoners of War discharged at Quebec - Name of prize ship: Land forces.

Weeman, Edward Prisoner: 1282 - Rank: Sergeant - By what ship or how taken: Troops - Time when: 19 Dec 1813 - Place where: Fort Niagara - Whether man of war, privateer, or merchant vessel: Taken on shore - When received: 29 Jan 1814 - From what ship or whence received: Montreal by land carriages. - Prisoner: 1282 - Rank: Sergeant - Name of Prize: Land forces - By what ship or how taken: Taken on shore - Discharged: 4 May 1814 - By what order: Returned to the United States - Source: List of American Prisoners of War discharged at Quebec - Name of prize ship: Land forces.

Weiant, Peter Prisoner: 1957 - Rank: Private - Name of Prize: Land forces - By what ship or how taken: Taken on shore - Discharged: 13 Mar 1815 - By what order: Returned to the United States - Source: List of American Prisoners of War discharged at Quebec - Name of prize ship: Land forces.

Welch, Henry Prisoner: 671 - Rank: Sergeant - Name of Prize: Land forces - By what ship or how taken: Taken on shore - Discharged: 10 Aug 1813 - By what order: HMS Regulus by order of his Excellency Sir George Prevost - Source: List of American Prisoners of War discharged at Quebec - Name of prize ship: Land forces.

Welch, Russel Prisoner: 381 - Rank: Private - Name of Prize: Land forces - By what ship or how taken: Taken on shore - Discharged: 4 May 1814 - By what order: Returned to the United States - Source: List of American Prisoners of War discharged at Quebec - Name of prize ship: Land forces.

Weldon, Ira Prisoner: 1697 - Rank: Private - Name of Prize: Land forces - By what ship or how taken: Taken on shore - Discharged: 8 Nov 1814 - By what order: George No. 515 by Sir George Prevost - Source: List of American Prisoners of War discharged at Quebec - Name of prize ship: Land forces.

Wells, Caleb Prisoner: 386 - Rank: Private - Source: Account of American prisoners of war who died at Quebec in the Months of July, August & September 1813 - Ship or Corps: Land forces - Vessel: Taken on shore - Place born: Rhode Island - Age: 45 - Where taken: Stoney Point - Date of death: 29 Jul 1813.

Welsh, Russel Prisoner: 381 - Rank: Private - Source: Account of American prisoners of war who died at Quebec between 14 February 1814 and 23 December 1814 - Ship or Corps: Land forces - Vessel: Taken on shore - Place born: Pennsylvania - Age: 21 - Where taken: Stoney Point - Date of death: 22 Mar 1814 - Disorder or casualty: Pneumonia.

Welsh, Zephaniah Prisoner: 34 - Rank: Private - Name of Prize: Land forces - By what ship or how taken: Taken on shore - Discharged: 31 Oct 1813 - By what order: HMS Malabar Transport by order of his Excellency Sir George Prevost - Source: List of American Prisoners of War discharged at Quebec - Name of prize ship: Land forces.

Went, George Prisoner: 1463 - Rank: Private - Name of Prize: Land forces - By what ship or how taken: Taken on shore - Discharged: 10 Nov 1814 - By what order: Stately No. 400 to Halifax by order of Sir George Prevost - Source: List of American Prisoners of War discharged at Quebec - Name of prize ship: Land forces.

West, Abiah Prisoner: 1921 - Rank: Private - Name of Prize: Land forces - By what ship or how taken: Taken on shore - Discharged: 10 Nov 1814 - By what order: Sovereign No. 628 to Halifax by order of Sir George Prevost - Source: List of American Prisoners of War discharged at Quebec - Name of prize ship: Land forces.

West, Abraham Prisoner: 640 - Rank: Private - Name of Prize: Land forces - By what ship or how taken: Taken on shore - Discharged: 10 Aug 1813 - By what order: HMS Regulus by order of his Excellency Sir George Prevost - Source: List of American Prisoners of War discharged at Quebec - Name of prize ship: Land forces.

West, Hugh S. Prisoner: 287 - Rank: Private - Name of Prize: Land forces - By what ship or how taken: Taken on shore - Discharged: 31 Oct 1813 - By what order: HMS Malabar Transport by order of his Excellency Sir George Prevost - Source: List of American Prisoners of War discharged at Quebec - Name of prize ship: Land forces.

Westbrook, Abraham Prisoner: 1088 - Rank: Private - Name of Prize: Land forces - By what ship or how taken: Taken on shore - Discharged: 31 Oct 1813 - By what order: HMS Malabar Transport by order of his Excellency Sir George Prevost - Source: List of American Prisoners of War discharged at Quebec - Name of prize ship: Land forces.

Wharf, Andrew Prisoner: 1434 - Rank: Passenger - Name of Prize: Lezare - By what ship or how taken: Privateer - Discharged: 24 May 1813 - By what order: Mulgrave Transport No. 311 - Source: List of American Prisoners of War discharged at Quebec - Name of prize ship: Lezare. - Prisoner: 1434 - Rank: Able seaman - By what ship or how taken: Prometheus - Time when: 5 May 1814 - Place where: off Halifax - Whether man of war, privateer, or merchant vessel: Privateer - When received: 24 May 1814 - From what ship or whence received: Mary Transport No. 368.

Wheeler, Anthony Prisoner: 512 - Rank: Private - Name of Prize: Land forces - By what ship or how taken: Taken on shore - Discharged: 10 Aug 1813 - By what order: HMS Regulus by order of his Excellency Sir George Prevost - Source: List of American Prisoners of War discharged at Quebec - Name of prize ship: Land forces.

Wheeler, Enoch   Prisoner: 1875 - Rank: Private - Name of Prize: Land forces - By what ship or how taken: Taken on shore - Discharged: 8 Nov 1814 - By what order: George No. 515 by Sir George Prevost - Source: List of American Prisoners of War discharged at Quebec - Name of prize ship: Land forces.

Wheeler, Nathaniel   Prisoner: 1195 - By what ship or how taken: Citizen - When received: 12 Dec 1813 - From what ship or whence received: Town goal. - Prisoner: 1195 - Rank: Private - Name of Prize: Land forces - By what ship or how taken: Taken on shore - Discharged: 4 May 1814 - By what order: Returned to the United States - Source: List of American Prisoners of War discharged at Quebec - Name of prize ship: Land forces.

Wheeler, Stephen   Prisoner: 47 - Rank: Private - Name of Prize: Land forces - By what ship or how taken: Taken on shore - Discharged: 31 Oct 1813 - By what order: HMS Malabar Transport by order of his Excellency Sir George Prevost - Source: List of American Prisoners of War discharged at Quebec - Name of prize ship: Land forces.

Wheeler, Willison   Prisoner: 286 - Rank: Private - Name of Prize: Land forces - By what ship or how taken: Taken on shore - Discharged: 31 Oct 1813 - By what order: HMS Malabar Transport by order of his Excellency Sir George Prevost - Source: List of American Prisoners of War discharged at Quebec - Name of prize ship: Land forces.

Wheelock, James   Prisoner: 656 - Rank: Private - Name of Prize: Land forces - By what ship or how taken: Taken on shore - Discharged: 31 Oct 1813 - By what order: HMS Malabar Transport by order of his Excellency Sir George Prevost - Source: List of American Prisoners of War discharged at Quebec - Name of prize ship: Land forces.

Whillhelm, Charles   Prisoner: 521 - Rank: Private - Name of Prize: Land forces - By what ship or how taken: Taken on shore - Discharged: 10 Aug 1813 - By what order: HMS Regulus by order of his Excellency Sir George Prevost - Source: List of American Prisoners of War discharged at Quebec - Name of prize ship: Land forces.

Whister, P. V.   Prisoner: 1946 - Rank: Sergeant - Name of Prize: Land forces - By what ship or how taken: Taken on shore - Discharged: 13 Mar 1815 - By what order: Returned to the United States - Source: List of American Prisoners of War discharged at Quebec - Name of prize ship: Land forces.

White, George   Prisoner: 1960 - Rank: Private - Name of Prize: Land forces - By what ship or how taken: Taken on shore - Discharged: 13 Mar 1815 - By what order: Returned to the United States - Source: List of American Prisoners of War discharged at Quebec - Name of prize ship: Land forces.

White, Isaac   Prisoner: 1329 - Rank: Sergeant - By what ship or how taken: Troops - Time when: 19 Dec 1813 - Place where: Fort Niagara - Whether man of war, privateer, or merchant vessel: Taken on shore - When received: 29 Jan 1814 - From what ship or whence received: Montreal by land carriages. - Prisoner: 1329 - Rank: Sergeant - Name of Prize: Land forces - By what ship or how taken: Taken on shore - Discharged: 4 May 1814 - By what order: Returned to the United States - Source: List of American Prisoners of War discharged at Quebec - Name of prize ship: Land forces.

White, John   Prisoner: 447 - Rank: Private - Name of Prize: Land forces - By what ship or how taken: Taken on shore - Discharged: 10 Aug 1813 - By what order: HMS Regulus by order of his Excellency Sir George Prevost - Source: List of American Prisoners of War discharged at Quebec - Name of prize ship: Land forces.

White, Joshua   Prisoner: 218 - Rank: Private - Name of Prize: Eagle - By what ship or how taken: Man of war - Discharged: 31 Oct 1813 - By what order: HMS Malabar Transport by order of his Excellency Sir George Prevost - Source: List of American Prisoners of War discharged at Quebec - Name of prize ship: Eagle.

White, Samuel   Prisoner: 1663 - Rank: Captain - Name of Prize: Land forces - By what ship or how taken: Taken on shore - Discharged: 10 Nov 1814 - By what order: Stately No. 400 to Halifax by order of Sir George Prevost - Source: List of American Prisoners of War discharged at Quebec - Name of prize ship: Land forces.

White, William   Prisoner: 1074 - Rank: Private - Name of Prize: Land forces - By what ship or how taken: Taken on shore - Discharged: 4 May 1814 - By what order: Returned to the United States - Source: List of American Prisoners of War discharged at Quebec - Name of prize ship: Land forces.

Whitley, Daniel R.   Prisoner: 372 - Rank: Private - Name of Prize: Land forces - By what ship or how taken: Taken on shore - Discharged: 31 Oct 1813 - By what order: HMS Malabar Transport by order of his Excellency Sir George Prevost - Source: List of American Prisoners of War discharged at Quebec - Name of prize ship: Land forces.

Whitman, Stephen   Prisoner: 610 - Rank: Private - Name of Prize: Land forces - By what ship or how taken: Taken on shore - Discharged: 10 Aug 1813 - By what order: HMS Regulus by order of his Excellency Sir George Prevost - Source: List of American Prisoners of War discharged at Quebec - Name of prize ship:

Land forces.

Whitney, Isaac   Prisoner: 1173 - Rank: Private - By what ship or how taken: Troops - Time when: 5 May 1813 - Place where: Rapids - Whether man of war, privateer, or merchant vessel: Taken on shore - When received: 25 Nov 1813 - From what ship or whence received: Town goal. - Prisoner: 1173 - Rank: Private - Name of Prize: Land forces - By what ship or how taken: Taken on shore - Discharged: 4 May 1814 - By what order: Returned to the United States - Source: List of American Prisoners of War discharged at Quebec - Name of prize ship: Land forces.

Whitney, Joel   Prisoner: 106 - Rank: Private - Name of Prize: Land forces - By what ship or how taken: Taken on shore - Discharged: 4 May 1814 - By what order: Returned to the United States - Source: List of American Prisoners of War discharged at Quebec - Name of prize ship: Land forces.

Whitton, Charles   Prisoner: 104 - Rank: Private - Name of Prize: Land forces - By what ship or how taken: Taken on shore - Discharged: 31 Oct 1813 - By what order: HMS Malabar Transport by order of his Excellency Sir George Prevost - Source: List of American Prisoners of War discharged at Quebec - Name of prize ship: Land forces.

Whitton, George   Prisoner: 206 - Rank: Private - Name of Prize: Growler - By what ship or how taken: Man of war - Discharged: 31 Oct 1813 - By what order: HMS Malabar Transport by order of his Excellency Sir George Prevost - Source: List of American Prisoners of War discharged at Quebec - Name of prize ship: Growler.

Wiklins, John   Prisoner: 617 - Rank: Private - Name of Prize: Land forces - By what ship or how taken: Taken on shore - Discharged: 10 Aug 1813 - By what order: HMS Regulus by order of his Excellency Sir George Prevost - Source: List of American Prisoners of War discharged at Quebec - Name of prize ship: Land forces.

Wilcox, Almyra   Prisoner: 1788 - Rank: Private - Name of Prize: Land forces - By what ship or how taken: Taken on shore - Discharged: 8 Nov 1814 - By what order: George No. 515 by Sir George Prevost - Source: List of American Prisoners of War discharged at Quebec - Name of prize ship: Land forces.

Wilcox, Burton   Prisoner: 1719 - Rank: Private - Name of Prize: Land forces - By what ship or how taken: Taken on shore - Discharged: 10 Nov 1814 - By what order: Stately No. 400 to Halifax by order of Sir George Prevost - Source: List of American Prisoners of War discharged at Quebec - Name of prize ship: Land forces.

Wilcox, David   Prisoner: 1169 - Rank: Private - By what ship or how taken: Troops - Time when: 5 May 1813 - Place where: Rapids - Whether man of war, privateer, or merchant vessel: Taken on shore - When received: 25 Nov 1813 - From what ship or whence received: Town goal. - Prisoner: 1169 - Rank: Private - Name of Prize: Land forces - By what ship or how taken: Taken on shore - Discharged: 4 May 1814 - By what order: Returned to the United States - Source: List of American Prisoners of War discharged at Quebec - Name of prize ship: Land forces.

Wilcox, John   Prisoner: 956 - Rank: Private - Name of Prize: Land forces - By what ship or how taken: Taken on shore - Discharged: 31 Oct 1813 - By what order: HMS Malabar Transport by order of his Excellency Sir George Prevost - Source: List of American Prisoners of War discharged at Quebec - Name of prize ship: Land forces.

Wilcox, Oliver   Prisoner: 1710 - Rank: Quartermaster - Name of Prize: Land forces - By what ship or how taken: Taken on shore - Discharged: 10 Nov 1814 - By what order: Stately No. 400 to Halifax by order of Sir George Prevost - Source: List of American Prisoners of War discharged at Quebec - Name of prize ship: Land forces.

Wilder, Elihu   Prisoner: 18 - Rank: Private - Name of Prize: Land forces - By what ship or how taken: Taken on shore - Discharged: 31 Oct 1813 - By what order: HMS Malabar Transport by order of his Excellency Sir George Prevost - Source: List of American Prisoners of War discharged at Quebec - Name of prize ship: Land forces.

Wilder, Ezra   Prisoner: 1938 - Rank: Sergeant - Name of Prize: Land forces - By what ship or how taken: Taken on shore - Discharged: 13 Mar 1815 - By what order: Returned to the United States - Source: List of American Prisoners of War discharged at Quebec - Name of prize ship: Land forces.

Wiley, Thomas   Prisoner: 1700 - Rank: Private - Name of Prize: Land forces - By what ship or how taken: Taken on shore - Discharged: 8 Nov 1814 - By what order: George No. 515 by Sir George Prevost - Source: List of American Prisoners of War discharged at Quebec - Name of prize ship: Land forces.

Wiley, William   Prisoner: 1403 - Rank: Private - By what ship or how taken: Troops - Time when: 19 Dec 1813 - Place where: Fort Niagara - Whether man of war, privateer, or merchant vessel: Taken on shore - When received: 29 Jan 1814 - From what ship or whence received: Montreal by land carriages. - Prisoner: 1403 - Rank: Private - Name of Prize: Land forces - By what ship or how taken: Taken on shore - Discharged: 4 May 1814 - By what order: Returned to the United States - Source: List of American Prisoners of War

discharged at Quebec - Name of prize ship: Land forces.

Wilhelm, Daniel   Prisoner: 1268 - Rank: Private - By what ship or how taken: Troops - Time when: 19 Dec 1813 - Place where: Fort Niagara - Whether man of war, privateer, or merchant vessel: Taken on shore - When received: 29 Jan 1814 - From what ship or whence received: Montreal by land carriages. - Prisoner: 1268 - Rank: Private - Name of Prize: Land forces - By what ship or how taken: Taken on shore - Discharged: 4 May 1814 - By what order: Returned to the United States - Source: List of American Prisoners of War discharged at Quebec - Name of prize ship: Land forces.

Wilkens, William   Prisoner: 968 - Rank: Private - Name of Prize: Land forces - By what ship or how taken: Taken on shore - Discharged: 31 Oct 1813 - By what order: HMS Malabar Transport by order of his Excellency Sir George Prevost - Source: List of American Prisoners of War discharged at Quebec - Name of prize ship: Land forces.

Wilkins, Aaron   Prisoner: 64 - Rank: Private - Name of Prize: Land forces - By what ship or how taken: Taken on shore - Discharged: 31 Oct 1813 - By what order: HMS Malabar Transport by order of his Excellency Sir George Prevost - Source: List of American Prisoners of War discharged at Quebec - Name of prize ship: Land forces.

Wilkins, Edward   Prisoner: 1183 - Rank: Private - By what ship or how taken: Troops - Time when: 5 May 1813 - Place where: Rapids - Whether man of war, privateer, or merchant vessel: Taken on shore - When received: 25 Nov 1813 - From what ship or whence received: Town goal. - Prisoner: 1183 - Rank: Private - Name of Prize: Land forces - By what ship or how taken: Taken on shore - Discharged: 4 May 1814 - By what order: Returned to the United States - Source: List of American Prisoners of War discharged at Quebec - Name of prize ship: Land forces.

Wilkinson, Andrew   Prisoner: 103 - Rank: Private - Name of Prize: Land forces - By what ship or how taken: Taken on shore - Discharged: 4 May 1814 - By what order: Returned to the United States - Source: List of American Prisoners of War discharged at Quebec - Name of prize ship: Land forces.

Wilkinson, Oliver   Prisoner: 326 - Rank: Private - Name of Prize: Land forces - By what ship or how taken: Taken on shore - Discharged: 31 Oct 1813 - By what order: HMS Malabar Transport by order of his Excellency Sir George Prevost - Source: List of American Prisoners of War discharged at Quebec - Name of prize ship: Land forces.

Wilkinson, Patrick   Prisoner: 432 - Rank: Private - Name of Prize: Land forces - By what ship or how taken: Taken on shore - Discharged: 10 Aug 1813 - By what order: HMS Regulus by order of his Excellency Sir George Prevost - Source: List of American Prisoners of War discharged at Quebec - Name of prize ship: Land forces.

Willet, Joseph   Prisoner: 1060 - Rank: Private - Name of Prize: Land forces - By what ship or how taken: Taken on shore - Discharged: 31 Oct 1813 - By what order: HMS Malabar Transport by order of his Excellency Sir George Prevost - Source: List of American Prisoners of War discharged at Quebec - Name of prize ship: Land forces.

Willet, Phil   Prisoner: 1095 - Rank: Private - Name of Prize: Land forces - By what ship or how taken: Taken on shore - Discharged: 31 Oct 1813 - By what order: HMS Malabar Transport by order of his Excellency Sir George Prevost - Source: List of American Prisoners of War discharged at Quebec - Name of prize ship: Land forces.

Williams, Andrew   Prisoner: 551 - Rank: Private - Name of Prize: Land forces - By what ship or how taken: Taken on shore - Discharged: 10 Aug 1813 - By what order: HMS Regulus by order of his Excellency Sir George Prevost - Source: List of American Prisoners of War discharged at Quebec - Name of prize ship: Land forces.

Williams, Benjamin   Prisoner: 1005 - Rank: Seaman - Name of Prize: Juliet - By what ship or how taken: Man of war - Discharged: 31 Oct 1813 - By what order: HMS Malabar Transport by order of his Excellency Sir George Prevost - Source: List of American Prisoners of War discharged at Quebec - Name of prize ship: Juliet.

Williams, Henry   Prisoner: 992 - Rank: Seaman - Name of Prize: Juliet - By what ship or how taken: Man of war - Discharged: 31 Oct 1813 - By what order: HMS Malabar Transport by order of his Excellency Sir George Prevost - Source: List of American Prisoners of War discharged at Quebec - Name of prize ship: Juliet.

Williams, Jack   Prisoner: 1989 - Rank: Seaman - Name of Prize: Armline - By what ship or how taken: Merchant Vessel - Discharged: 13 Mar 1815 - By what order: Returned to the United States - Source: List of American Prisoners of War discharged at Quebec - Name of prize ship: Armline.

Williams, Jesse   Prisoner: 1734 - Rank: Seaman - Name of Prize: Scorpion - By what ship or how taken: Man of war - Discharged: 7 Nov 1813 - By what order: HMS Freedom No. 582 by order of his Excellency Sir George Prevost - Source: List of American Prisoners of War discharged at Quebec - Name of prize ship:

American Prisoners of War held at Montreal and Quebec during the War of 1812

Scorpion.

Williams, John W.   Prisoner: 1766 - Rank: Sergeant - Name of Prize: Land forces - By what ship or how taken: Taken on shore - Discharged: 8 Nov 1814 - By what order: George No. 515 by Sir George Prevost - Source: List of American Prisoners of War discharged at Quebec - Name of prize ship: Land forces.

Williams, Samuel (1)   Prisoner: 94 - Rank: Private - Name of Prize: Land forces - By what ship or how taken: Taken on shore - Discharged: 31 Oct 1813 - By what order: HMS Malabar Transport by order of his Excellency Sir George Prevost - Source: List of American Prisoners of War discharged at Quebec - Name of prize ship: Land forces.

Williams, Samuel (2)   Prisoner: 1725 - Rank: Seaman - Name of Prize: Scorpion - By what ship or how taken: Man of war - Discharged: 7 Nov 1813 - By what order: HMS Freedom No. 582 by order of his Excellency Sir George Prevost - Source: List of American Prisoners of War discharged at Quebec - Name of prize ship: Scorpion.

Williams, Thomas   Prisoner: 1767 - Rank: Sergeant - Name of Prize: Land forces - By what ship or how taken: Taken on shore - Discharged: 8 Nov 1814 - By what order: George No. 515 by Sir George Prevost - Source: List of American Prisoners of War discharged at Quebec - Name of prize ship: Land forces.

Williams, Elijah   Prisoner: 1490 - Rank: Sergeant - Name of Prize: Land forces - By what ship or how taken: Taken on shore - Discharged: 13 Mar 1815 - By what order: Returned to the United States - Source: List of American Prisoners of War discharged at Quebec - Name of prize ship: Land forces.

Williamson, John T.   Prisoner: 1206 - Rank: Lieutenant - By what ship or how taken: Troops - Time when: 19 Dec 1813 - Place where: Fort Niagara - Whether man of war, privateer, or merchant vessel: Taken on shore - When received: 18 Jan 1814 - From what ship or whence received: Montreal by land carriages. - Prisoner: 1206 - Rank: Lieutenant - Name of Prize: Land forces - By what ship or how taken: Taken on shore - Discharged: 4 May 1814 - By what order: Returned to the United States - Source: List of American Prisoners of War discharged at Quebec - Name of prize ship: Land forces.

Williby, George   Prisoner: 355 - Rank: Corporal - Name of Prize: Land forces - By what ship or how taken: Taken on shore - Discharged: 31 Oct 1813 - By what order: HMS Malabar Transport by order of his Excellency Sir George Prevost - Source: List of American Prisoners of War discharged at Quebec - Name of prize ship: Land forces.

Willis, Alfred   Prisoner: 659 - Rank: Private - Name of Prize: Land forces - By what ship or how taken: Taken on shore - Discharged: 10 Aug 1813 - By what order: HMS Regulus by order of his Excellency Sir George Prevost - Source: List of American Prisoners of War discharged at Quebec - Name of prize ship: Land forces.

Wilson, Ebenezer   Prisoner: 1709 - Rank: Major - Name of Prize: Land forces - By what ship or how taken: Taken on shore - Discharged: 10 Nov 1814 - By what order: Stately No. 400 to Halifax by order of Sir George Prevost - Source: List of American Prisoners of War discharged at Quebec - Name of prize ship: Land forces.

Wilson, Horace   Prisoner: 1837 - Rank: Private - Name of Prize: Land forces - By what ship or how taken: Taken on shore - Discharged: 8 Nov 1814 - By what order: George No. 515 by Sir George Prevost - Source: List of American Prisoners of War discharged at Quebec - Name of prize ship: Land forces.

Wilson, James   Prisoner: 560 - Rank: Private - Name of Prize: Land forces - By what ship or how taken: Taken on shore - Discharged: 10 Aug 1813 - By what order: HMS Regulus by order of his Excellency Sir George Prevost - Source: List of American Prisoners of War discharged at Quebec - Name of prize ship: Land forces.

Wilson, William (1)   Prisoner: 1128 - Rank: Private - By what ship or how taken: Troops - Time when: 5 May 1813 - Place where: Rapids, River Raisin - Whether man of war, privateer, or merchant vessel: Taken on shore - When received: 25 Nov 1813 - From what ship or whence received: Town goal.

Wilson, William (2)   Prisoner: 1145 - Rank: Private - By what ship or how taken: Troops - Time when: 5 May 1813 - Place where: Rapids, River Raisin - Whether man of war, privateer, or merchant vessel: Taken on shore - When received: 25 Nov 1813 - From what ship or whence received: Town goal. - Prisoner: 1145 - Rank: Private - Name of Prize: Land forces - By what ship or how taken: Taken on shore - Discharged: 4 May 1814 - By what order: Returned to the United States - Source: List of American Prisoners of War discharged at Quebec - Name of prize ship: Land forces.

Winchester, James   Prisoner: 246 - Rank: Brigadier General - Name of Prize: Land forces - By what ship or how taken: Taken on shore - Discharged: 3 Apr 1814 - By what order: Returned to the United States - Source: List of American Prisoners of War discharged at Quebec - Name of prize ship: Land forces.

Winder, William H.   Prisoner: 255 - Rank: Brigadier General - Name of Prize: Land forces - By what ship or how taken: Taken on shore - Discharged: 3 Apr 1814 - By what order: Returned to the United States - Source: List of American Prisoners of War discharged at Quebec - Name of prize ship: Land forces. - Prisoner: 1425 - Rank: Brigadier General - By what ship or how taken: Troops - Time when: 19 Dec 1813 - Place where: Fort

ererer

Niagara - Whether man of war, privateer, or merchant vessel: Taken on shore - When received: 29 Jan 1814 - From what ship or whence received: Montreal by land carriages.

Wings, Daniel   Prisoner: 606 - Rank: Private - Name of Prize: Land forces - By what ship or how taken: Taken on shore - Discharged: 31 Oct 1813 - By what order: HMS Malabar Transport by order of his Excellency Sir George Prevost - Source: List of American Prisoners of War discharged at Quebec - Name of prize ship: Land forces.

Winn, Clement   Prisoner: 479 - Rank: Private - Name of Prize: Land forces - By what ship or how taken: Taken on shore - Discharged: 10 Aug 1813 - By what order: HMS Regulus by order of his Excellency Sir George Prevost - Source: List of American Prisoners of War discharged at Quebec - Name of prize ship: Land forces.

Winner, Michael   Prisoner: 614 - Rank: Private - Name of Prize: Land forces - By what ship or how taken: Taken on shore - Discharged: 10 Aug 1813 - By what order: HMS Regulus by order of his Excellency Sir George Prevost - Source: List of American Prisoners of War discharged at Quebec - Name of prize ship: Land forces.

Winter, Christopher   Prisoner: 1360 - Rank: Private - By what ship or how taken: Troops - Time when: 19 Dec 1813 - Place where: Fort Niagara - Whether man of war, privateer, or merchant vessel: Taken on shore - When received: 29 Jan 1814 - From what ship or whence received: Montreal by land carriages. - Prisoner: 1360 - Rank: Private - Name of Prize: Land forces - By what ship or how taken: Taken on shore - Discharged: 4 May 1814 - By what order: Returned to the United States - Source: List of American Prisoners of War discharged at Quebec - Name of prize ship: Land forces.

Winton, John   Prisoner: 351 - Rank: Private - Name of Prize: Land forces - By what ship or how taken: Taken on shore - Discharged: 31 Oct 1813 - By what order: HMS Malabar Transport by order of his Excellency Sir George Prevost - Source: List of American Prisoners of War discharged at Quebec - Name of prize ship: Land forces.

Witherall, Gerard   Prisoner: 341 - Rank: Private - Name of Prize: Land forces - By what ship or how taken: Taken on shore - Discharged: 31 Oct 1813 - By what order: HMS Malabar Transport by order of his Excellency Sir George Prevost - Source: List of American Prisoners of War discharged at Quebec - Name of prize ship: Land forces.

Withington, Robert   Prisoner: 177 - Rank: Seaman - Name of Prize: Growler - By what ship or how taken: Man of war - Discharged: 31 Oct 1813 - By what order: HMS Malabar Transport by order of his Excellency Sir George Prevost - Source: List of American Prisoners of War discharged at Quebec - Name of prize ship: Growler.

Withington, Thomas   Prisoner: 1150 - Rank: Private - By what ship or how taken: Troops - Time when: 5 May 1813 - Place where: Rapids, River Raisin - Whether man of war, privateer, or merchant vessel: Taken on shore - When received: 25 Nov 1813 - From what ship or whence received: Town goal. - Prisoner: 1150 - Rank: Private - Name of Prize: Land forces - By what ship or how taken: Taken on shore - Discharged: 4 May 1814 - By what order: Returned to the United States - Source: List of American Prisoners of War discharged at Quebec - Name of prize ship: Land forces.

Witturn, Redford   Prisoner: 1964 - Rank: Private - Name of Prize: Land forces - By what ship or how taken: Taken on shore - Discharged: 13 Mar 1815 - By what order: Returned to the United States - Source: List of American Prisoners of War discharged at Quebec - Name of prize ship: Land forces.

Wolfram, William   Prisoner: 626 - Rank: Private - Name of Prize: Land forces - By what ship or how taken: Taken on shore - Discharged: 10 Aug 1813 - By what order: HMS Regulus by order of his Excellency Sir George Prevost - Source: List of American Prisoners of War discharged at Quebec - Name of prize ship: Land forces.

Wood, Amory   Prisoner: 979 - Rank: Private - Name of Prize: Land forces - By what ship or how taken: Taken on shore - Discharged: 31 Oct 1813 - By what order: HMS Malabar Transport by order of his Excellency Sir George Prevost - Source: List of American Prisoners of War discharged at Quebec - Name of prize ship: Land forces.

Wood, Emery   Prisoner: 1773 - Rank: Private - Name of Prize: Land forces - By what ship or how taken: Taken on shore - Discharged: 8 Nov 1814 - By what order: George No. 515 by Sir George Prevost - Source: List of American Prisoners of War discharged at Quebec - Name of prize ship: Land forces.

Wood, George W.   Prisoner: 1249 - Rank: Private - By what ship or how taken: Troops - Time when: 19 Dec 1813 - Place where: Fort Niagara - Whether man of war, privateer, or merchant vessel: Taken on shore - When received: 29 Jan 1814 - From what ship or whence received: Montreal by land carriages. - Prisoner: 1249 - Rank: Private - Name of Prize: Land forces - By what ship or how taken: Taken on shore - Discharged: 4 May 1814 - By what order: Returned to the United States - Source: List of American Prisoners of War discharged at Quebec - Name of prize ship: Land forces.

Wood, Israel   Prisoner: 102 - Rank: Private - Name of Prize: Land forces - By what ship or how taken: Taken on

shore - Discharged: 31 Oct 1813 - By what order: HMS Malabar Transport by order of his Excellency Sir George Prevost - Source: List of American Prisoners of War discharged at Quebec - Name of prize ship: Land forces.

Wood, James W. Prisoner: 947 - Rank: Doctor - Name of Prize: Taken in his own boat - Discharged: 31 Jan 1814 - By what order: Returned to the United States - Source: List of American Prisoners of War discharged at Quebec - Name of prize ship: Taken in his own boat.

Wood, Pratt Prisoner: 580 - Rank: Private - Name of Prize: Land forces - By what ship or how taken: Taken on shore - Discharged: 10 Aug 1813 - By what order: HMS Regulus by order of his Excellency Sir George Prevost - Source: List of American Prisoners of War discharged at Quebec - Name of prize ship: Land forces.

Woodland, Leban Prisoner: 394 - Rank: Private - Name of Prize: Land forces - By what ship or how taken: Taken on shore - Discharged: 31 Oct 1813 - By what order: HMS Malabar Transport by order of his Excellency Sir George Prevost - Source: List of American Prisoners of War discharged at Quebec - Name of prize ship: Land forces.

Woodland, William Prisoner: 445 - Rank: Private - Name of Prize: Land forces - By what ship or how taken: Taken on shore - Discharged: 10 Aug 1813 - By what order: HMS Regulus by order of his Excellency Sir George Prevost - Source: List of American Prisoners of War discharged at Quebec - Name of prize ship: Land forces.

Woodley, Daniel Prisoner: 1231 - Rank: Private - By what ship or how taken: Troops - Time when: 19 Dec 1813 - Place where: Fort Niagara - Whether man of war, privateer, or merchant vessel: Taken on shore - When received: 29 Jan 1814 - From what ship or whence received: Montreal by land carriages. - Prisoner: 1231 - Rank: Private - Name of Prize: Land forces - By what ship or how taken: Taken on shore - Discharged: 4 May 1814 - By what order: Returned to the United States - Source: List of American Prisoners of War discharged at Quebec - Name of prize ship: Land forces.

Woodman, Benjamin Prisoner: 238 - Rank: Private - Name of Prize: Eagle - By what ship or how taken: Man of war - Discharged: 31 Oct 1813 - By what order: HMS Malabar Transport by order of his Excellency Sir George Prevost - Source: List of American Prisoners of War discharged at Quebec - Name of prize ship: Eagle.

Woodman, Jeremiah Prisoner: 1775 - Rank: Private - Name of Prize: Land forces - By what ship or how taken: Taken on shore - Discharged: 8 Nov 1814 - By what order: George No. 515 by Sir George Prevost - Source: List of American Prisoners of War discharged at Quebec - Name of prize ship: Land forces.

Woragoul, John Prisoner: 1674 - Rank: Seaman - Name of Prize: Taken in a gig (a ship's long boat) - By what ship or how taken: Man of war - Discharged: 7 Nov 1813 - By what order: HMS Freedom No. 582 by order of his Excellency Sir George Prevost - Source: List of American Prisoners of War discharged at Quebec - Name of prize ship: Taken in a gig (a ship's long boat).

Wormsly, Richard Prisoner: 1669 - Rank: Seaman - Name of Prize: Taken in a gig (a ship's long boat) - By what ship or how taken: Man of war - Discharged: 7 Nov 1813 - By what order: HMS Freedom No. 582 by order of his Excellency Sir George Prevost - Source: List of American Prisoners of War discharged at Quebec - Name of prize ship: Taken in a gig (a ship's long boat).

Wright, Oliver Prisoner: 178 - Rank: Seaman - Name of Prize: Growler - By what ship or how taken: Man of war - Discharged: 31 Oct 1813 - By what order: HMS Malabar Transport by order of his Excellency Sir George Prevost - Source: List of American Prisoners of War discharged at Quebec - Name of prize ship: Growler.

Wright, William Prisoner: 1293 - Rank: Private - By what ship or how taken: Troops - Time when: 19 Dec 1813 - Place where: Fort Niagara - Whether man of war, privateer, or merchant vessel: Taken on shore - When received: 29 Jan 1814 - From what ship or whence received: Montreal by land carriages. - Prisoner: 1293 - Rank: Private - Name of Prize: Land forces - By what ship or how taken: Taken on shore - Discharged: 9 Mar 1814 - By what order: Volunteered for the New Brunswick Fencibles - Source: List of American Prisoners of War discharged at Quebec - Name of prize ship: Land forces.

Yarrington, Alva Prisoner: 653 - Rank: Drummer - Name of Prize: Land forces - By what ship or how taken: Taken on shore - Discharged: 10 Aug 1813 - By what order: HMS Regulus by order of his Excellency Sir George Prevost - Source: List of American Prisoners of War discharged at Quebec - Name of prize ship: Land forces.

Yates, Francis Prisoner: 1267 - Rank: Private - By what ship or how taken: Troops - Time when: 19 Dec 1813 - Place where: Fort Niagara - Whether man of war, privateer, or merchant vessel: Taken on shore - When received: 29 Jan 1814 - From what ship or whence received: Montreal by land carriages. - Prisoner: 1267 - Rank: Private - Name of Prize: Land forces - By what ship or how taken: Taken on shore - Discharged: 4 May 1814 - By what order: Returned to the United States - Source: List of American Prisoners of War

discharged at Quebec - Name of prize ship: Land forces.

Young, Christian   Prisoner: 1903 - Rank: Private - Name of Prize: Land forces - By what ship or how taken: Taken on shore - Discharged: 8 Nov 1814 - By what order: George No. 515 by Sir George Prevost - Source: List of American Prisoners of War discharged at Quebec - Name of prize ship: Land forces.

Young, David   Prisoner: 1866 - Rank: Private - Name of Prize: Land forces - By what ship or how taken: Taken on shore - Discharged: 8 Nov 1814 - By what order: George No. 515 by Sir George Prevost - Source: List of American Prisoners of War discharged at Quebec - Name of prize ship: Land forces.

Young, Ephraim   Prisoner: 105 - Rank: Private - Source: Account of American prisoners of war who died at Quebec in the Months of July, August & September 1813 - Ship or Corps: Land forces - Vessel: Taken on shore - Place born: Erey, MA - Age: 17 - Where taken: Stoney Point - Date of death: 10 Aug 1813.

Young, Thomas   Prisoner: 1962 - Rank: Sergeant - Name of Prize: Land forces - By what ship or how taken: Taken on shore - Discharged: 13 Mar 1815 - By what order: Returned to the United States - Source: List of American Prisoners of War discharged at Quebec - Name of prize ship: Land forces.

Young, William   Prisoner: 635 - Rank: Private - Name of Prize: Land forces - By what ship or how taken: Taken on shore - Discharged: 10 Aug 1813 - By what order: HMS Regulus by order of his Excellency Sir George Prevost - Source: List of American Prisoners of War discharged at Quebec - Name of prize ship: Land forces.